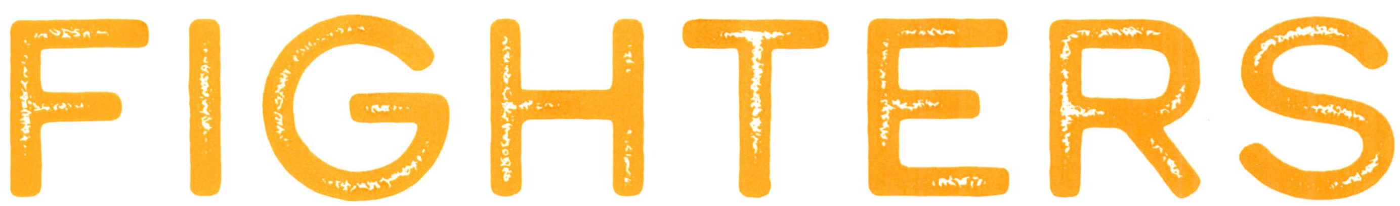
FIGHTERS

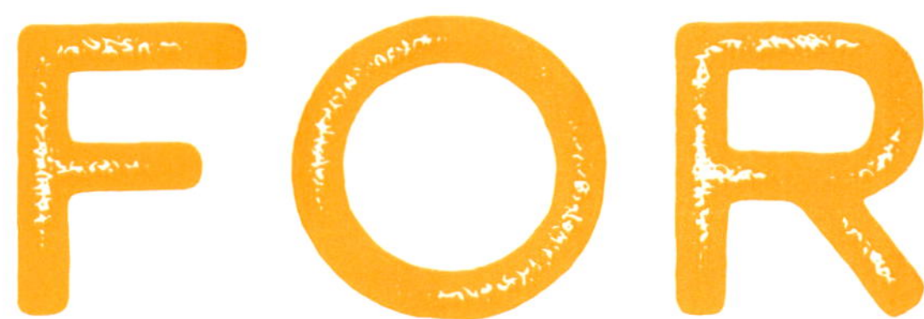
FOR

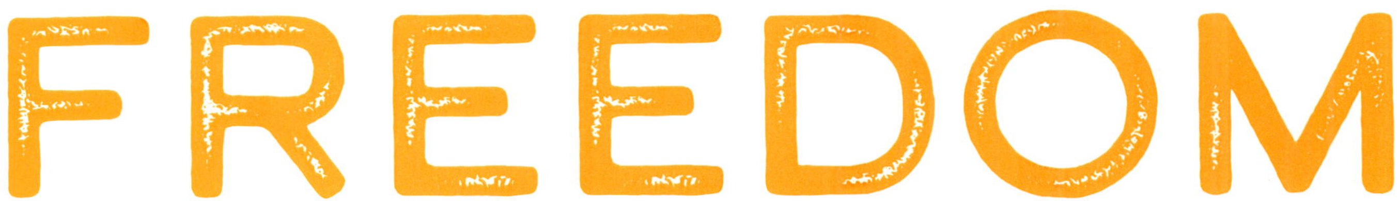
FREEDOM

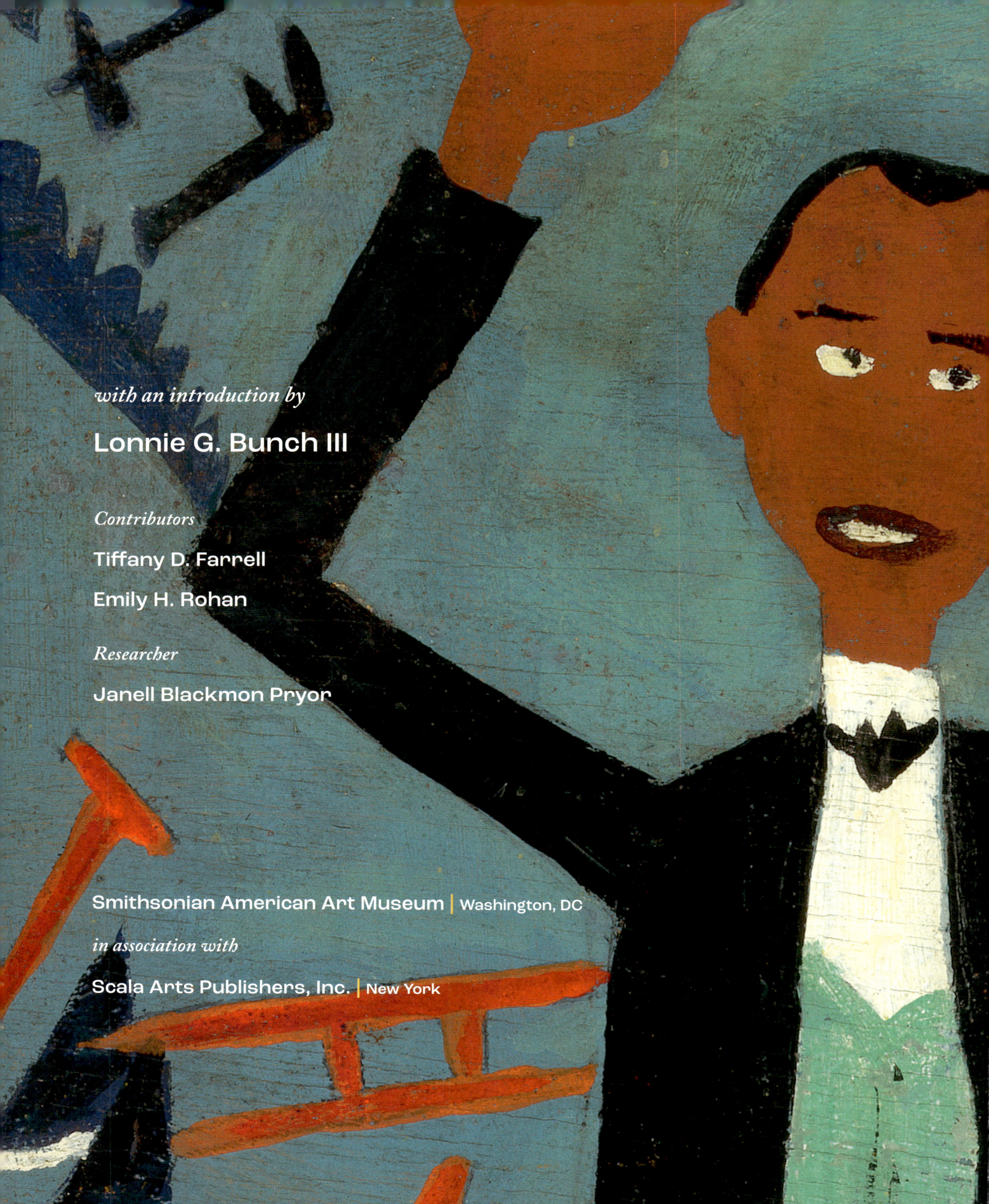

with an introduction by

Lonnie G. Bunch III

Contributors

Tiffany D. Farrell

Emily H. Rohan

Researcher

Janell Blackmon Pryor

Smithsonian American Art Museum | Washington, DC

in association with

Scala Arts Publishers, Inc. | New York

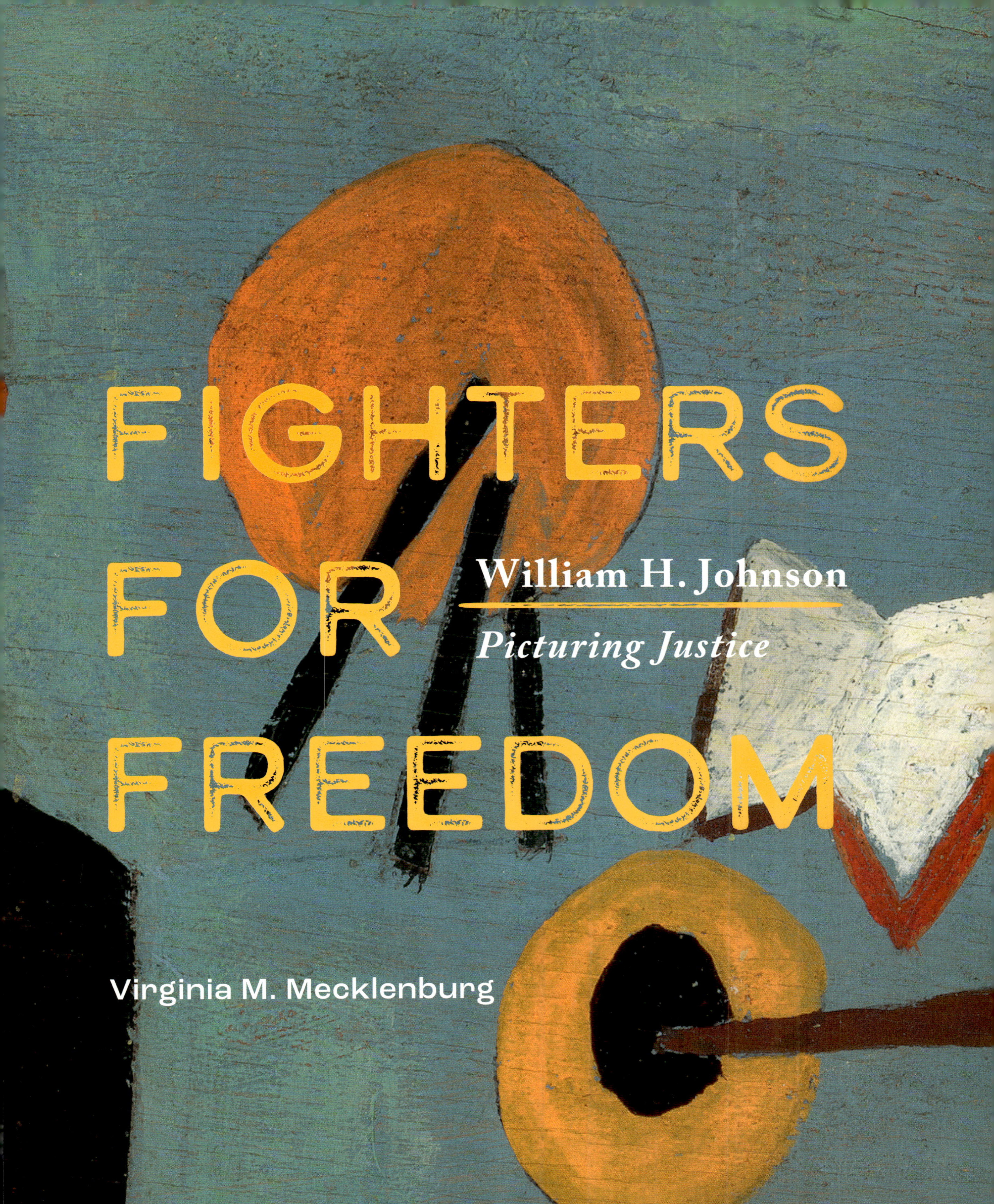
FIGHTERS FOR FREEDOM
William H. Johnson
Picturing Justice
Virginia M. Mecklenburg

Fighters for Freedom: William H. Johnson Picturing Justice is organized by the Smithsonian American Art Museum with generous support from

Art Bridges

Faye and Robert Davidson

William R. Kenan Jr.
Endowment Fund

Jacob and Gwendolyn Lawrence
Foundation

Whitney and Elizabeth MacMillan
Foundation

Margery and Edgar Masinter
Exhibition Endowment

Sara Roby Foundation

Share Fund

Art Bridges

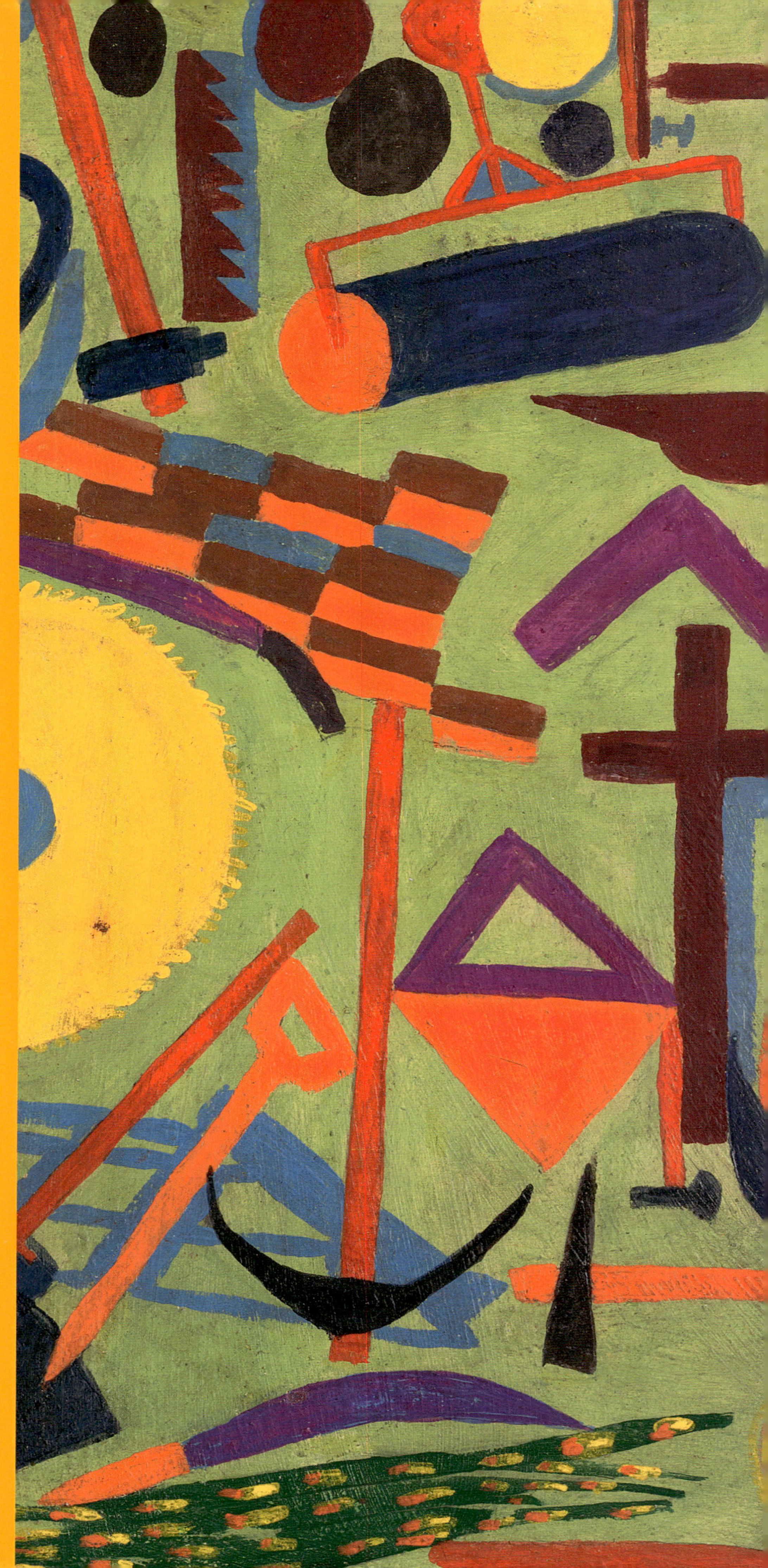

CONTENTS

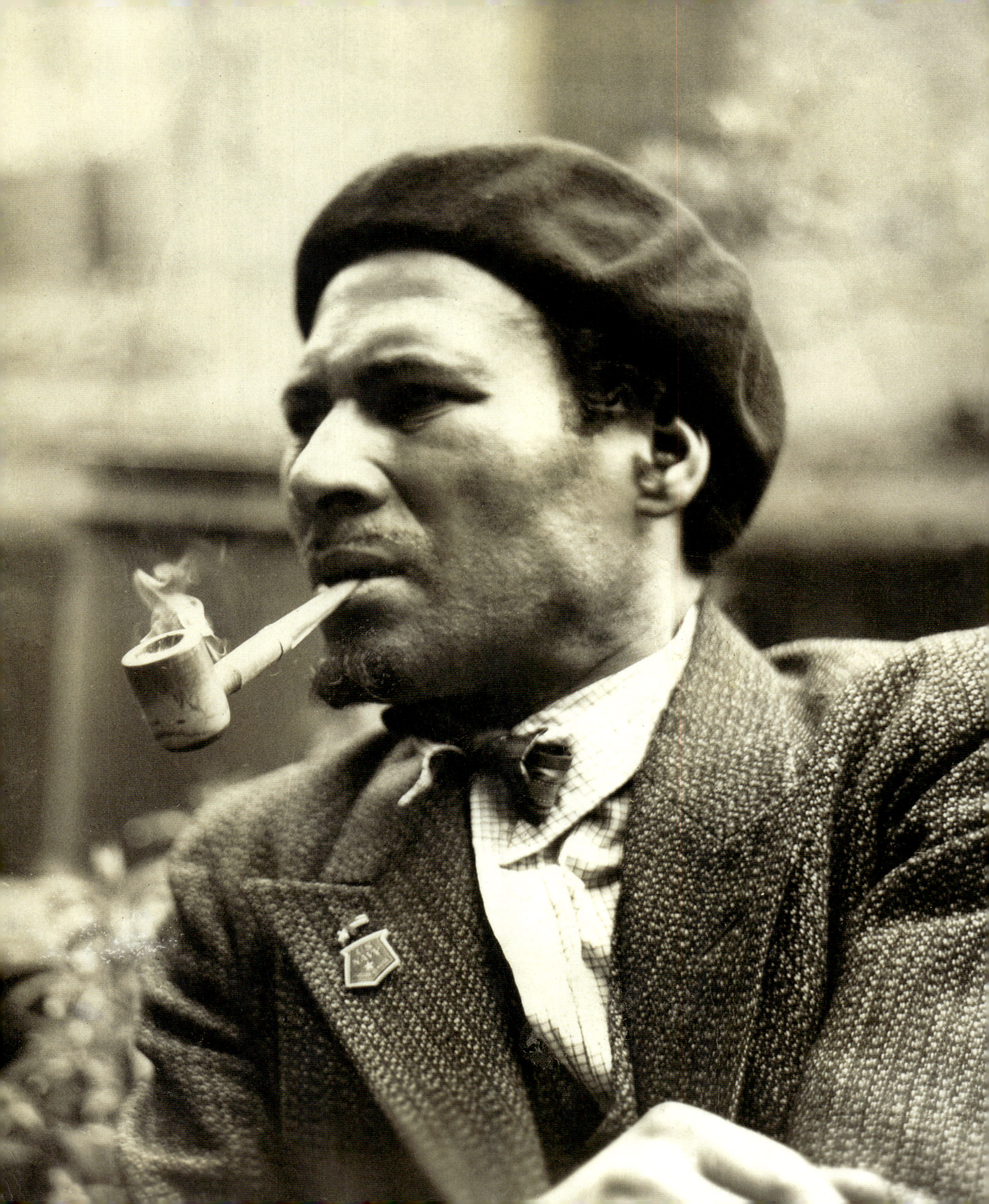

DIRECTOR'S FOREWORD

Stephanie Stebich

Margaret and Terry Stent Director
Smithsonian American Art Museum

THE PAINTING SERIES *Fighters for Freedom* is the culmination of a career that took William H. Johnson (1901–1970) from Florence, South Carolina, to New York, Paris, Denmark, Norway, and ultimately back home, where he painted the lives of those he called "my people." Even as a boy, Johnson had a vision. He left the Jim Crow South at age seventeen, determined to become an artist. He excelled at the National Academy of Design in New York City, then honed his skills in France and Scandinavia. When he returned to the United States in 1938, he dedicated himself to a singular goal—to paint what it meant to be Black in the United States. With the *Fighters* series he went even further. By telling the stories of those who fought for social justice, both historically and in his own time, he confirmed that African Americans have always been central to the American narrative.

Johnson's own life was one of both triumph and tragedy. The press, in Scandinavia where he lived in the 1930s, and later in New York, enthusiastically covered his exhibitions. But at age forty-six he was diagnosed with a degenerative brain disease and hospitalized for the remainder of his life. In 1967 the William E. Harmon Foundation, the patron of African American artists that cared for Johnson's work after his hospitalization, entrusted his entire collection of more than one thousand paintings, watercolors, prints, and drawings to the Smithsonian American Art Museum (SAAM). The museum, in turn, offered almost one hundred and fifty paintings and prints to other institutions. As a result, Fisk, Hampton, Howard, Morgan State, and other historically Black universities have rich collections of Johnson's work. The Harmon Foundation also gave Johnson's personal scrapbook and a rich trove of documentary materials to SAAM. These now reside with the Smithsonian Institution's Archives of American Art, which makes these primary sources available online. It is an awesome and humbling responsibility to preserve, display, and interpret the lifetime work of this American master.

William H. Johnson, ca. 1945,
Harmon Foundation Collection,
National Archives, Washington, DC

Like many of his contemporaries, Johnson pushed the boundaries of conventional art-making. In his commitment to painting Black life, he reclaimed people and truths too often dismissed by mainstream white culture. Throughout his career Johnson ignored social assumptions and racial barriers to follow his own star. He learned then broke free of conventional art-making, experimented with color and movement, and moved from one style to another in a constant challenge to push himself further. As a result, the paintings from his youthful years at the National Academy look very different from those he painted in France, Denmark, and Norway, while his images of Black life in New York and the South are dramatically unlike anything he had created before. In *Fighters for Freedom*, Johnson's last body of work, he explored yet another direction, one that was uniquely suited to episodically telling the powerful stories of those who fought for freedom and personal agency in the United States and around the world.

Many of the Fighters Johnson identified now seem obvious choices. John Brown, Harriet Tubman, and Frederick Douglass were well-known activists in the American struggle for social and racial justice even during their lifetimes. International figures—Mohandas Gandhi, Haile Selassie, and others—extended the quest for freedom and individual choice on the world stage. Some of the Fighters are included in spite of inconvenient truths about their lives. He honored George Washington, even though he was an enslaver. He featured Marcus Garvey, who offered hope to millions that they could escape systemic discrimination by moving to Africa, even though Garvey was jailed for securities fraud. British prime minister Winston Churchill, who was a key figure in the Allied victory in World War II, appears as a Fighter even though for years Churchill vocally refused to liberate India from British colonial rule. Yet Johnson honored them as he did others because their achievements were colossal in spite of their personal failings.

In tracing the Fighters' lives, Johnson tracked high points of American history and individual achievement from the Revolutionary War through World War II. But he refused to pull punches. Through small vignettes he confronted the prejudice and brutality that challenged the Fighters and undermined democracy's fundamental values of life, liberty, and the pursuit of happiness.

We still have much to learn about Johnson's *Fighters for Freedom*. We don't know exactly when Johnson painted each one. *Crispus Attucks* and *Swearing in George Washington* appear to be several years earlier than the dense, scrapbook-like images of 1944 and 1945. Magazine articles he used as source materials suggest he was thinking about the series at least as early as 1939, and possibly even before he returned to the United States from Scandinavia the previous year. We don't know the order in which he painted them or how he chose which Fighters to feature. Nor do we have information about his relationships with the contemporary Fighters. He met Paul Robeson in Copenhagen, but did Johnson see Robeson in the role of Othello on Broadway? Did he meet Josephine Baker in Paris and see her perform? Did he watch newsreel clips of Joe Louis winning the world heavyweight championship or hear radio speeches that Mary McLeod Bethune delivered in her deep, sonorous voice?

Johnson left no diary that recorded his thoughts or personal encounters, but he kept a scrapbook in which he saved his awards and reviews of his exhibitions. Photographs and postcards, his marriage contract, and articles he clipped about current events provide important insights into his life.

We all owe a huge debt to those who ensured that Johnson's artworks and legacy would survive. Mary Beattie Brady and Evelyn S. Brown of the Harmon Foundation supported Johnson and promoted his work during his lifetime. An early prize and cash award from the Harmon Foundation allowed him to travel to Denmark in 1930. Brady and Brown featured Johnson's paintings in the

Harmon Foundation's annual exhibitions and sent them to shows elsewhere when Johnson lived abroad. Most significant, however, they assumed responsibility for the care of Johnson's entire body of work for a full decade.

When Johnson was hospitalized in 1947, his artworks were placed in storage with costs covered by money he had earned working at the Brooklyn Navy Yard. When funds ran out and the artworks were about to be discarded, Helen and David Harriton, whom Johnson and his wife had met in 1937, alerted the Harmon Foundation. The New York Surrogate's Court subsequently awarded ownership to the foundation.

In 1967, when the foundation ceased operation, Brady and Brown offered Johnson's artworks to the Smithsonian American Art Museum. Director David Scott and Curator of Contemporary Art Adelyn Dohme Breeskin accepted more than one thousand paintings, drawings, and prints, as well as Johnson's scrapbook and source materials. Many were in wretched condition from years of storage under abysmal conditions. It was an act of faith on their part to commit to the preservation of Johnson's work and to ensure that his vision would survive for future generations.

Much of what we know about Johnson's story comes from publications by pioneering scholars of African American art Dr. Leslie King-Hammond and Dr. Richard J. Powell, whose PhD dissertations and subsequent books and articles have probed the nuances of Johnson's art and life. Building on their groundwork and Breeskin's catalogue for SAAM's 1971 exhibition *William H. Johnson, 1901–1970*, others followed. In articles and catalogue essays David Driskell, Tritobia Hayes Benjamin, Lowery Stokes Sims, and Lizzetta LeFalle-Collins have examined the subjects, themes, and places Johnson painted and situated him in terms of his contemporary artists and moment. In her master's thesis Cristie Owen Adams identified many of the figures Johnson included in the

Fighters for Freedom paintings; Makeda Best's discussion of Johnson's scrapbooking approach in the *Fighters* panels offers cultural as well as stylistic insights into this fascinating body of work. Pre- and postdoctoral fellows at SAAM and elsewhere will carry the work of these scholars forward, offering fresh insights into this powerful and provocative agent of American art and culture.

Fighters for Freedom: William H. Johnson Picturing Justice brings these remarkable paintings together as a group for the first time since 1946. It is an honor to present them in Washington, DC, and to share Johnson's paintings and his remarkable story with museums across the United States.

Many people have made the exhibition possible. It is a special pleasure to thank Robert C. Davidson Jr., chair of the SAAM Board of Commissioners, and his wife, Faye, for supporting the project from its outset. Dr. Walter O. Evans and the Jacob and Gwendolyn Knight Lawrence Foundation, Joe Roby of the Sara Roby Foundation, the Share Fund, the William R. Kenan Jr. Endowment Fund, the Whitney and Elizabeth MacMillan Foundation, and the Margery and Edgar Masinter Exhibition Endowment provided invaluable assistance. The Art Bridges Foundation enabled the exhibition to tour to a dozen venues around the country. Funding from the Kress Foundation allowed us to bring Keara Teeter to SAAM's Lunder Conservation Center to treat more than thirty *Fighters for Freedom* paintings under Amber Kerr's expert supervision.

We are deeply grateful to President Darrell K. Williams and Dr. Vanessa Thaxton-Ward of Hampton University for allowing us to present *Three Great Freedom Fighter*s and *Against the Odds* in the Washington, DC, exhibition. Special thanks also go to Hampton's curator of collections Kenlontae' Turner for his unflagging enthusiasm and assistance.

The presentation at SAAM owes a huge debt to Phoebe Hilleman, Emily K. Berg, and Anne Showalter, who have created educational materials and in-gallery

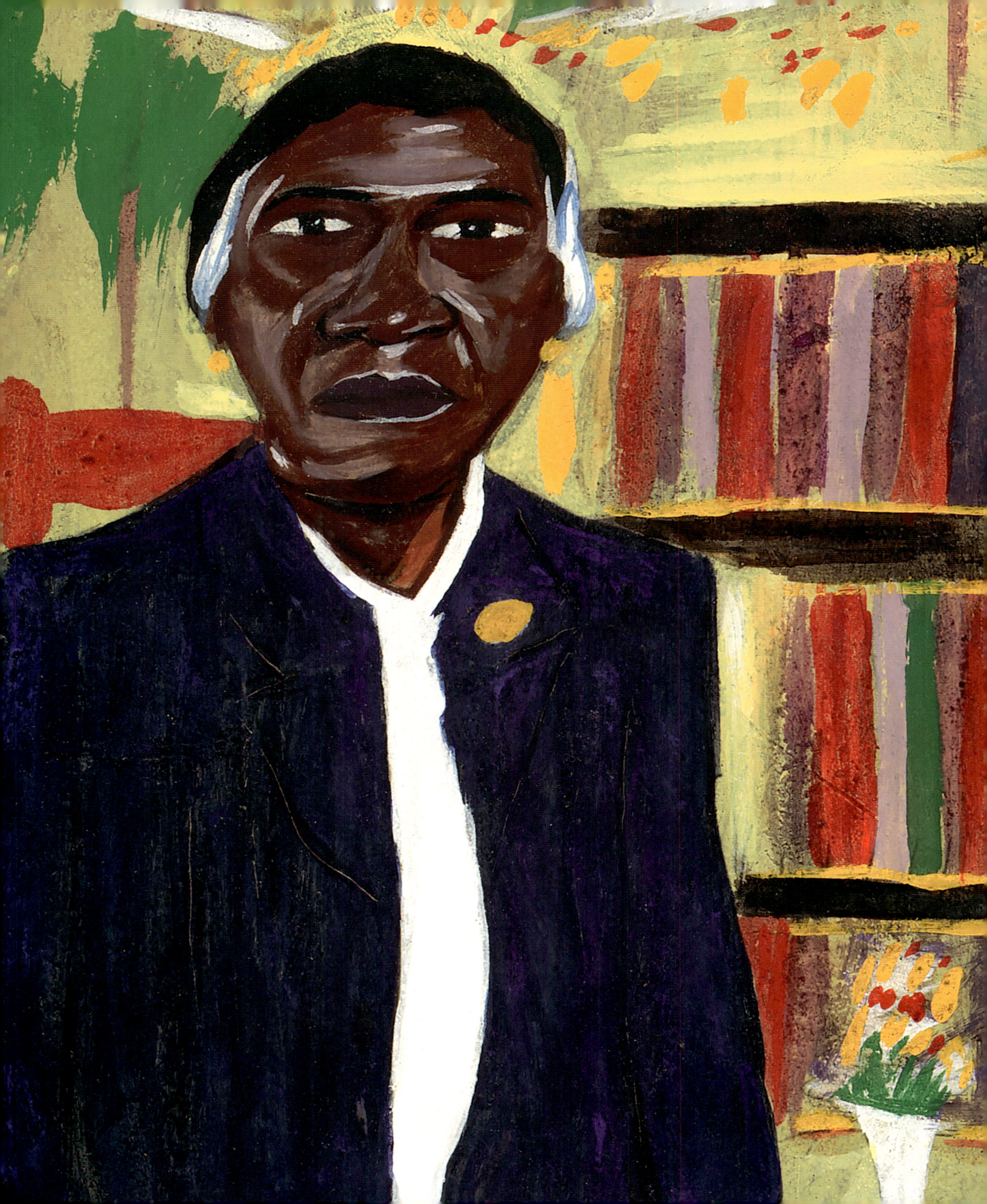

interpretation strategies that bring Johnson's Fighters to life and help us understand that the American narrative includes sacrifice and suffering as well as individual and collective triumph. In our exhibitions office, the creative design team of Sara Gray and Nathaniel Phillips developed a beautiful installation that brings Johnson's own aesthetic for the *Fighters for Freedom* into focus in the galleries. Martin Kotler, frame conservator extraordinaire, ensured the powerful presentation of each artwork. Senior Curator Virginia Mecklenburg has long championed Johnson's work and has written and spoken beautifully about his important place in the story of American art. We are grateful she thoughtfully conceived the exhibition and, with Collections Coordinator Laura Augustin, uncovered the stories told here and coordinated the efforts of this dedicated group. Special thanks, as always, go to registrars Jenni Lee and Ed Bray, who coordinated logistics and organized the national tour, and to collections managers Jim Concha and Claire Denny for their assistance with all things related to storing, accessing, and shipping this collection.

And to the book team—Tiffany Farrell, head of SAAM's publications office; editor Emily Rohan; scholar Janell Blackmon Pryor; designer Denise Arnot; and Virginia Mecklenburg—you've created a volume that beautifully illuminates the stories Johnson told in his *Fighters for Freedom* paintings. Emily K. Berg and Phoebe Hillemann, thank you for writing the insightful Smithsonian Connections sidebars, linking items from other Smithsonian museums to Johnson's Fighters. Finally, to our colleagues at Scala Arts Publishers, we appreciate your care and assistance in producing and marketing this book.

I also express our thanks to Smithsonian Institution Secretary Lonnie G. Bunch III for his eloquent introduction about the nation's historical and ongoing struggles for equality and for his unwavering support for the Smithsonian American Art Museum.

Historical Scene with Mary McLeod Bethune (detail); see p. 109

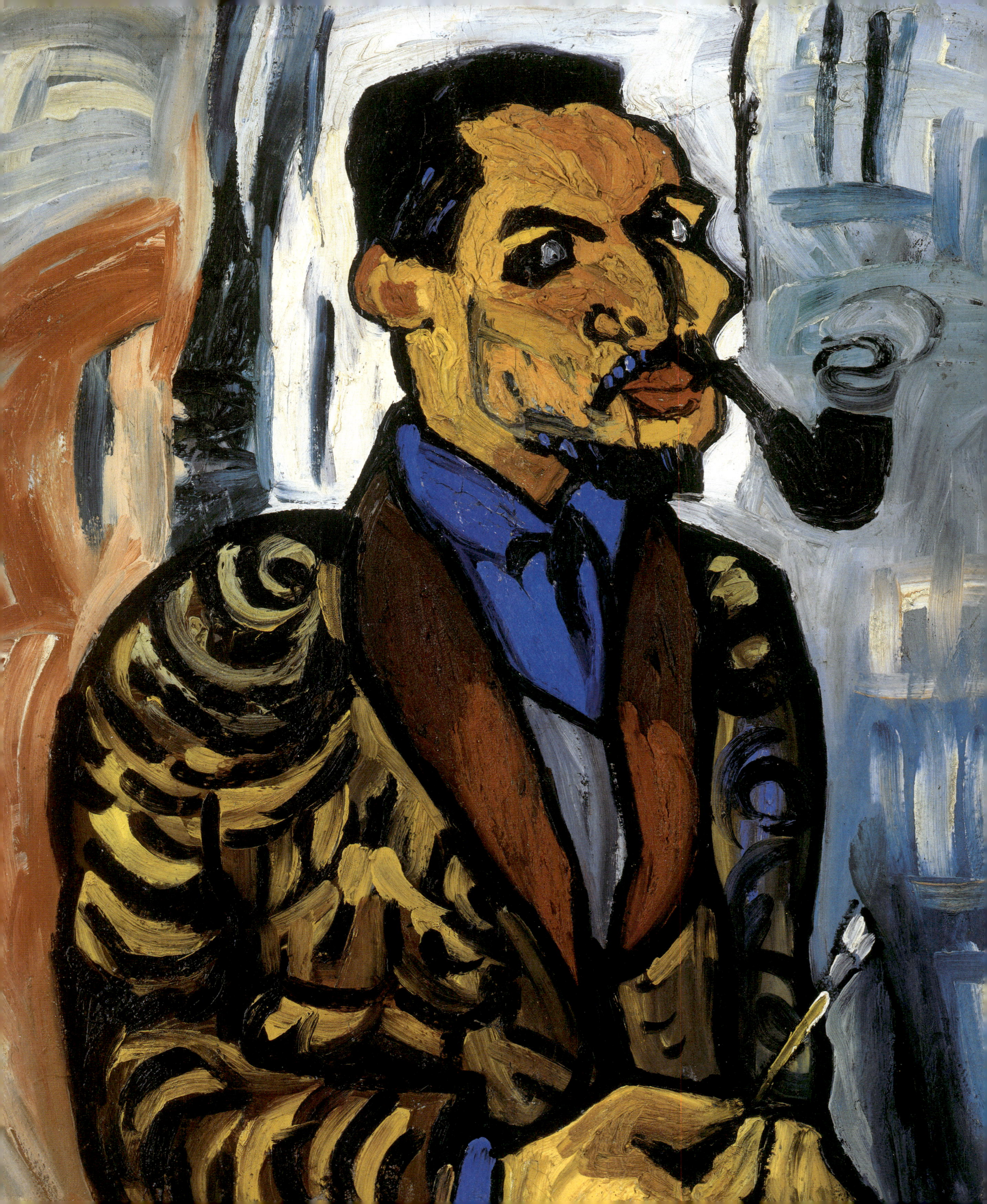

INTRODUCTION

Lonnie G. Bunch III

Secretary
Smithsonian Institution

WILLIAM H. JOHNSON'S remarkable series of paintings, *Fighters for Freedom*, is a timeless and universal celebration of the innate human need to be free. It is also a specific response to the era in which he lived. During the 1940s, the images of African Americans that proliferated were often negative, a collection of racist stereotypes intended to minimize Black people and rob them of their humanity. Johnson offered an important counternarrative, showing how much African Americans had contributed to the nation's history and character, thus earning them equal and fair treatment in American society. By including non-African American figures in this series, he stated emphatically that the Black people he memorialized on the canvas were every bit as deserving of full citizenship. With these significant artworks, Johnson also claimed his place as an accomplished global citizen and American in his own right.

From its inception, the United States has been defined by intertwined struggles for freedom and over who should benefit from that freedom. Much of the work to build a more equitable nation, whether by expanding voting rights, advocating for equal justice under the law, or fighting for access to economic opportunity, was undertaken by those to whom freedoms were denied, including African Americans, Indigenous peoples, and women. American history is rife with stories about people both famous and obscure who, despite their country not believing in them, believed in their country and fought to compel it to live up to its noblest ideals.

The desire to be free is one of the things we all have in common. When freedom is taken away, understandably, our yearning for it only grows stronger. This truth was most evident among enslaved African Americans; historical accounts confirm they regularly discussed freedom in their cramped quarters. Their belief when there was no reason to believe and their resilience in the face of the ultimate injustice prove that the other component of fighting for freedom has always been hope.

Self-Portrait with Pipe (detail); see p. 34

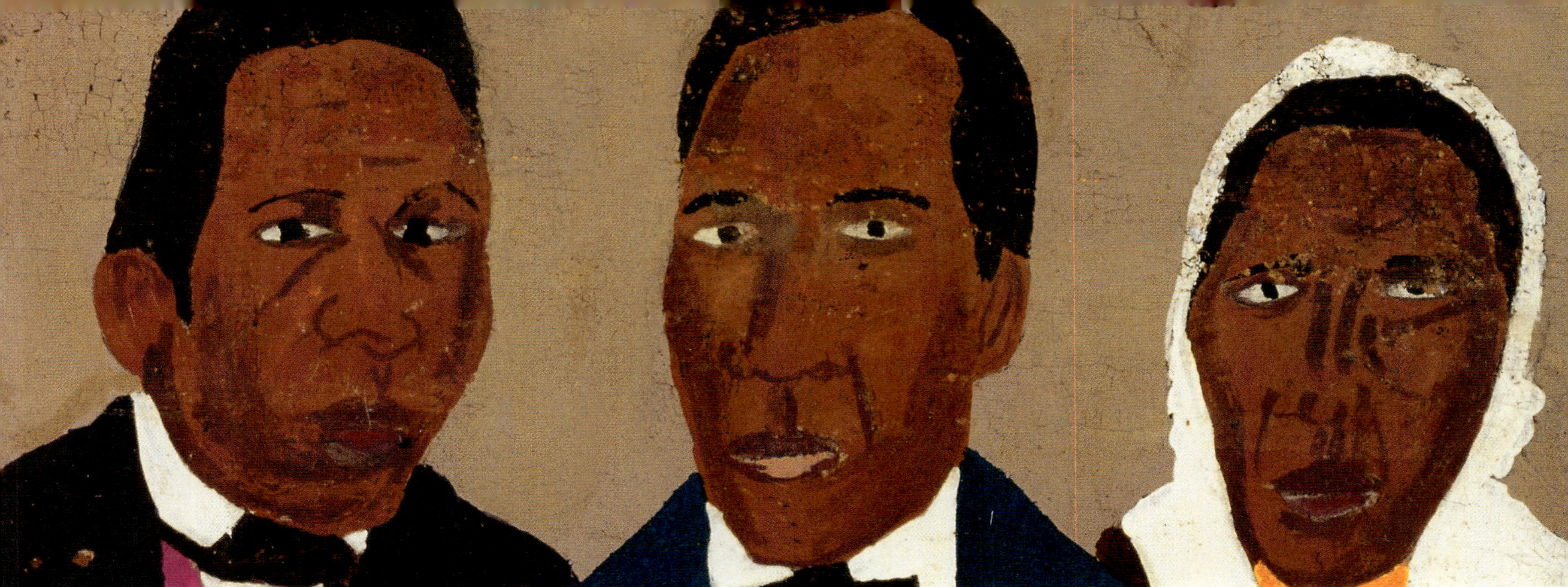

Underground Railroad (details); see p. 69

Slavery is the most heinous and inhuman example of the deprivation of liberty, so when I think about some of our nation's great freedom fighters, I think about the abolitionists who fought to undo this moral blight, among them Harriet Tubman, John Brown, Frederick Douglass, and Abraham Lincoln. They and their successors in the Civil Rights Movement who fought to end the segregation and discrimination of the Jim Crow era—A. Philip Randolph, Ella Baker, Bayard Rustin, John Lewis, and so many others—changed the course of a nation, and in so doing, helped bend the moral arc of the universe toward justice.

A central issue of those fighting for civil rights, of course, was to enfranchise those who had been prevented from taking part in our purest and most essential expression of democracy, the vote. From poll taxes to literacy tests, courageous men and women fought to overcome obstacles that stood in the way of the right to self-govern. Those who toiled to secure the franchise are also heroes; freedom fighters who worked for voting rights and to pass the Fifteenth and Nineteenth Amendments like Sojourner Truth, Ida B. Wells, Mary Church Terrell, and Lucy Stone must never be forgotten. Their legacy continues today with the people still battling voter suppression and other attempts to turn back the clock on the constitutional rights central to our democratic republic.

Another group deserving of our collective gratitude are those who donned uniforms, fought in foreign lands, and risked their lives for the nation and its aspirational principles, despite unequal treatment back home—literal freedom

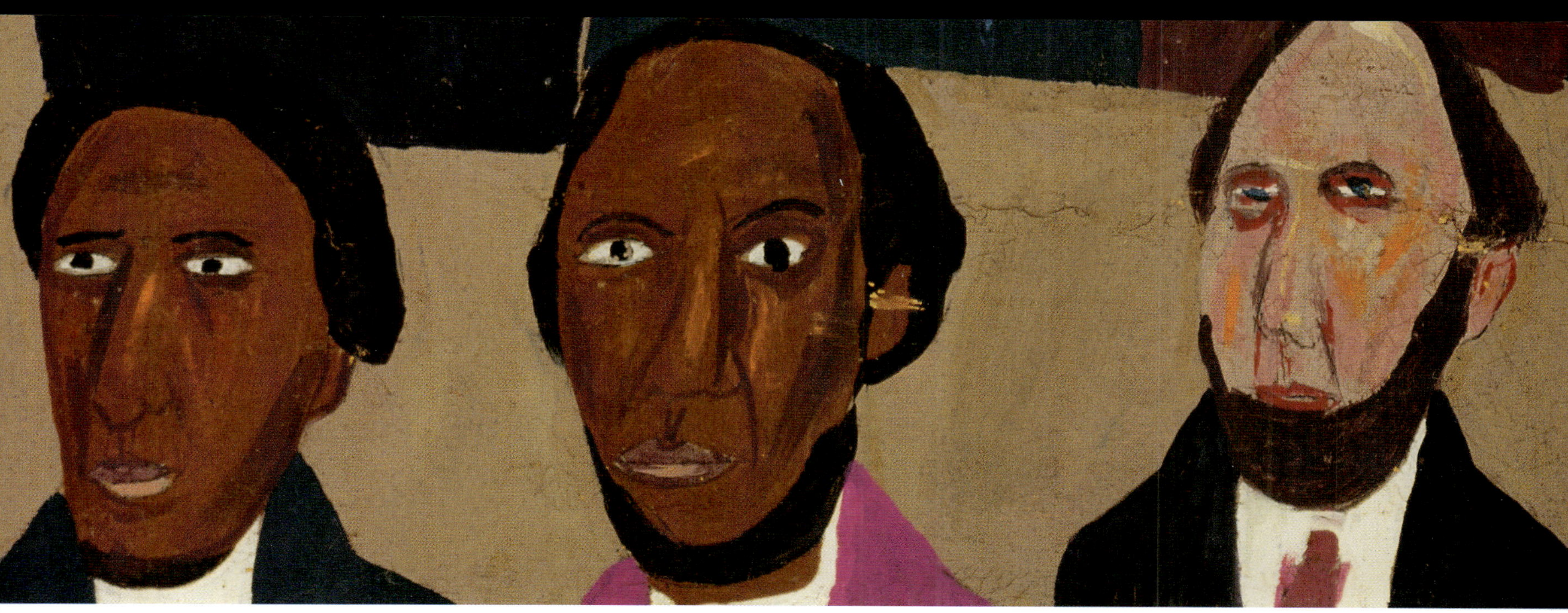

fighters. I think of the Indigenous people who, despite having been granted citizenship less than a century ago, serve in the U.S. military at a rate five times the national average. Or World War I's segregated 369th Infantry Regiment from New York, known as the Harlem Hellfighters, who were treated with an unfamiliar dignity and respect while stationed in France. They came home with a renewed determination to combat the widespread injustice of a segregated America, paving the way for a new generation of people who created a robust Civil Rights Movement.

Stories like these are as vital today as they have ever been because the struggle for freedom continues. History has always been my preferred weapon in the fight for social justice and in helping highlight the roles so many have played in making our nation better. As a historian who has spent my career in the museum field, I have witnessed time and again the wondrous power of bringing accounts like these to light. They spark curiosity about who we are, where we come from, and what our future may look like. It is so important to research, preserve, and tell the stories about people who changed the course of history, whether in textbooks, museums, popular media, or on canvas like the vibrant works of William H. Johnson.

Johnson's *Fighters for Freedom* series is a striking example of art at its most potent, using a colorful palette to create evocative scenes and craft important narratives about equality, justice, achievement, and the sacrifices made in the continuing effort to bring about a more perfect union. It speaks to the time

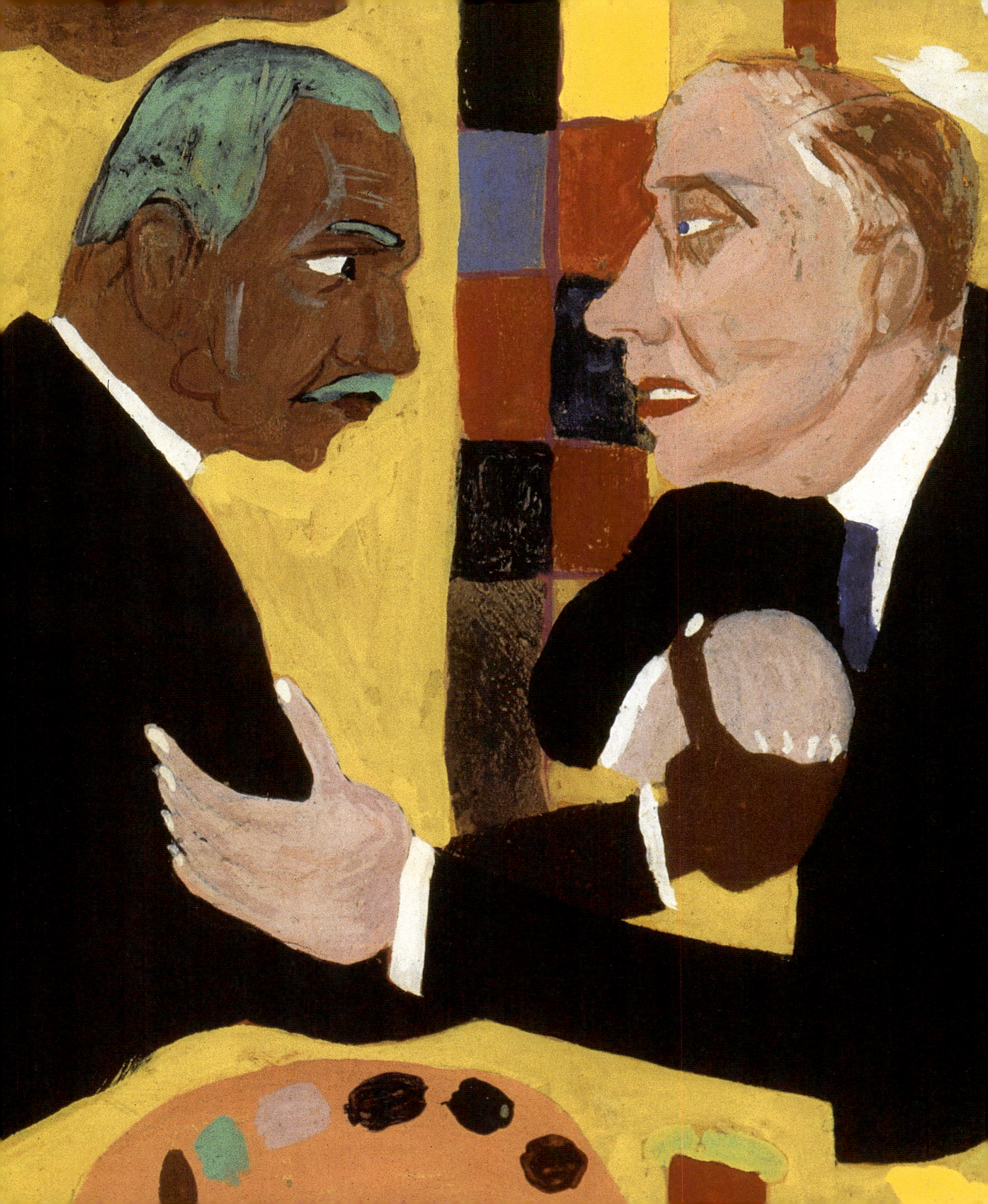

in which he lived, created from his unique vantage point as someone who straddled two worlds—the son of South Carolina who knew firsthand the disparity between the ideals of freedom and its unequal attainability, and the outsider who lived in Europe and saw the potential in a freer and more accepting society.

The stories he chose to commemorate in this series highlight those who did the hard work of changing the country, bit by bit, generation by generation: Little-known travelers in the Underground Railroad who made the journey from enslavement to freedom. World-renowned singer Marian Anderson, who performed for seventy-five thousand people on the steps of the Lincoln Memorial in 1939 after being denied the right to sing at Constitution Hall. Black women, such as educator Mary McLeod Bethune, housing advocate Jane Edna Hunter, and Maggie Lena Walker, the first woman to found and run a bank, who built impressive institutions despite being discriminated against for both the color of their skin and their gender.

Fighters for Freedom celebrates those who challenged the nation to extend its blessings of liberty, freedom, and democracy to everyone, despite the danger they faced in doing so. I hope the traveling exhibition organized by Virginia Mecklenburg, senior curator at the Smithsonian American Art Museum, inspires a new generation to seek out the lives and deeds of William H. Johnson's subjects. Their courage and moral clarity remain a beacon for anyone seeking to make the United States live up to the ideal that Frederick Douglass envisioned as "the perfect national illustration of the unity and dignity of the human family that the world has ever seen."

Dr. George Washington Carver (detail); see p. 90

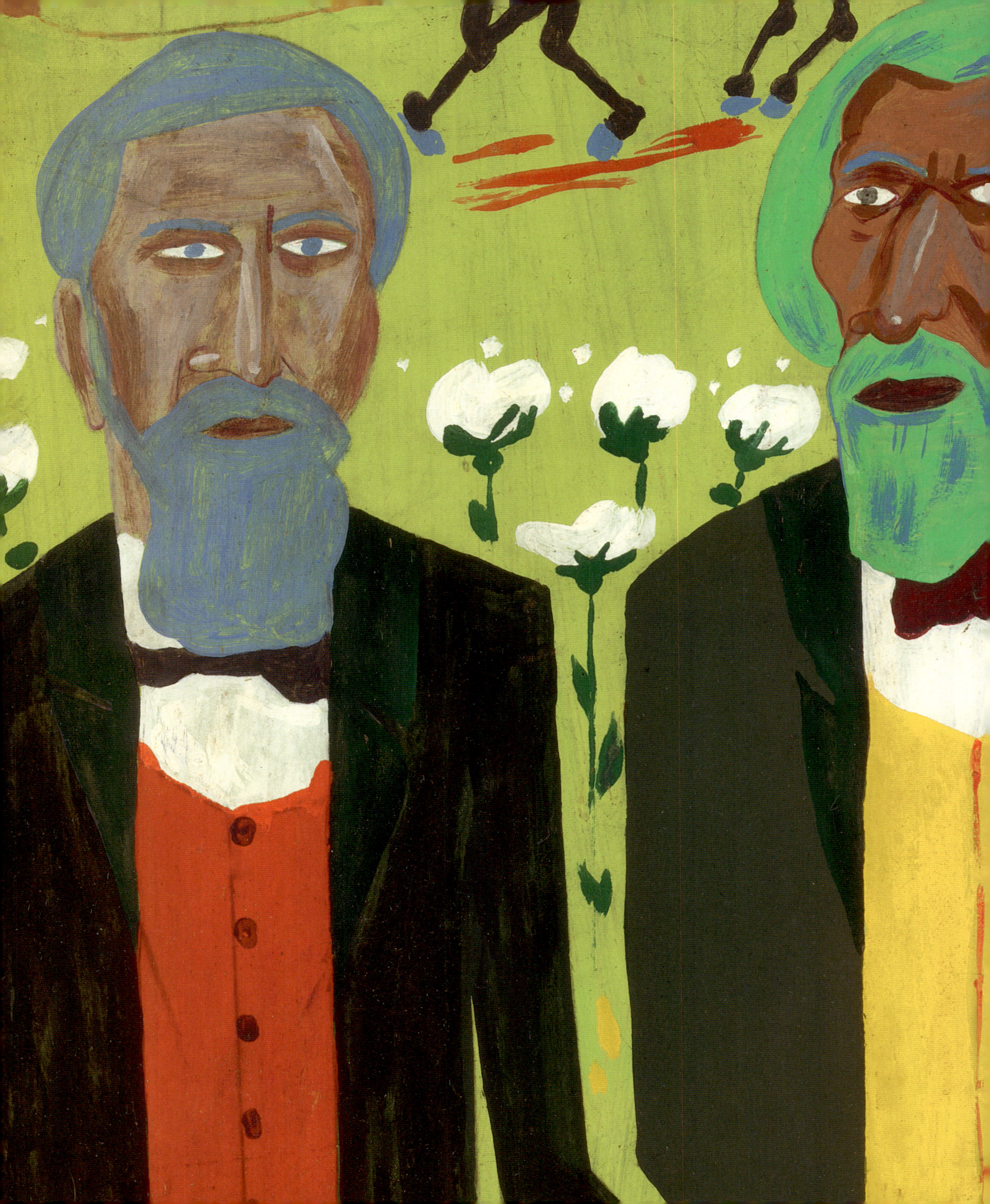

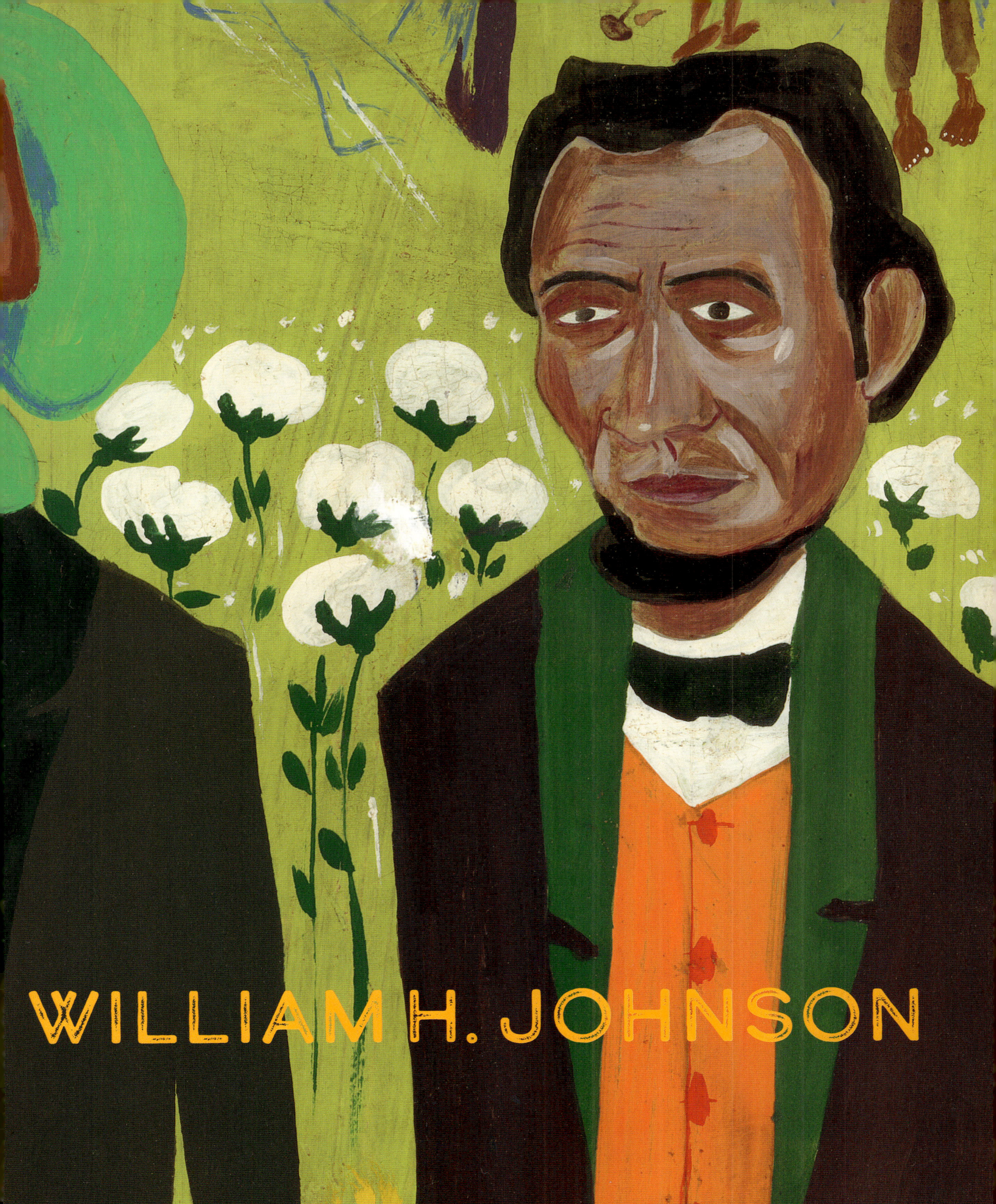
WILLIAM H. JOHNSON

AN INDEPENDENT MAN

In all my years of painting, I have had one absorbing and inspired idea, and have worked towards it with unyielding zeal—to give, in simple and stark form—the story of the Negro as he has existed.

William H. Johnson, 1946[1]

Virginia M. Mecklenburg

Senior Curator, Smithsonian American Art Museum

WILLIAM H. JOHNSON (1901–1970) (Fig. 1) painted his *Fighters for Freedom* series in the mid-1940s as a tribute to African American activists, scientists, teachers, and performers and to recognize the efforts of international figures working against colonialism and armed aggression during World War II. He celebrated their accomplishments, but he also acknowledged the realities of racism, violence, and oppression they faced. We know the stories of some of his Fighters—Harriet Tubman, George Washington Carver, and Marian Anderson are legends. But today fewer of us remember the pioneering educator Nannie Helen Burroughs, or Jane Edna Hunter, who provided affordable, safe housing for Black women working in Cleveland, Ohio.

Through Johnson's *Fighters for Freedom* paintings, we learn about people who changed lives, promoted equality, valued legacy, and demonstrated unflagging determination in the face of almost insurmountable challenges. Johnson shows us who they were and offers historical insights into their lives. Ultimately, he helps us understand that the pursuit of freedom is ongoing across generations, and in doing so, he implicitly charges us to think about the struggle for social justice in our own time. With *Fighters for Freedom* Johnson tells us that the continued fight for equity, dignity, and equality for all is central to the American story.

Who Was William H. Johnson?

Like the individuals he called "fighters for freedom," Johnson, too, understood sacrifice and determination. He was born in 1901 in Florence, South Carolina,

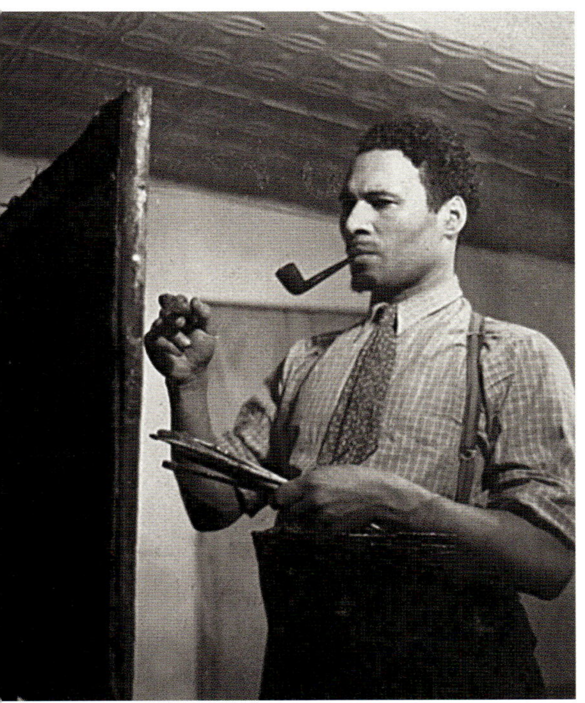

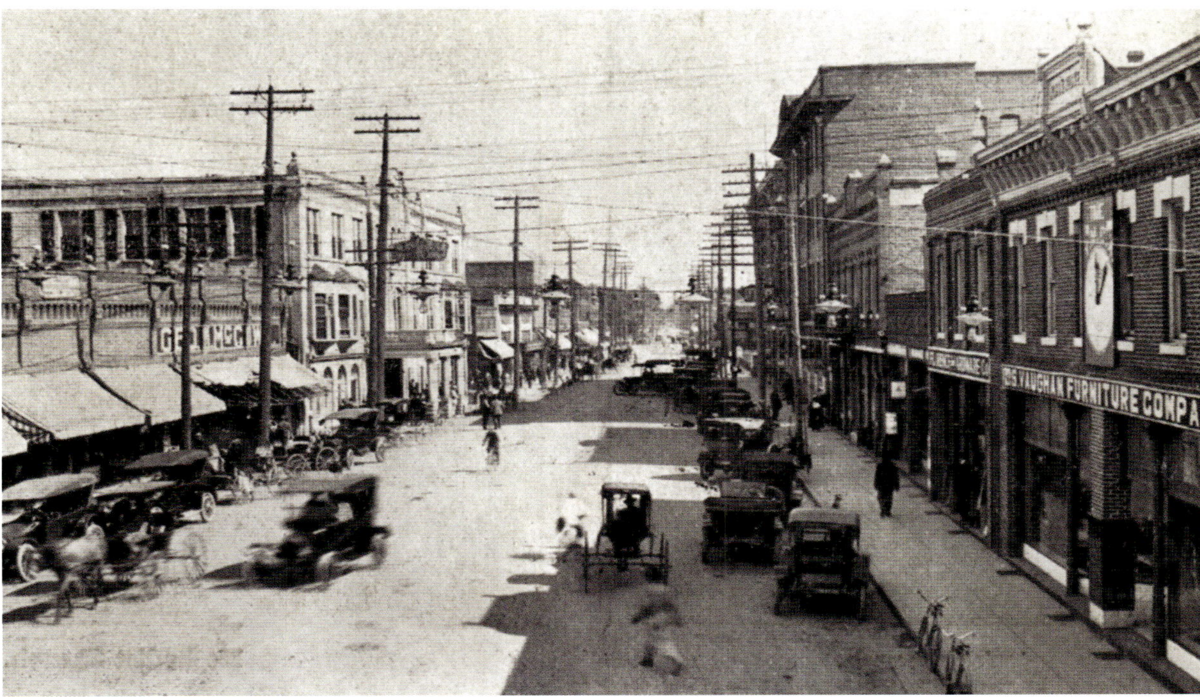

Fig. 1

William H. Johnson, ca. 1937, William H. Johnson papers, Archives of American Art

Fig. 2

Florence, South Carolina, 1914, Courtesy Florence County Museum

a bustling commercial center that was a hub for the Atlantic Coast Line Railroad (**Fig. 2**).[2] His parents, Henry and Alice Johnson, modeled hard work—his father shoveled coal for the railroad, his mother worked as a cook at the local YMCA and in domestic service. As a kid Johnson ran errands and worked in a bowling alley. But he learned about the world beyond the segregated southern community where he grew up from his uncle Willie Smoot, a Pullman porter on the New York to Miami route. Smoot regaled his namesake with tales about the great city to the north and fueled Johnson's dreams.

Johnson left for New York City when he was seventeen, one of hundreds of thousands of African Americans who abandoned low-paying jobs and subsistence farm life for greater opportunities in urban centers in the North, Midwest, East, and even as far west as California. Chicago and Detroit were destinations, as were San Francisco and Los Angeles. But for many, the vibrant streets of Harlem in New York offered the greatest inducement to leave home. There were jobs to be had, but even more, Harlem offered a space where Black Americans could savor food, create music, and pursue religious practices born in the African American community. Although not entirely free of discrimination, it was a place where creativity and individuality flourished. For Johnson, who hoped to become a commercial cartoonist, New York offered galleries and museums and art schools—places where he could look at art and learn skills that tapped into his talent for drawing.

Fig. 3

Still Life, ca. 1923–26, oil on canvas, 25 3/8 × 31 7/8 in., Smithsonian American Art Museum, Gift of the Harmon Foundation, 1967.59.684

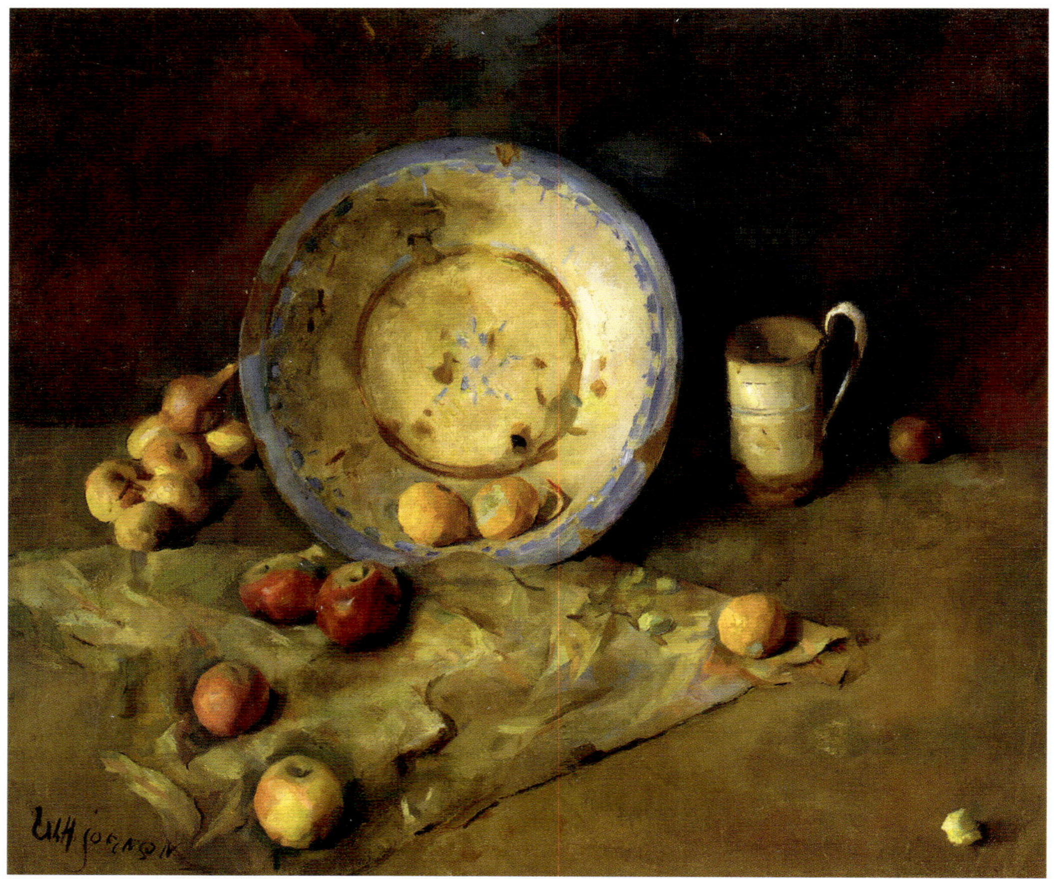

It took three years for Johnson to achieve his dream of becoming an art student. He worked as a laborer, saved money, and, on October 4, 1921, after passing an exam that required him to make quick sketches on the spot, he was accepted at the National Academy of Design. The academy experience was eye-opening. For the first time Johnson was thrown together with people of very different backgrounds and experiences. He studied alongside Russian-born Jewish artist Raphael Soyer; Paul Cadmus, an openly gay man; and Malvin Gray Johnson, an African American from North Carolina whose upbringing paralleled Johnson's own. Johnson soon learned, he said later, that "in the artistic realm, race ultimately isn't very important."[3]

Although it was tough working and going to art school at the same time, Johnson excelled (Fig. 3). By the time he graduated in 1926, he had won almost all the prizes the academy awarded. He also earned the support of one of the academy's newest instructors, Charles W. Hawthorne, a highly respected painter who pushed his students to think beyond conventional ways of making art. Hawthorne advised his students to work emotionally and spontaneously, as art historian and Johnson scholar Richard J. Powell writes, to "raise the mundane to the level of the profound."[4]

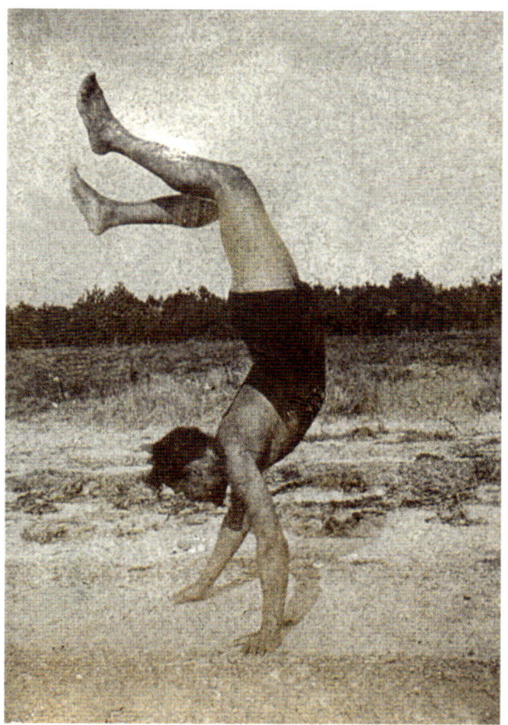

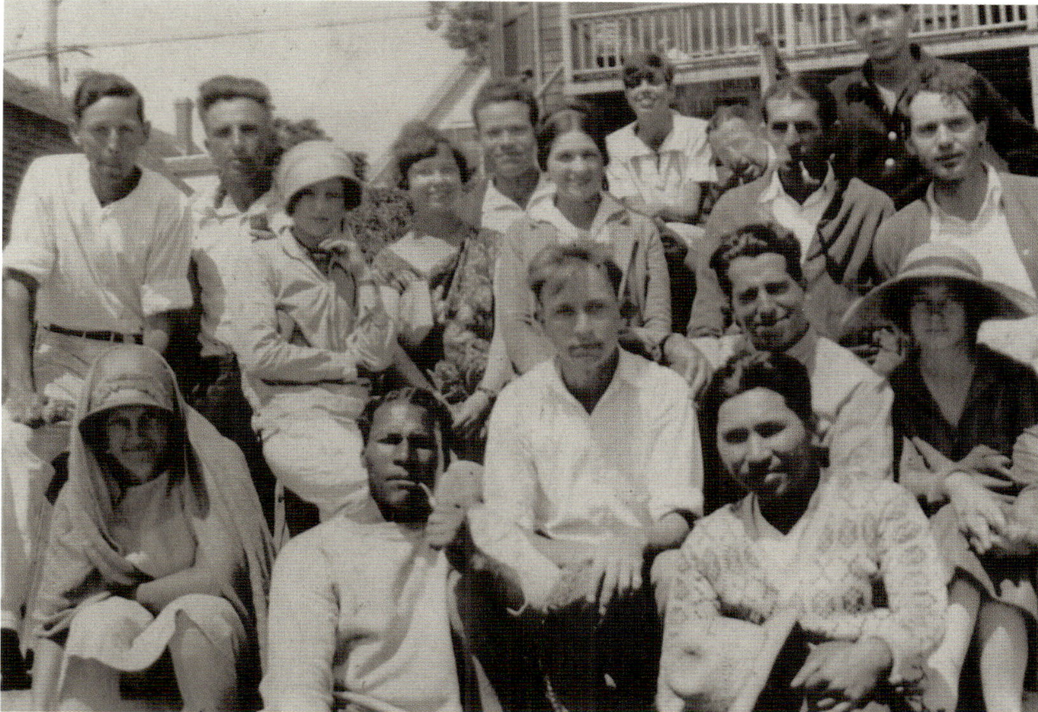

Fig. 4

Johnson at the beach, undated photograph, William H. Johnson papers, Archives of American Art

Fig. 5

Charles Hawthorne's class at Provincetown, MA, ca. 1923–26, William H. Johnson papers, Archives of American Art. Johnson is seated at lower left.

The Years Abroad

Hawthorne believed in Johnson's potential. He hired the young painter to help with his summer school in Provincetown on Cape Cod, paid him as an assistant, and raised funds for Johnson to go to Europe (**Figs. 4, 5**). To make his money go further, Johnson got a job as a ship's porter to pay for his passage across the Atlantic Ocean, and, in November 1926, like many aspiring artists of his generation, he headed for Europe. He later described his first year in Paris:

> *It was some experience. New life. The Dôme* [a bistro frequented by artists]. *Sit down with a "café," with Eye[s] open you see the world in Cavalcade. Before a few hours I had met fellow artists from New York, Provincetown.... first winter in Paris, sharing James M. Whistler's first studio in Montparnasse—painting... as an* ***independent man*** [emphasis mine].... *continued still-life, portrait painting, with many visits to art museums and galleries, with a little French on the side.*[5]

Although Johnson had shown his work in the academy's student exhibitions, his first real show was at the American-run Students and Artists Club in Paris in 1927. His new paintings, filled with brilliant color and unconventional perspectives, marked him as an up-and-coming modernist (**Fig. 6**).

After a year living under the gray skies of the French capital, Johnson longed for sunshine. In 1927 he headed south to Cagnes-sur-Mer. The town was an

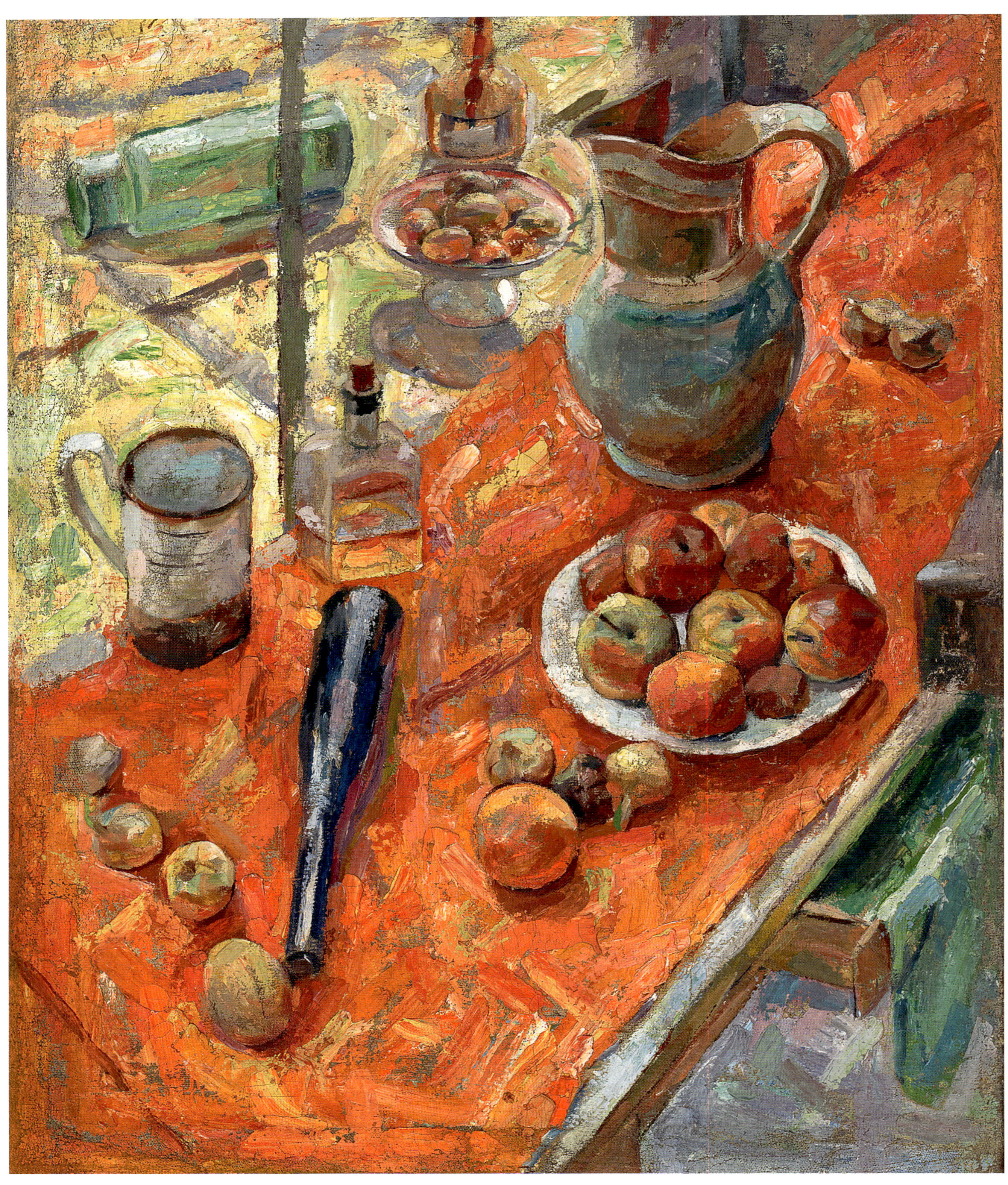

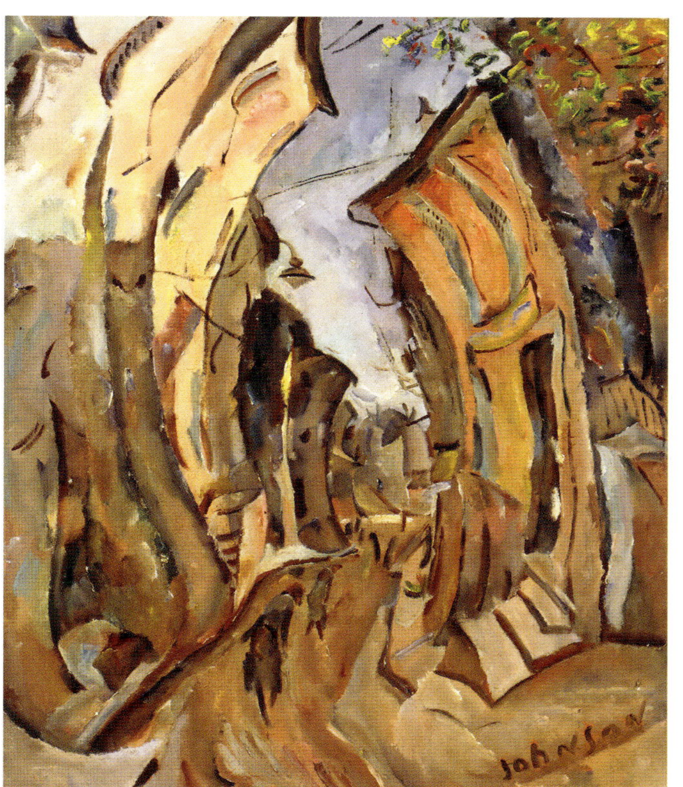

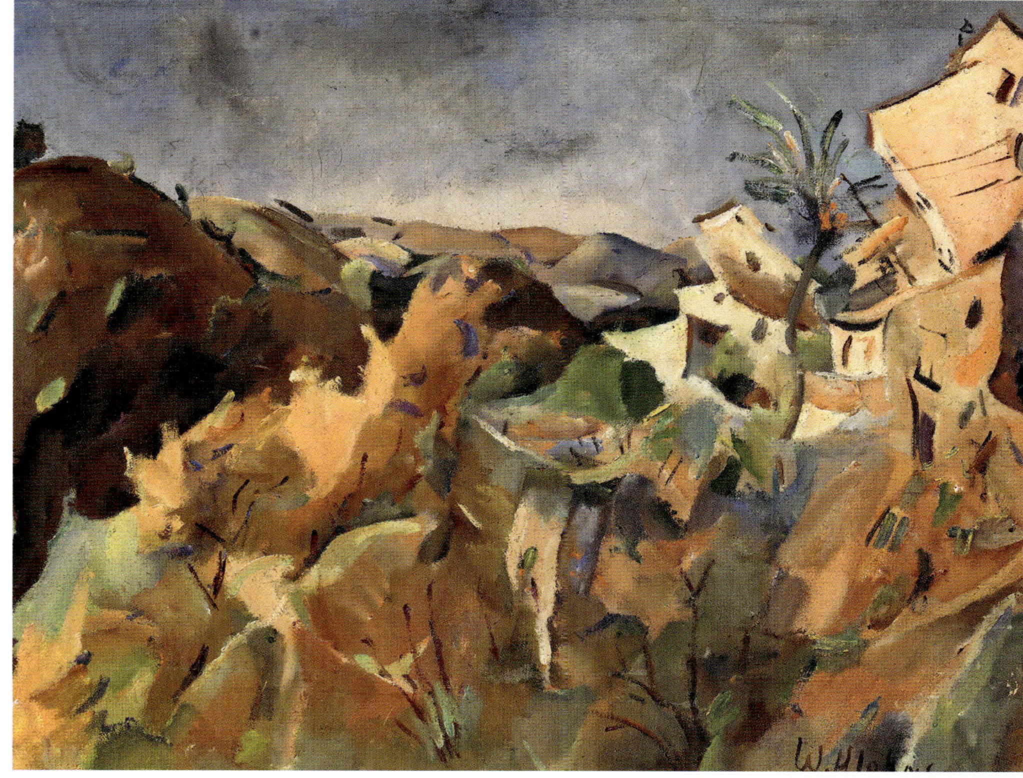

Fig. 6

Still Life, ca. 1927, oil on canvas, 32 × 25 ⅛ in., Smithsonian American Art Museum, Gift of the Harmon Foundation, 1967.59.686

Fig. 7

Cagnes sur Mer ca. 1926–29, oil on canvas, 28 × 23 ⅛ in., Smithsonian American Art Museum, Gift of the Harmon Foundation, 1967.59.713

Fig. 8

Long View from St. Anne, Cagnes sur Mer, ca. 1926–27, oil on canvas, 23 ⅛ × 31 in., Smithsonian American Art Museum, Gift of the Harmon Foundation, 1967.59.688

exciting place for an aspiring modernist to experiment; French impressionist Pierre-Auguste Renoir had worked there, as had the cubist André Derain. But most compelling for Johnson was Chaïm Soutine, who painted buildings, trees, and the land itself as if distorted by the action of an earthquake. Fascinated by Soutine, Johnson applied a newfound sense of movement to his work, creating landscapes and structures that undulate in space (**Figs. 7, 8**). "I am not afraid," he wrote to Hawthorne, "to exaggerate a contour, a form, or anything that gives more character and movement to the canvas." Even so, he was not willing to give up nature. He had, he said, "a reverence [for] the minute detail of the color variation in the sun light."[6]

Although he painted constantly, Johnson found time to enjoy the cafés and street life of the southern French town. In 1929, he met Holcha Krake, a Danish textile artist, and her sister Erna and brother-in-law Christoph Voll, who were traveling around Europe that summer. They became friends immediately; the Danish sisters and German-born sculptor invited Johnson to join them on a trip to the island of Corsica. There, he later recalled, he and Krake "painted together…enjoyed the sun, the beauty of the landscape, and the simple peasant life."[7] After Corsica the group continued on, only to bid each other goodbye in the fall. Krake returned to Denmark, the Volls went back to Germany, and Johnson headed home to the States.

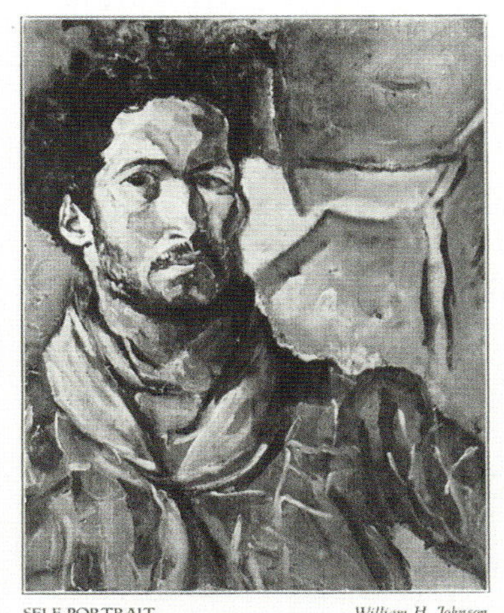

SELF-PORTRAIT William H. Johnson

EXHIBIT OF FINE ARTS
by
American Negro Artists
Presented by the
Harmon Foundation
and
The Commission on Race Relations
Federal Council of Churches

After three years abroad, Johnson was eager to see his family and reconnect with his American friends. He stopped first in New York, where he rented a minimally adequate loft on West 120th Street in Harlem (he had to paint by candlelight under a leaky roof). He also contacted George Luks, a well-known painter and satirical cartoonist he had worked for briefly before heading to Europe. Luks was a juror that year for the Harmon Foundation's Award for Distinguished Achievements among Negroes in the Fine Arts Field.[8] Excited by Johnson's new paintings, Luks immediately nominated him, even though the deadline had passed. The competition was stiff—Allan Rohan Crite, Sargent Johnson, Loïs Mailou Jones, and Augusta Savage were also in the running that year—but the jury unanimously granted the top prize and cash award of four hundred dollars to Johnson. "We think he is one of our coming great painters," announced the press release. "He is a real modernist…spontaneous, vigorous, firm, direct; he has shown a great thing in art—it is the expression of the man himself"[9] (**Fig. 9**). When the foundation's annual show opened in January 1930

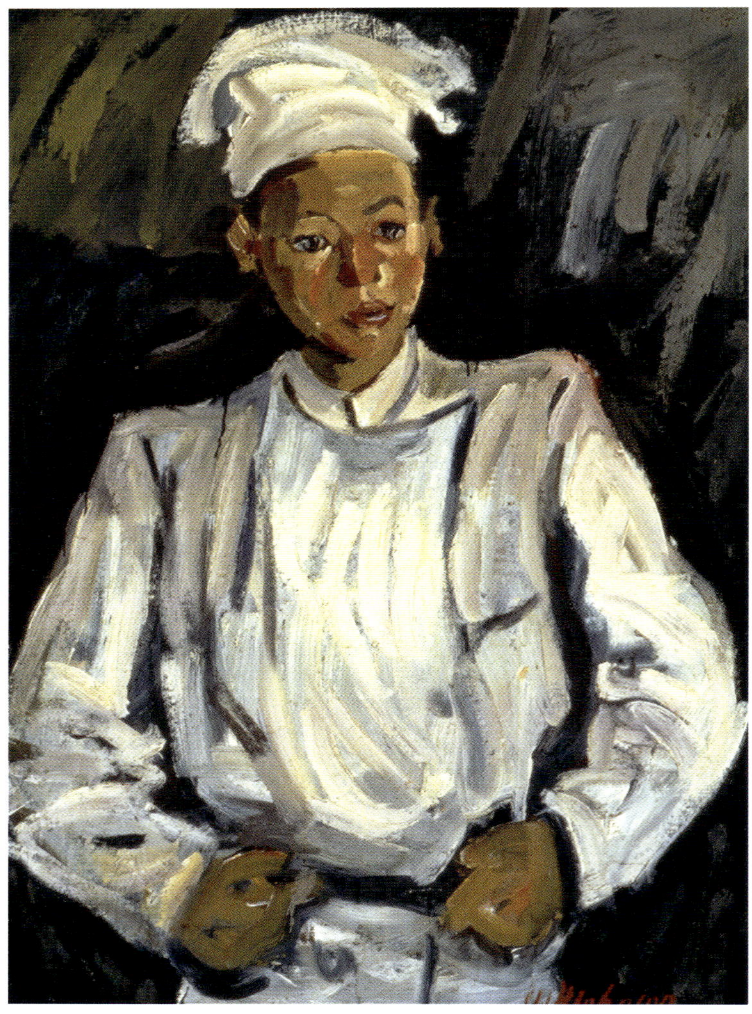

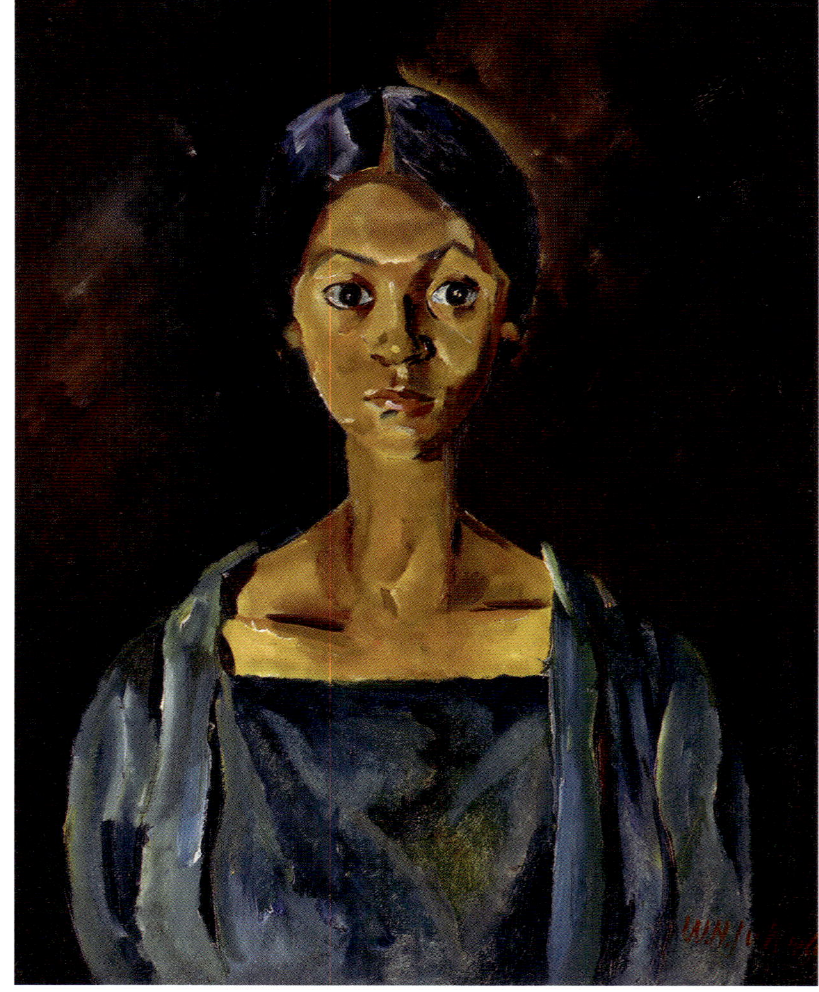

Fig. 9

Harmon Foundation exhibition catalogue featuring a self-portrait by Johnson, 1930, William H. Johnson papers, Archives of American Art

Fig. 10

Young Pastry Cook, ca. 1928–30, oil on canvas, 31 3/4 × 22 5/8 in., Smithsonian American Art Museum, Gift of the Harmon Foundation, 1967.59.693

Fig. 11

Girl in a Green Dress (Portrait Study No. 22), 1930, oil on canvas, 24 1/4 × 19 1/8 in., Smithsonian American Art Museum, Gift of the Harmon Foundation, 1967.59.747

Fig. 12

Johnson and his wife, Holcha Krake, at their home in Denmark, ca. 1935–38, William H. Johnson papers, Archives of American Art

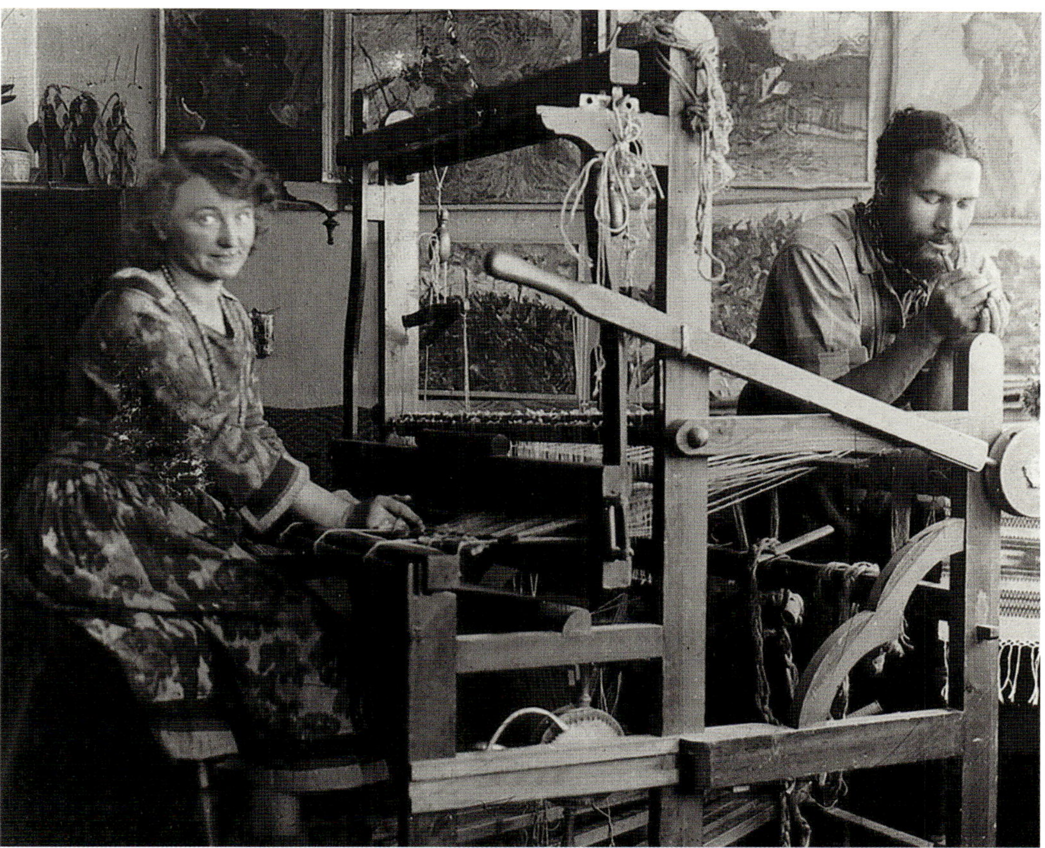

in New York (it subsequently traveled to sixteen other cities), reviews of Johnson's self-portraits and depictions of the undulating architecture of Cagnes-sur-Mer were mixed. Some called him a trailblazer; others lamented his artistic debt to French modernism.

In February, a month after the show opened, Johnson returned home. He visited his family in Florence, painted landscapes and portraits, and, in mid-April, had a one-day exhibition of 135 paintings at the YMCA (**Figs. 10, 11**). Even though the show was on view for only three hours, the announcement in the *Florence Morning News* noted that Johnson's "real genius may someday make the city of his birth famous."[10] On his way back to New York after spending less than three months in Florence, Johnson made a quick stop in Washington, DC. He stayed with Howard University professor Alain Locke, editor of the anthology *The New Negro*. Locke agreed to help sell Johnson's paintings and introduced him to Harlem Renaissance poet Langston Hughes.

Scandinavia

Flush with cash from the Harmon Foundation award, in the spring of 1930 Johnson again sailed for Europe. He met up with Holcha Krake in Denmark, and in June they married (**Fig. 12**). For the next eight years, the couple lived in

Fig. 13

Sun Setting, Denmark, ca. 1930, oil on burlap, 20 3/4 × 25 3/8 in., Smithsonian American Art Museum, Gift of the Harmon Foundation, 1967.59.720

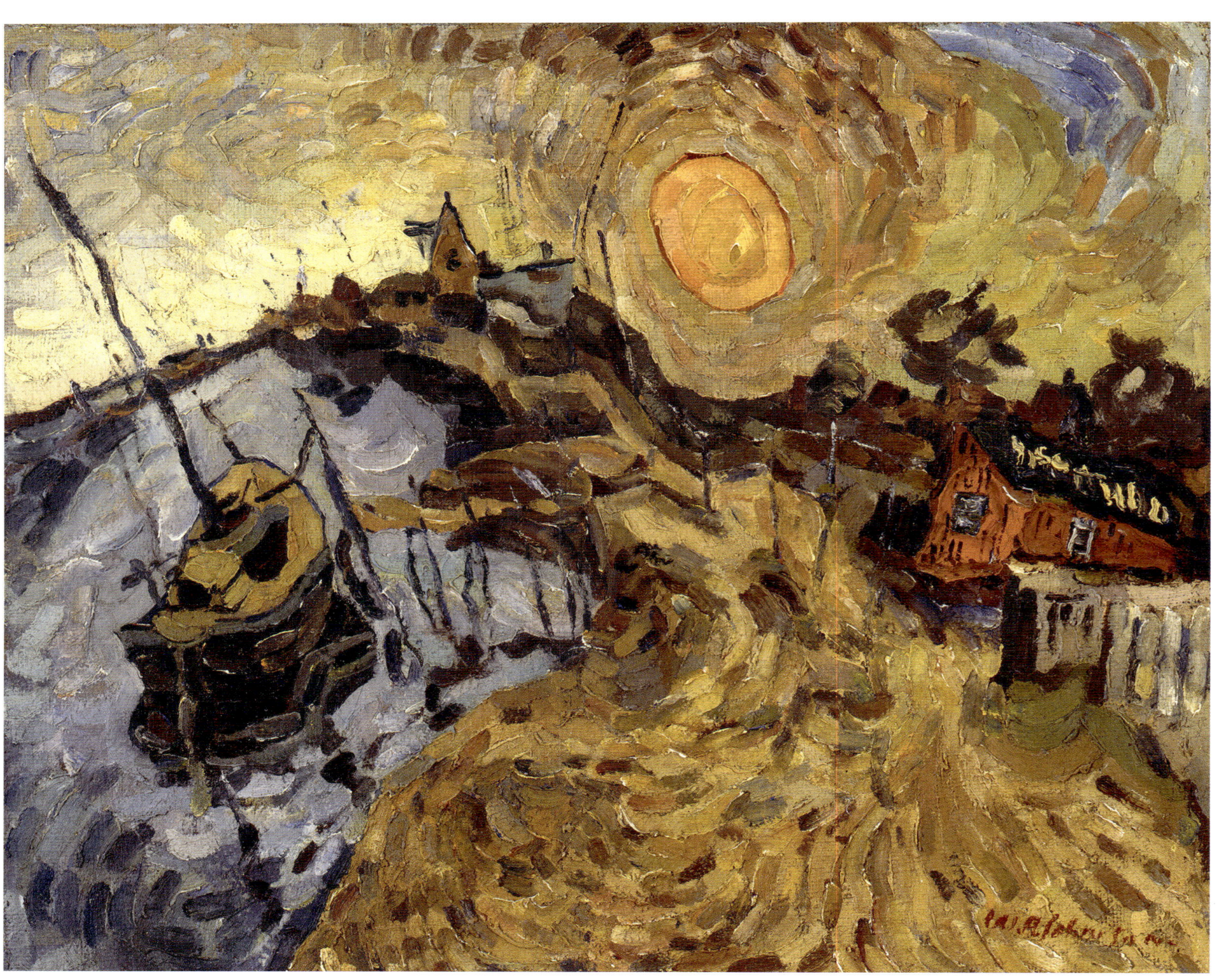

Fig. 14

Tunis, 1932, hand-colored woodcut on paper, 14 5/8 × 19 1/2 in., Smithsonian American Art Museum, Gift of the Harmon Foundation, 1967.59.855

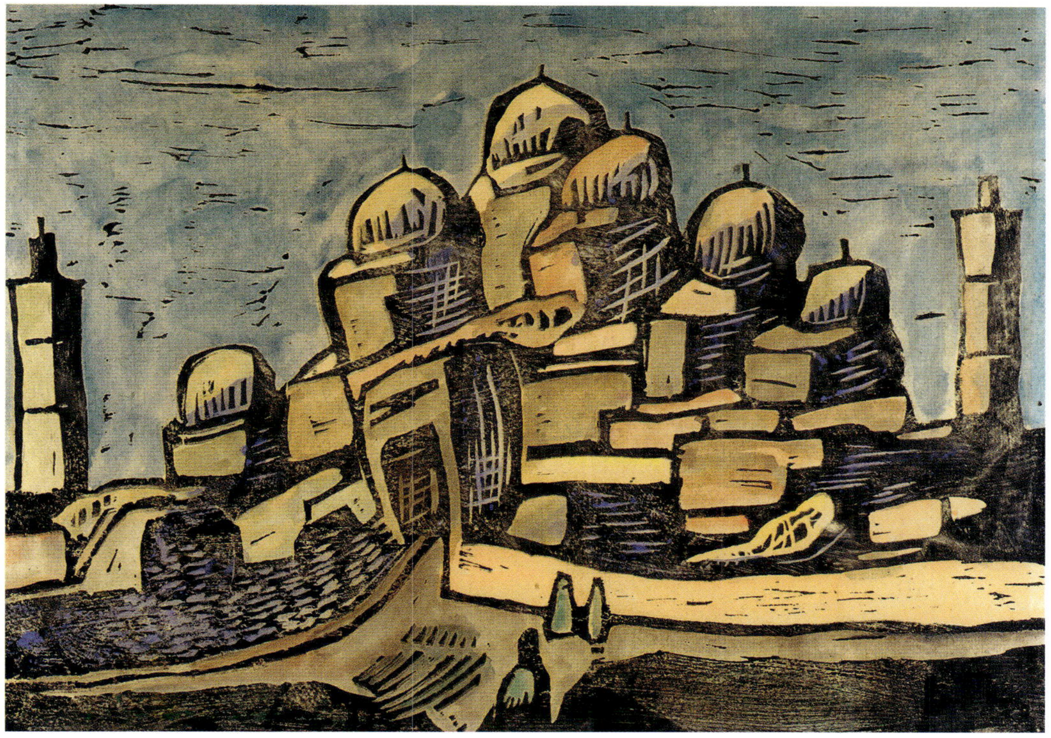

Kerteminde, a small fishing village on the Danish island of Fyn; in Oslo, the capital of Norway; and among the mountains and fjords to the north. Wherever they lived, Johnson continued to push the limits of his art. Experimental Danish landscapes and exuberant canvases of the mountains of northern Norway as well as delicate watercolors of flowers and Danish fishermen demonstrate both his evolving abilities with a brush and his increasing confidence as a painter (**Fig. 13**). When time and funds permitted, the couple traveled. On a trip to Tunisia in North Africa in 1932, they visited mosques and markets (**Fig. 14**), and in the Netherlands they studied paintings by Vincent van Gogh, which confirmed Johnson's commitment to the power of color and expressive form (**Fig. 15**). In 1935 in Oslo, Krake and Johnson met the reclusive Norwegian Edvard Munch (whose painting *The Scream* continues to fascinate). The couple exhibited their work, sometimes singly, sometimes together, in exhibitions in Denmark, Norway, and occasionally Sweden. Although sales were infrequent in Depression-era Scandinavia, museums in Trondheim, Norway, and Stockholm, Sweden, bought Johnson paintings.

Johnson stood out as a Black man in the white world of Scandinavia, but he found himself relatively free from the structural discrimination he would inevitably have experienced in the United States. Although articles about his shows often mentioned his African American roots, critics nonetheless focused on Johnson's formal achievements rather than his race.

Fig. 15 (following pages)

Midnight Sun, Lofoten, 1937, oil on burlap, 41 5/8 × 59 1/8 in., Smithsonian American Art Museum, Gift of the Harmon Foundation, 1967.59.907

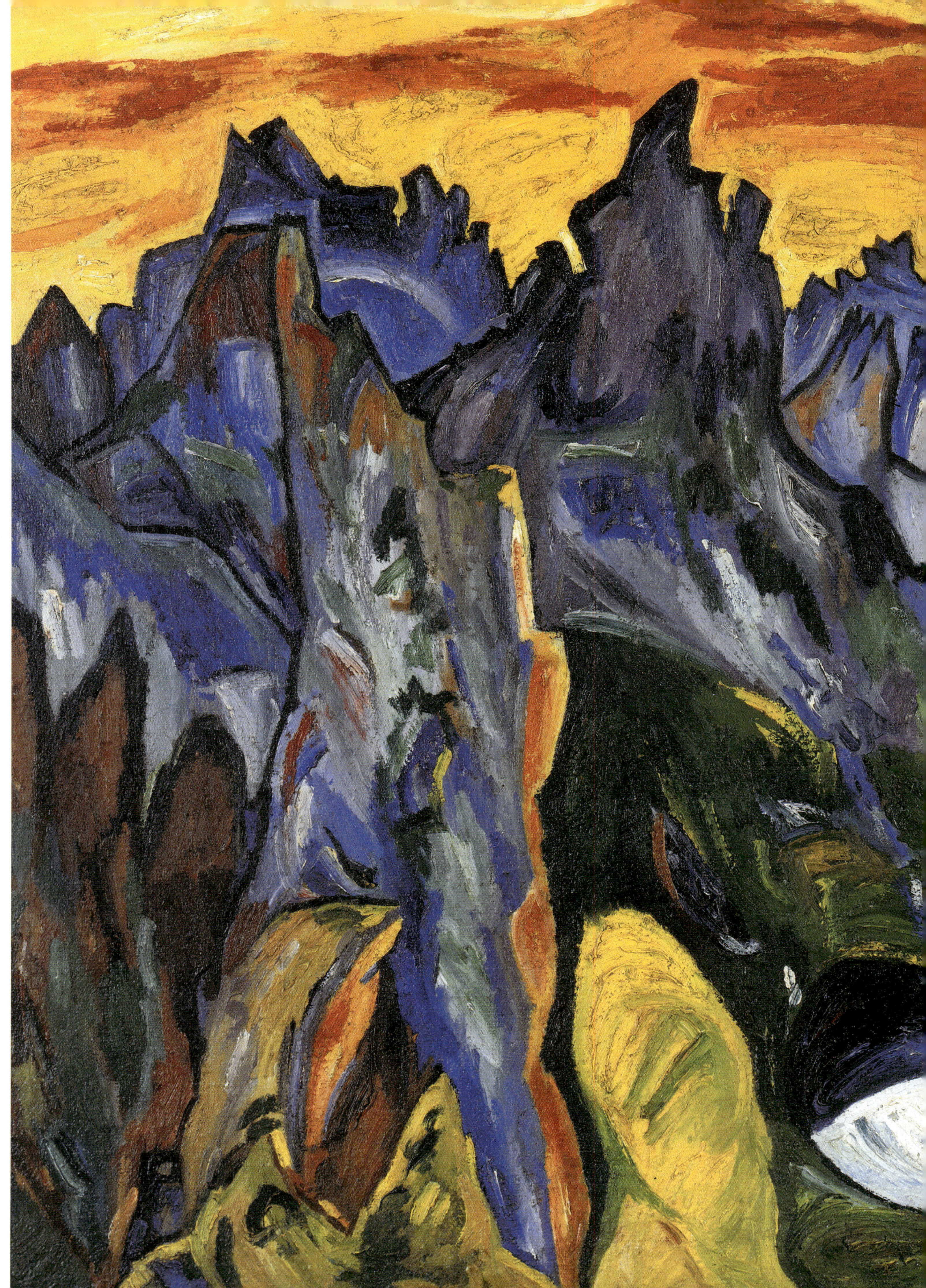

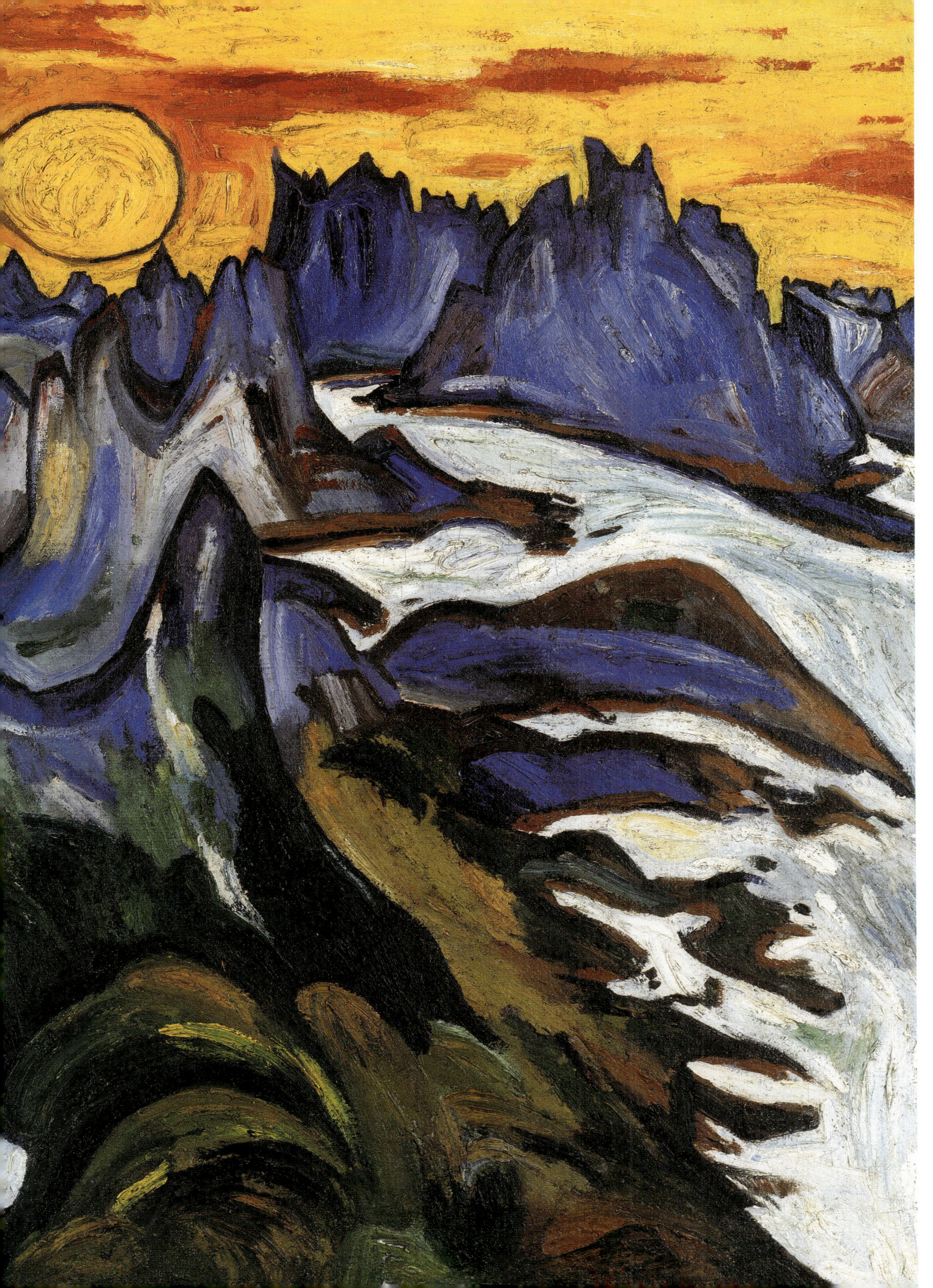

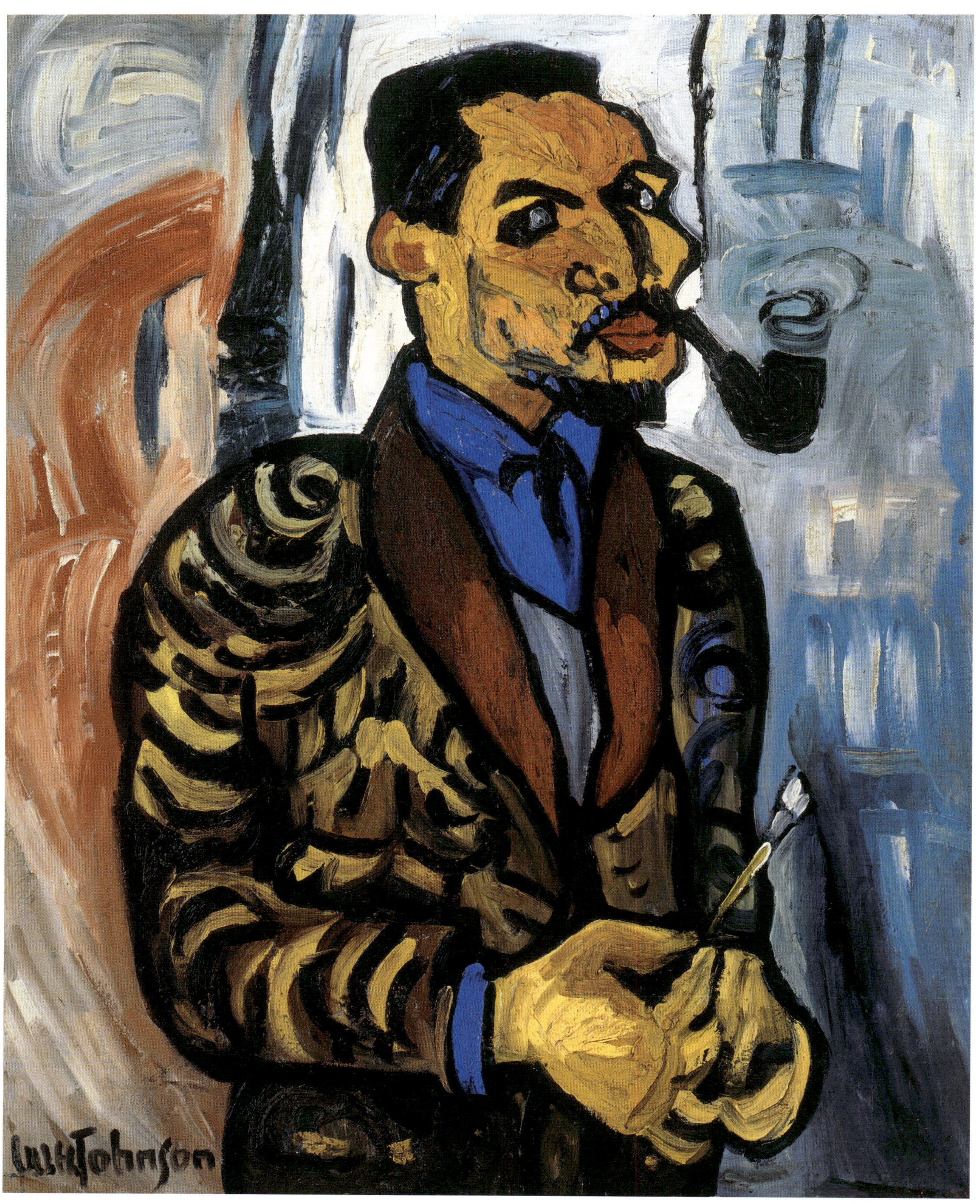
WHJohnson

Fig. 16

Self-Portrait with Pipe, ca. 1937, oil on canvas, 35 × 28 in., Smithsonian American Art Museum, Gift of the Harmon Foundation, 1967.59.913

By 1937 Johnson had lived abroad for over a decade. This time in Scandinavia allowed him to develop formidable skills, but the political situation in Europe was becoming increasingly tense. Adolf Hitler's Nazi Party organized an exhibition of "Degenerate Art" as a condemnation of artists who (like Johnson) worked in an expressionist style, and in 1938, boxer Joe Louis's heavyweight bout against the German Max Schmeling was billed as a battle of ideologies—the American Brown Bomber against Hitler's "master race." On a personal level, Krake's brother-in-law Christoph Voll, one of the so-called degenerate artists, was harassed by the Nazis and his artwork confiscated.

Johnson was also thinking about who he was as an artist, a man, and an African American (Fig. 16). Partly influenced by Holcha's commitment to the folk culture and traditions of Denmark, he began thinking about the relationship between artists and the people who saw their work. In an interview with a Norwegian newspaper critic, he said "people have to be taught how to see their own country through the eyes of a painter."[11] He may have been thinking of making paintings that spoke directly to Black audiences (for him the equivalent of Holcha's Danish "folk"), but he also realized a more pressing need—to create images of African Americans for a white world that rarely acknowledged the lives or circumstances of the people he cared most about. Clearly it was time to come home.

Back in New York

In late 1938, the couple returned to New York. Johnson had, he later said, a "burning desire to commence where I left off.... [with] the painting of my people. My travels taught me that to create, an artist must live and paint in his own environment."[12]

Within six months, he jettisoned the exuberant brushstrokes and vibrant forms of his recent Scandinavian landscapes to focus on the lives of African Americans in New York and the South. For the next seven years he painted rural sharecroppers (Figs. 17, 18), fashionable New Yorkers (Fig. 19), Black soldiers training for war (Figs. 20, 21), and religious scenes (Fig. 22), many of them inspired by spirituals, using bright unmodulated colors and flat simplified forms that spoke to those untutored in art as well as to modernist sophisticates. Like Holcha, whose weavings connected with the Danish folk movement, Johnson had committed to painting in a style he believed would speak directly to Black audiences.

Johnson's conversion to Black subjects and a direct style coincided with his immersion for the first time in an art environment that was primarily African American. In May 1939, six months after arriving in New York, he was hired to

Fig. 17

Sowing, ca. 1940, oil on burlap, 38 1/2 × 45 3/4 in., Smithsonian American Art Museum, Gift of the Harmon Foundation, 1967.59.1002

Fig. 18

Going to Church, ca. 1940–41, oil on burlap, 38 1/8 × 45 3/8 in., Smithsonian American Art Museum, Gift of the Harmon Foundation, 1967.59.1003

Fig. 19

Café, ca. 1939–40, oil on paperboard, 36 1/2 × 28 3/8 in., Smithsonian American Art Museum, Gift of the Harmon Foundation, 1967.59.669

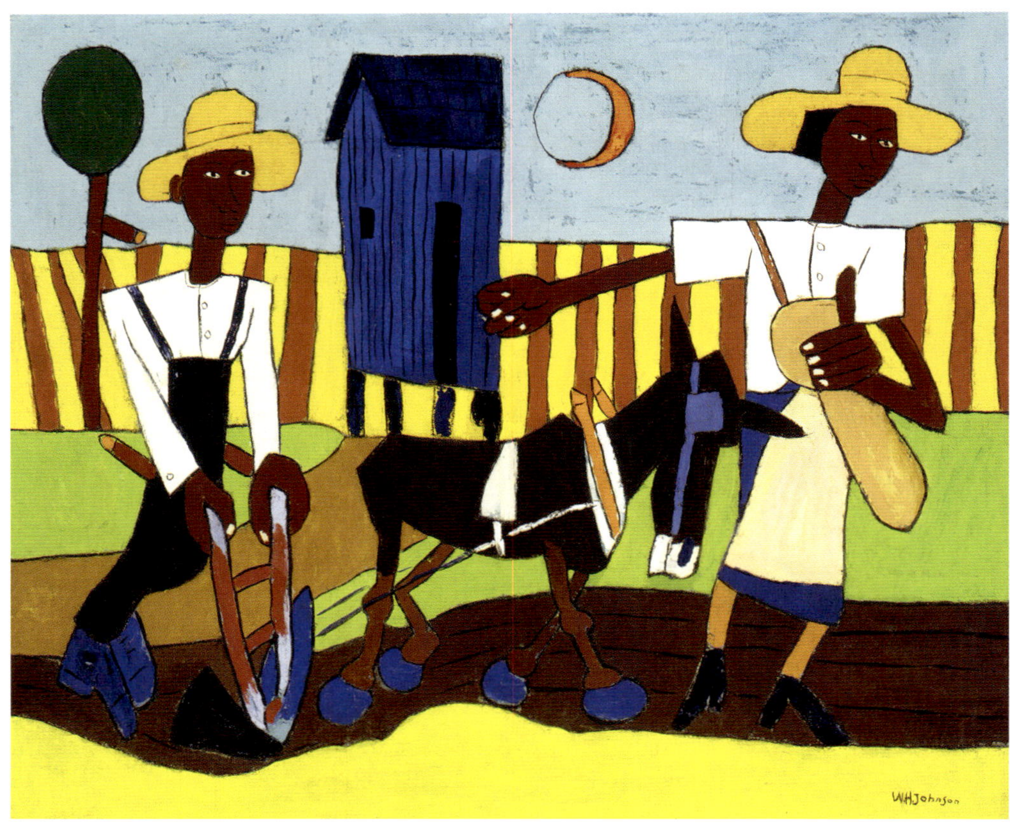

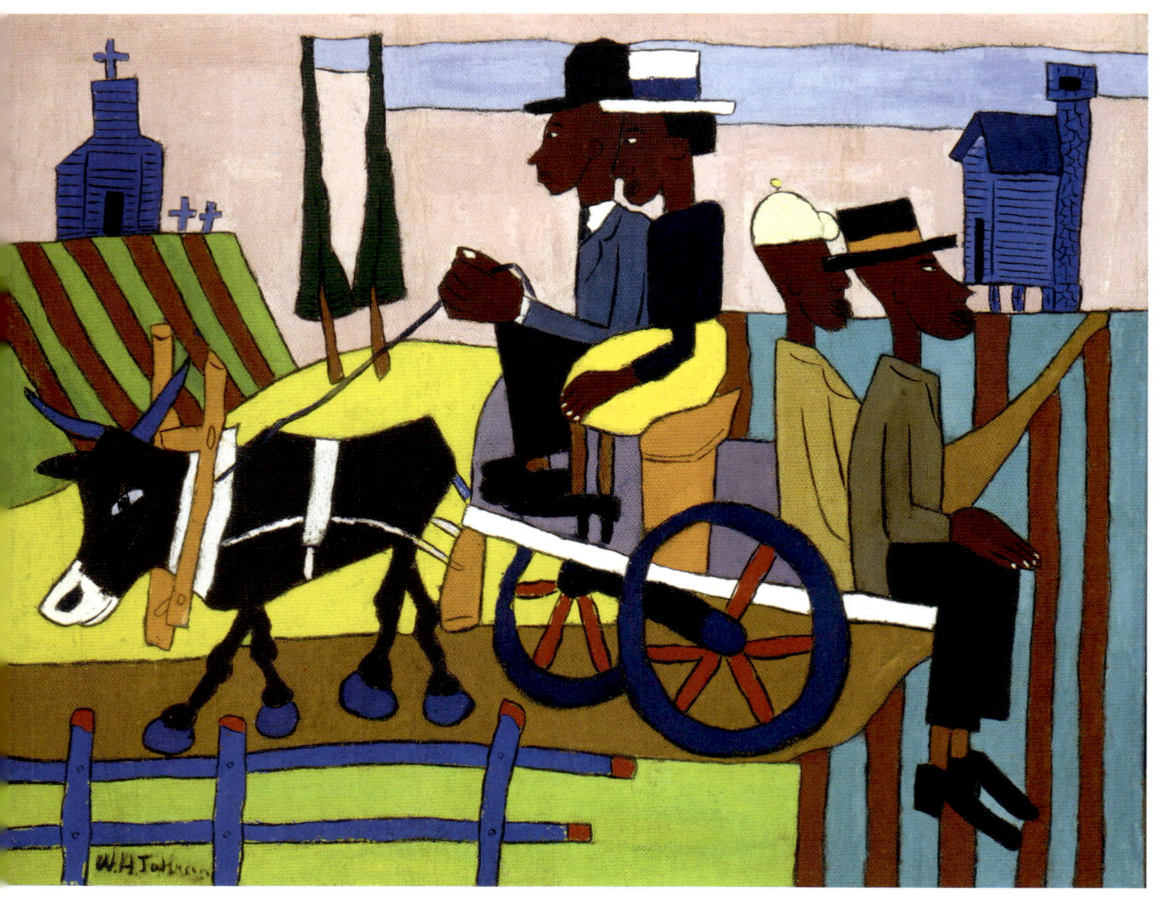

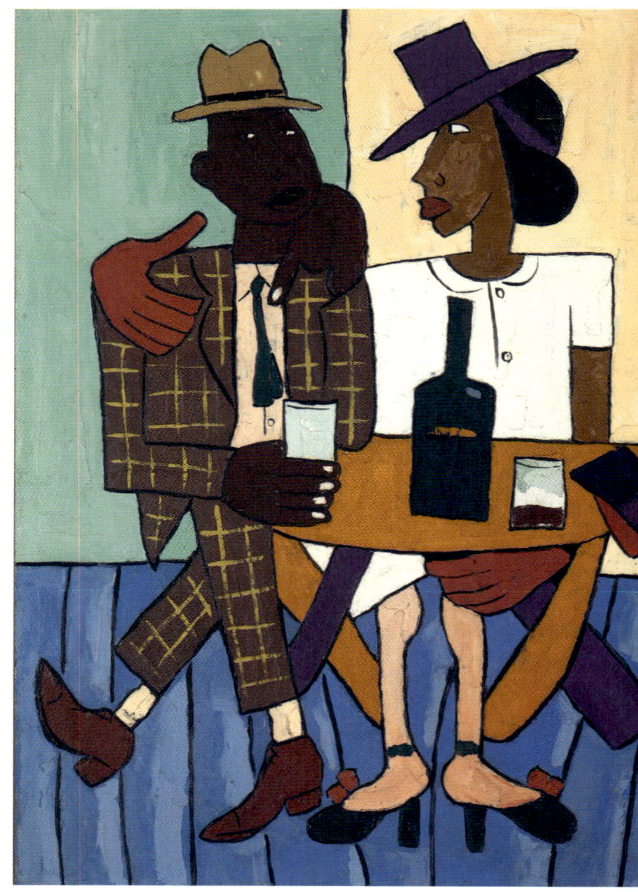

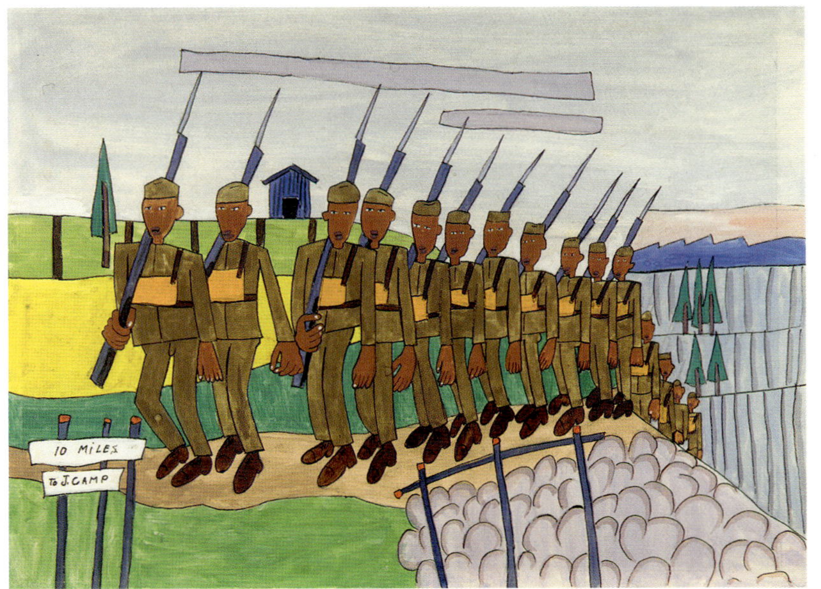

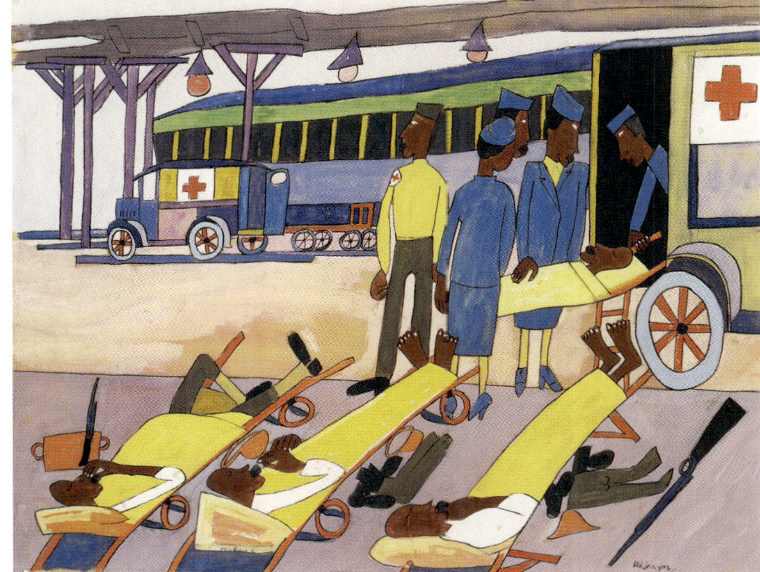

Fig. 20

Ten Miles to J. Camp, ca. 1942, tempera and pen and ink with pencil on paper, 13 ¾ × 17 ⅞ in., Smithsonian American Art Museum, Gift of the Harmon Foundation, 1967.59.1071

Fig. 21

Station Stop, Red Cross Ambulance, ca. 1942, tempera and pen and ink on paper, 18 ¾ × 22 ⅜ in., Smithsonian American Art Museum, Gift of the Harmon Foundation, 1967.59.1120R

teach at the Harlem Community Art Center.[13] He met Charles Alston, Aaron Douglas, and other instructors as well as the young Jacob Lawrence and Romare Bearden. Downtown, where the couple lived, he reconnected with sculptor Selma Burke and other artist friends both Black and white. He had left New York ten years earlier still a student; he returned a mature artist confident of his skills and future direction.

Johnson's first major solo exhibition in New York, which opened at Alma Reed Gallery on 57th Street in May 1941, introduced the artist's southern "folk"-inspired paintings. Richmond Barthé, Romare Bearden, Robert Blackburn, Selma Burke, Aaron Douglas, Palmer Hayden, Norman Lewis, and Augusta Savage—leading visual artists of the Harlem Renaissance—all signed the guest book. Over the next several years Johnson exhibited frequently to wide acclaim. Although critics invariably mentioned Johnson's race, most focused on the emotional power of his work. A writer for the *Chicago Sunday Times* said Johnson's paintings "captivate our imagination and intelligence." Emily Genauer, well-known reviewer for the *New York World-Telegram*, said, "Each [painting is] a mosaic of bold, clear color thickly applied in amazingly inventive patterns, full of warmth and wit." Howard Devree at the *New York Times* was even more impressed: "More than 'primitive' painting they at first seem to be, the temperas by William H. Johnson reveal…a lot of keen observation and shrewd setting forth of ideas"; Devree also remarked the "quiet dignity" with which Johnson treated his figures.[14]

In 1942, with the United States embroiled in war in Europe and the Pacific, national priorities shifted. The Federal Art Project, which provided money for

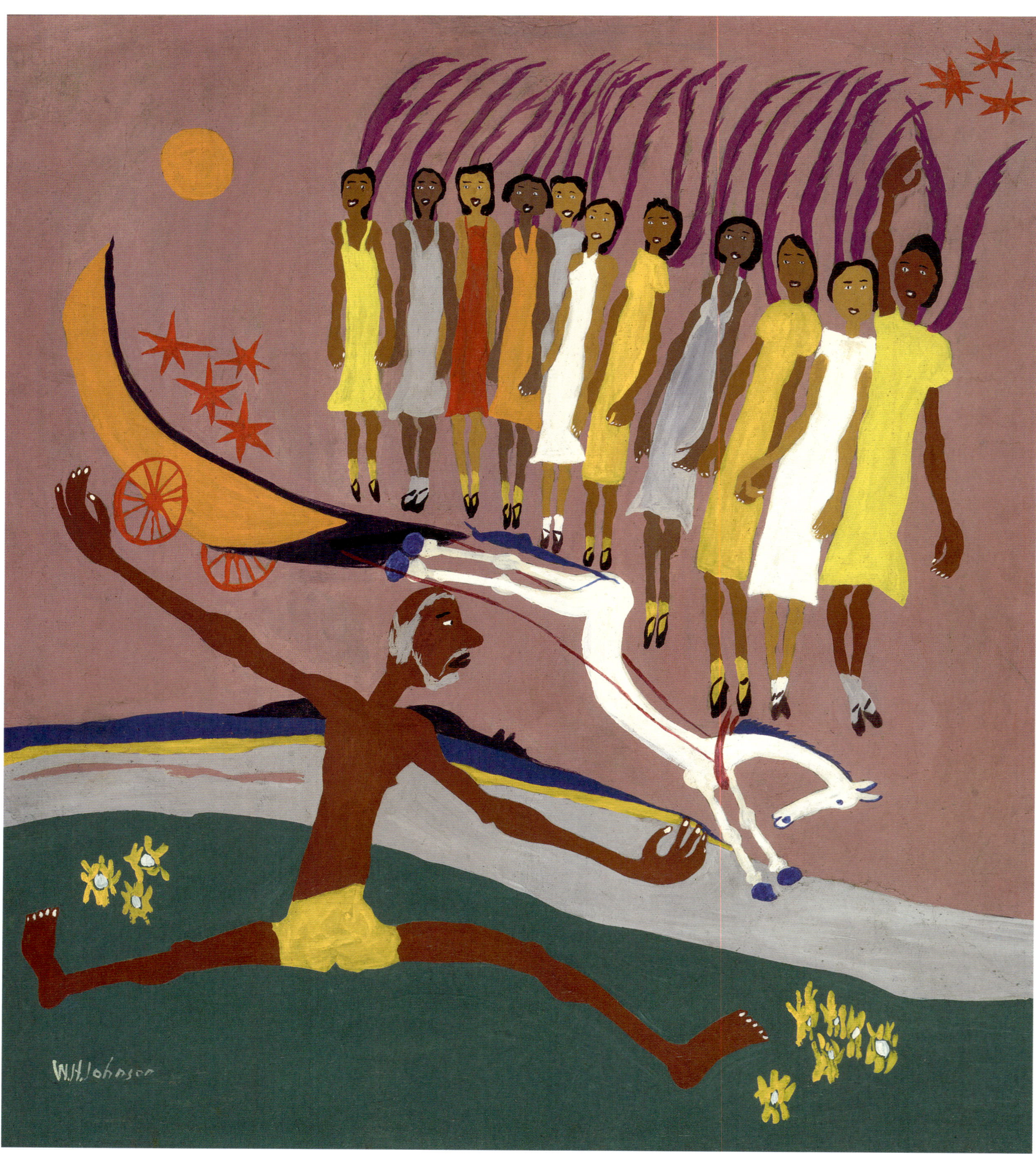
W.H.Johnson

Fig. 22

Swing Low, Sweet Chariot, ca. 1944, oil on paperboard, 28 5/8 × 26 1/2 in., Smithsonian American Art Museum, Gift of the Harmon Foundation, 1983.95.52

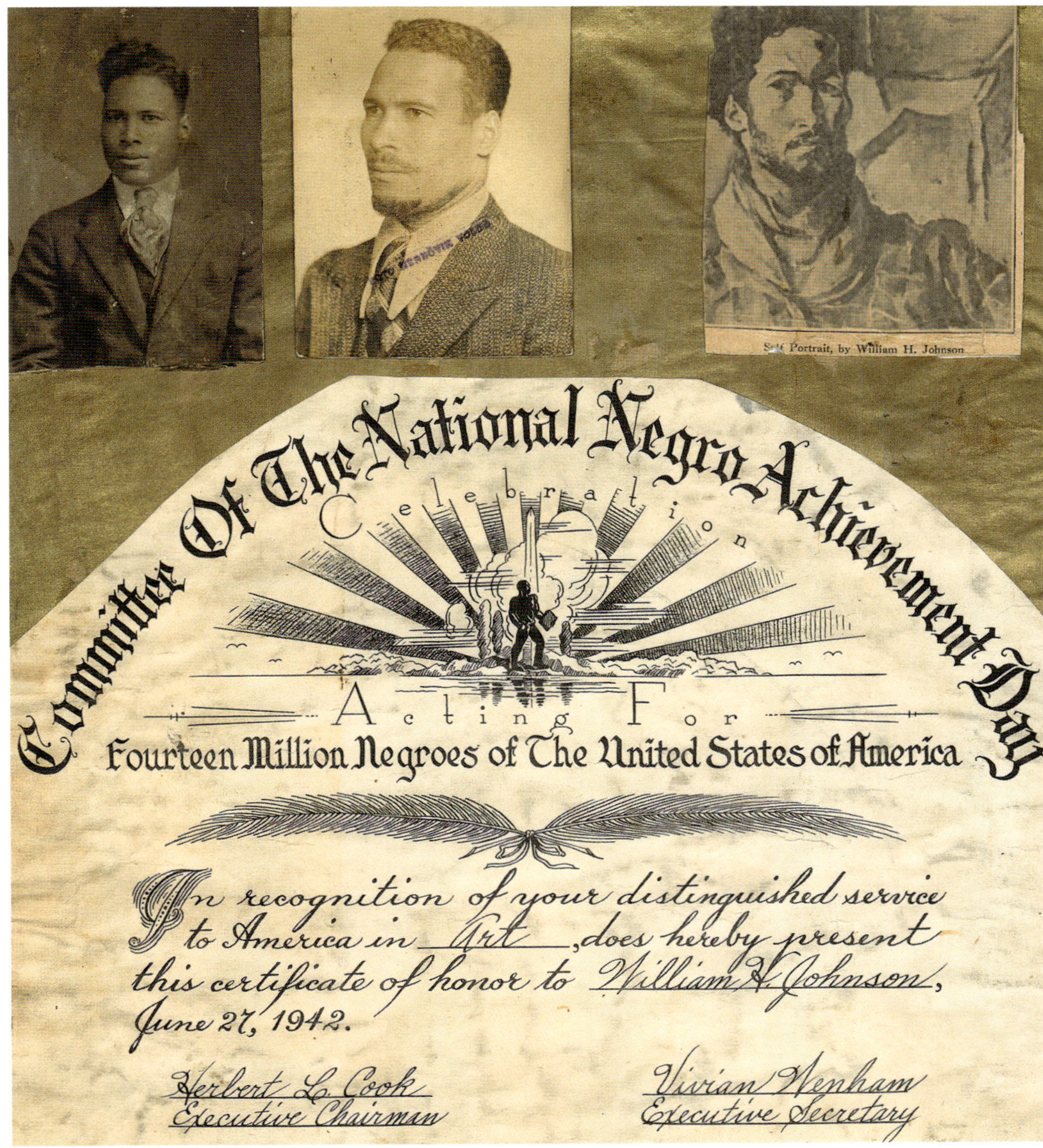

Committee Of The National Negro Achievement Day

Celebration

Acting For

Fourteen Million Negroes of The United States of America

In recognition of your distinguished service to America in Art, does hereby present this certificate of honor to William H. Johnson, June 27, 1942.

Herbert L. Cook
Executive Chairman

Vivian Wenham
Executive Secretary

Fig. 23

Page from Johnson's scrapbook featuring certificate from the Committee of the National Negro Achievement Day, William H. Johnson papers, Archives of American Art

teacher salaries at the Harlem Community Art Center, was winding down, and at the end of the year the center closed. But Johnson was already making his mark. The Committee of the National Negro Achievement Day, June 27, 1942, "acting for fourteen million Negroes of the United States of America," presented Johnson with a scroll honoring his "distinguished service to America in Art" (**Fig. 23**). Johnson was in good company. Mary McLeod Bethune, Dr. George Washington Carver, Joe Louis, Paul Robeson, and Adam Clayton Powell Jr. were also honored that day.

Johnson was also attracting serious attention on the gallery scene. He exhibited at the New York World's Fair in 1940, and in 1941 was featured in an important show of work by African American artists at Edith Halpert's Downtown Gallery. In the spring of 1943, the young art dealer Betty Parsons offered Johnson an exhibition at Wakefield Gallery. The show, which featured about thirty works, was widely and favorably reviewed and, much to the Johnsons' relief, many of the paintings sold. Paul Robeson, whom the couple had previously met in Denmark, dropped by between performances as Othello on Broadway and bought two paintings; the managing editor of *Fortune* magazine purchased a watercolor; and Carl Van Vechten, a noted photographer of African American cultural figures, invited Johnson to sit for a photograph.

Then tragedy struck. Late in 1943, Holcha was hospitalized with advanced-stage breast cancer and in January 1944 she died. Johnson was devastated, even as the demand for his work escalated. Over the next six months he showed at Atlanta University (March–April), at the Newark Museum (April–May), at the G Place Gallery in Washington, DC (May), and in a solo show at Wakefield Gallery (May). A joint show of Johnson's paintings and Holcha's textiles and ceramics opened at Marquié Gallery in New York in December.[15]

The Fighters for Freedom

Against this backdrop Johnson began the *Fighters for Freedom* paintings. We don't know what specifically precipitated his desire to paint historical figures.[16] After painting Black recruits and soldiers at war, Johnson might have been thinking about the sacrifices young African American men made for a segregated country that continued to marginalize their lives and work. Marian Anderson's performance on the steps of the Lincoln Memorial before a crowd of some seventy-five thousand on Easter Sunday 1939 (six months after Johnson returned to New York) might have prompted him to consider the challenges she had faced even after becoming an international star. A *Saturday Evening Post* article about history instruction in American schools, which remains in his papers, might have caused him to think about those whose stories were not told in the classrooms of a country that systematically excluded the contributions of African Americans from its history.[17] Whatever the case, the idea of painting a series that addressed American history, and specifically African American history, had been percolating since shortly after (or possibly even before) he returned from Scandinavia. He made images of George Washington as early as 1940 or 1941 and exhibited a painting of Booker T. Washington in the spring of 1941; clippings he used as source images for his compositions date from as early as 1939 (*Haile Selassie* is an example) and possibly earlier.

Johnson was not alone in his commitment to recounting the contributions Black Americans made to the national narrative. Historian Carter G. Woodson had founded the *Journal of Negro History* in 1916 and initiated "Negro History

Week" in New York in 1926. Historian Arturo Schomburg, Alain Locke, and others promoted teaching African American history to a broad, cross-racial public through lectures and publications, with the aim to instill in Black Americans a sense of heritage and racial pride. In 1940, to celebrate the seventy-fifth anniversary of the Thirteenth Amendment to the U.S. Constitution, which abolished slavery in the United States, Black churches, schools, and civic groups throughout the country organized pageants and parades. Novelists, poets, jazz artists, and film and Broadway stars we now consider luminaries of American culture created a rich landscape for the reexamination and affirmation of African American life.[18]

Aaron Douglas, Charles White, and other Black artists soon joined the cause, often painting the same individuals Johnson would go on to feature in his *Fighters for Freedom* series. Malvin Gray Johnson, a friend of Johnson's from the academy, and Earle Richardson designed murals featuring Black revolutionaries Nat Turner, Toussaint L'Ouverture, Harriet Tubman, and others. White's mural *Progress of the American Negro: Five Great American Negroes* (1939–40, Howard University Gallery of Art) featured Sojourner Truth, Booker T. Washington, Frederick Douglass, George Washington Carver, and Marian Anderson. Jacob Lawrence—best known for *The Migration Series* (1940–41, Phillips Collection and Museum of Modern Art)—also painted the lives of Toussaint L'Ouverture (1938, forty-one panels) and Harriet Tubman (1940, thirty-one panels).[19]

Crafting the Fighters

In contrast to Lawrence's multipart serial narratives and the epic statements made by muralists who presented large-format historical sagas on public walls, Johnson's paintings are intimate and personal. He told each Fighter's story within a single painting and selected episodes and symbols that document their struggles and achievements, creating discontinuous, scrapbook-like images. In doing so he traced the arc of African American contributions within American history from the Revolutionary War to the present.

And he did his research. Working in the 135th Street branch of the New York Public Library, Johnson studied books and scoured newspapers, magazines, old prints, and even photographs by the young Gordon Parks for narratives and images to ensure the accuracy and legibility of his subjects. Sadie Iola Daniel's 1931 book, *Women Builders*, for example, provided portraits and information for the painting of the same title (p. 105), as did William Still's 1872 volume *The Underground Rail Road* (p. 69) (**Fig. 24**).

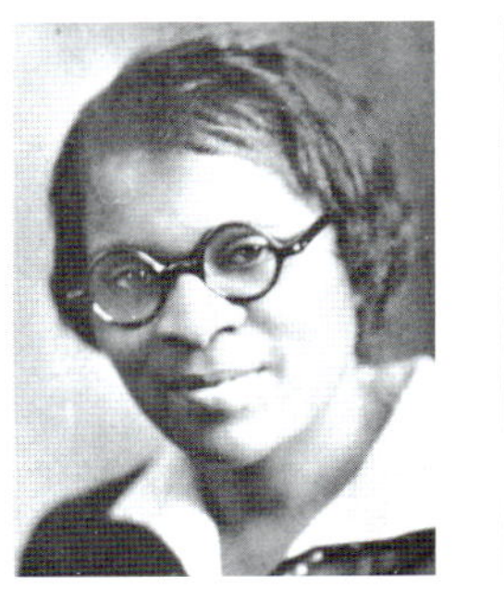
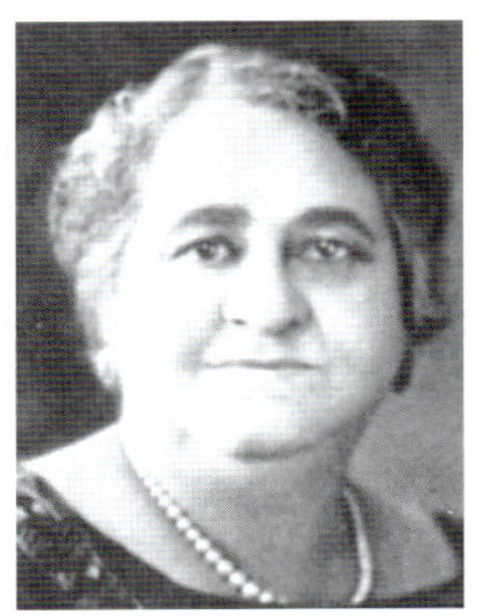
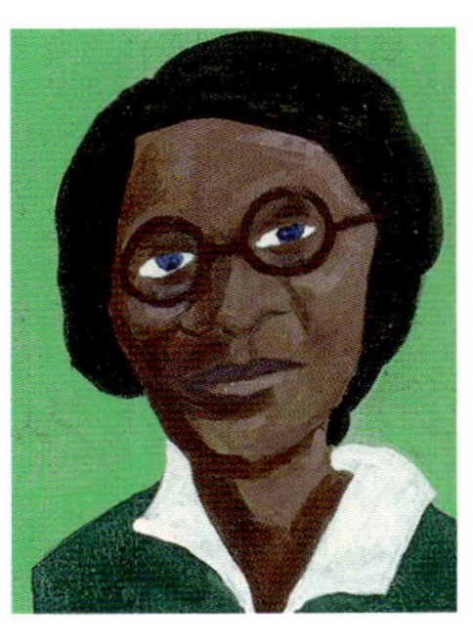
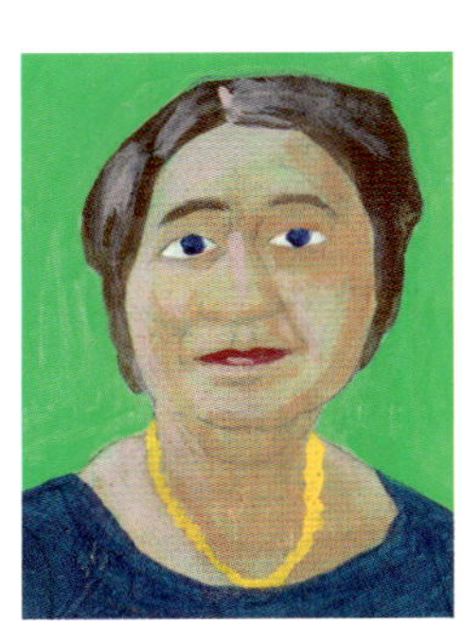
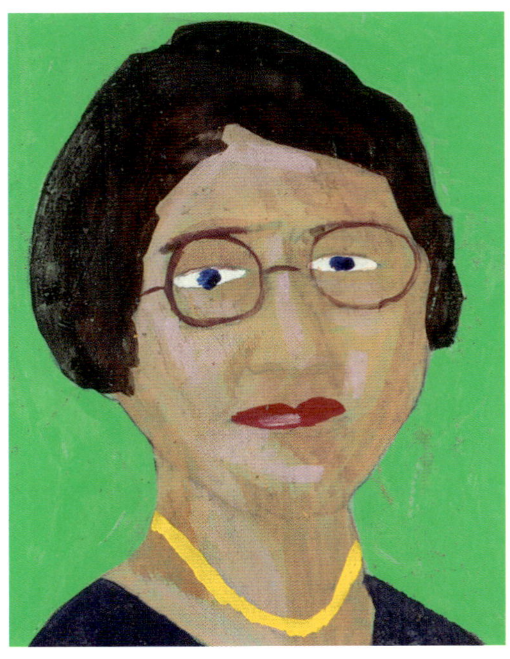
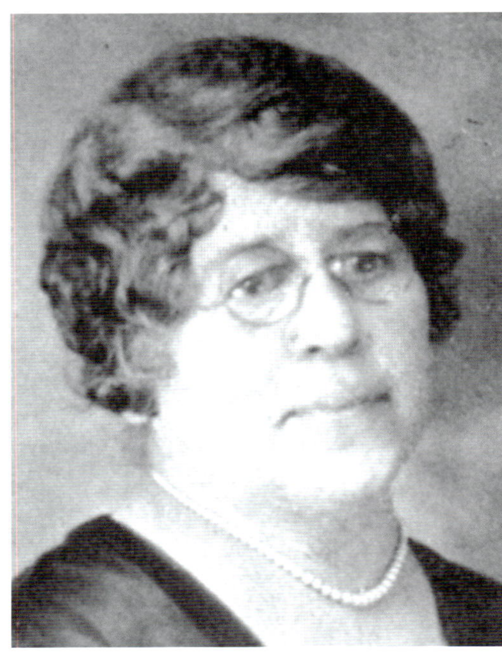

Fig. 24

Photographs of Charlotte Hawkins Brown, Maggie L. Walker, and Janie Porter Barrett (left to right) featured in Sadie Iola Daniel's *Women Builders* (1931). Johnson reproduced these portraits in his painting of the same name; see p. 105.

Johnson was particularly attuned to Fighters who were making history in his day. He painted Jack Johnson, Joe Louis, Paul Robeson, and Marian Anderson, and focused the spotlight on inequities suffered at home by these internationally celebrated performers and sports figures. For *Three Allies in Cairo,* he used a photograph from *LIFE* magazine to capture the likenesses and spatial relationships of world leaders meeting in Egypt (**Figs. 25, 26**). He showed Jawaharlal Nehru and Mohandas Gandhi, both of whom had been imprisoned for demanding that Great Britain relinquish its colonial hold on India, and he collected news photographs of heavyweight champ Joe Louis, which he used as the basis for *Boxers* (p. 113).[20] Each of the *Fighters* paintings is declarative, punctuated by small vignettes, flags, miniature buildings, and other symbolic indicators that locate them geographically and reveal significant encounters in the Fighter's life.

The *Fighters for Freedom* paintings do more, though. Johnson used them and the particular format in which they appear to send universal messages. *Crispus Attucks* (p. 52), which depicts the first person to be killed in the run-up to the Revolutionary War, shows us that Black Americans have died defending their country since before it became a republic. *Nat Turner* (p. 63) presents the rebellion leader hanging from a gallows surrounded by a field of crosses, white on the left, brown and tan on the right. Through Turner, Johnson shows us that oppressed people will seek freedom from bondage by any means necessary, even if death is a likely outcome. *Three Great Abolitionists* (p. 85), in which Frederick Douglass joins the hands of radical abolitionist John Brown and Abraham Lincoln, speaks to reconciliation. Although Douglass had supported

Fig. 25

"'Fighting Friends' in Tehran," *LIFE* magazine, December 20, 1943. Johnson referenced the lower photo in *Three Allies in Cairo* (see photo enlargement at bottom).

Fig. 26

Three Allies in Cairo; see p. 147

Lincoln for president in 1860, he was bitterly disappointed that Lincoln was unwilling to categorically denounce slavery at the outset of his presidency and condemned the president in lectures and in print. Not until Lincoln issued the Emancipation Proclamation on January 1, 1863, did the two reconcile. This joining of hands is symbolic, telling us that ultimately we must come together, even if we vigorously disagree, when a cause is just.

Johnson did at least three paintings of Marian Anderson. The first two, painted in fragile tempera (one shown on p. 123), show the Black contralto singing before a massive crowd on the steps of the Lincoln Memorial with the great statue of Lincoln large in the background (**Figs. 27, 28**). For the third image, which he painted in the permanent medium of oil, Johnson shows Anderson not at the Lincoln Memorial, but as an international figure surrounded by tiny buildings and flags that represent countries where she performed (**Fig. 29**). At the center right is a vignette of Anderson shaking hands with First Lady Eleanor Roosevelt, one of many who were outraged by the refusal of the all-white Daughters of the American Revolution to allow Anderson to perform at Constitution Hall, their

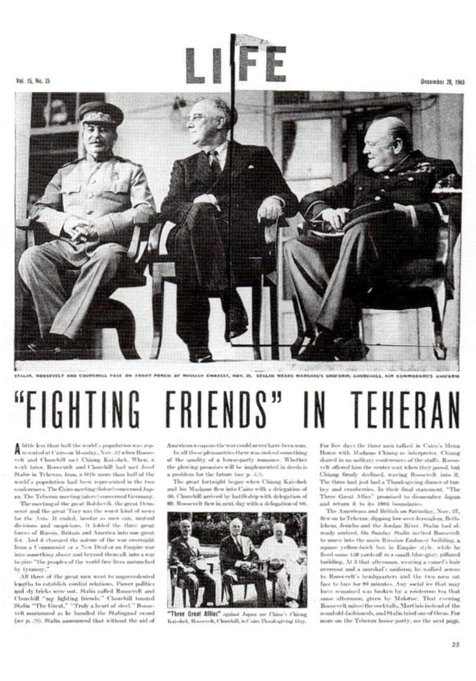

LIFE

STALIN, ROOSEVELT AND CHURCHILL POSE ON FRONT PORCH OF RUSSIAN EMBASSY, NOV. 29. STALIN WEARS MARSHAL'S UNIFORM; CHURCHILL, AIR COMMODORE'S UNIFORM

"FIGHTING FRIENDS" IN TEHERAN

A little less than half the world's population was represented at Cairo on Monday, Nov. 22 when Roosevelt and Churchill met Chiang Kai-shek. When, a week later, Roosevelt and Churchill had met Josef Stalin in Teheran, Iran, a little more than half of the world's population had been represented in the two conferences. The Cairo meeting (*below*) concerned Japan. The Teheran meeting (*above*) concerned Germany.

The meeting of the great Bolshevik, the great Democrat and the great Tory was the worst kind of news for the Axis. It ended, insofar as men can, mutual divisions and suspicions. It folded the three great forces of Russia, Britain and America into one great fist. And it changed the nature of the war overnight from a Communist or a New Deal or an Empire war into something above and beyond them all, into a war to give "the peoples of the world free lives untouched by tyranny."

All three of the great men went to unprecedented lengths to establish cordial relations. Power politics and sly tricks were out. Stalin called Roosevelt and Churchill "my fighting friends." Churchill toasted Stalin "The Great," "Truly a heart of steel." Roosevelt murmured as he handled the Stalingrad sword (*see p. 29*). Stalin announced that without the aid of American weapons the war could never have been won.

In all these pleasantries there was indeed something of the quality of a house-party romance. Whether the glowing promises will be implemented in deeds is a problem for the future (*see p. 43*).

The great fortnight began when Chiang Kai-shek and his Madame flew into Cairo with a delegation of 20. Churchill arrived by battleship with delegation of 80. Roosevelt flew in next day with a delegation of 60.

"Three Great Allies" against Japan are China's Chiang Kai-shek, Roosevelt, Churchill, in Cairo Thanksgiving Day.

For five days the three men talked in Cairo's Mena House with Madame Chiang as interpreter. Chiang shared in no military conferences of the staffs. Roosevelt offered him the center seat when they posed, but Chiang firmly declined, waving Roosevelt into it. The three had just had a Thanksgiving dinner of turkey and cranberries. In their final statement, "The Three Great Allies" promised to dismember Japan and return it to its 1894 boundaries.

The Americans and British on Saturday, Nov. 27, flew on to Teheran, dipping low over Jerusalem, Bethlehem, Jericho and the Jordan River. Stalin had already arrived. On Sunday Stalin invited Roosevelt to move into the main Russian Embassy building, a square yellow-brick box in Empire style, while he lived some 150 yards off in a small, blue-gray, pillared building. At 3 that afternoon, wearing a camel's hair overcoat and a marshal's uniform, he walked across to Roosevelt's headquarters and the two men sat face to face for 90 minutes. Any social ice that may have remained was broken by a roisterous tea that same afternoon, given by Molotov. That evening Roosevelt mixed the cocktails, Martinis instead of the usual old-fashioneds, and Stalin tried one of them. For more on the Teheran house party, see the next page.

25

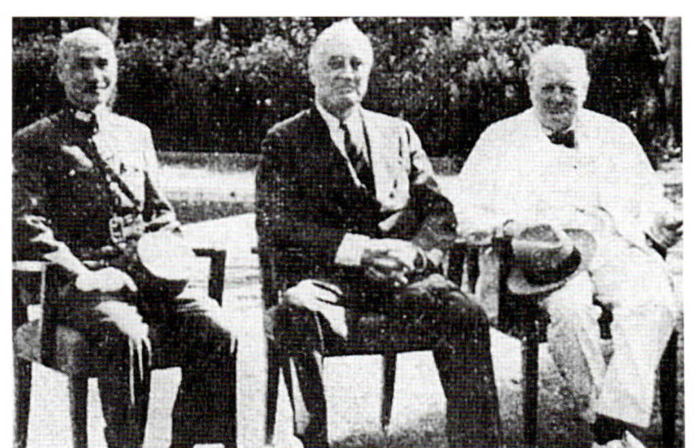

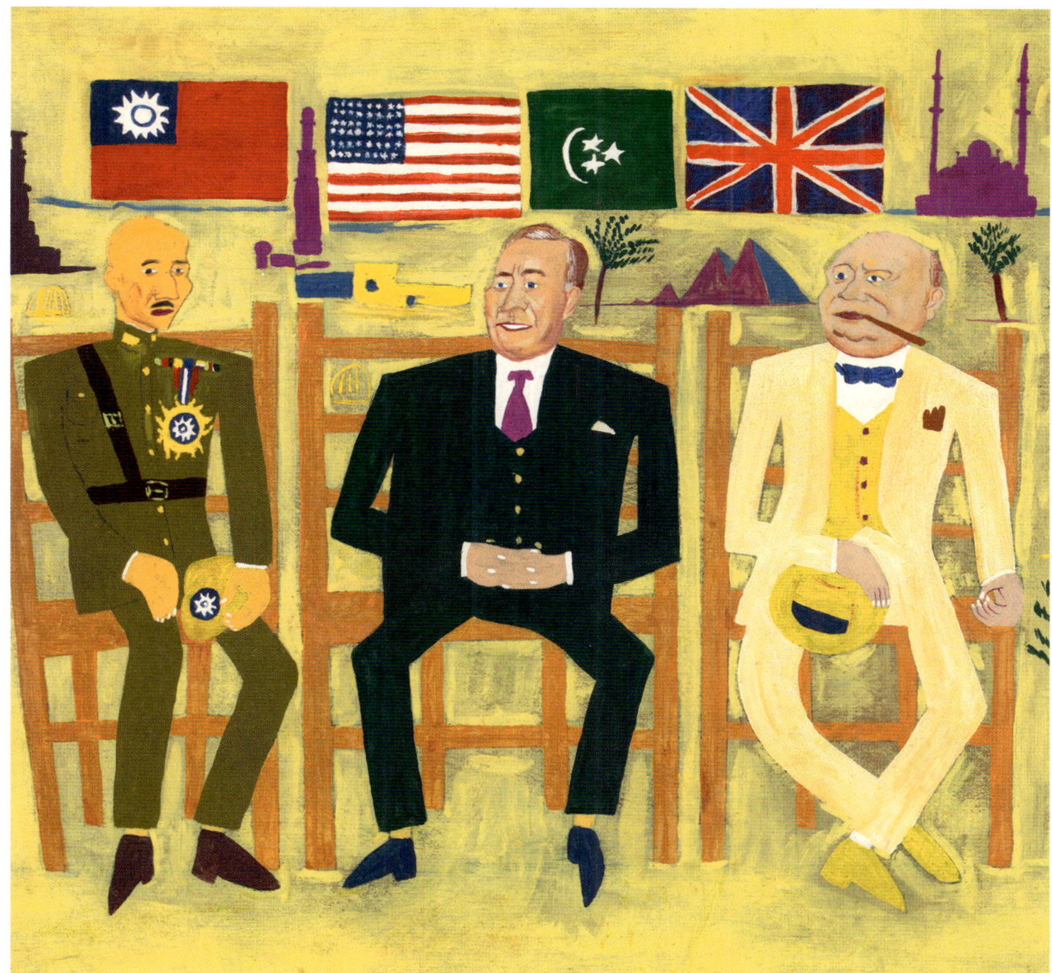

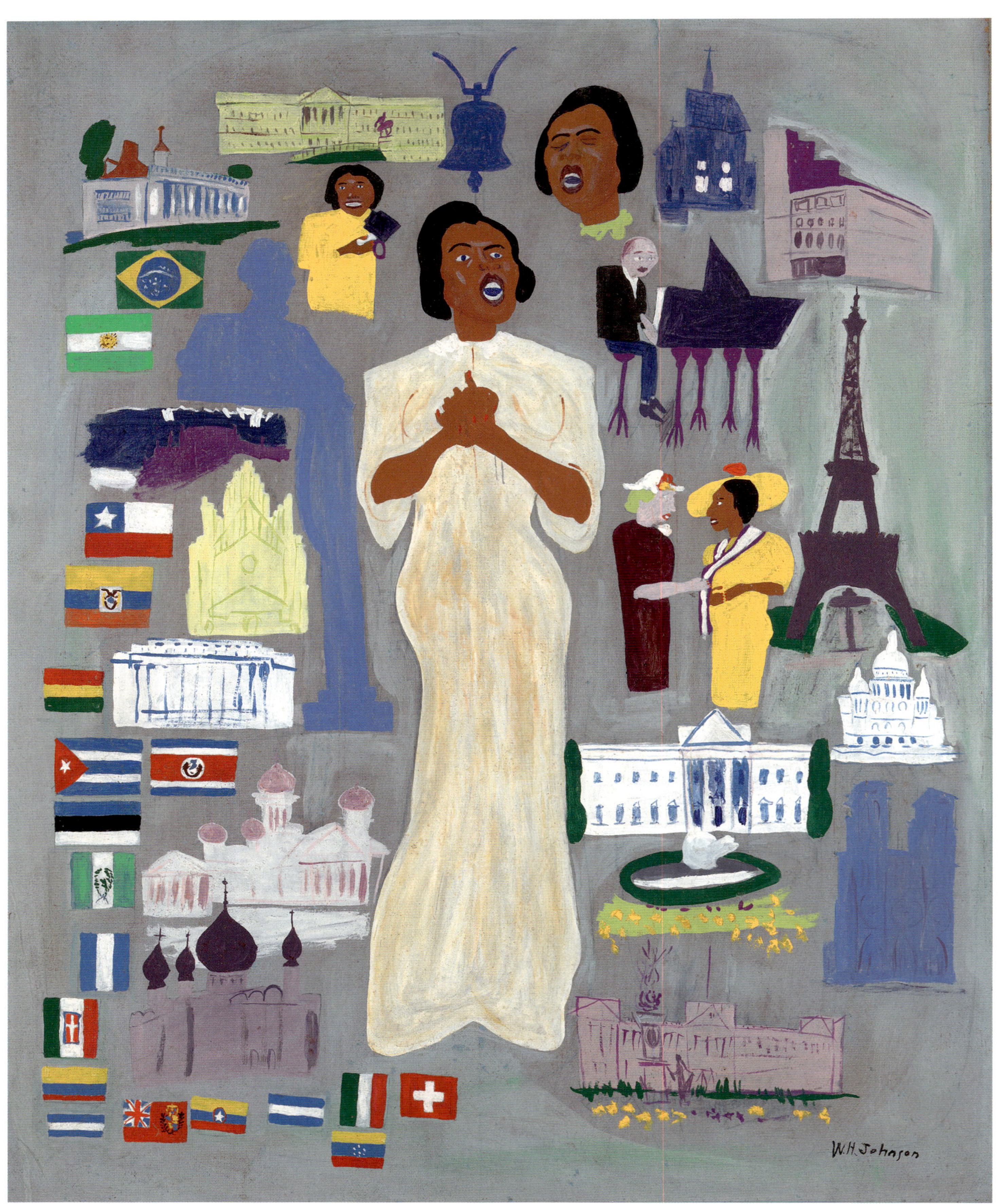
W.H. Johnson

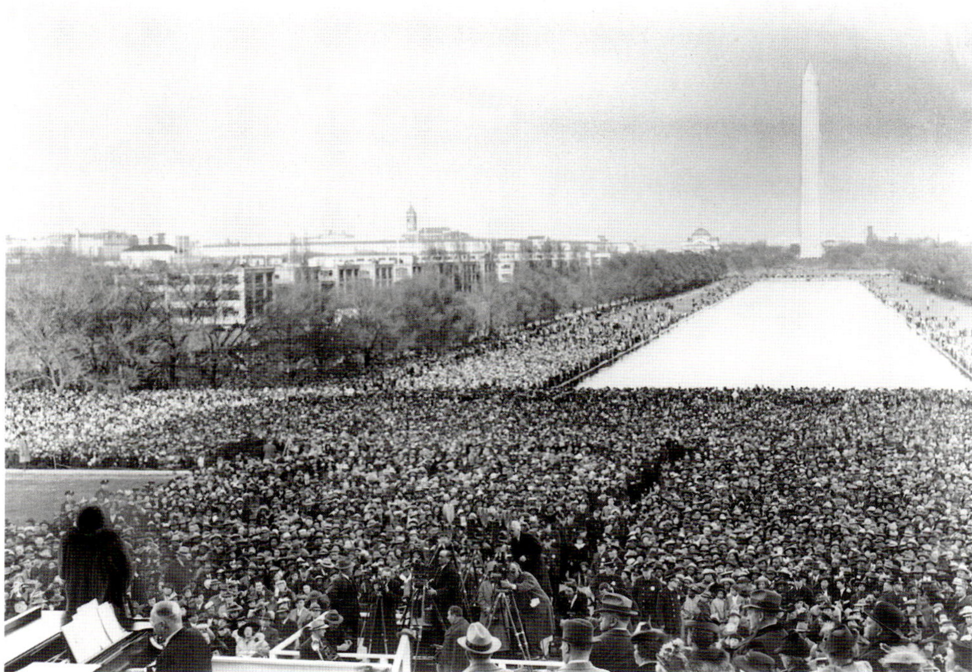

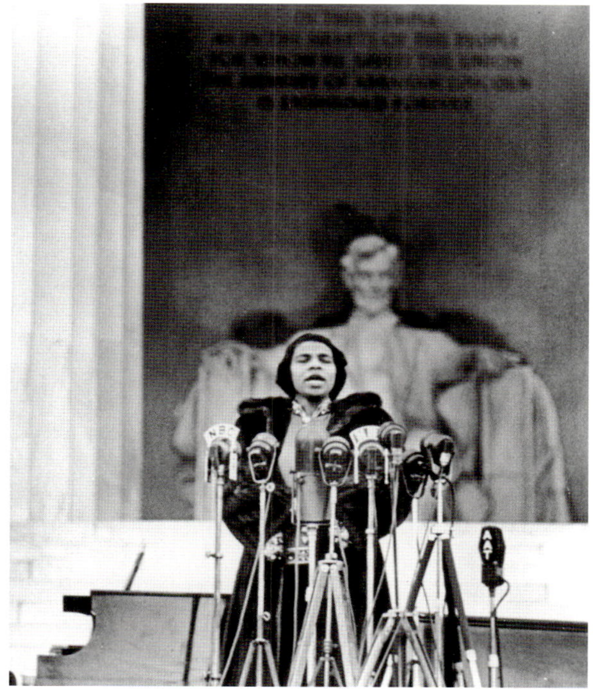

Figs. 27, 28

Marian Anderson singing to an audience of 75,000 from the steps of the Lincoln Memorial, Washington, DC, April 9, 1939

national headquarters in Washington, because of her race. For the oil version of Marian Anderson, Johnson chose to paint the celebrated performer not in this moment of nationwide visibility, but as a star renowned throughout the world.

Johnson exhibited a group of the *Fighters* along with paintings of Southern sharecroppers, fashionable Harlemites, military recruits, and religious subjects at the 135th Street branch of the New York Public Library during Negro History Week in 1946 (**Fig. 30**). He declared in an interview for the *New York Amsterdam News*, "I am a Negro and proud." The article concluded with the interviewer saying, "You could not help but feel the man has reached the highest degree of personal concept, shorn of all imitation and maudlin sentiment."[21]

Johnson contemplated returning to Denmark after Holcha's death in 1944. In 1946 he was finally ready. He wrote to his late wife's family:

> *I [have] now completed it all from my people's phite [fight] early 1800 to date. Spirituals, poor workers, sharecroppers, city lives, jitter bugs, dancers, war scenes, Red Cross, religious themes, families down south—portraits of all I could paint [of] history's Great men, women—**fighter[s] for Freedom*** [emphasis mine]. *I...depicted the character[s] who accomplished great deeds for the freedom [fight]—up to the United Nations. Now all this completed—all!*[22]

It had been clear to those who knew him well that Johnson had been behaving oddly for several years. Before her death Holcha had confided to a friend that William had been experiencing erratic mood swings and sudden outbursts of

Fig. 29

Marian Anderson; see p. 120

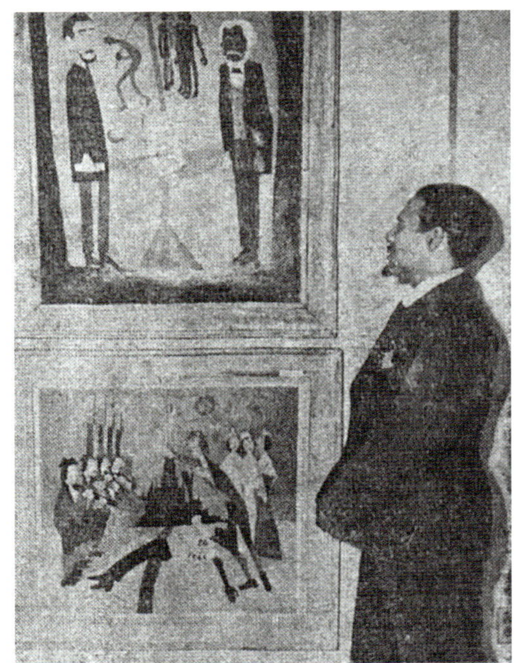

WILLIAM H. JOHNSON
an artist of the world scene

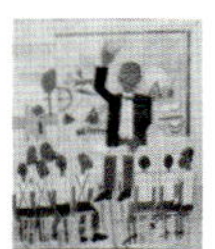

B.T. WASHINGTON LEGEND - *Gouache*

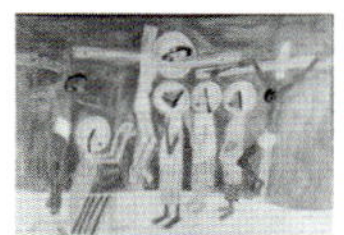

MT. CALVARY - *Gouache*

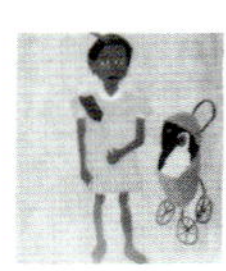

LI'L SIS - *Oil on board*

William H. Johnson, the American artist of Negro origin, saw a colorful lyrical world, as he made his way from the Deep South, across Europe and North Africa, and into the clear mountain air of Norway above the Arctic Circle. On this twenty year odyssey, he observed life and customs through the universal language of art. He painted hundreds of oils, watercolors, gouaches and pen and ink sketches; and further recorded his impressions with block prints and silk screens—each motif representing a novel artistic experience.

Johnson was born in the Negro section of Florence, South Carolina, in 1901. His parents were poor, simple-living folk. His schooling had to be brief, because as the eldest of five children, his working and earning from an early age was necessary. In those years, at the start of the century, there was no ray of opportunity that he might grasp to lift himself out of these circumstances. Yet, he aspired to be an artist! He worked at this strange ambition the best way he could.

He Set His Course In Art Copying Cartoons

"I began copying the humorous drawings in our newspapers," he says, "And the joy I derived from these may without a doubt be ascribed to the way we primitive people always adore caricatures." So he set his course in the field of art.

"You have to search your way forward," he said once many years later in an interview in Stockholm, Sweden. "You have to dare something when you are young."

From copying cartoons as a method of self-training in art, he derived the ability to tell a story in a picture. He also carried a caricature-like lilt throughout his entire art career. He had five years of formal training at the National Academy of Design in New York, working during all of that time at any kind of job he could find, for he still had to send money home. He won outstanding art prizes while a student there and in 1926, through the interest of friends of the late Charles W. Hawthorne, outstanding artist of the time, a fund was raised to send him abroad for study.

Johnson's short story technique in his painting became apparent in his first impressionistic work in France and Corsica with his strong blue skies of the Riviera, the crooked streets running a rick-rack course up a hill and carrying the sun-baked buildings along with them. He seemed to know how to get down to the bare essentials and to pull out what he needed. In late 1929, he returned to this country to startle and interest the art world in his work. He received in January 1930 the *Gold Award in Art* of the Harmon Foundation.

He Marries A Danish Artist

That same year he went back to Europe and married the Danish ceramic and textile artist, Holcha Krake. They had met the year before at Cagnes-sur-Mer, the artist colony in Southern France where she had gone with her sister and brother-in-law, a German sculptor and had all traveled together across France and Belgium and finally to Holcha's home in Odense where Johnson was warmly received by her family.

In the smiling little fishing village of Kerteminde, Denmark, where the Johnsons made their home, he intrigued the native folk with what his painter's eye saw in the gardens, the old houses and the clusters of red roofs.

"His art is a form of expressionism, a dynamic one, which never really has flowered here in Denmark," wrote a Danish art critic. "For him and all those who can master it, that close feeling of life evident in lines and colors is something very important which makes the motif live in one's consciousness. Just take a look at the street which waves in and out among the red roofs of Kerteminde. They make the gray line of the street swing out and glow through the

Fig. 30

Johnson at the opening of his exhibition at the New York Public Library's 135th Street branch, 1946, from Nora Holt, "Primitives on Exhibition," *New York Amsterdam News*, March 9, 1946

Fig. 31

Harmon Foundation brochure, "William H. Johnson: An Artist of the World Scene," 1956, Smithsonian Institution Archives

anger. By fall 1946, his mental health had deteriorated. He returned to Denmark, spent six months with the Krake family, then went to Norway, where, increasingly confused and combative, he lived on the street. Picked up in Oslo for vagrancy, he was diagnosed with a degenerative brain disease and hospitalized. In November he was returned to the United States and on December 1, 1947, was admitted to Central Islip State Hospital in New York. He remained there, without painting, until his death in 1970.

Johnson's Legacy

Throughout his difficult final journey, Johnson kept his and Holcha's artwork with him. In the 1950s, a court-appointed attorney who had been assigned to oversee Johnson's possessions at the time of his hospitalization recommended that the artwork be destroyed when funds for storing them ran out. At this point the Johnsons' longtime friend Helen Harriton stepped in.[23] She alerted the Harmon Foundation, which agreed to take custody on the condition that the New York Surrogate's Court grant the foundation unconditional rights to the work. Holcha's weavings and ceramics were returned to her family (a significant body is now in the collection of the Florence County Museum in South Carolina). Under the watchful eye of Harmon Foundation employee and longtime Johnson friend Palmer Hayden, Johnson's paintings, drawings, and watercolors that had been poorly cared for almost a decade were sorted. Those items that could not be salvaged were discarded; minimal conservation, matting, and framing were undertaken on others to prevent further deterioration and prepare them for exhibition. The foundation organized a retrospective of Johnson's work at the Countee Cullen branch of the New York Public Library in December 1956, and for the next several years the exhibition traveled to colleges, libraries, and community centers in New York, New England, the Midwest, and the South (**Fig. 31**).

In 1966, when the Harmon Foundation announced it would close the following year, director Mary Beattie Brady and assistant director Evelyn Brown began making plans for the long-term future of the artworks in their care. The holdings were extensive: more than one thousand works by William H. Johnson, a substantial collection of paintings by Malvin Gray Johnson, as well as six hundred-plus works by contemporary African artists.[24] They offered Johnson's work to the Smithsonian Institution's National Collection of Fine Arts (NCFA, now the Smithsonian American Art Museum) on the condition that the museum carry on the foundation's mission to catalogue, exhibit, lend, and publish Johnson's work.[25]

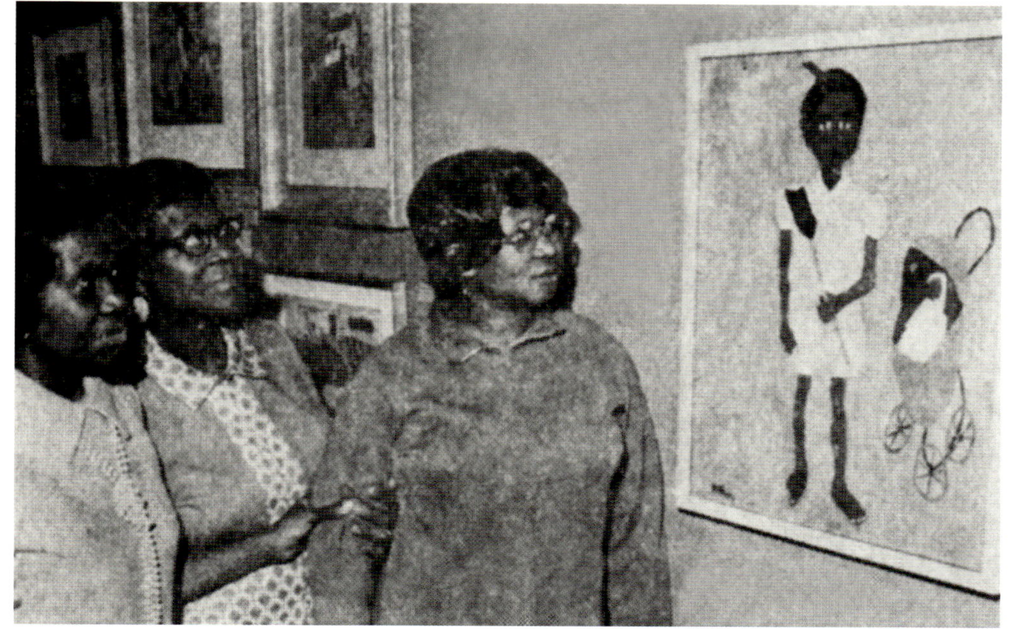

In June 1967, sixty-nine crates were shipped from the foundation's New York headquarters to the District of Columbia, where NCFA launched a long-range conservation initiative (which continues to this day) and offered works to other museum collections. Historically Black colleges and universities responded enthusiastically, resulting in the transfer of more than one hundred fifty paintings and prints.[26] Several more were given to members of Johnson's family. In November 1971, NCFA opened *William H. Johnson, 1901–1970*, a major retrospective that traced the arc of Johnson's career and subsequently toured to cities in Africa, Europe, and the United States (Figs. 32, 33).[27] Since that time, the Smithsonian American Art Museum (SAAM) has featured Johnson's work in solo and group exhibitions that have traveled to dozens of museums around the country. SAAM's 1991 exhibition *Homecoming: William H. Johnson and Afro-America*, organized by guest curator Dr. Richard J. Powell, was a blockbuster that reintroduced Johnson's late work to a national audience. Powell's book, *Homecoming: The Art and Life of William H. Johnson*, which accompanied the show, remains the most important account of Johnson's life and work. Visitors to SAAM continue to discover this remarkable artist, whose paintings are always on view.

Fighters for Freedom represents the culmination of Johnson's lifelong commitment to African America. As a student at the academy, he developed skills that would make him an effective painter. As a modernist in Scandinavia, he embraced an international perspective that gave him insight into the long traditions and experimental possibilities of art. As a celebrated painter on the New York gallery scene, he focused on African American subjects, transforming the mundane worlds of southern agriculture and New York street life into profound statements about the human condition. With *Fighters for Freedom* Johnson confirms the centrality of struggle and social justice within the American story. He tells us that Black lives matter, that determination and perseverance can change hearts and minds, and that the pursuit of freedom touches people everywhere. Through his paintings he calls on us to take up the challenge he began and continue the fight for equity, dignity, and equality for all.

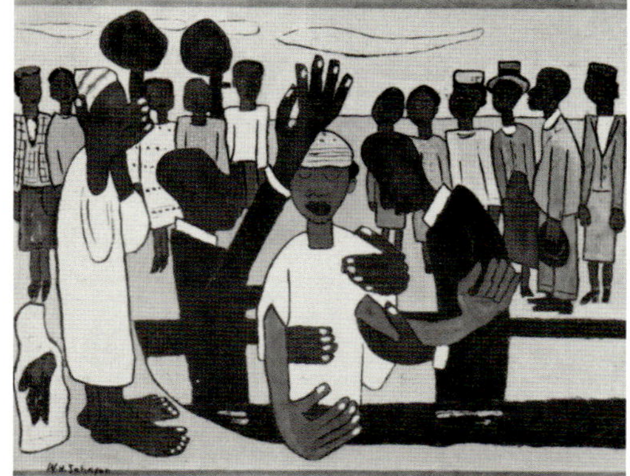

Fig. 32

Johnson's niece Lillian Cooper with a painting of herself, *Li'L Sis* (1967.59.1023), at the National Collection of Fine Arts, November 1971, Smithsonian Institution Archives

Fig. 33

Catalogue for the exhibition *William H. Johnson: A Retrospective Exhibition*, held at the Nigerian National Museum, Lagos, May 29–June 21, 1972, Smithsonian Institution Archives

Endnotes

1 William H. Johnson quoted in Nora Holt, "Primitives on Exhibit," *New York Amsterdam News*, March 9, 1946, 16.

2 Much of the biographical information sketched out here is drawn from Adelyn D. Breeskin, *William H. Johnson, 1901–1970* (Washington, DC: Smithsonian Institution Press for the National Collection of Fine Arts, 1971) and Richard J. Powell, *Homecoming: The Art and Life of William H. Johnson* (New York: Rizzoli for the National Museum of American Art, 1991). The Archives of American Art holds extensive Johnson materials, including clippings from exhibitions in Scandinavia and the United States, photographs, and a scrapbook that Johnson kept. Note that the National Collection of Fine Arts and the National Museum of American Art designate the museum now identified as the Smithsonian American Art Museum. I am deeply grateful to pioneering research on Johnson by Breeskin, Powell, Leslie King-Hammond, and Makeda Best, whose recent article offers an in-depth examination of Johnson's *Fighters for Freedom* paintings; see "Cut Aesthetics: William H. Johnson's Scrapbook History Paintings," *Archives of American Art Journal* 58, no. 1 (Spring 2019): 4–27.

3 Kay P., "Med Kerteminde-Malerier til U.S.A. Negermaleren fortæller om Kunst og Race," *Demokraten* (Aarhus, Denmark), December 7, 1934, 3, translated by Richard J. Powell and quoted in Powell, *Homecoming*, 12. The original clipping is included in Johnson's papers in the Archives of American Art. William H. Johnson papers, 1922–1972, bulk 1926–1956, box 1, folder 20, Archives of American Art, Smithsonian Institution (hereafter William H. Johnson Papers). The vast majority of Johnson's papers have been digitized and are available on the Archives of American Art's website, https://aaa.si.edu.

4 The discussion of Hawthorne's approach to teaching appears in Powell, *Homecoming*, 12–14.

5 William H. Johnson, undated handwritten résumé, ca. 1940, excerpted in Breeskin, *William H. Johnson*, 12.

6 William H. Johnson to Charles W. Hawthorne, August 13, 1928, quoted in Powell, *Homecoming*, 31.

7 Biography of Holcha Krake Johnson (after 1943), William H. Johnson Papers, box 1, folder 2, quoted in Powell, *Homecoming*, 36.

8 The William E. Harmon Foundation, which was established in 1921, offered awards in literature, music, fine arts, business and industry, science and innovation, education, religious service, and race relations under Mary Beattie Brady, who served as director from 1922 to 1967. The foundation's program to increase opportunities for African American artists had the greatest impact. In addition to awards that carried cash prizes, the foundation sponsored traveling exhibitions that brought the work of African American artists to communities around the country. For further information on the Harmon Foundation, see Gary A. Reynolds and Beryl J. Wright, *Against the Odds: African-American Artists and the Harmon Foundation* (Newark, NJ: The Newark Museum, 1989).

9 Harmon Foundation, "Exhibition to Be Held of Work of Negro Artists," press release, January 4, 1930, box 31, folder 5, Harmon Foundation, Inc. records, 1913–1967, Manuscript Division, Library of Congress (hereafter Harmon Foundation Papers), quoted in Powell, *Homecoming*, 41.

10 "Y.M.C.A. Officers Announce Exhibit by Negro Artist," *Florence Morning News*, April 13, 1930, 8, and "Artist Johnson," *Florence Morning News*, April 15, 1930, 4, quoted in Powell, *Homecoming*, 51.

11 "Eksotisk maler utstiller i Trondheim. Og laerer oss å se vart eget lands farveprakt," *Nidaros*, September 15, 1937, quoted in Richard J. Powell, "William H. Johnson: Expressionist and Artist of the Blues Aesthetic" (PhD diss., Yale University, 1988), 125.

12 William H. Johnson, Rosenwald Fellowship application, January 6, 1942, Harmon Foundation Collection, quoted in Powell, *Homecoming*, 150.

13 The Harlem Community Art Center opened in December 1937, a year before Johnson's return. First Lady Eleanor Roosevelt attended the grand opening, as did President A. Philip Randolph of the Brotherhood of Sleeping Car Porters, author and civil rights activist James Weldon Johnson, and noted sculptor Augusta Savage, who was the center's first director. With support from multiple civic groups as well as the government's Federal Art Project, the Harlem Community Art Center quickly became a cultural hub for musicians, writers, and visual artists as well as the Harlem community itself. Within its first sixteen months, some 1,500 children and adults enrolled in classes and another 24,000 had gathered for lectures, exhibitions, and demonstrations. "Harlem's Artistic Community in the 1930s," in Patricia Hills, *Painting Harlem Modern, The Art of Jacob Lawrence* (Berkeley: University of California Press, 2009), 8–31, offers an excellent overview of the Harlem Community Art Center and its activities. For the participation figures, she cites Gwendolyn Bennett, "The Harlem Community Art Center," in *Art for the Millions: Essays from the 1930s by Artists and Administrators of the WPA Federal Art Project*, ed. Francis V. O'Connor (Greenwich, CT: New York Graphic Society, 1973), 213–15.

14 *Chicago Sunday Times*, July 21, 1940; Emily Genauer, "At Alma Reed Gallery," *New York World-Telegram*, May 10, 1941; Howard Devree, "A Reviewer's Notebook," *New York Times*, May 2, 1943, and "One by One Painters Show Work," *New York Times*, May 7, 1944. The clippings can be found in Johnson's papers in the Archives of American Art. National magazines *Art News* and *Art Digest* routinely covered his shows, as did other New York dailies. The Black press was equally attentive: The *Pittsburgh Gazette*; *Opportunity: A Journal of Negro Life*; and *The Crisis*, which reached audiences across the country, covered Johnson's exhibitions.

15 Atlanta University, "Third Annual Atlanta University Exhibition," March–April 1944; Newark Museum, "American Negro Art: Contemporary Painting and Sculpture," April–May, 1944; Wakefield Gallery, New York, "Small Oil Paintings," May 1944; and G Place Gallery, Washington, DC, "New Names in American Art," May 1944.

16 Johnson had explored American historical subjects not long after returning from Europe. He created multiple images of Lincoln at Gettysburg (see SAAM 1967.59.565R-V, 1967.59.556R-V, and 1967.59.177R-V), and the swearing in of George Washington (1967.59.364R-V, 1967.59.653, 1967.59.155R-V, and 1967.59.546), along with *John Brown* (1967.59.1148), and the screenprint *On a John Brown Flight* (1971.137) around 1940 to 1941. However, not until about 1944 or 1945, following race riots in Harlem which Johnson depicted in the painting *Moon over Harlem* (1943–44, SAAM 1967.59.577), did his commitment to telling the stories of notable African Americans and world leaders coalesce in the group he called *Fighters for Freedom*. The Smithsonian American Art Museum collection includes more than thirty-five paintings and a number of drawings from the *Fighters* series.

17 Henry B. Pringle, "Why Not Teach American History?" *Saturday Evening Post*, January 20, 1945, 14, William H. Johnson Papers, box 1, folder 11.

18 Zora Neale Hurston's *Moses, Man of the Mountain*, which recasts the biblical Book of Exodus from an African American perspective, came out in 1939, as did Arna Bontemps's *Drums at Dusk* based on Toussaint L'Ouverture's slave rebellion. Writers Countee Cullen, Langston Hughes, James Weldon Johnson, band leaders Duke Ellington and Count Basie, singers Ella Fitzgerald and Billie Holliday, as well as the Cotton Club's Cab Calloway thrilled millions with their radio appearances and nightclub performances. Hattie McDaniel won the 1939 Academy Award for Best Supporting Actress for her role in *Gone with the Wind*.

19 Among other major historical murals painted at the time are Aaron Douglas's 1934 four-panel mural *Aspects of Negro Life* (Schomburg Center for Research in African American History and Culture, New York Public Library), Hale Woodruff's account of the story of the slave ship *Amistad* in three murals for Talladega College (1938), and Charles White's *Contributions of the Negro to Democracy in America* (1943, Clarke Hall, Hampton University).

20 Johnson often used clippings as the basis for sketches of fighters and world leaders, for example *Franklin Delano Roosevelt* (1967.59.352), *Gandhi* (1967.59.380), and *Two Boxers* (1967.59.505R-V), Smithsonian American Art Museum.

21 Holt, "Primitives on Exhibit," William H. Johnson Papers, box 1, folder 14.

22 William H. Johnson to Thora and Nanna Krake, September 28, 1946, private collection, Denmark, quoted in Powell, *Homecoming*, 237n50.

23 The Johnsons met Helen and Dave Harriton in June 1937 on a fjord steamer in Norway. They stayed in touch and when the Johnsons returned to New York, the Harritons met their ship and invited them to stay at their home until they found an apartment. Helen Harriton to Mary Beattie Brady, Sept. 30, 1956, Harmon Foundation Papers, box 77, folder 3. Much of the information about this last chapter of Johnson's life comes from Powell, *Homecoming*, 223–29.

24 The foundation also owned work by Ellis Wilson, Palmer Hayden, and Albert Alexander Smith, a Black artist who worked primarily in Spain. Paintings by Palmer Hayden, Claude Clark, Malvin Gray Johnson, and Laura Wheeler Waring were given to the Smithsonian American Art Museum. More than forty paintings by Betsy Graves Reyneau and Laura Wheeler Waring that the foundation had commissioned for the exhibition *Portraits of Outstanding Americans of Negro Origin* were given to the Smithsonian's National Portrait Gallery; a suite of prints by Mizufune Rokushu is now in the collection of the Smithsonian's National Museum of Asian Art.

25 SAAM's acquisitions files contain correspondence and other documentation related to the transfer from the Harmon Foundation to SAAM of more than one thousand paintings, watercolors, prints, and sketches and SAAM's transfer of some one hundred forty to other museums. See Evelyn S. Brown to David W. Scott, April 19, 1967, offering the collection to SAAM (then the National Collection of Fine Arts), and David Scott to Evelyn Brown, May 10, 1967, accepting her proposal. The vision of Adelyn Dohme Breeskin, who joined the staff of NCFA as consulting curator of contemporary art following her 1962 retirement as director of the Baltimore Museum of Art, is largely responsible for the museum's decision to accept such a large body of work. She and curator Jan Muhlert conducted extensive research and interviews for *William H. Johnson, 1901–1970*, the first comprehensive publication on Johnson's work, which accompanied the 1971 exhibition of the same title.

26 Professor James A. Porter selected thirty works for Howard University, including two from the *Fighters for Freedom* series: *Abraham Lincoln Lives Revelation* and *On a John Brown Flight*. Dr. Richard Long identified nineteen paintings for Hampton University, including *Against the Odds* and *Three Great Freedom Fighters* as well as sixteen paintings for Atlanta University (now Clark Atlanta University). David Driskell selected twenty paintings for Fisk University, including an untitled Gettysburg Address scene, *Booker T. Washington Legend*, and *Negro Genius*. James E. Lewis selected twenty works for Morgan State University; twenty more were given to Tuskegee University. Additional works were transferred to the DuSable Black History Museum, South Carolina State University, North Carolina Central University, the Gibbes Museum of Art, the Florence County Museum in South Carolina, the Frederick Douglass Institute, and several other institutions.

27 The touring exhibition, which included fifty-five paintings, watercolors, prints, and drawings, spanned the full range of Johnson's career. It was presented in the following cities in Africa and Europe: Addis Ababa, Ethiopia; Angers, France; Lagos, Nigeria; Onikan, Nigeria; Rouen, France; Cape Town, South Africa; Tunis, Tunisia, and Zagreb, Croatia. In the United States it was shown in Baltimore, Maryland; Midland, Texas; Oakland, California; and six cities in South Carolina (Columbia, Florence, Greenville, Orangeburg, Spartanburg, and Charleston).

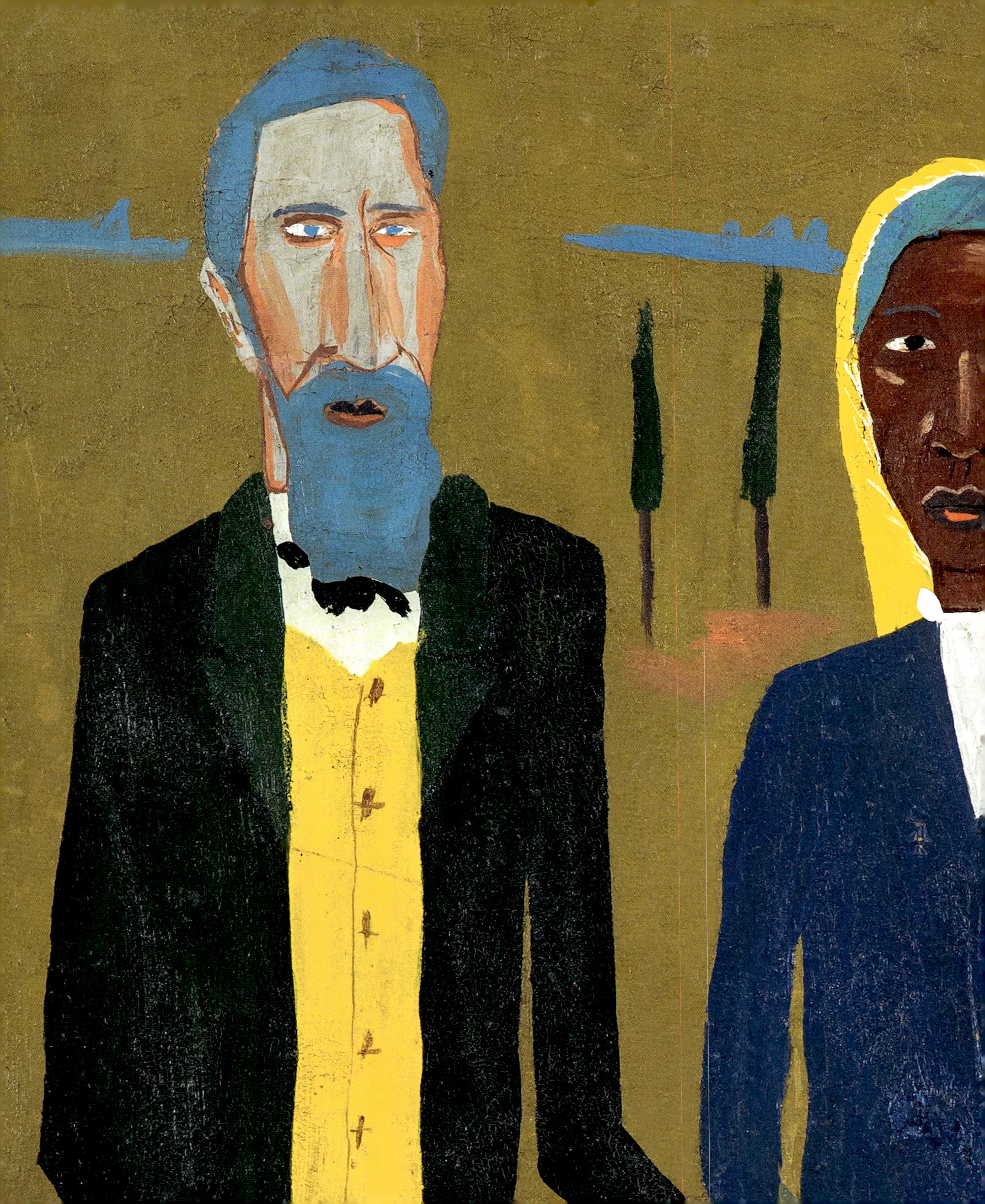

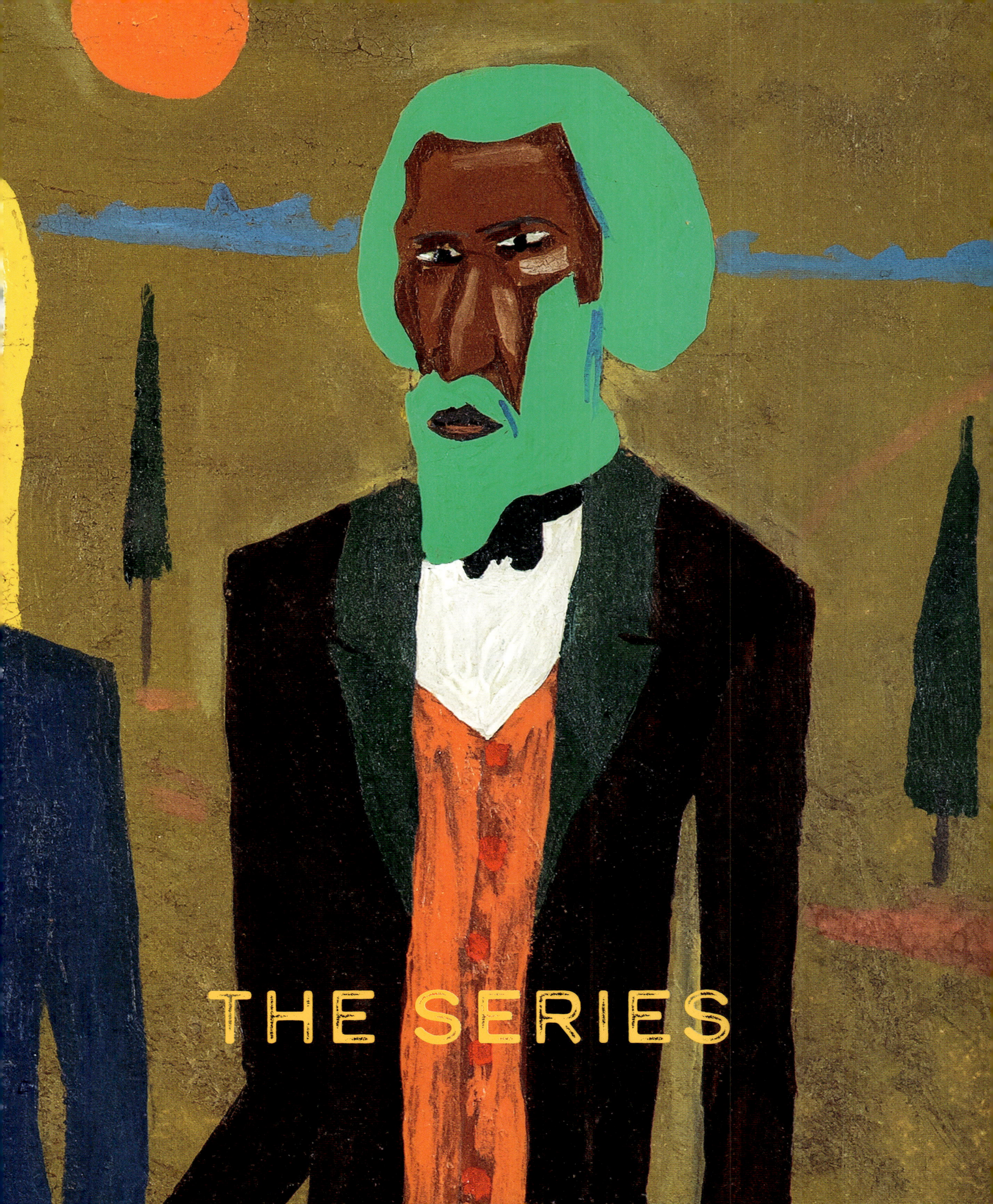

THE SERIES

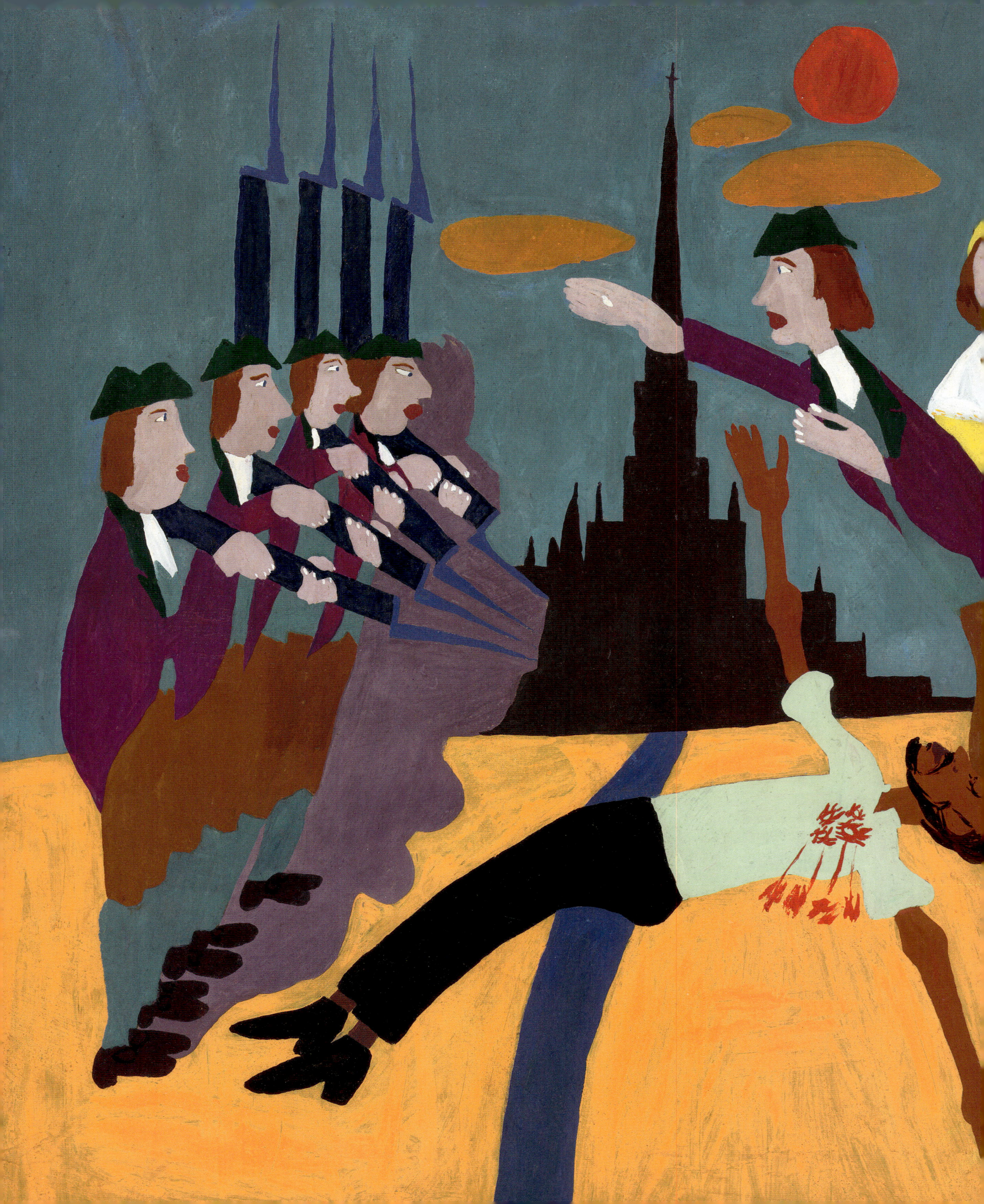

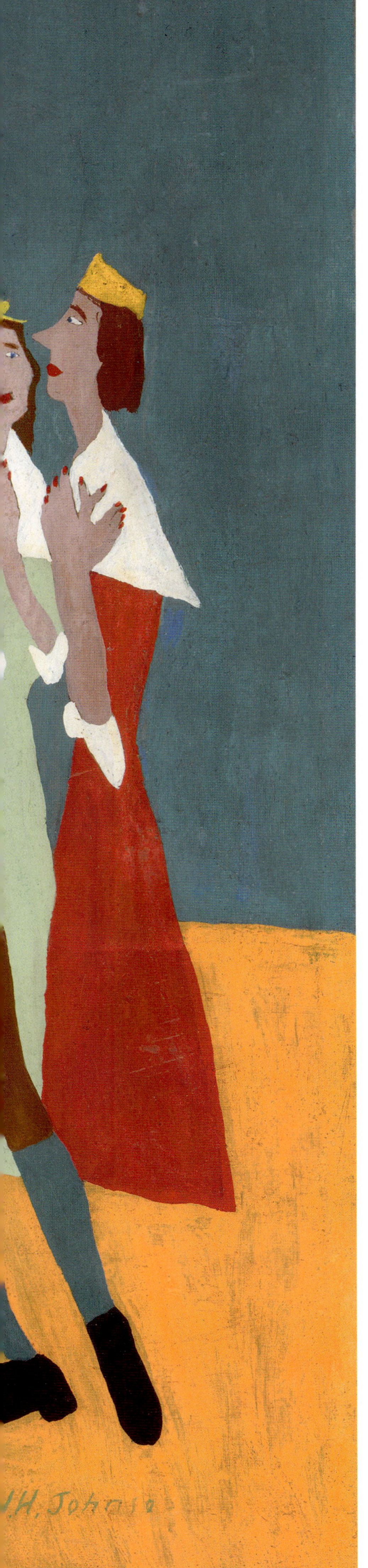

CRISPUS ATTUCKS

ca. 1945
oil on paperboard
29 ½ × 30 ⅞ in.
Smithsonian American Art Museum
Gift of the Harmon Foundation

LITTLE IS KNOWN about Crispus Attucks, whom many consider the first casualty of the American Revolution. Born around 1723 in Massachusetts, he likely was of African and Native American descent, stood over six feet tall, and had been enslaved before escaping to Boston, where he worked on whaling ships. On March 5, 1770, Attucks was part of a group of colonists who, wielding snowballs and sticks, confronted soldiers standing guard outside the King Street Customs House in Boston. Britain's King George III had sent troops to the city two years earlier to quell unrest over his burdensome taxes on essential goods like paper, tea, and glass. Bostonians of all classes resented this conspicuous military presence, which only increased the tension between colonists and the crown. Precisely what happened outside the customs house is unclear, but during a clash the troops fired into the crowd, killing five. Attucks was the first to die. Three days after the incident, nearly three-quarters of the city's population attended the victims' funeral. They formed a procession that traveled from King Street to Boston's Granary Burying Ground, where Attucks and four others were buried in a common grave. Months later, the soldiers involved in the killings were tried for murder and acquitted (though two were found guilty of manslaughter and sent back to England).

News of the incident, now known as the Boston Massacre, spread through the colonies and lit the fuse of revolution. Attucks's name and story, however, soon faded away and were largely

“Crispus Attucks, the First Martyr of the American Revolution, King (now State) Street, Boston, March 5, 1770,” from William Cooper Nell, *Colored Patriots of the American Revolution* (1855)

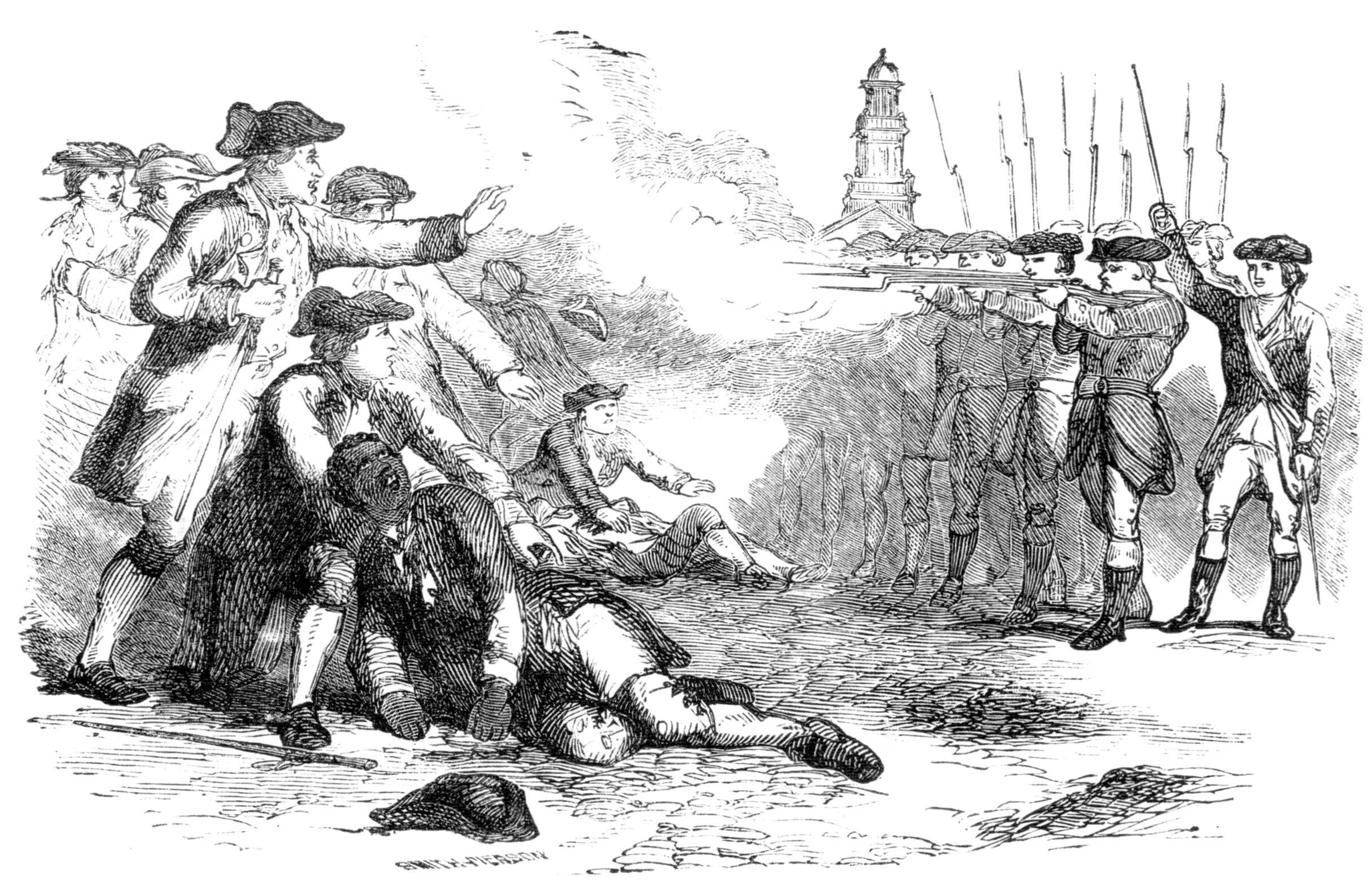

forgotten for more than eighty years, until the abolitionist William Cooper Nell brought them to light. In 1855, Nell published *The Colored Patriots of the American Revolution*, which hailed Attucks as the first martyr in the battle against British tyranny. The book argued that African Americans deserved equal rights and full citizenship because they had fought and died for the sake of independence just as others had.

Johnson likely based his painting on an engraving from Nell's *Colored Patriots* (opposite). The original engraving presents a chaotic scene. Soldiers fire on the frenzied customs house protestors, who cry out and tend to the wounded; amid plumes of smoke at center, a fleeing man's hat flies through the air. Attucks reclines in the foreground, arms and legs limp from his injuries, while another man lies dying behind him. Johnson pared down the scene, magnifying biblical themes of sacrifice. In the artist's stylized version, Attucks lies dead in the center foreground with his arms outstretched, Christ-like. At left, soldiers point their bayonets at the slain, unarmed man; at right, a white colonist extends his arm in a gesture of outrage, or perhaps reconciliation, while three mourning women look on. Boston's skyline hovers in the distance, recalling the Puritan idea of New England as a "city on a hill," a beacon of Christian virtue for the rest of the world. By placing Attucks at the foot of that city, his hand reaching to the cross that sits atop its highest spire, Johnson linked his fate—visually and morally—to that of the colonies and the American experiment writ large.

Attucks served as an emblem of sacrifice through the Civil War, the Jim Crow era, and beyond. In the early nineteenth century, when African Americans were not yet permitted to serve in the military, they formed independent militias; many, including the Attucks Guards of New York and Cincinnati's Attucks Blues, were named after the martyred sailor. By including Attucks in his *Fighters for Freedom* series, Johnson joined this chorus, asserting that Black people have been fighting and dying for the nation since its inception.

—EHR

SWEARING IN GEORGE WASHINGTON

ca. 1945
oil on paperboard
27 5/8 × 31 7/8 in.
Smithsonian American Art Museum
Gift of the Harmon Foundation

FOLLOWING THE Revolutionary War, in which the American colonies threw off British colonial rule to establish the United States, the new country's government took the form of a confederation, a "league of friendship" in which states functioned as independent and sovereign entities. Without a strong central government, however, disputes over territory, taxation, and trade among the states soon threatened to destroy the young nation. After two years of debate, delegates from twelve states ratified a new governing document—the United States Constitution. It established a federal government composed of three coequal parts—the executive, legislative, and judicial branches—with a president, chosen by the Electoral College, heading the executive branch. George Washington was the

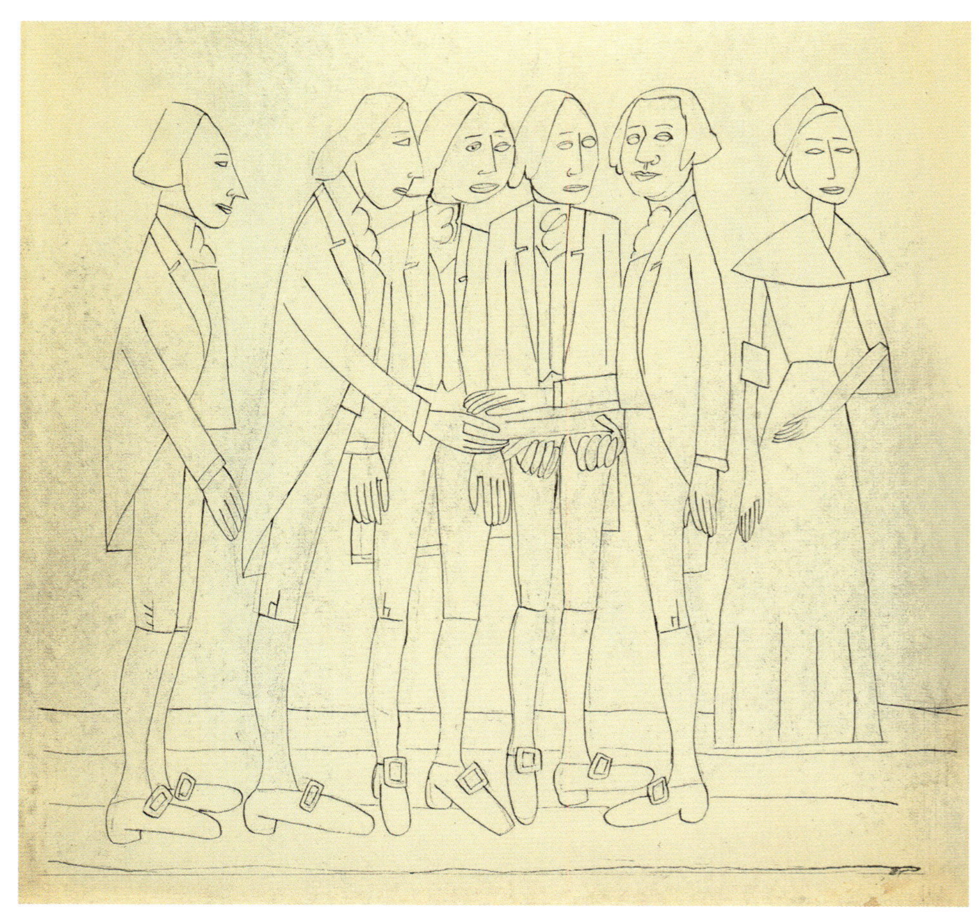

Swearing in George Washington, ca. 1942–1943, pen and ink and pencil on paper, 17 7/8 × 17 1/8 in., Smithsonian American Art Museum, Gift of the Harmon Foundation, 1967.59.546

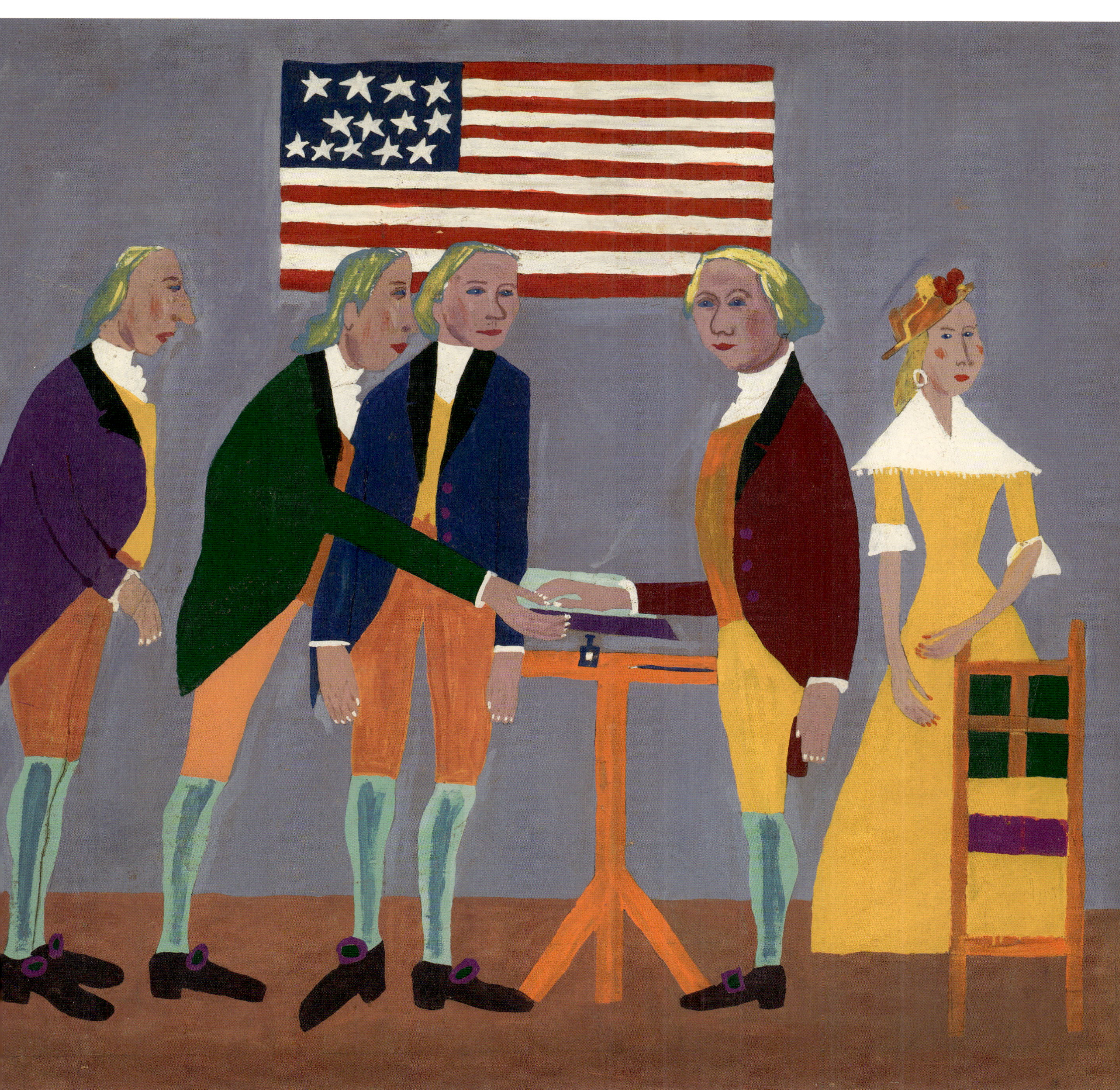

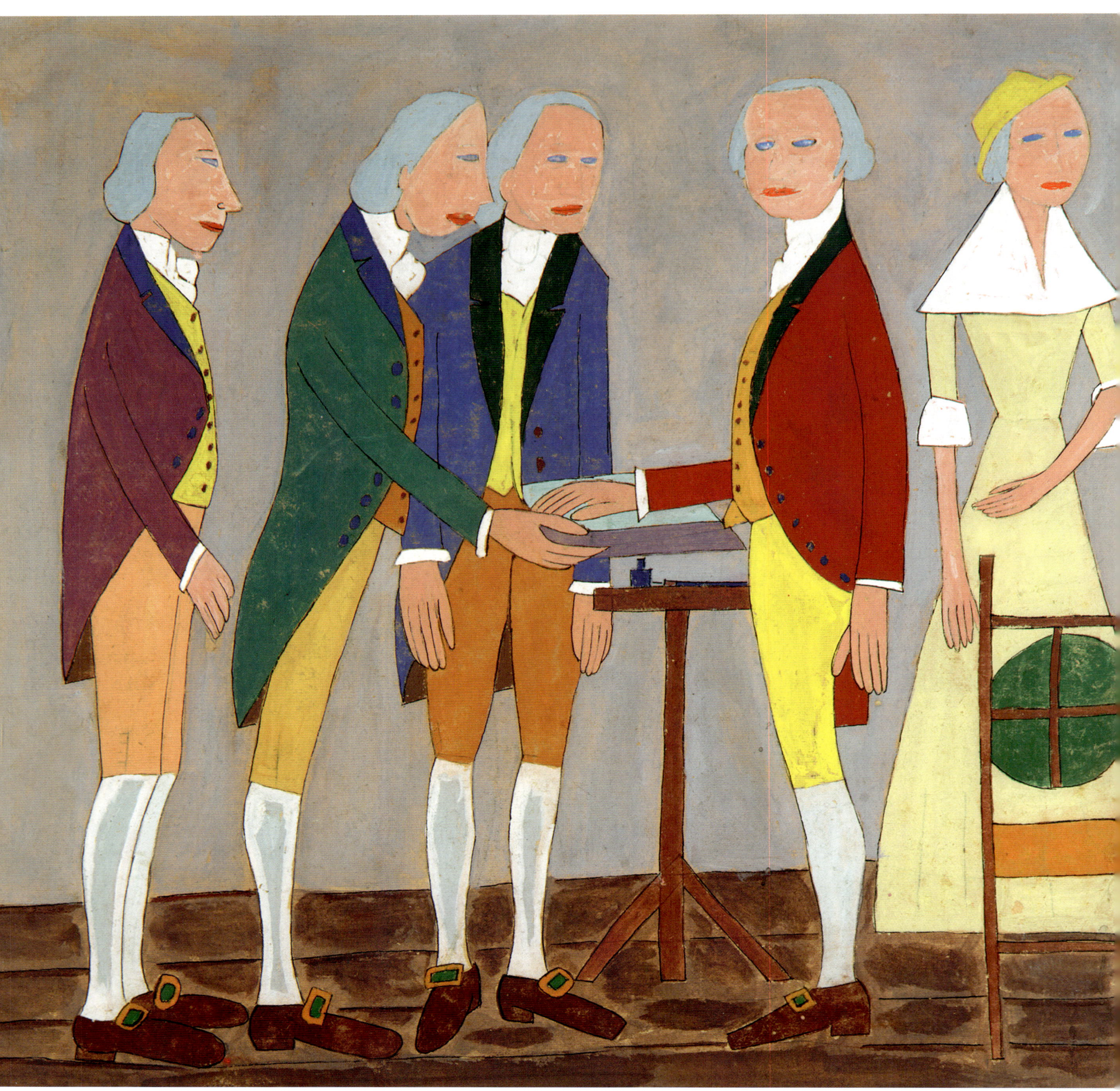

Swearing in George Washington, ca. 1942–43, tempera and pen and ink with pencil on paper, 16 3/8 × 16 5/8 in., Smithsonian American Art Museum, Gift of the Harmon Foundation, 1967.59.155R-V

unanimous choice to become the first president. Although the former commander in chief of the Continental Army had retired to his plantation, Mount Vernon, he was committed to the success of the country he had helped create, so he accepted the post, albeit reluctantly. Thousands of people came out to greet Washington as he traveled from Virginia to the country's temporary capital in New York City, where he took the oath of office on April 30, 1789.

Swearing in George Washington (p. 57) is a simple composition. Washington stands in the center looking out at us as he is sworn in. His right hand is on a book (a Bible) held by Robert R. Livingston, chancellor of New York State. At far left is newly elected vice president John Adams; Martha Washington, in a stylish hat and earrings, observes the historic moment.

The artist gave no indication that Washington took the oath of office outdoors, on a balcony at Federal Hall so throngs of people in the street below could watch the ceremony, nor did he show the fireworks that lit up the sky later that night. Instead, this simplified scene emphasizes the solemnity and dignity of a moment that launched the form of government that continues to this day.

Johnson made two preparatory drawings and a preliminary painting (pp. 56, 58) as he worked out his final arrangement, yet the final painting lacks the complexity of others in the series. Although most of his *Fighters for Freedom* paintings depict scenes that trace the subjects' achievements and, in some cases, shortcomings, here Johnson chose not to show the battles that Washington's troops fought or to acknowledge other episodes in his illustrious life. Instead, in the final version, Johnson added an American flag, a symbol of the heroic effort of establishing a new nation.

—VMM

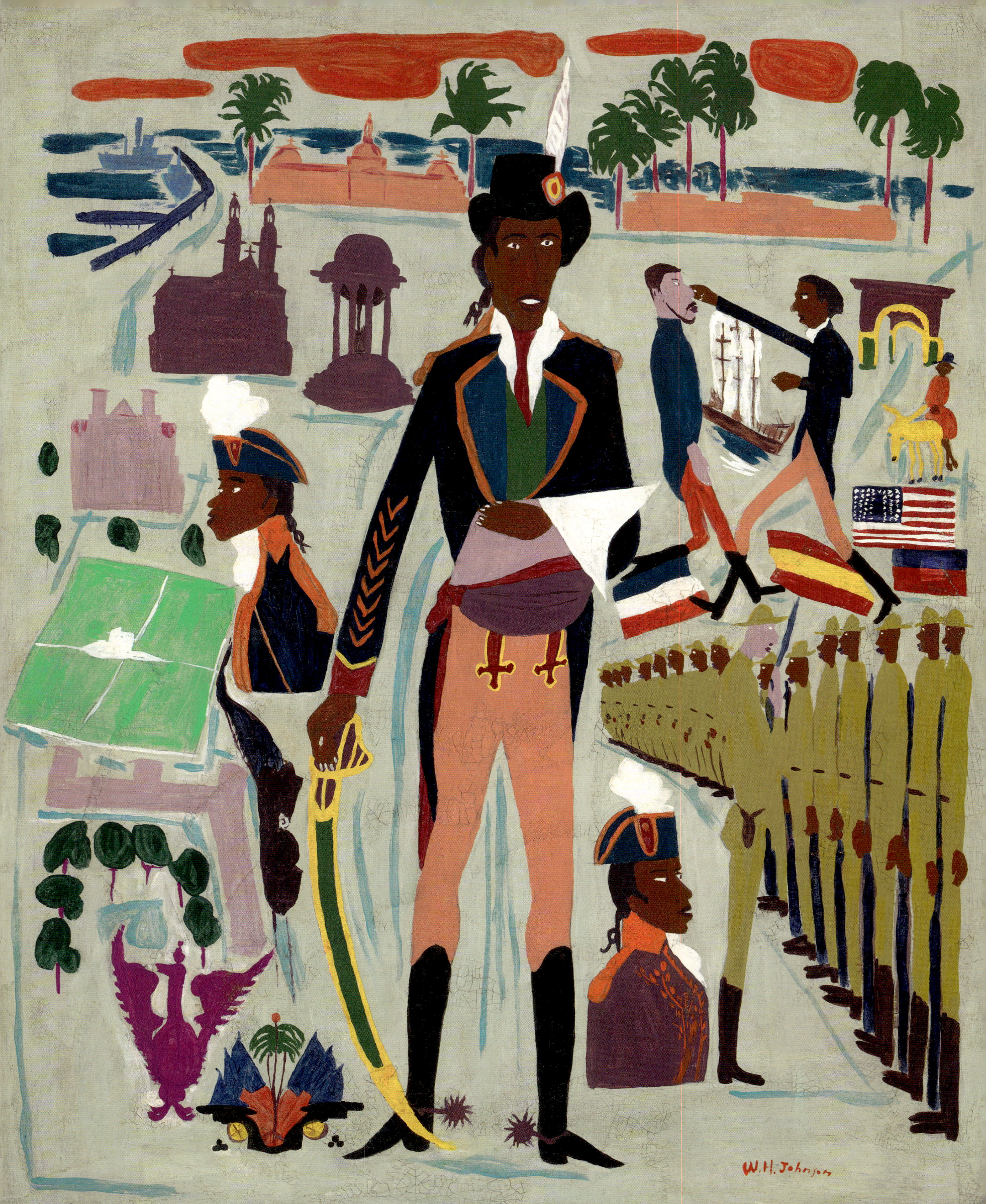
W. H. Johnson

TOUSSAINT L'OUVERTURE, HAITI

ca. 1945
oil on paperboard
38 ¼ × 30 ⅛ in.
Smithsonian American Art Museum
Gift of the Harmon Foundation

GENERAL TOUSSAINT L'Ouverture (1743–1803), born François Dominique Toussaint Bréda, masterminded the only successful revolt of enslaved people in history, on the French colony of Saint-Domingue (modern-day Haiti). L'Ouverture, who had been enslaved on a sugar plantation, harnessed his knowledge of the island's mountainous landscape and skill at guerilla-style warfare to lead the uprising, which began in 1791. He aimed to unite the colony's Black population, gain a degree of autonomy from France, and abolish slavery. After three years of fighting, the French government conceded, granting freedom and full citizenship to Saint-Domingue's inhabitants of African descent and recognizing L'Ouverture as the colony's governor general. He wrote a constitution that abolished slavery and for seven years ruled as though Saint-Domingue was an independent nation. This provoked the ire of Napoleon Bonaparte, who ordered him captured and deported to France. He died there, in a squalid prison, in 1803. The next year L'Ouverture's lieutenant, Jean-Jacques Dessalines, finally succeeded in throwing off French rule and established Haiti, the world's first Black republic.

As an early martyr in the struggle against slavery in the Americas, L'Ouverture has long been an icon for those fighting oppression. Marcus Garvey wrote in his newspaper *Negro World* in 1925 that his "brilliancy as a soldier and statesman outshone that of a Cromwell, Napoleon, and Washington; hence, he is entitled to the highest place as a hero among men." Johnson's painting portrays L'Ouverture as soldier and statesman, rebel and governor. At center, an elegantly attired L'Ouverture holds a piece of paper that likely represents the abolitionist constitution he authored. At right, he is a plainly dressed fighter locked in combat with a European soldier, while a slave ship in the distance alludes to the stakes of their struggle. At lower right, Johnson painted what appear to be World War II–era soldiers, a row of African American recruits standing before a white officer. The U.S. military was segregated until after World War II, and white officers commonly led African American units. By placing this modern scene among images of a brilliant Black commander, Johnson might have been critiquing a discriminatory practice of his day.

—EHR

NAT TURNER

ca. 1945
oil on paperboard
31 ⅜ × 25 ⅞ in.
Smithsonian American Art Museum
Gift of the Harmon Foundation

THIS DISTURBING scene represents a watershed moment in American history, the hanging of Nat Turner (1800–1831). A controversial figure in the antislavery movement, Turner launched a rebellion against white enslavers in rural Southampton County, Virginia, in August 1831. He and his followers attacked and killed fifty-five men, women, and children—an event that sent shock waves throughout the country, but especially the South.

Remarkably little is known about this Fighter, though the outlines of his life have become legendary. Turner was born enslaved on October 2, 1800, on a plantation in southeastern Virginia. When Turner was a boy, the man who was probably his father, Abraham, self-emancipated; his son never saw him again. More separations followed, as Turner suffered the cruel fate of many enslaved people; he was transferred or sold at least three times, forcing him from his remaining family, friends, and likely even his wife and children. While still a child, Turner used his extraordinary reading and writing skills to study the Bible. With a deep religious conviction, he later preached to his community and began to have spiritual visions. "Ol' Prophet Nat" eventually came to believe that God called him to free his people from bondage.

Turner recalled one of his early visions, from about 1825: "I saw white spirits and black spirits engaged in battle, and the sun was darkened—the thunder rolled in the Heavens, and blood flowed in streams—and I heard a voice saying, 'Such is your luck, such you are called to see, and let it come rough or smooth, you must surely [bear] it.'" This and other revelations, likely combined with brutal life experiences, later convinced Turner to plan, with a group of six trusted friends, to upend the system of slavery with a violent surprise attack. Secrecy was crucial to success, so they involved few at the outset and stored no guns. They intended to use weapons and farm tools found at the victims' homes.

During the night of August 21, 1831, or in the predawn hours of August 22, the conspirators began by killing Turner's then-enslavers, the Travis family, at their plantation. There they recruited one of Turner's friends to the ongoing insurgency before moving to nearby farms, continuing the violence, and gaining forty or more followers. But they did not convince as many to join

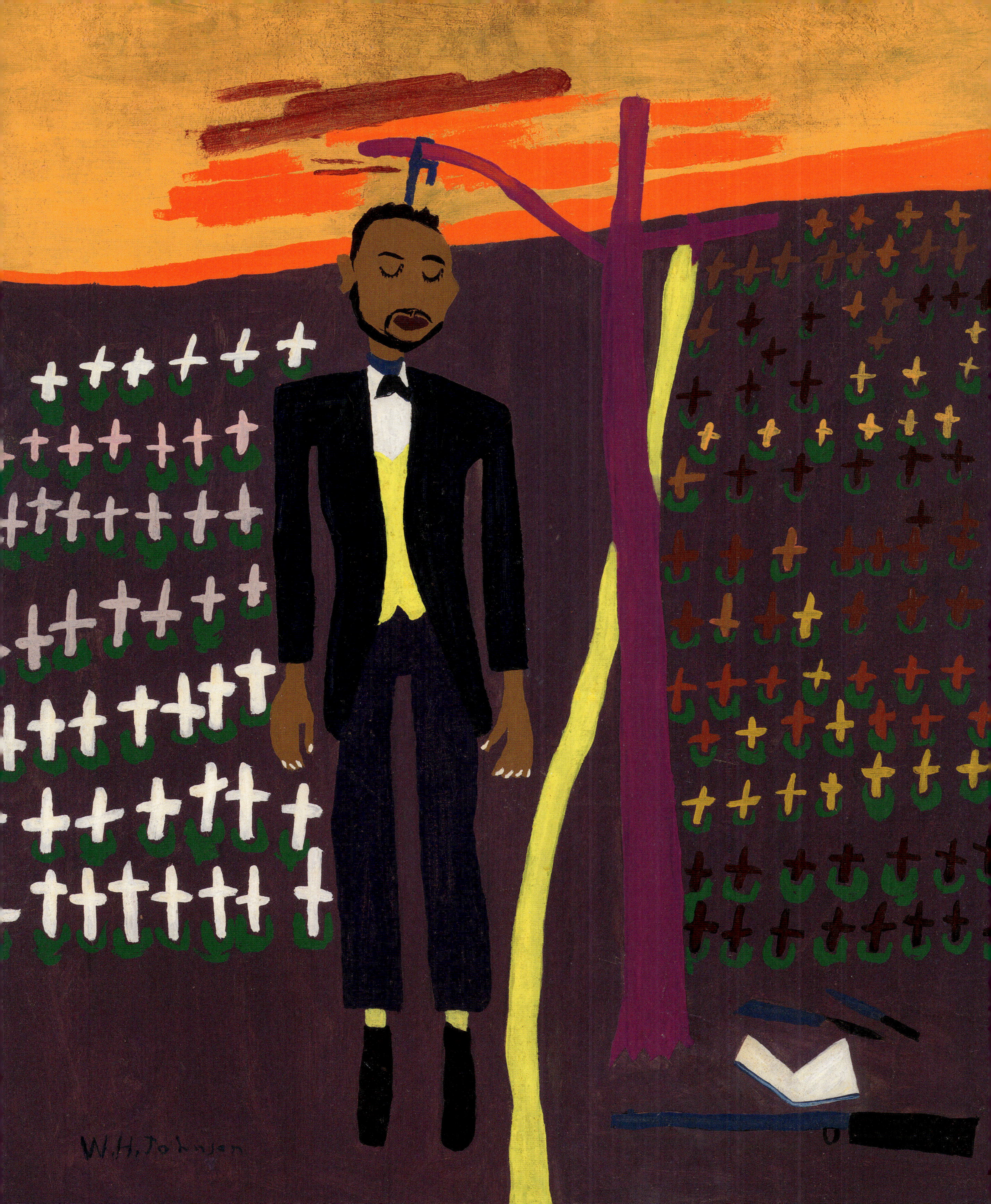
W.H. Johnson

as they hoped. A militia dispersed and defeated the raiders by midday on August 23, yet Turner evaded capture for two months. He was finally apprehended on October 30 and taken to the county jail, where Thomas R. Gray, a white lawyer, wrote down his confession.

Newspaper headlines expressed horror at the murder of women and children, although some acknowledged the raiders had cause. *The African Sentinel and Journal of Liberty*, published by a free Black man in Albany, New York, wrote, "Slaves…have done vastly wrong in the late insurrection [but] their struggle for freedom is the same in principle as the struggle of our fathers in '76." *The Ohio State Journal* agreed: "We believe that the people of these United States ought no longer to shut their eyes to the dreadful evils of slavery."

After speedy trials, with enslavers as jury members, Turner and nineteen others were convicted and executed. (More were convicted but had their sentences commuted.) Turner met his end on November 11, 1831. Meanwhile, in retaliation for the violence against whites, vigilantes across the South

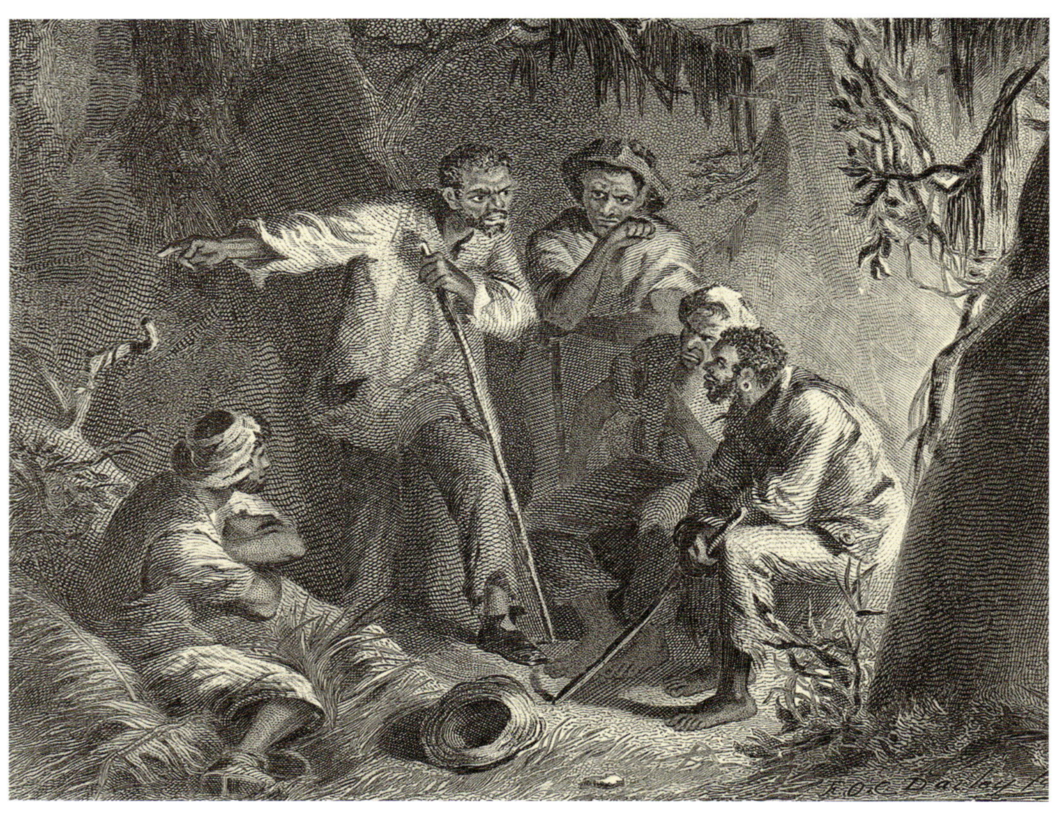

Below left: "Nat Turner and His Confederates in Conference," engraving by F. O. C. Darley, from Orville J. Victor, *History of American Conspiracies* (1863)

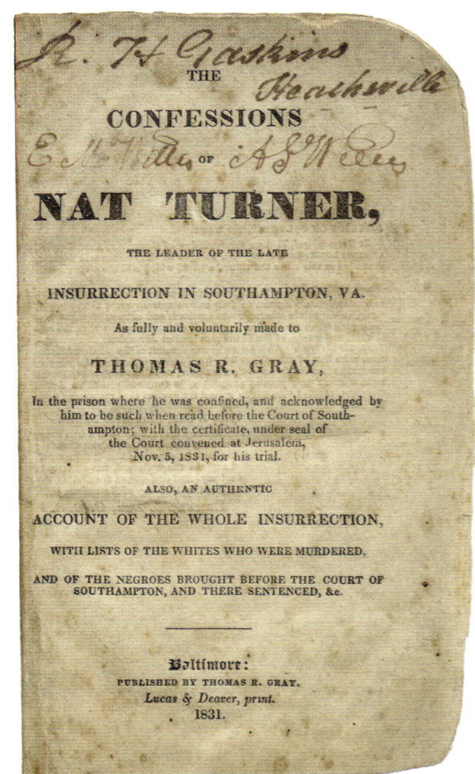

THE

CONFESSIONS

OF

NAT TURNER,

THE LEADER OF THE LATE

INSURRECTION IN SOUTHAMPTON, VA.

As fully and voluntarily made to

THOMAS R. GRAY,

In the prison where he was confined, and acknowledged by him to be such when read before the Court of Southampton; with the certificate, under seal of the Court convened at Jerusalem, Nov. 5, 1831, for his trial.

ALSO, AN AUTHENTIC

ACCOUNT OF THE WHOLE INSURRECTION,

WITH LISTS OF THE WHITES WHO WERE MURDERED,

AND OF THE NEGROES BROUGHT BEFORE THE COURT OF SOUTHAMPTON, AND THERE SENTENCED, &c.

Baltimore:

PUBLISHED BY THOMAS R. GRAY.

Lucas & Deaver, print.

1831.

Below right: Title page, *The Confessions of Nat Turner* (1831)

Smithsonian Connections

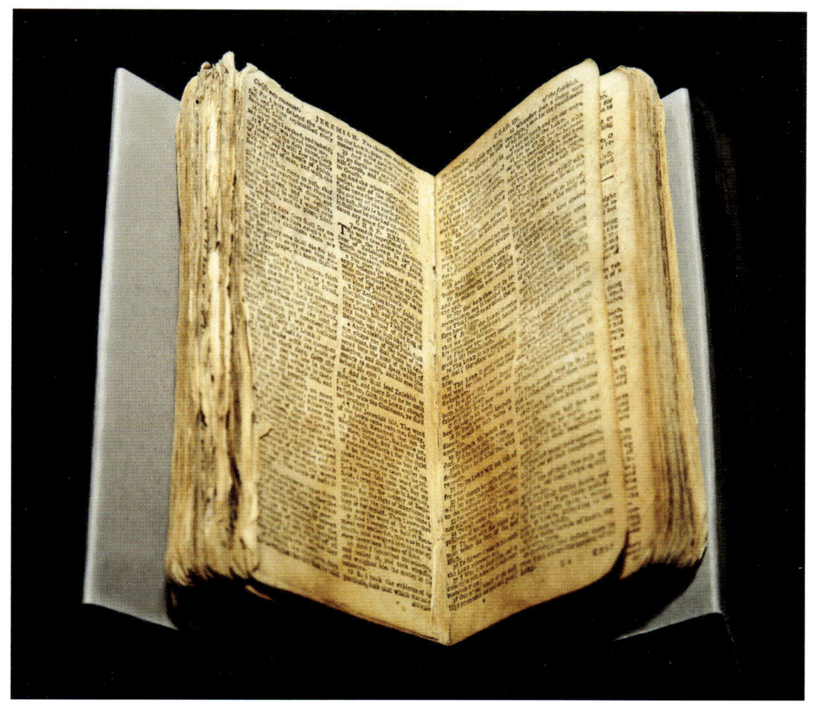

When Nat Turner was captured, this worn Bible was found in his possession. Most people in bondage were not taught to read or write, but Turner learned to do both as a child. His literacy enabled him to interpret the Bible directly and preach his spiritual convictions about liberation. Enslavers recognized the power and danger of literacy. Fearing further uprisings after Turner's rebellion, most Southern states passed laws making it illegal to teach enslaved people to read.

William H. Johnson includes the Bible in his painting of a hanged Nat Turner, alluding to its role in inspiring Turner to free his people at any cost.

Bible belonging to Nat Turner, 1830s, ink on paper, Collection of the Smithsonian National Museum of African American History and Culture, Gift of Maurice A. Person and Noah and Brooke Porter, 2011.28

tortured and murdered hundreds of African Americans, free and enslaved, whether they had joined Turner or not. Nat Turner's radical measures indicate how much those in bondage reviled slavery; the brutal aftermath proved the bravery required to fight it.

In the wake of Turner's revolt, some Virginians began to speak out against slavery. At the urging of editorials (in the *Richmond Enquirer*, for example) and about two thousand petitioners, by early 1832 the Virginia legislature debated abolition; however, there was not enough support to pursue it. Instead the representatives further restricted African Americans, free and enslaved alike. Indeed, across the South, fears of similar revolts prompted new laws intended to further oppress African Americans in their education, movements, and religion.

Historians have found no likeness of Turner from his lifetime, so Johnson's rendering likely sprang from his imagination. Under an eerie sky, the painting depicts fifty white crosses for the enslavers and their family members who died in the rebellion. In the opposite field, more than ninety crosses in shades of brown stand for the others who were executed, whether by legal or extralegal means. The upright tree trunk, underscored by a bright yellow line, suggests the stark division between races in the South and foreshadows the nation's rupture in the Civil War. Turner's sword, musket, and Bible refer to the uprising, its violence, and the moral justification for the later war. Johnson painted Turner sympathetically, with the dignity of formal attire, to memorialize the preacher's ultimate sacrifice for the cause of freedom.

—TDF

JOHN BROWN LEGEND

ca. 1945
oil on paperboard
38 5/8 × 36 1/4 in.
Smithsonian American Art Museum
Gift of the Harmon Foundation

UNLIKE OTHER abolitionists, most of whom shunned violence, John Brown (1800–1859) was willing to kill in the name of liberating enslaved people. A devout Puritan, he felt that God had called on him to rid the United States of its great evil, slavery. Brown never joined a formal abolitionist group; he instead waged a personal holy war on racism and oppression. After the Kansas-Nebraska Act of 1854 left open the question of slavery in the western territories, Brown and his sons traveled to Kansas and led attacks on pro-slavery groups that had settled there.

Four years later, Brown electrified the nation with his raid on Harpers Ferry, Virginia (now West Virginia), the site of a major federal armory below the Mason-Dixon Line. He had hoped to take over the armory with a group of allies, rally enslaved people from surrounding areas to widespread rebellion, and establish a new, free nation. The plan failed. Few people joined, and within two days all members of Brown's twenty-two-person team were either killed or captured, or had fled. Brown himself was captured, severely beaten, and sentenced to hang for treason. During and after his trial, he became a lightning rod for the already roiling national debate over slavery. Some hailed him as a martyr—a song, "John Brown's Body," was a rallying cry for Union soldiers during the Civil War—while others condemned him a terrorist and murderer.

Johnson depicted Brown as a saintly figure. A halo of hair encircles his head, which he bows beneath a cross of stars on the way to his execution. The artist derived many of his images from a book published in 1910 by Oswald Garrison Villard, grandson of abolitionist William Lloyd Garrison, titled *John Brown, 1800–1859: A Biography Fifty Years After*. These include portraits of fellow abolitionists and supporters (upper left), Brown's sons who joined his crusade (lower left), and members of Brown's team who died in the raid on Harpers Ferry (middle-lower right). A landscape of the town, also drawn from Villard's pages, appears at upper right. After Brown's death, it was widely told that he had stopped to kiss an enslaved child on his way to the gallows. *John Brown Legend* centers this tender moment. To the left of that scene, a gun represents Brown's commitment to arming enslaved people, while on the right, a Bible beside Brown's headstone symbolizes the deep faith that drove his actions.

—EHR

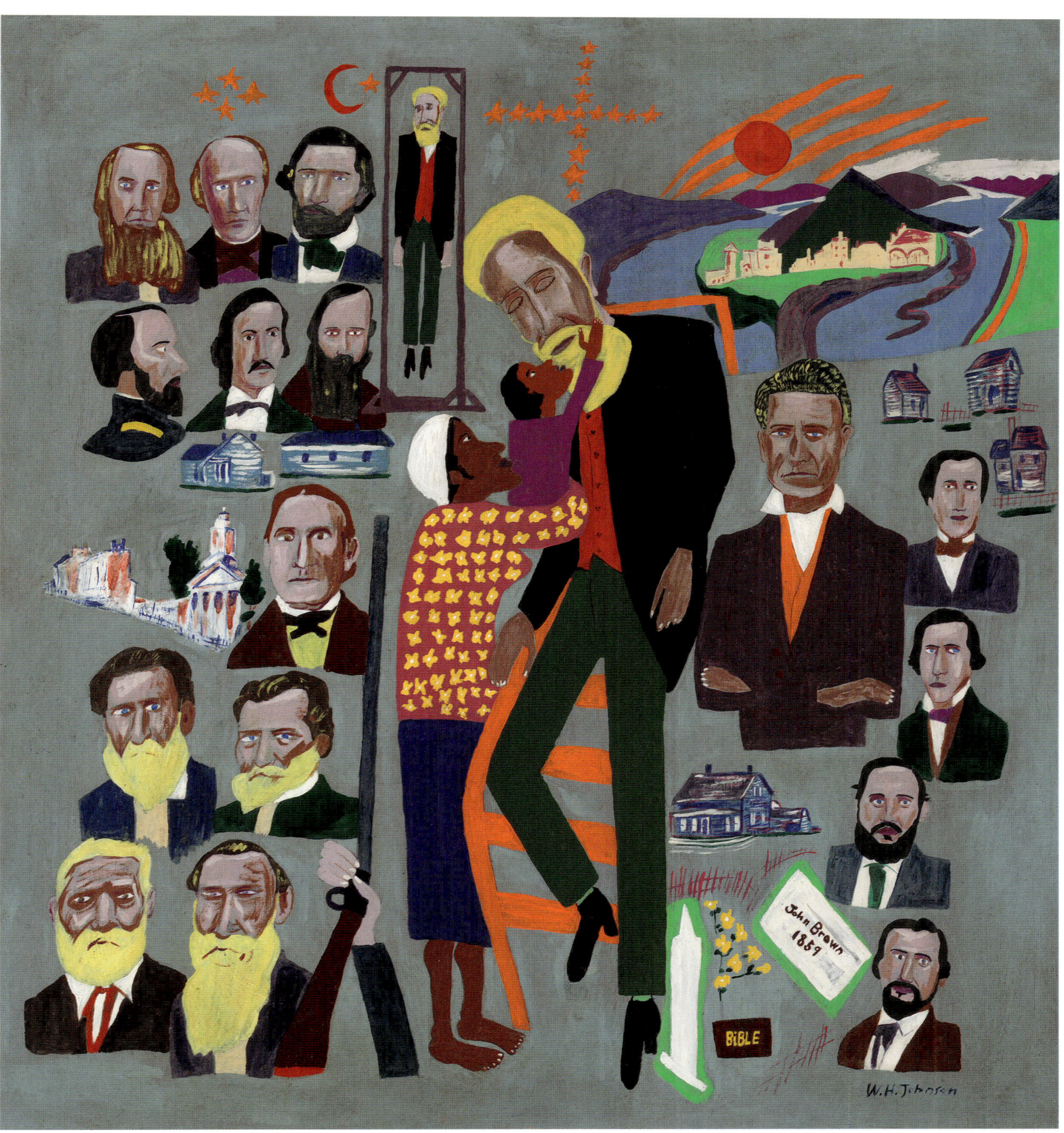
John Brown
1859
BIBLE
W.H. Johnson

UNDERGROUND RAILROAD

ca. 1945
oil on paperboard
33 ³⁄₈ × 36 ³⁄₈ in.
Smithsonian American Art Museum
Gift of the Harmon Foundation

IN *UNDERGROUND RAILROAD*, Johnson combined portraits and vignettes to create a cinematic tableau of abolitionists, self-emancipators, and modes of escape. Surrounded by purple railroad tracks, all of these figures risked their lives serving the Underground Railroad or traveling along that secret network of organizers, guides, and safe houses that helped enslaved people reach freedom. Johnson found a rich source in the 1872 book *The Underground Rail Road* by African American abolitionist William Still (1821–1902).

Born in New Jersey to a father who bought his own freedom and a mother who twice escaped her enslavers, William Still dedicated fourteen years to helping hundreds of self-emancipators find freedom. From his post as clerk at the Pennsylvania Antislavery Society in Philadelphia, a nexus for Underground Railroad operations, Still kept a diary and letters to preserve escapees' names and stories. Johnson shows Still in a turquoise jacket on the right side of the painting (third row from the bottom, second from the right) between Still's older brother, Peter, and his mother, Charity. Still's volume offers insight to the hearts and experiences of self-emancipators and of those, both Black and white, who helped them.

One such story is that of Henry "Box" Brown (shown at center in a red box), who, with help from a merchant, shipped himself to freedom in a wooden crate, traveling twenty-six hours via train, steamer, and finally cart from Richmond, Virginia, to the Antislavery Society in Philadelphia. Describing the crate's safe delivery and Brown's "resurrection" upon its opening. Still wrote, "Rising up in his box, [Brown] reached out his hand, saying, 'How do you do, gentlemen?'"

That elation belies the extreme risks self-emancipators faced; many encountered violence if not recapture, torture, or death. Two boats at center top of the painting relate a story of six former slaves fleeing from Worcester County, Maryland. After purchasing a boat, they attempted to row across the Delaware Bay at night. Attacked by five white men in another boat, the escapees battled despite injuries, and the foes retreated.

Clever disguises enabled other daring maneuvers, including one in front of the White House.

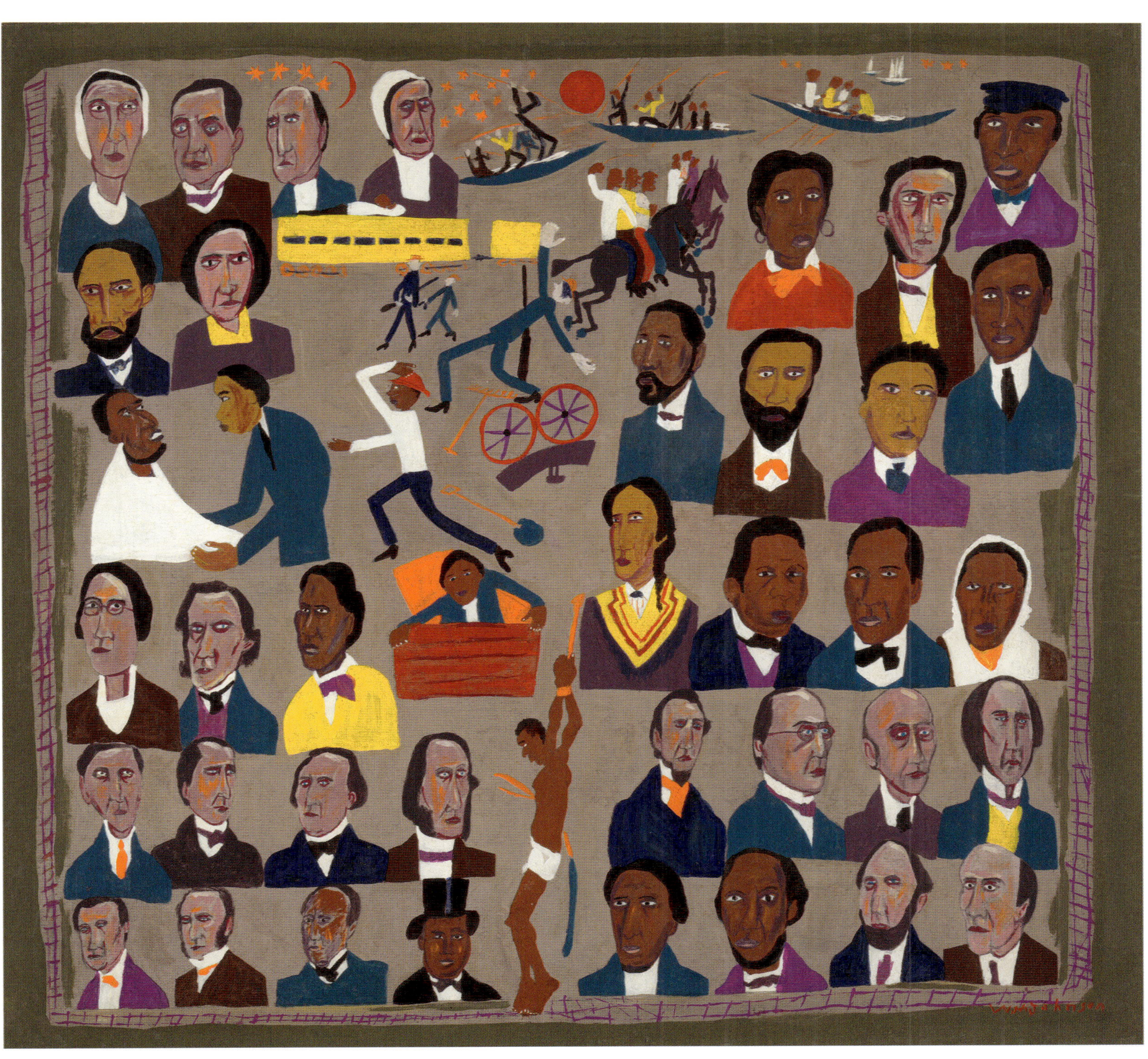

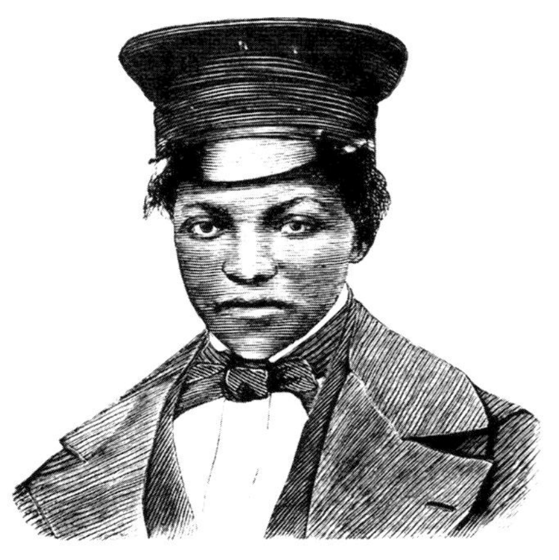

MARIA WEEMS ESCAPING IN MALE ATTIRE.

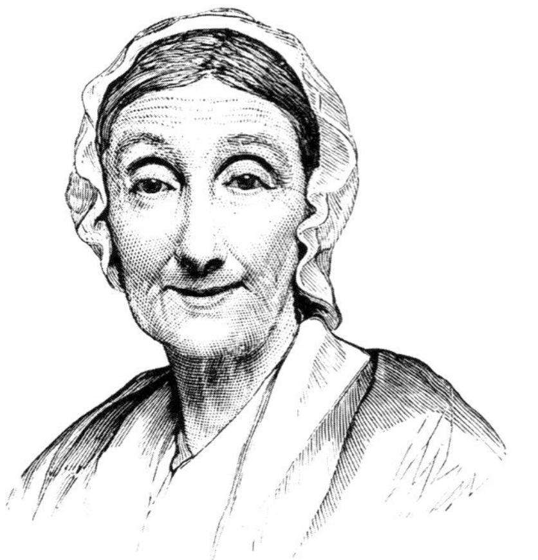

ABIGAIL GOODWIN.

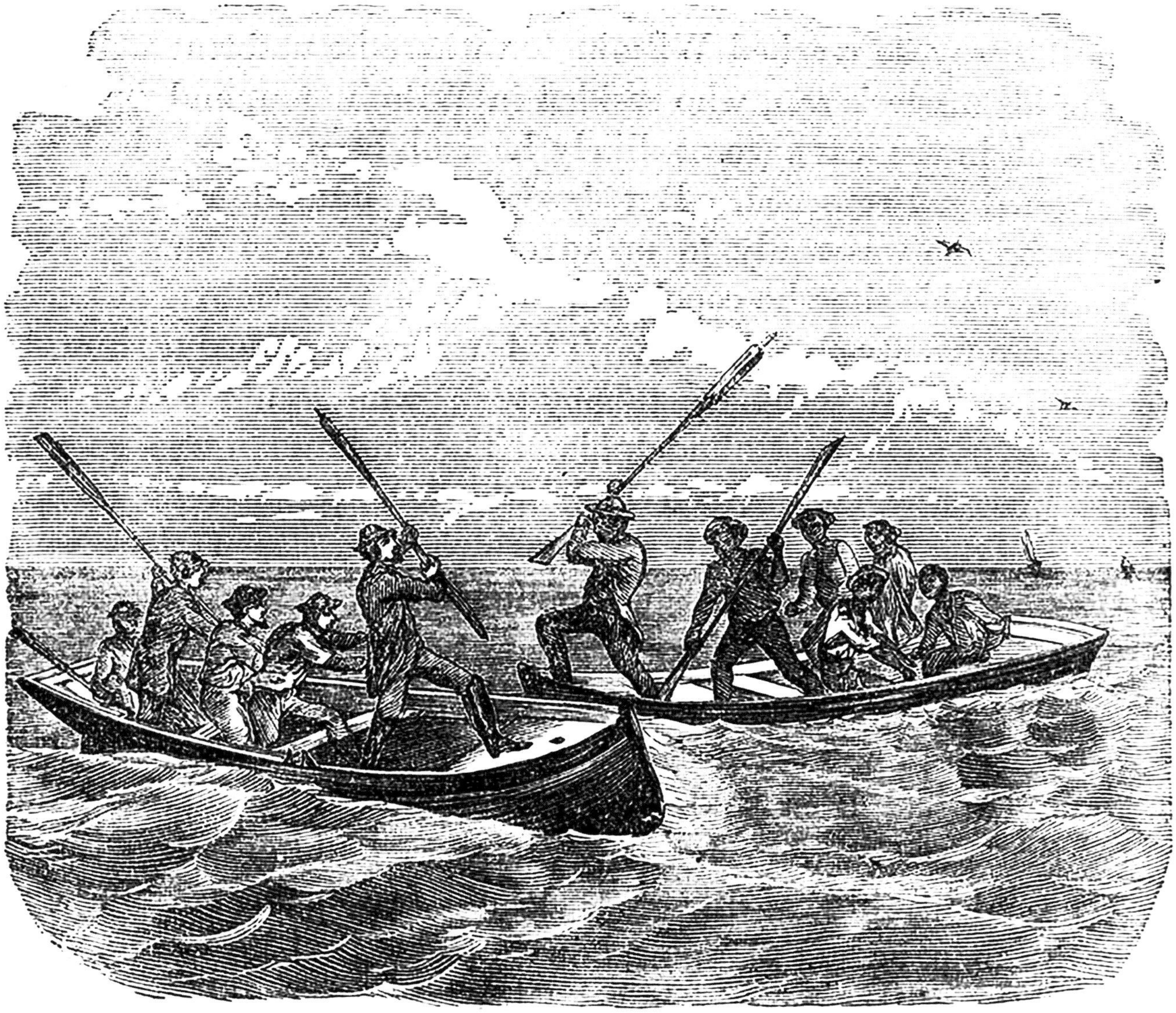

Engravings from William Still's *Underground Rail Road* (1872). Far left: "Maria Weems Escaping in Male Attire"; left: portrait of Abigail Goodwin; below: "Fight in Chesapeake Bay; Crossing the Bay in a Batteau"; opposite: "Resurrection of Henry Box Brown"

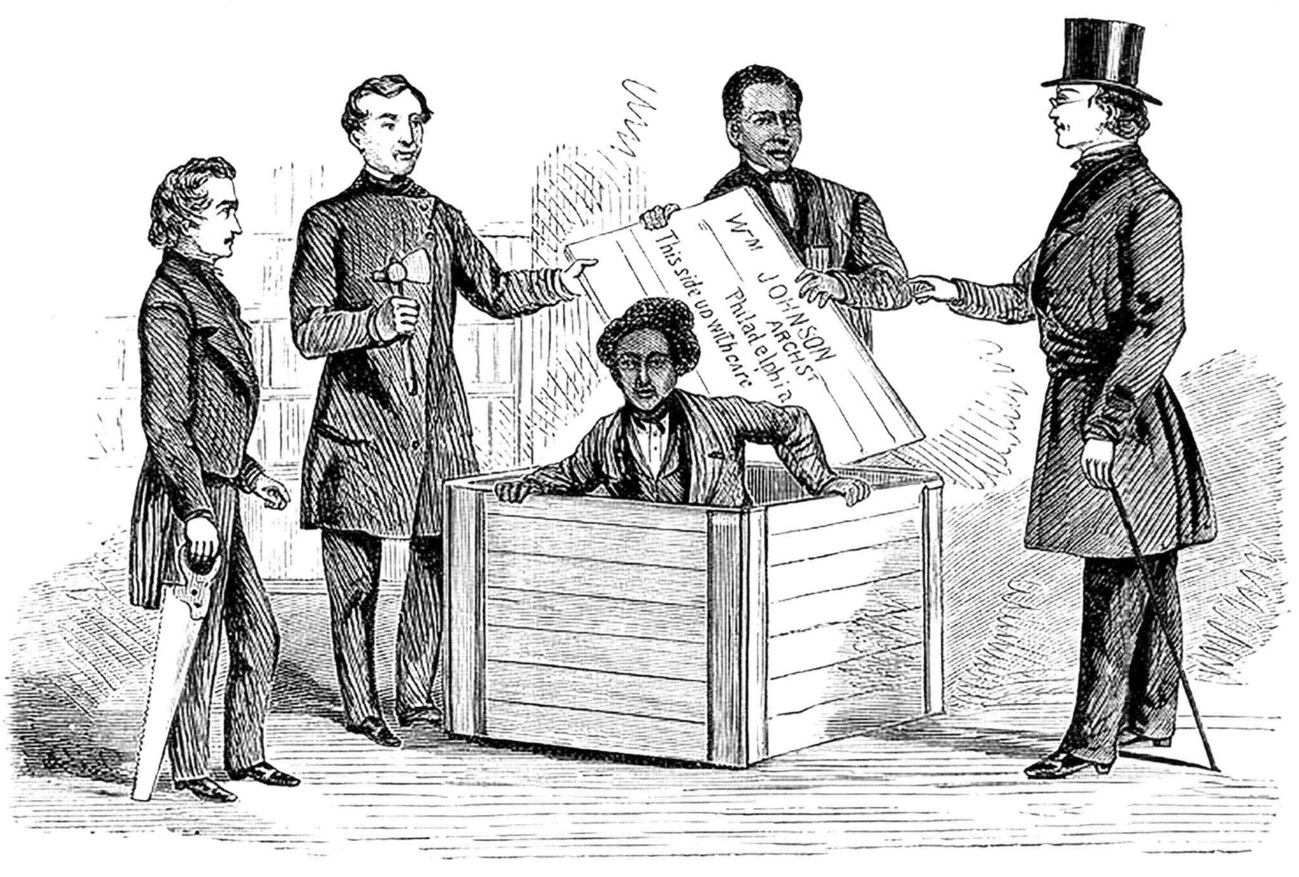

RESURRECTION OF HENRY BOX BROWN.

Maria Weems, shown in a hat in the painting's top right corner, was separated from her family at a slave auction when she was thirteen. Abolitionists had bought freedom for Maria's mother and sister. Two years later, an Underground Railroad operative met the still-enslaved Maria in Washington, DC, and hatched a bold plan. Wearing boy's clothing, Weems became "Joe" the driver, and, Still recounts, "in the most polite and natural manner, with the fleetness of a young deer, he ["Joe"] jumped into the carriage, took the reins and whip," and drove out of the city with the accomplice inside.

Still also applauds the dedication of conductors (route guides), station masters (who owned safe houses), stockholders (who financed operations), and other activists. Still talks about famous Quaker abolitionist Lucretia Mott (top row, fourth from left), but also lesser-known white women like Abigail Goodwin (same row, far left and opposite) and Graceanna Lewis (third row from bottom, far left). Although a free man, conductor Samuel D. Burris was once caught by enslavers himself (bottom row with top hat). Station master Thomas Garrett (top row, second from left) penned many letters in the book, and James Miller McKim (second row from bottom, fourth from left), also of the Pennsylvania Antislavery Society, appears in many stories. Altogether these thirty-six busts and seven vignettes signify the expansive scope of one hub of the Underground Railroad. The figures' actions also reveal boundless courage in claiming freedom—whether for themselves or others.

—TDF

HARRIET TUBMAN

ca. 1945
oil on paperboard
28 ⅞ × 23 ⅜ in.
Smithsonian American Art Museum
Gift of the Harmon Foundation

JOHNSON'S DOUBLE PORTRAIT captures the abolitionist, Civil War scout, and suffragist Harriet Tubman (1822–1913) in her multifaceted heroism and power. The younger Tubman's commanding stance comes from a woodcut (right) honoring her Civil War service. But Johnson cleverly changed the setting to that of her prewar role as a guide, or "conductor," on the Underground Railroad, a network of free African Americans and some white people who secretly helped enslaved persons escape to freedom. The rifle, part of the print's original composition, provides an angular element around which Johnson forms abstracted fields, pathways, and railroad tracks stretching toward the North Star. Along the dark edges of the painting, purple marks also form train tracks. Johnson added the cross on Tubman's messenger bag to emphasize the religious faith that guided her on these dangerous missions. He also painted a flag-inspired outfit—a red-and-white striped skirt and navy coat—to underscore her lifelong fight for liberty.

Tubman first sought freedom for herself. In 1849, at age twenty-seven, she self-emancipated from a plantation in Dorchester County, Maryland, and traveled alone under cover of night until she reached Pennsylvania. Risking her life, she returned to Maryland more than a dozen times over ten years to free about seventy family members and friends. In September 1850, Congress passed the Fugitive Slave Act, which required that escapees be returned to their enslavers, even if they were found in the North.

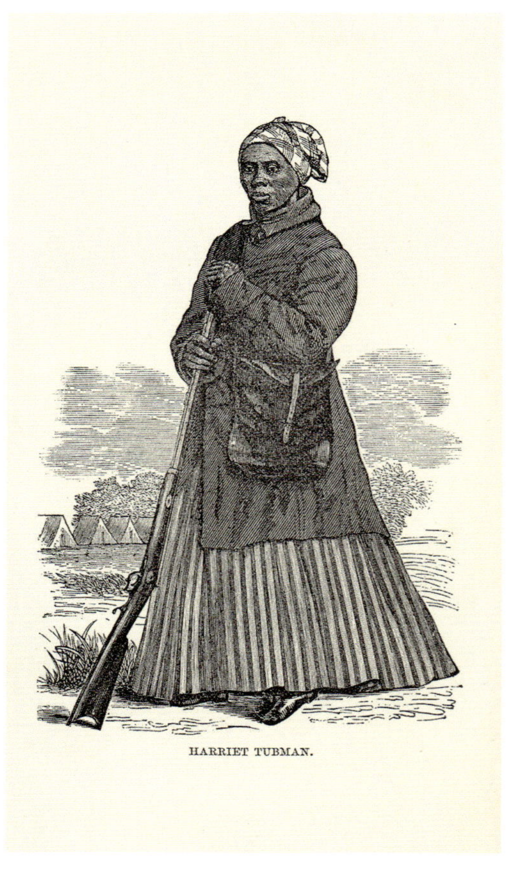

John G. Darby, *Harriet Tubman*, engraving from Sarah H. Bradford, *Scenes in the Life of Harriet Tubman* (1869), General Research Division, The New York Public Library

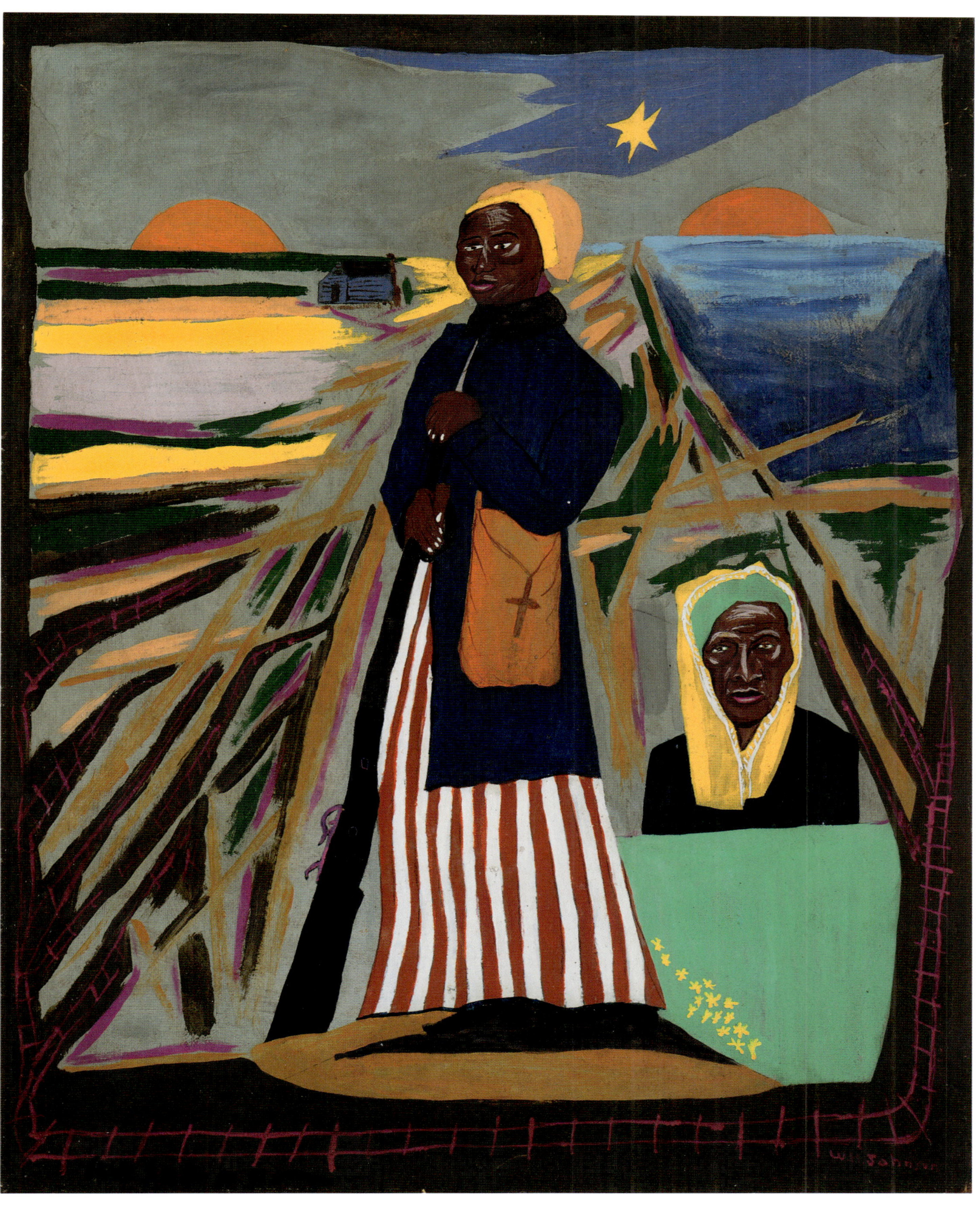

Smithsonian Connections

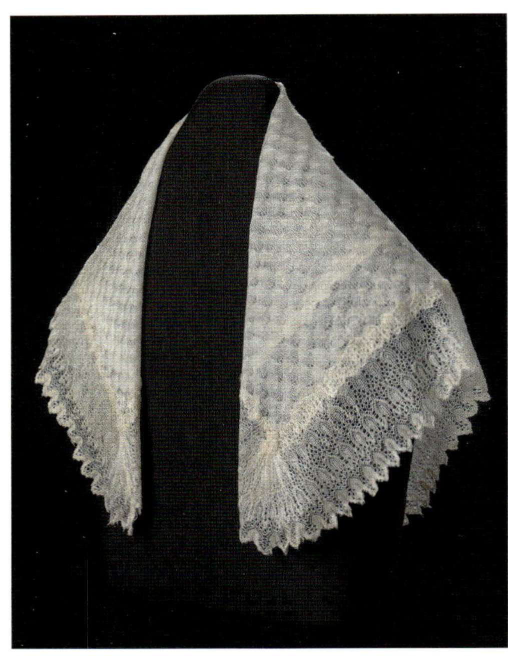

This white silk and lace scarf, given to Harriet Tubman by Queen Victoria around 1897 in recognition of Tubman's liberating hundreds of enslaved people, represents the freedom fighter's strength and delicateness. Mary Elliott, curator of American slavery at the National Museum of African American History and Culture, describes this shawl as a "powerful way to humanize [Tubman]. You get a sense of her size. You get a sense of this small but mighty powerhouse of a woman, [who is] still delicate and feminine."

Tubman fulfilled many roles in her life as a wife, sister, daughter, fighter, liberator, activist, and community member. The courage, strength, and dignity she displayed in the face of enormous barriers have made her a hero to all who are dedicated to freedom and equality.

Shawl given to Harriet Tubman by Queen Victoria, ca. 1897, silk lace and linen, Collection of the Smithsonian National Museum of African American History and Culture, Gift of Charles L. Blockson, 2009.50.39

Thereafter, Tubman led some of her passengers as far as Canada to avoid recapture. Of her Underground Railroad expeditions, she said, "I never ran my train off the track and I never lost a passenger."

Tubman's stealth and bravery on the Underground Railroad were assets in her next chapter as a scout and nurse for the Union Army during the Civil War. In 1863 she created a spy network in South Carolina that informed the Union of enemy troop movements and activities. Based on this intelligence, Tubman and Colonel James Montgomery planned an attack; in June, Tubman and a Union force of mostly local African Americans (including the Second South Carolina Volunteers) successfully navigated up the Combahee River on gunboats, then destroyed bridges and seized Confederate supplies. As the victorious Union boats were leaving, enslaved plantation workers hastily pursued them and climbed aboard. Tubman became the first African American and the first woman to lead a military assault while also freeing more than seven hundred people.

After the Civil War, Tubman raised money for freedmen, ran a nursing home for African Americans in Auburn, New York, and campaigned for women's suffrage. Johnson's sketch of Tubman in a scarf recalls photographs from her elder years (opposite), when her daring achievements were widely acclaimed both in the United States and abroad.

—TDF

Harriet Tubman, ca. 1911, Library of Congress Rare Book and Special Collection Division, Miller NAWSA Suffrage Scrapbooks, 1897–1911

Harriet Tubman, ca. 1945, pencil on paper, 8 × 5 in., Smithsonian American Art Museum, Gift of the Harmon Foundation, 1967.59.394R–V

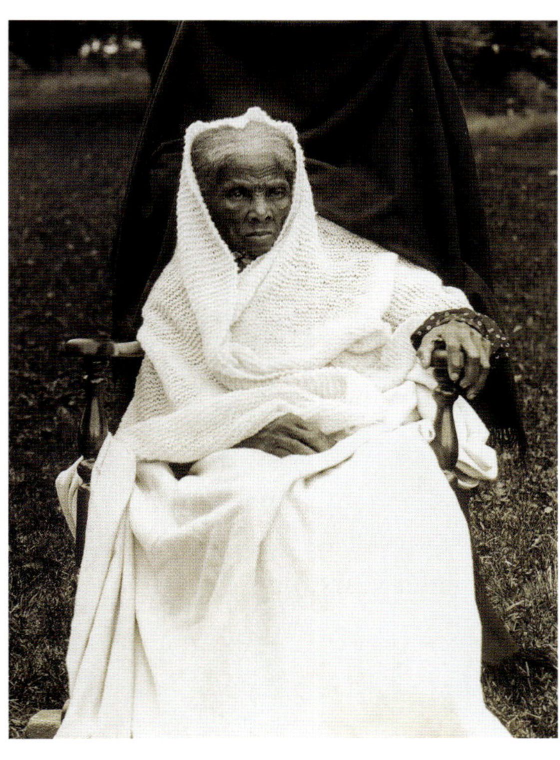

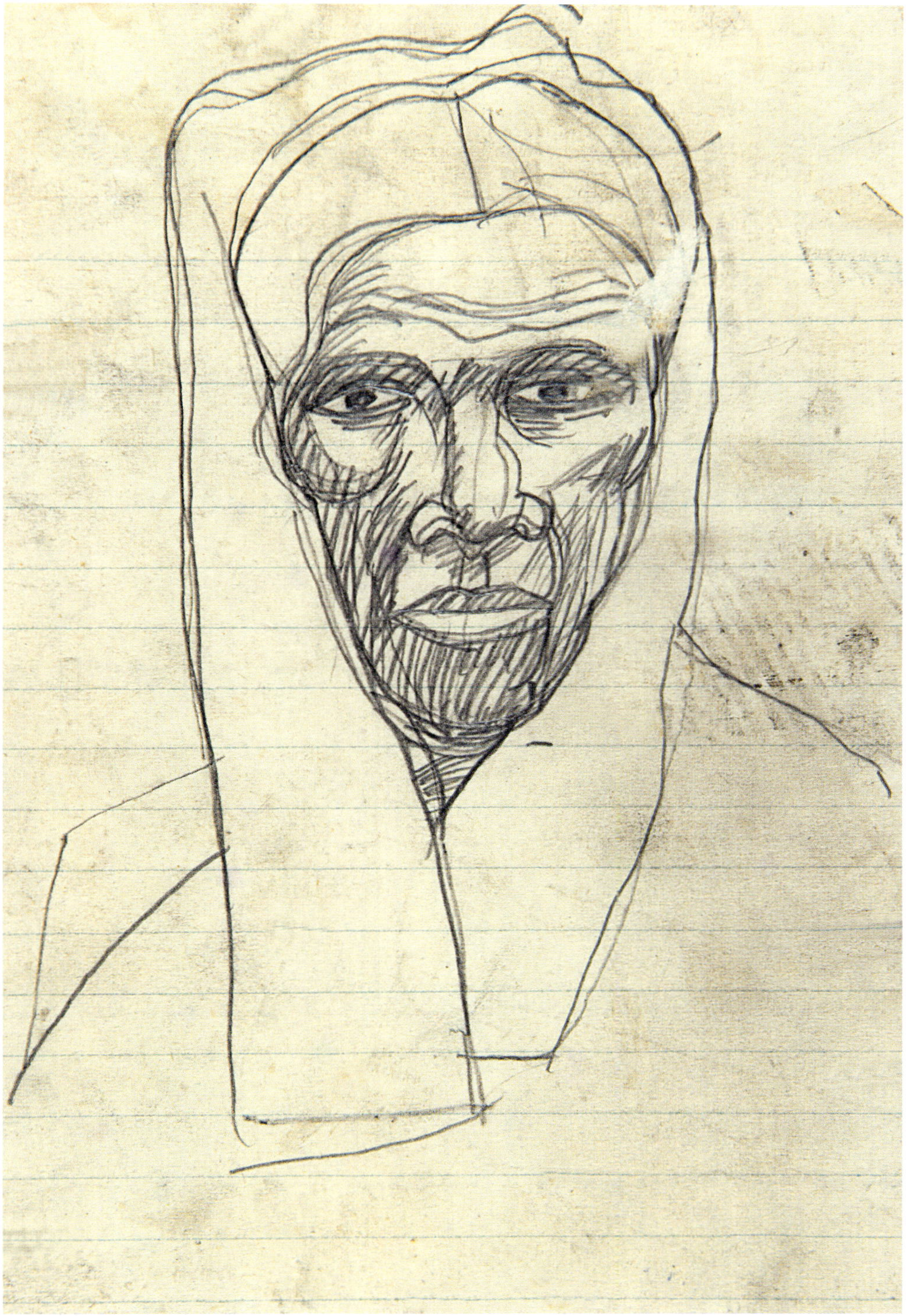

THREE GREAT FREEDOM FIGHTERS

ca. 1945
oil on paperboard
41 ½ × 33 ⅜ in.
Collection of the
Hampton University Art Museum

The difference between us is very marked. Most that I have done and suffered in the service of our cause has been in public, and I have received much encouragement at every step of the way. You on the other hand have labored in a private way. I have wrought in the day—you in the night.... The midnight sky and the silent stars have been the witnesses of your devotion to freedom and of your heroism. Excepting John Brown—of sacred memory—I know of no one who has willingly encountered more perils and hardships to serve our enslaved people than you have. —Frederick Douglass to Harriet Tubman

THREE GREAT FREEDOM FIGHTERS is powerful in its simplicity. John Brown (1800–1859), Harriet Tubman (1822–1913), and Frederick Douglass (1818–1895) stand tall with hands clasped together, linked by a thin blue line behind their heads. Except for a few fir trees and an orange sun, the background is empty. Johnson provides no time or location. Instead, he shows the three icons of freedom united against a common evil. Each one had devoted their life to fighting slavery, but they followed distinct paths to doing so. For John Brown (p. 66), who had grown up in an abolitionist household that offered safe haven to fugitives on the Underground Railroad, violence was the answer. For him, only direct action—not peaceful protest—offered a way forward, even though it resulted in his capture and execution.

Harriet Tubman (p. 72), who grew up enslaved on a Maryland plantation, realized that forests and fields offered places where she could hide as she conducted small bands of self-emancipators traveling north. Another Eastern Shore native, Frederick Douglass (p. 78) harnessed his eloquence as a speaker and impassioned writer to draw huge numbers to his message. Having self-emancipated as a young man, he eventually made his way to Massachusetts, where abolitionist groups invited him to speak. He electrified those who heard him, and in the following decades he traveled the country advocating for freedom and equality.

Yet in spite of their very different beginnings, the three were allies in a common cause and shared personal ties. Brown hoped to enlist Douglass's support for the raid on Harpers Ferry and stayed at the Douglass home for two weeks while he planned the mission that ultimately ended in his death. Tubman met Brown around the same time and helped recruit supporters for the raid. She and Douglass went back even further. In December 1851, Tubman led a band of eleven fleeing to Canada and probably stayed in Douglass's home along the way. Although details are sketchy, the timing and size of the group make it likely that it was Tubman's group Douglass described harboring in his autobiography. He had tremendous admiration for "General" Tubman, a title bestowed upon her by John Brown.

—VMM

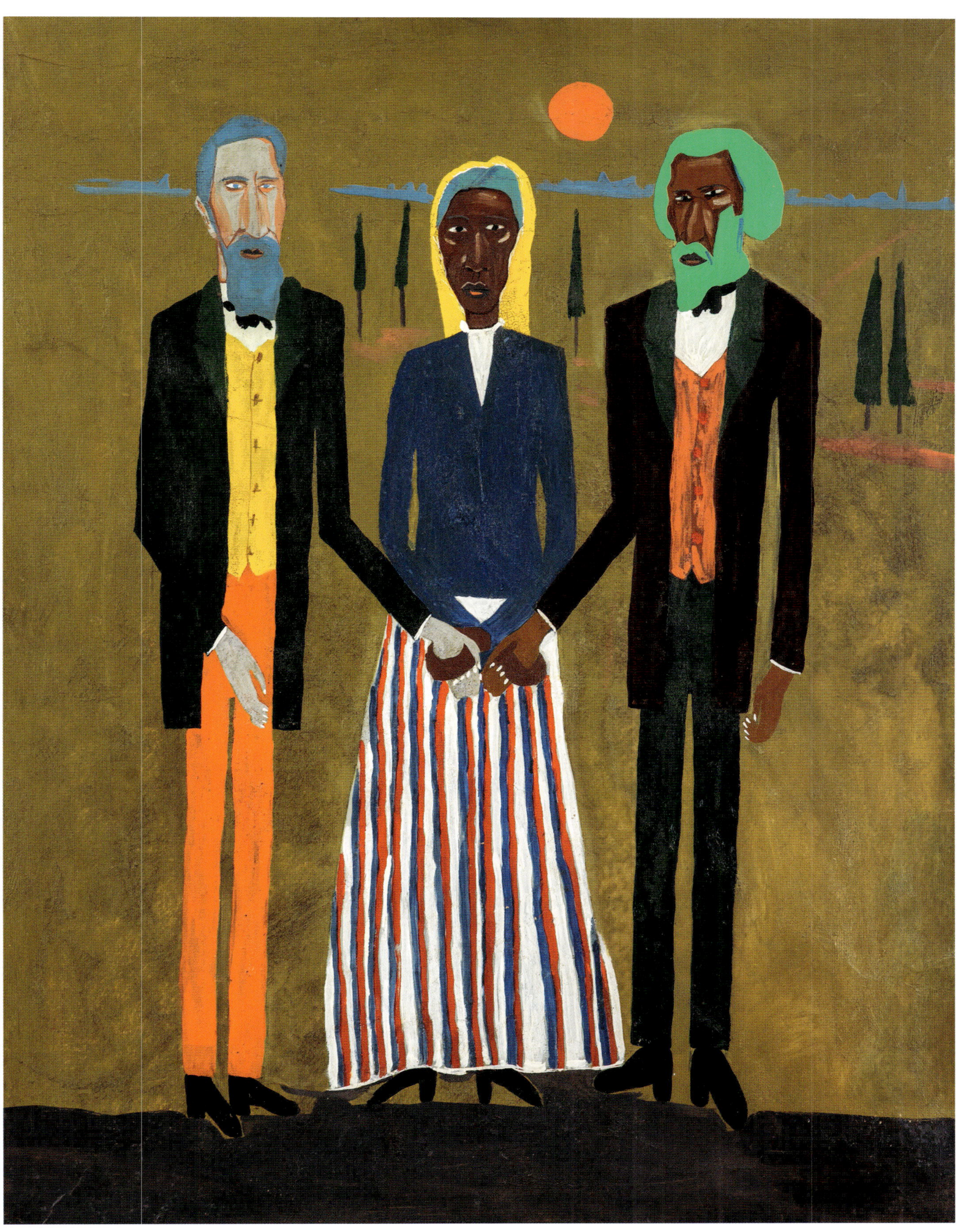

LET MY PEOPLE FREE

ca. 1945
oil on fiberboard
38 ¼ × 30 in.
Smithsonian American Art Museum
Gift of the Harmon Foundation

IN *LET MY PEOPLE FREE,* Johnson acknowledged the fraught relationship between abolitionist Frederick Douglass and Abraham Lincoln during the early years of Lincoln's presidency. He placed the figures on opposite sides of a table. Between them, suspended eerily above the table, are bound, lynched, and fleeing figures that represent slavery in all its brutality. Lincoln and Douglass initially disagreed over what to do about the "peculiar institution" of slavery in the United States. Johnson illustrated the grave stakes of that disagreement.

Frederick Douglass (1818–1895), was born into slavery on the Eastern Shore of Maryland. In 1838, he escaped to Massachusetts via the Underground Railroad, first by boarding a northbound train from Baltimore disguised

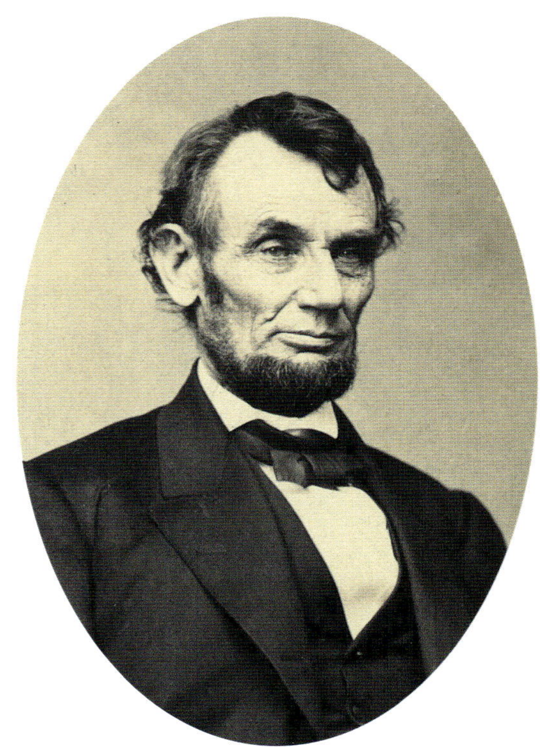

Anthony Berger, *Abraham Lincoln*, 1864, albumen silver print, 7 ½ × 5 ⅜ in., National Portrait Gallery, Smithsonian Institution

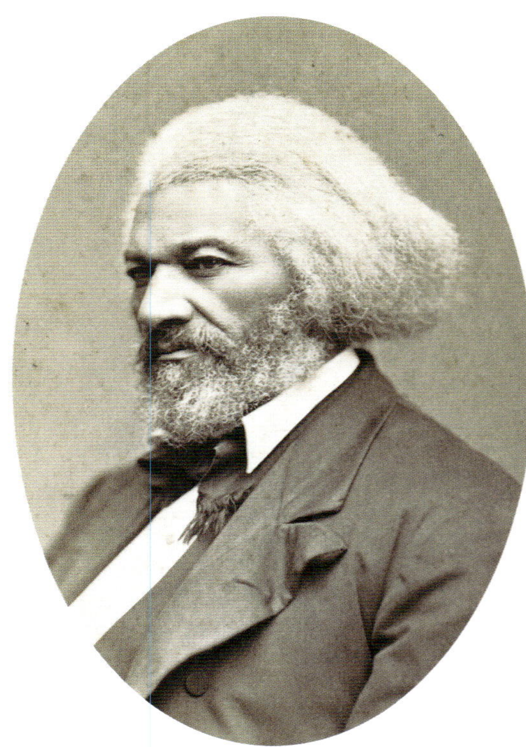

George Kendall Warren, *Frederick Douglass*, ca. 1876, albumen print on card mount, 7 × 4 in., Library of Congress Prints and Photographs Division, Liljenquist Family Collection

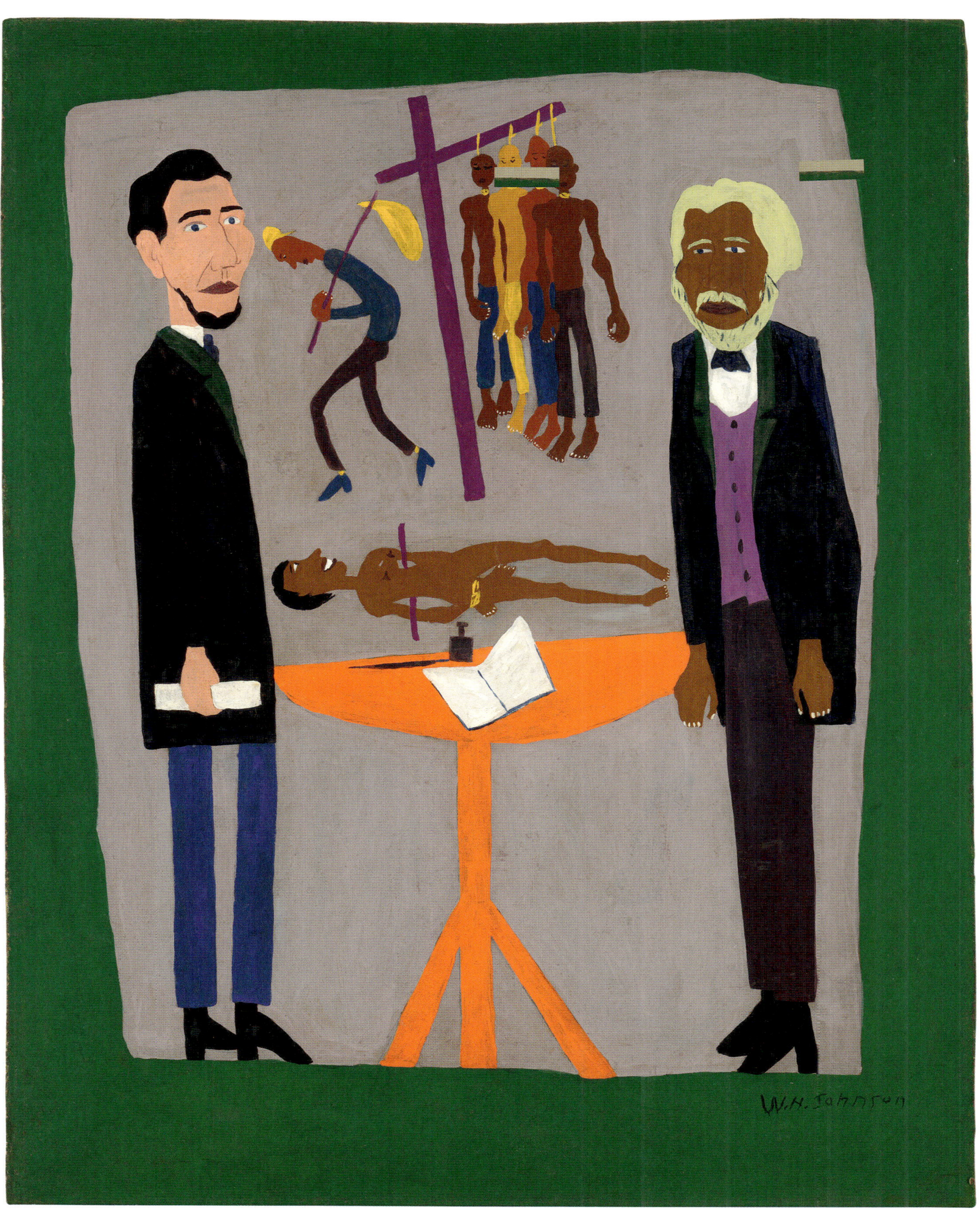
W.H. Johnson

Smithsonian Connections

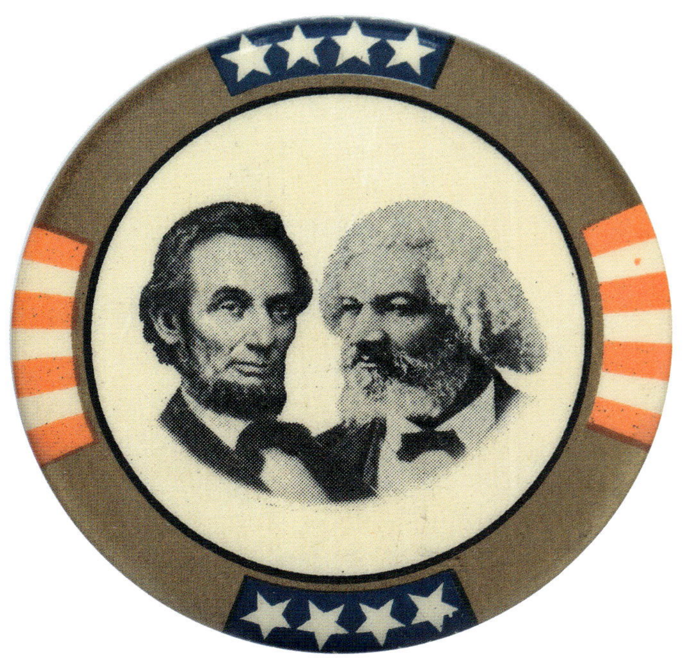

Easily mass-produced and disseminated, pinback buttons have long been used for activism, self-expression, and political campaigning. Wearing a button connects people to a cause and visually associates them with others who hold similar beliefs.

While President Abraham Lincoln and abolitionist and orator Frederick Douglass shared a complex relationship, they remain two of the most influential figures in abolition history. This 1960s button depicting Lincoln and Douglass was produced during the height of the Civil Rights Movement, a powerful symbol of people working across racial lines to fight for African Americans' equality. The struggle for freedom and social justice continues to this day, long after emancipation. Lincoln and Douglass serve as enduring symbols of the movement.

Pinback button featuring Abraham Lincoln and Frederick Douglass, 1960s, ink on paper with metal and plastic, Collection of the Smithsonian National Museum of African American History and Culture, 2010.77.2

as a free sailor. While still a fugitive, he joined the abolitionist lecture circuit, delivering speeches that detailed the horrific treatment he had experienced at his enslavers' hands. He became a national figure in 1845, when he published his autobiography, *Narrative of the Life of Frederick Douglass, an American Slave.* By 1860, when Abraham Lincoln was elected president, Douglass was the most prominent antislavery crusader in the United States, and possibly the most famous Black person in the world. Although he had endorsed Lincoln's candidacy, Douglass vehemently criticized Lincoln's plan to keep the Union together by allowing Southern states to perpetuate slavery, calling the president "a genuine representative of American prejudice and Negro hatred." Despite abhorring slavery, Lincoln initially tolerated it, believing that abolishing it outright would destroy the Union. He entertained the idea of a gradual emancipation in which enslavers would be compensated for their "losses," and Lincoln considered sending formerly enslaved people to Africa and elsewhere outside the United States (a plan known as colonization). These ideas drew Douglass's scathing public criticism.

A turning point came with the Emancipation Proclamation, issued on January 1, 1863, in which Lincoln declared all those enslaved in Confederate states to be free. Douglass praised the move, saying, "it is difficult to grasp the full and complete significance of President Lincoln's proclamation. The change in attitude…is vast and startling." Douglass urged African American men to volunteer for the Union army and fight for their full citizenship, even recruiting two of his sons, Lewis and Charles, to the Fifty-Fourth Massachusetts Regiment. By August 1863, though, he had

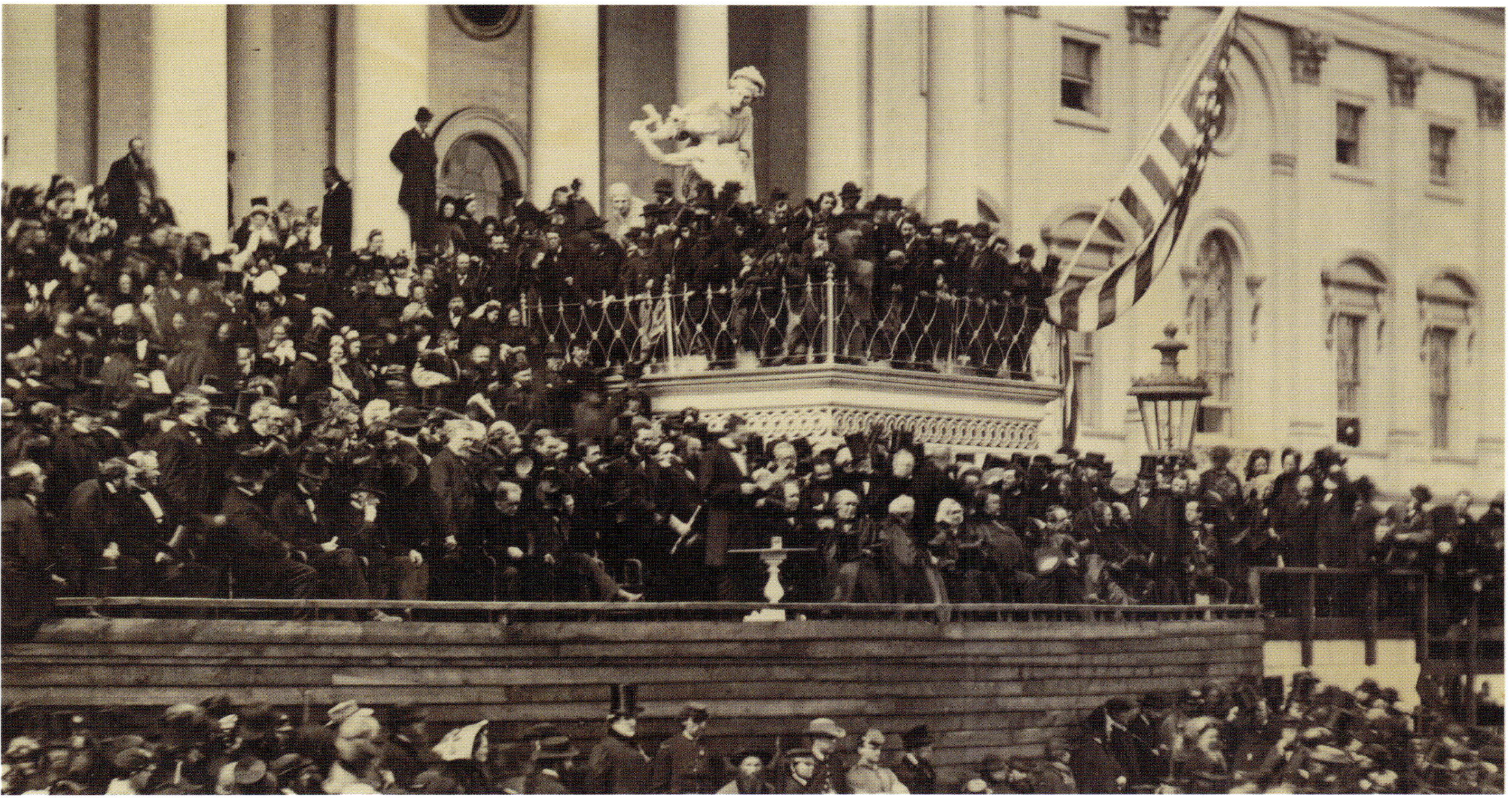

Alexander Gardner, *Lincoln delivering his second inaugural address as President of the United States, Washington DC*, 1865, albumen silver print, 7 × 9 in., Library of Congress Prints and Photographs Division

ceased recruiting, infuriated by the unequal treatment African American soldiers faced. They were paid far less than white soldiers, given no opportunities for promotion, and lacked formal protections against being tortured, killed, or enslaved if captured by Confederates. Douglass took his concerns directly to President Lincoln, making an unsolicited visit to the White House on August 10, 1863. Though the men disagreed on some matters, Lincoln listened intently and impressed Douglass with his openness and decency. Confident that the president had taken his concerns seriously, Douglass resumed his recruiting efforts. The two met again in 1864, when, fearing that he would not win reelection, Lincoln invited Douglass to the White House to discuss a daring proposal: If Lincoln lost and his plans for emancipation stalled, could Douglass and his allies somehow rally enslaved people in Southern states to flee north en masse? The president's onetime critic was now a trusted ally and coconspirator. The plan proved unnecessary, however, when Lincoln won a second term. He invited Douglass to his second inauguration on March 4, 1865. The Union's victory was imminent, and in his address, Lincoln called for peaceful reconstruction after the war's end. "With malice toward none, with charity for all," he said, "let us…bind up the nation's wounds" and "do all which may achieve and cherish a just and lasting peace among ourselves and with all nations." At an event in the White House's East Room that day (which police initially barred Douglass from entering), the president, addressing the formerly enslaved man as "my friend," asked Douglass what he thought of his speech. "There is no man in the country," Lincoln said, "whose opinion I value more than yours."

—EHR

ABRAHAM LINCOLN

ca. 1945
oil on paperboard
36 1/4 × 33 3/8 in.
Smithsonian American Art Museum
Gift of the Harmon Foundation

ABRAHAM LINCOLN (1809–1865), sixteenth president of the United States, appears several times in the *Fighters for Freedom* series. During four years in office, Lincoln—the self-educated son of a Kentucky frontiersman—led the Union to a bloody, hard-fought victory over the Confederacy in the Civil War, which brought an end to slavery.

Here, Lincoln is surrounded by key episodes from his life and the aftermath of his death. The left side of the painting illustrates Lincoln's path to becoming the "Great Emancipator," from the log cabin where he grew up to the U.S. House of Representatives (represented by the U.S. Capitol), where he served from 1847 to 1849.

Below the Capitol, a pair of hands hold a piece of paper alongside a quill—a nod to Lincoln's gift for writing and oratory. The paper could symbolize the Emancipation Proclamation, issued during the height of the war, in which President Lincoln declared "all persons held as slaves within any State…[to] be then, thenceforward, and forever free." Or it could be the Gettysburg Address, which Lincoln delivered at the site where more than fifty thousand Union and Confederate troops died in the three-day Battle of Gettysburg. The Union was fighting, Lincoln said in his address, for the idea that a nation "conceived in liberty" and "dedicated to the proposition that all men are created equal" could endure.

A row of crosses at lower left evokes the enormous cost of the war, which by some estimates left 750,000 soldiers dead. The fight against slavery ultimately claimed Lincoln's life, too. He was shot by John Wilkes Booth, an actor and Confederate sympathizer, on April 14, 1865, just five days after the war's end.

At right, Johnson illustrates the grim aftermath of Lincoln's killing. A Union soldier drags Booth from the burning barn in which he was shot after a twelve-day manhunt. Below are barred prison windows and a gallows from which Booth's four coconspirators hang.

—EHR

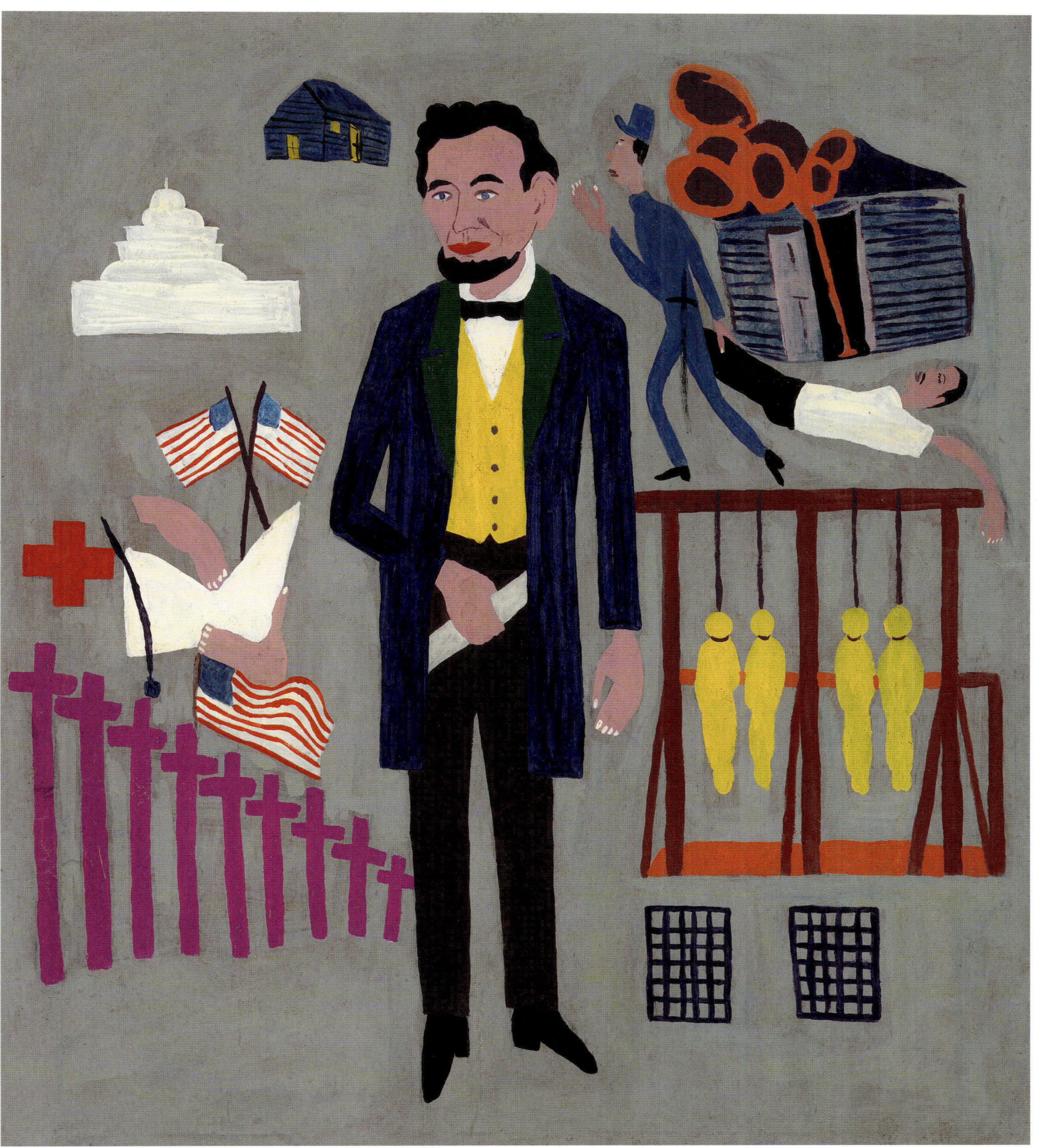

THREE GREAT ABOLITIONISTS: A. LINCOLN, F. DOUGLASS, J. BROWN

ca. 1945
oil on paperboard
37 3/8 × 34 1/4 in.
Smithsonian American Art Museum
Gift of the Harmon Foundation

IN *THREE GREAT ABOLITIONISTS* Frederick Douglass (1818–1895) clasps hands with John Brown (1800–1859) and President Abraham Lincoln (1809–1865). Brown, at left, represents the lead-up to the Civil War with his violent raid on Harpers Ferry; Lincoln, at right, signals its end and with it the abolition of slavery. Surrounding these figures, cotton bolls and men plowing indicate the backbreaking toil of enslaved agricultural workers. In the lower left corner, African American women raise their arms in praise.

The three men held different, sometimes conflicting ideas about how to rid the United States of slavery. Brown and Douglass were close acquaintances who shared a deep commitment to racial equality, but when Brown asked Douglass to join the raid on Harpers Ferry, Douglass declined. He was unwilling to undertake what he correctly predicted was a suicide mission. Lincoln publicly condemned Brown's violent approach, arguing that it was damaging to enslaved people and the abolitionist cause alike. At the same time, Douglass criticized Lincoln, who was elected in 1860 on a promise to prevent the spread of slavery rather than end slavery itself. After Lincoln changed his position and issued the Emancipation Proclamation on January 1, 1863, Douglass threw his full support behind the president. *Three Great Abolitionists* offers an image of solidarity, with Brown, Douglass, and Lincoln united in their opposition to slavery and exalted for their contributions to the cause of African American freedom.

—EHR

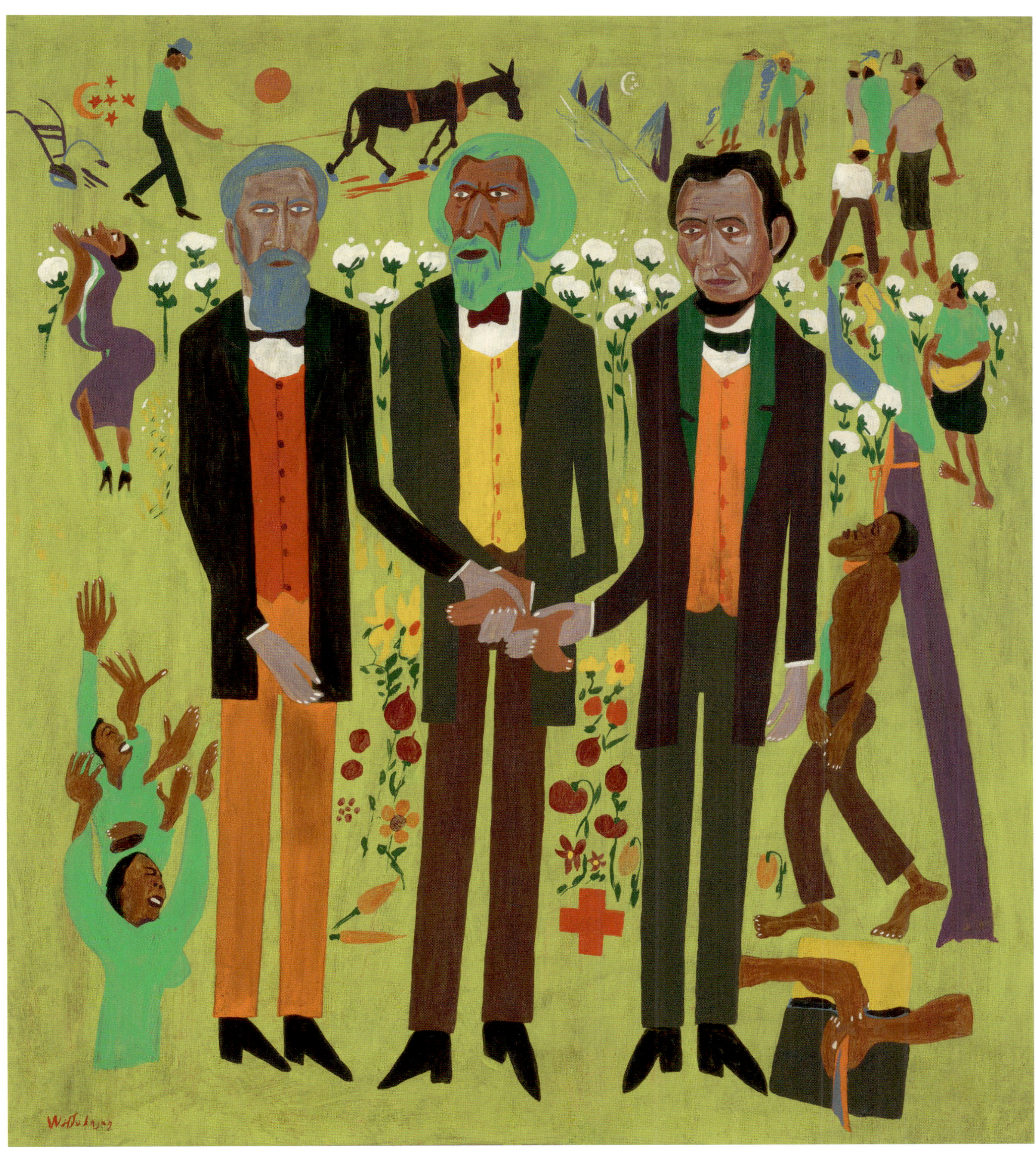

BOOKER T. WASHINGTON

Booker T. Washington Revelation
ca. 1945
oil on fiberboard
39 ⅞ × 30 ⅞ in.
Smithsonian American Art Museum
Gift of the Harmon Foundation

BY THE TURN OF THE twentieth century, Booker Taliaferro Washington (1856–1915) had become the most influential activist for African American education and advancement. Both of Johnson's paintings of Washington emphasize his role as a teacher and later founder and first president of Tuskegee Normal and Industrial Institute (now Tuskegee University) in Alabama.

The small cabin shown at the left in *Booker T. Washington Legend* (p. 88) suggests his humble beginnings. He was born enslaved on a tobacco plantation in Franklin County, Virginia, and later moved with his family to West Virginia, where he worked in the mines before going to school each morning. According to his 1901 autobiography, *Up from Slavery*, Washington overheard other miners discussing a school for African Americans in Hampton, Virginia, and in 1872 traveled alone by stagecoach, wagon, and finally on foot to the school to seek admission. Three years later he graduated with honors from the Hampton Institute (now Hampton University) and dedicated his life to educating African Americans. He first taught in West Virginia and then at Hampton Institute before founding the Tuskegee Institute in 1881. That coeducational school focused on training in vocational and agricultural skills to improve income and living standards, but it also prepared new generations of teachers for the important work of educating African American youths nationwide. The tools on the chalkboard in Johnson's painting reflect the school's practical curriculum, while Washington's raised hand suggests he developed his famed oratorical skills in the classroom. His confidence and charisma on stage won support from many white benefactors and many African Americans.

Booker T. Washington Revelation depicts the figure at the height of his national influence. Although by this time Washington was known for authoring books and counseling political figures, including President Theodore Roosevelt, Johnson surrounds him with the buildings of Tuskegee Institute, his most enduring achievement. Johnson based the buildings on photographs he found in Washington's 1911 publication, *My Larger Education*. The artist also shows people the educator admired and described in that same book. They include farmer and community leader Rufus Herron and

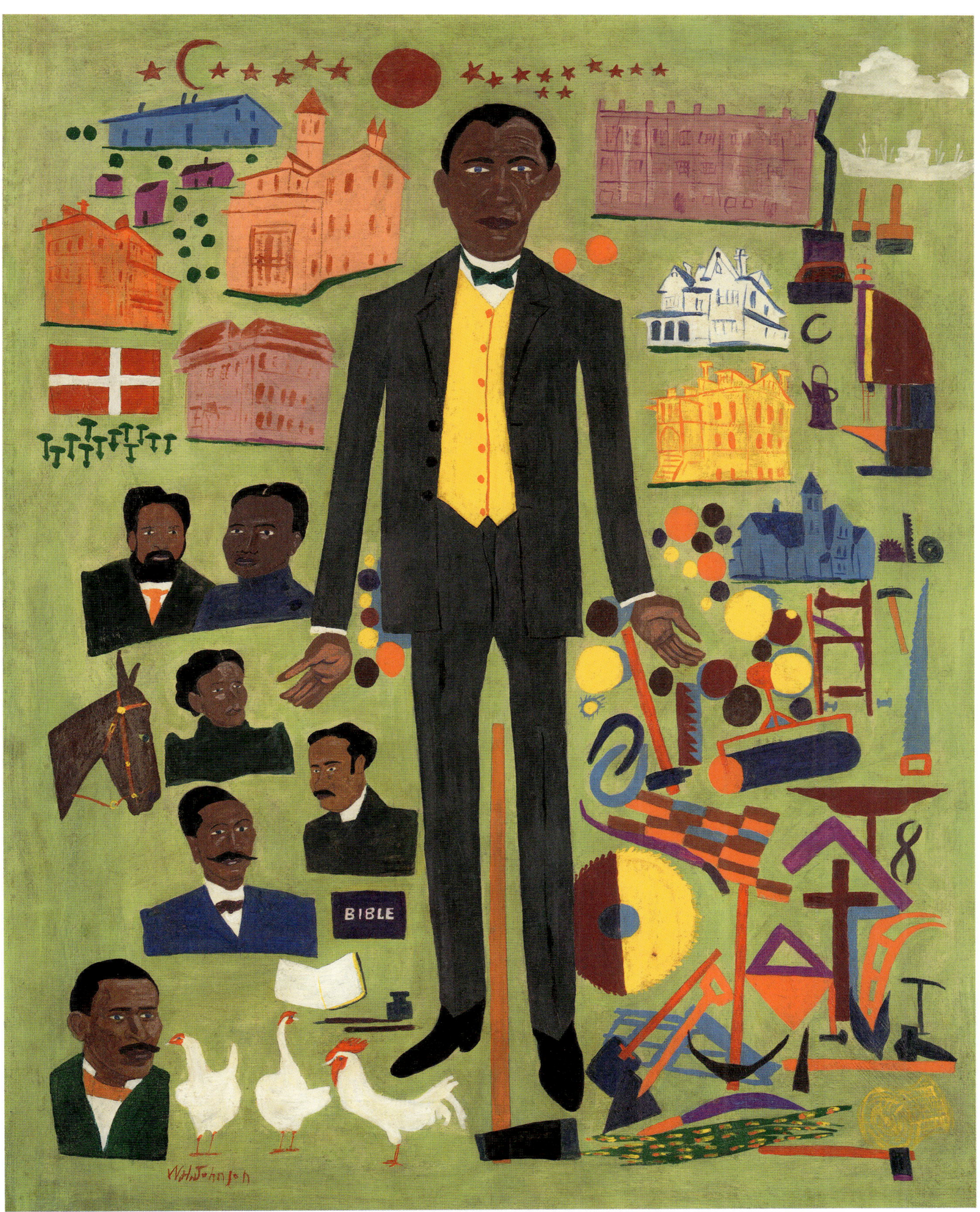
BIBLE
W.H.Johnson

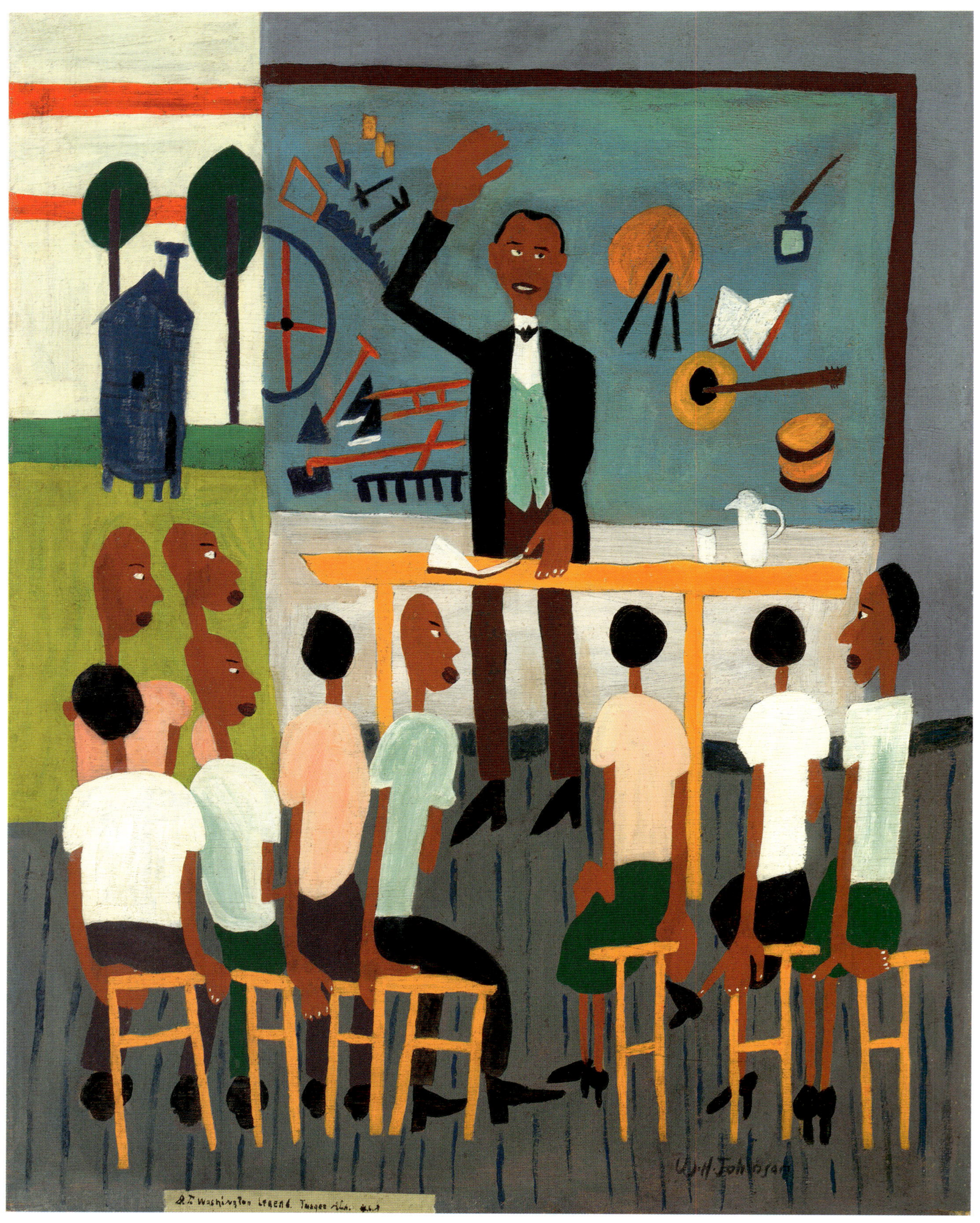
B.T. Washington Legend.

Booker T. Washington Legend
ca. 1944–45
oil on plywood
32 5/8 × 25 1/4 in.
Smithsonian American Art Museum
Gift of the Harmon Foundation

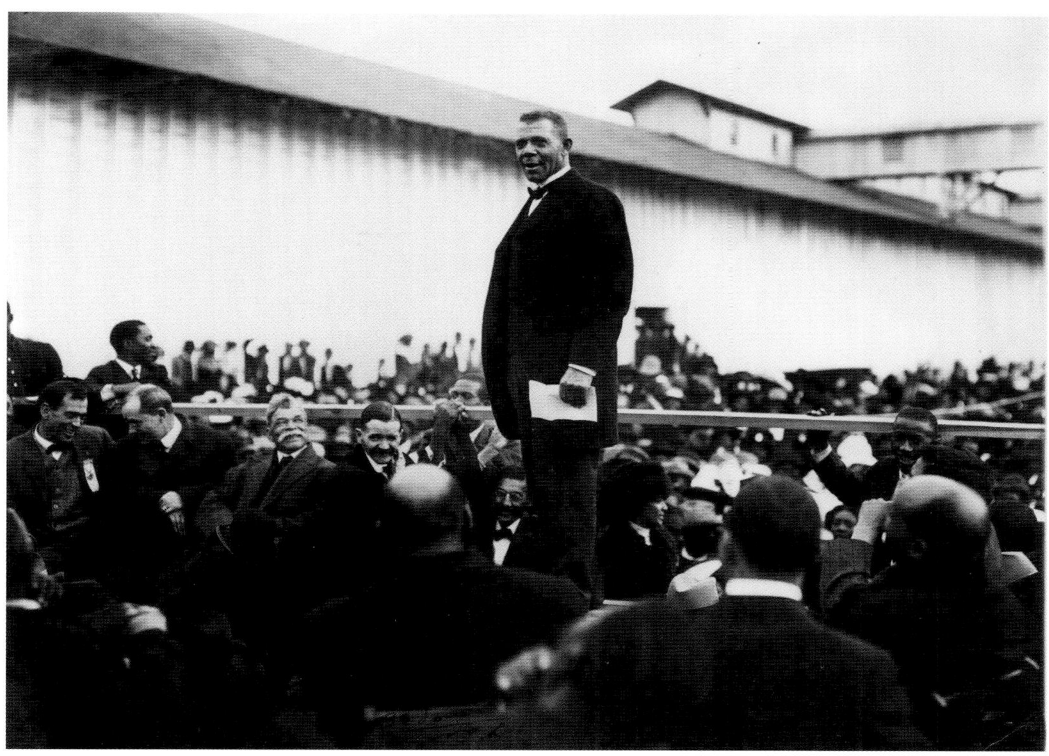

Booker T. Washington speaking in Mound Bayou, Mississippi, 1912.
Library of Congress Prints and Photographs Division

Hampton Institute teacher Major Robert Russa Moton (top left and right), Bishop George W. Clinton (above Bible), and Dr. George Washington Carver (lower left, in blue). The woman at center is likely Washington's third wife, Margaret Murray Washington, also a distinguished educator and administrator at Tuskegee Institute.

Among African American leaders in the late 1800s, Washington was, publicly at least, more conservative. In an important speech given at the Cotton States and International Exposition in Atlanta, Georgia, in 1895, Washington urged African Americans to focus on better jobs and financial gains, unlinked from issues of equal rights (at least initially). He said, "The wisest among my race understand that the agitation of questions of social equality is the extremist folly, and that progress in the enjoyment of all the privileges that will come to us must be the result of severe and constant struggle rather than of artificial forcing." He continued, "The opportunity to earn a dollar in a factory just now is worth infinitely more than the opportunity to spend a dollar in an opera house." Washington argued that when African Americans had greater skills and more money, their influence and acceptance in wider society would grow. Other race leaders strongly disagreed and demanded voting rights and an immediate end to racial violence and segregation. Washington's speech became known as the "Atlanta Compromise" because it bowed to the existing power structure. With *Booker T. Washington Revelation*, Johnson emphasized vocational trades and farming in the lower right quadrant, referring to Tuskegee's curriculum but also conjuring the theme of Washington's Atlanta speech. In *Booker T. Washington Legend*, the artist may subtly refer to leaders' disagreement on the chalkboard, where the tools of building trades and farming on the left are split from symbols of academic coursework—literature, music, and "painting—on the right.

—TDF

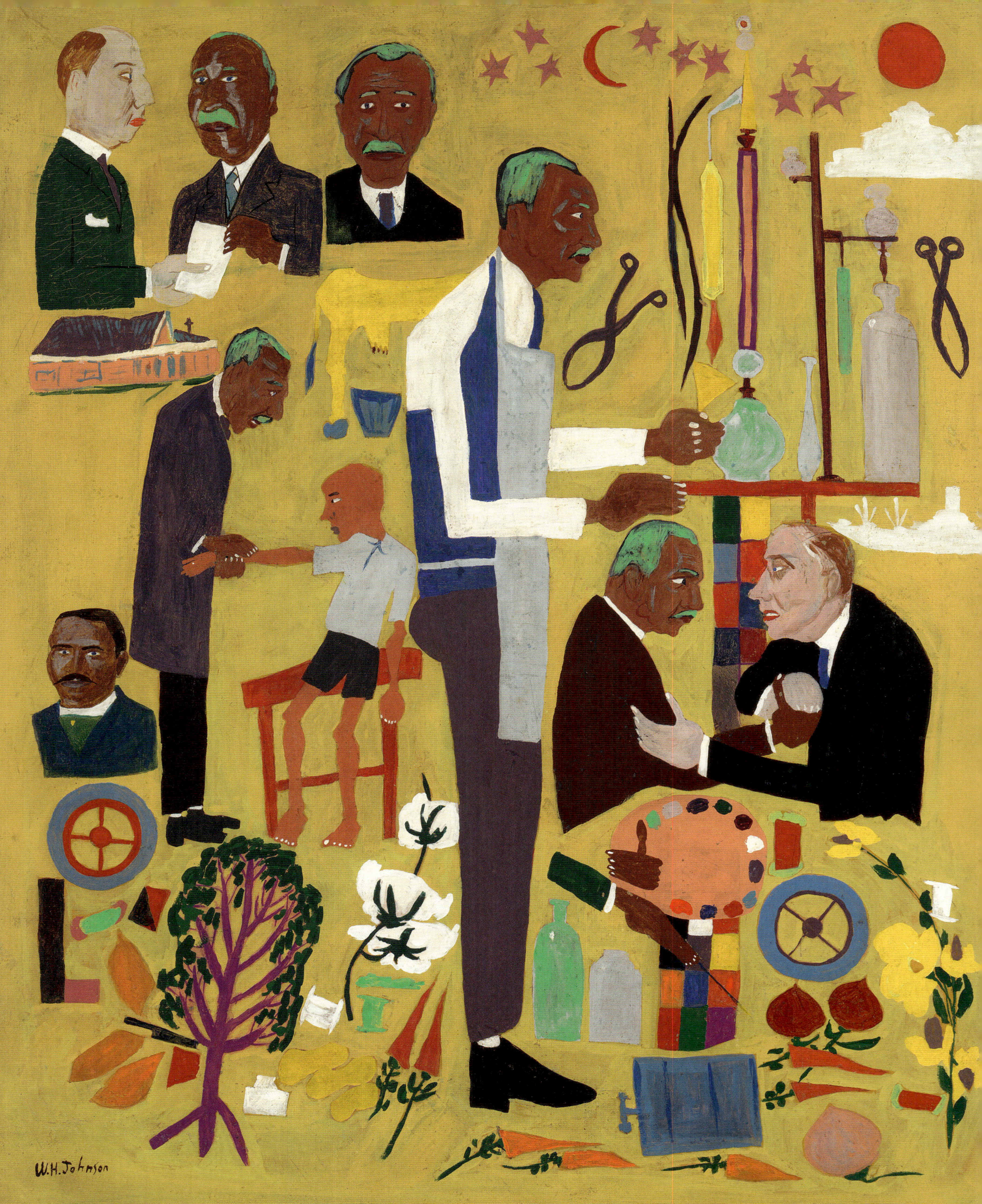
W.H. Johnson

DR. GEORGE WASHINGTON CARVER

ca. 1945
oil on paperboard
35 ½ × 28 ½ in.
Smithsonian American Art Museum
Gift of the Harmon Foundation

SCIENTIST AND INVENTOR George Washington Carver (ca. 1864–1943) made immeasurable contributions to Southern agriculture and environmentalism. His work on crop rotation—alternating cotton with soybeans, peanuts, and sweet potatoes to return nitrogen to depleted soil—revitalized cotton farming in the South after years of declining production. His motivation was not simply to improve the economics of cotton cultivation; he was committed to helping undernourished subsistence farmers—many of whom suffered under exploitative land leasing policies—improve their diets, crop yields, and economic fortunes. "The one great ideal of my life," Carver wrote, "[is] to be of the greatest good to the greatest number of 'my people' possible." He understood that a healthy and sustainable relationship to the land could empower African American farmers in the South and beyond.

Carver was born into slavery in southwestern Missouri. When he was just a few weeks old his mother was kidnapped, leaving him effectively orphaned. He spent his childhood in a series of foster homes, attending school whenever and wherever he could. He eventually made his way north to Iowa, where in his late twenties he enrolled at Iowa Agricultural College (now Iowa State University). After graduating with a master's degree in agriculture, he accepted an offer from Booker T. Washington to teach at the Tuskegee Institute in Alabama, where he would remain for the rest of his career. Carver's teaching was cutting-edge and community focused. From

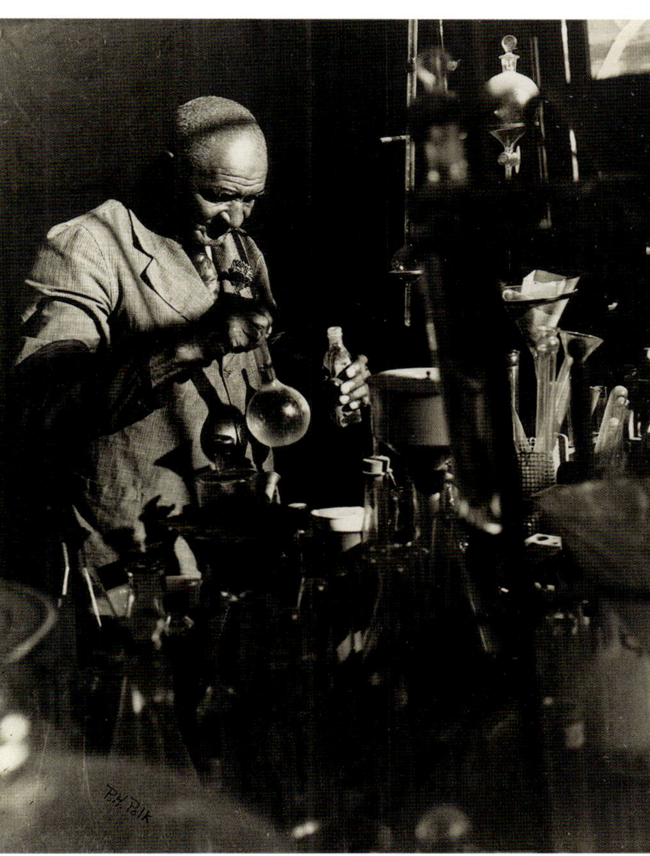

Prentice H. Polk, *George Washington Carver*, ca. 1930, gelatin silver print, 9 ⅝ × 7 13/16 in., National Portrait Gallery, Smithsonian Institution, NPG.95.89

Dr. George Washington Carver
ca. 1945
oil on plywood
32 ½ × 26 ¾ in.
Smithsonian American Art Museum
Gift of the Harmon Foundation

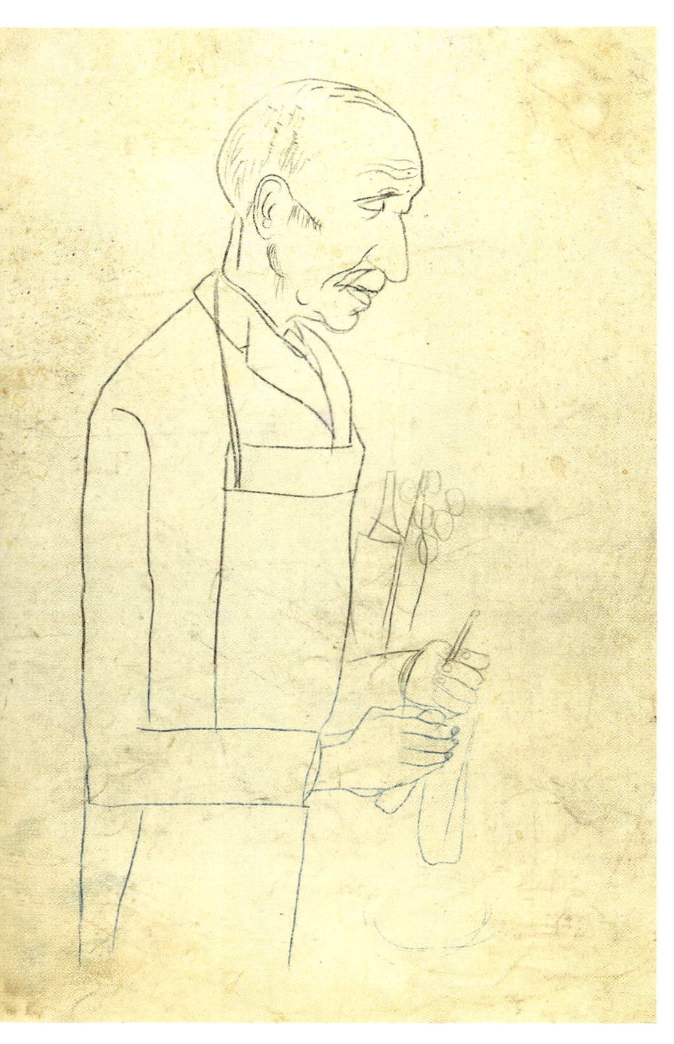

Tuskegee's campus he ventured into the countryside to teach cultivation techniques and livestock care to nearby farmers. He devised a first-of-its-kind mobile classroom, the Jesup Agricultural Wagon, to aid this work. Carver taught poor farmers not only which crops to grow and how to grow them, but also how to make best use of their output. His many uses for peanuts are most famous, but he created hundreds of other recipes for cheap, plant-derived products like soap, paint, fertilizer, and glue. Carver himself lived frugally. Upon his death in 1943 he left sixty thousand dollars to the Tuskegee Institute to continue his agricultural research.

Dr. George Washington Carver, ca. 1945, carbon tracing on paper, 17 ½ × 11 ¼ in., Smithsonian American Art Museum, Gift of the Harmon Foundation, 1967.59.534R–V

In his two paintings on the subject, Johnson emphasized Carver's dynamism, showing him as a scientist, teacher, healer, even artist. (He had studied painting before turning to agriculture.) The mustachioed Carver tinkers with chemistry equipment, pollinates a flower, and applies a peanut oil remedy to the arm of a young polio patient. The fruits of his research—bolls of cotton, abundant produce, a laboratory and museum at Tuskegee—surround him. Carver's inventions earned him wide acclaim in his lifetime, as indicated by scenes of Carver shaking hands with Henry Ford (pictured wearing a green jacket) and President Franklin Delano Roosevelt, who in 1939 awarded him the Roosevelt Medal for Outstanding Contribution to Southern Agriculture.

—EHR

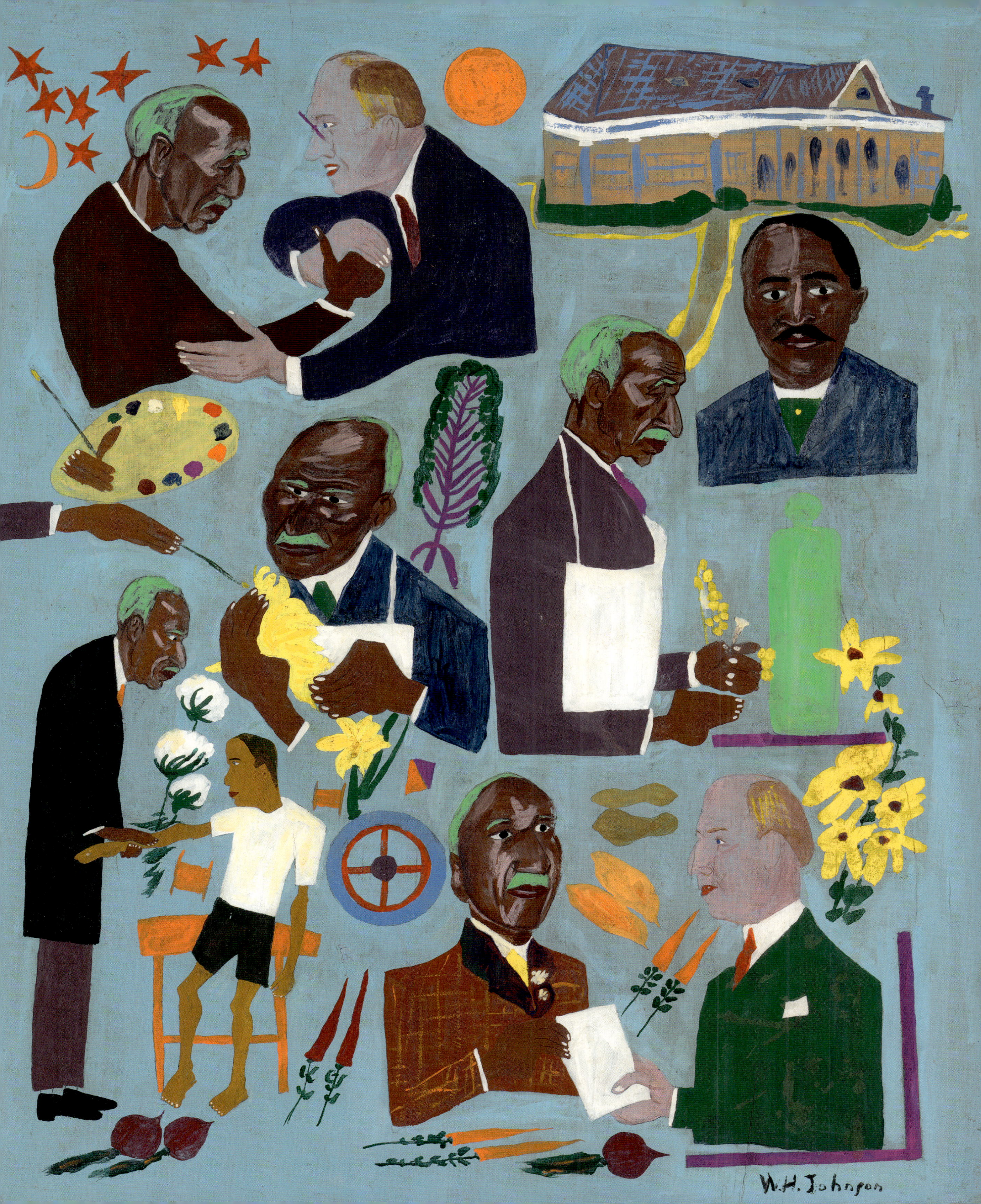
W.H. Johnson

COMMODORE PEARY AND HENSON AT THE NORTH POLE

ca. 1945
oil on paperboard
27 5⁄8 × 35 1⁄2 in.
Smithsonian American Art Museum
Gift of the Harmon Foundation

THIS PAINTING presents explorers Matthew Henson (1866–1955) and Rear Admiral Robert Peary (1856–1920) in an icy landscape that alludes to their greatest achievement, the discovery of the North Pole. The two were an unlikely pair. Henson, at left, was born to free tenant farmers in rural Maryland just one year after slavery was abolished nationwide. At age twelve he ran away to Baltimore, where he found work on a ship, the *Katie Hines*. During five years at sea, Henson traveled the world, learned to read and write and do mathematics, and acquired a host of technical skills, including carpentry and navigation. Back ashore, he found work at a hat and clothing store in Washington, DC. It was there, in 1887, that he encountered naval officer Robert Peary, who promptly hired him to be his assistant. Over the next twenty-two years, the two men undertook many expeditions—including eight attempts to reach the North Pole—and became coequal partners in exploration.

Henson proved indispensable in the Arctic especially, for in addition to being an expert carpenter and navigator, he was fluent in the language spoken by the Inuit people who lived near the Pole and was well versed in their survival practices. Each expedition required months of preparation. The explorers and their Inuit companions would stockpile food and supplies through the Arctic winter before making their final pushes north. From their base-camp igloos, they traveled on dogsleds for up to fourteen hours a day, sometimes in temperatures as low as sixty-five degrees below zero. It was Henson who, by several accounts, was at the head of the expedition crew when it finally reached what they believed was the North Pole on April 6, 1909 (whether the group actually made it to the Pole is still debated). Back in the United States, Peary alone was credited with the discovery, while Henson—written off as the white explorer's servant—faded into relative obscurity. It took nearly thirty years for him to win formal recognition. The prestigious Explorers Club named him a member in 1937, and in 1944 Congress awarded him a silver medal for his contributions to polar exploration. In 1954, President Dwight D. Eisenhower presented him with a special commendation at the White House.

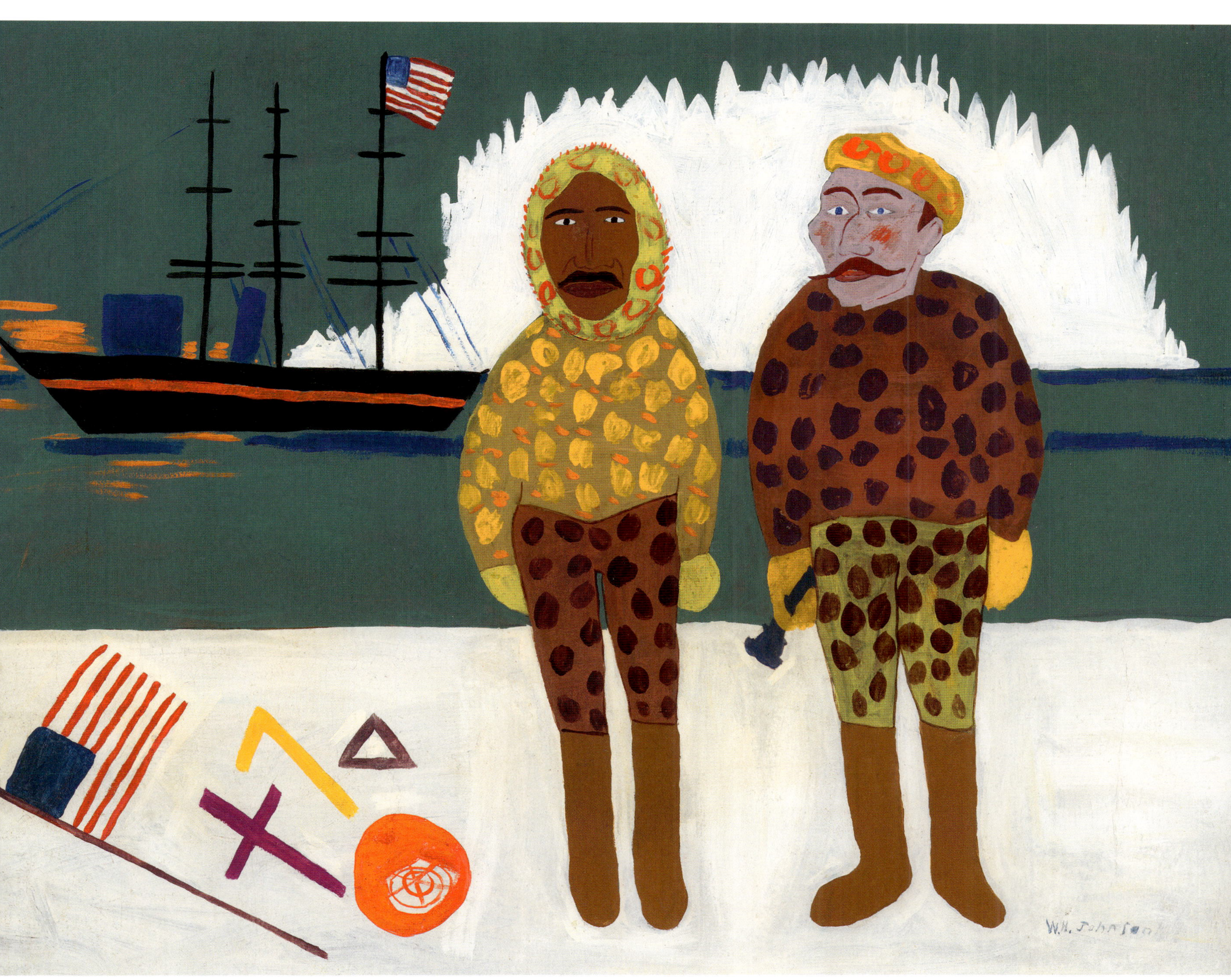

Matthew Henson, photograph from *A Negro Explorer at the North Pole* (1912), National Portrait Gallery, Smithsonian Institution, NPG.99.170.3

Robert E. Peary, Cape Sheridan, Canada, 1909

George Grantham Bain, photographer, "On the sledge that went to the North Pole," ca. January 1910, Library of Congress Prints and Photographs Division. Henson is at the far right.

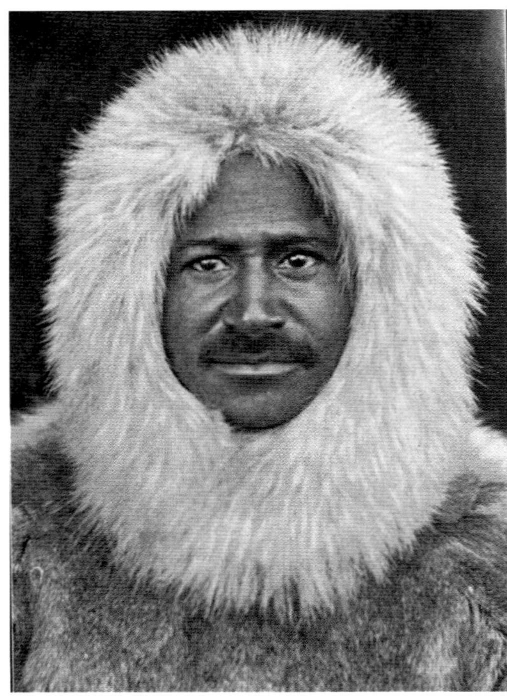

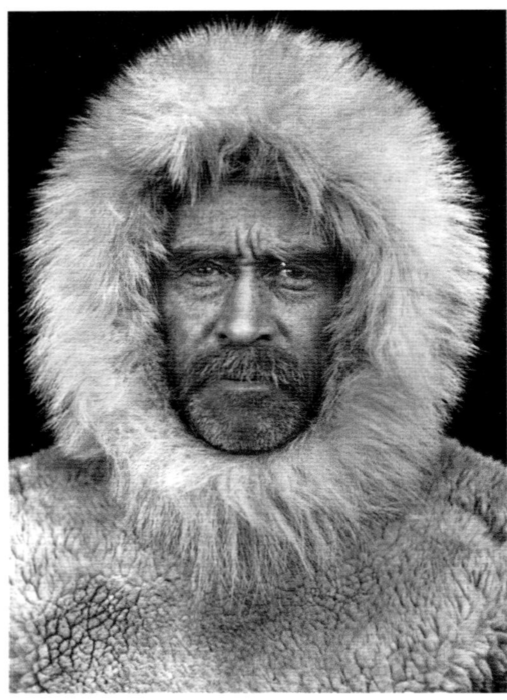

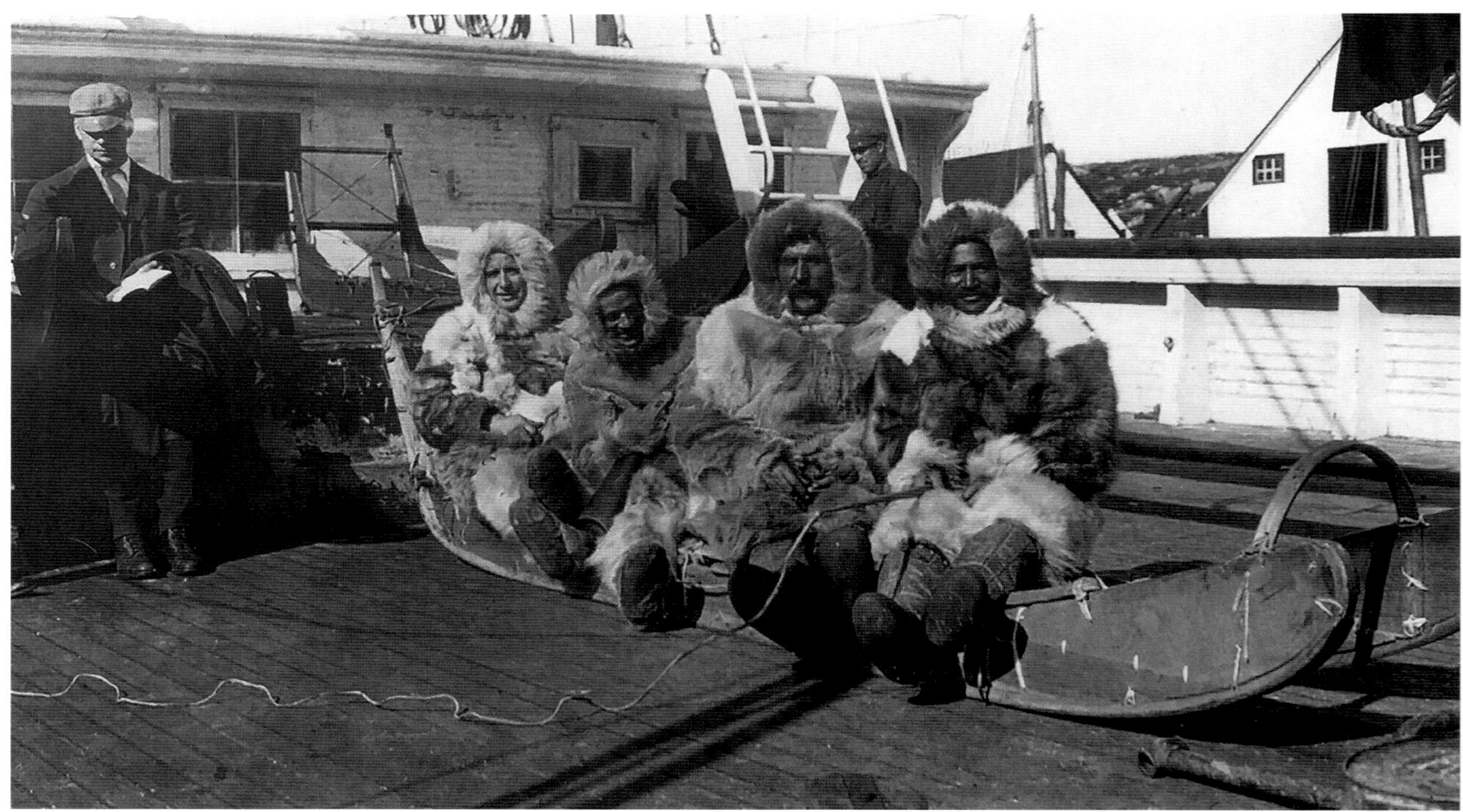

Smithsonian Connections

This silver pocket watch was likely carried by American explorer Matthew Henson on his pioneering 1908 to 1909 expedition to the North Pole with Rear Admiral Robert Peary. The side of the watch is engraved with Henson's initials and last name, and the back reads "R. E. PEARY / NORTH POLE / EXPEDITION / 1908." While Peary was widely credited for discovering the North Pole at the time, it was his longtime assistant and navigator Henson who is now understood to have reached their destination first. Henson headed up the expedition party of six that completed the grueling journey. This watch, an essential explorer's tool, commemorates Henson's remarkable skill and fortitude.

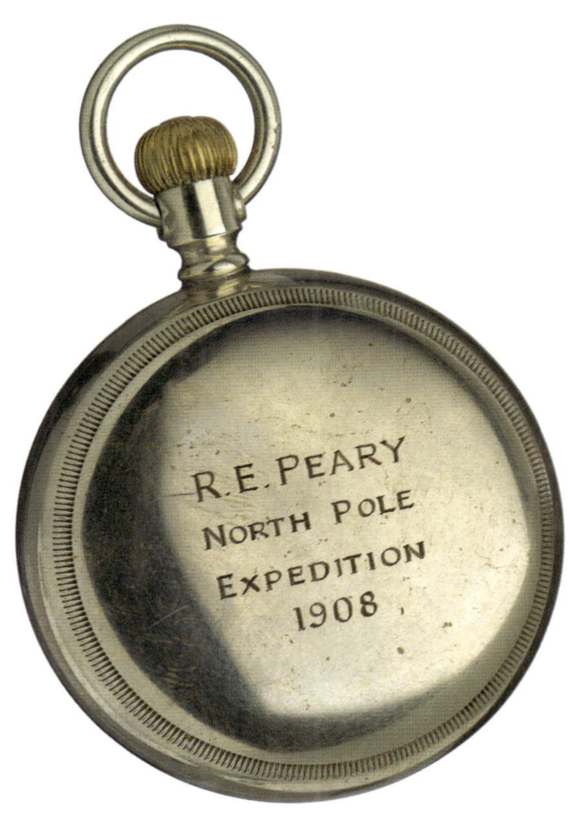

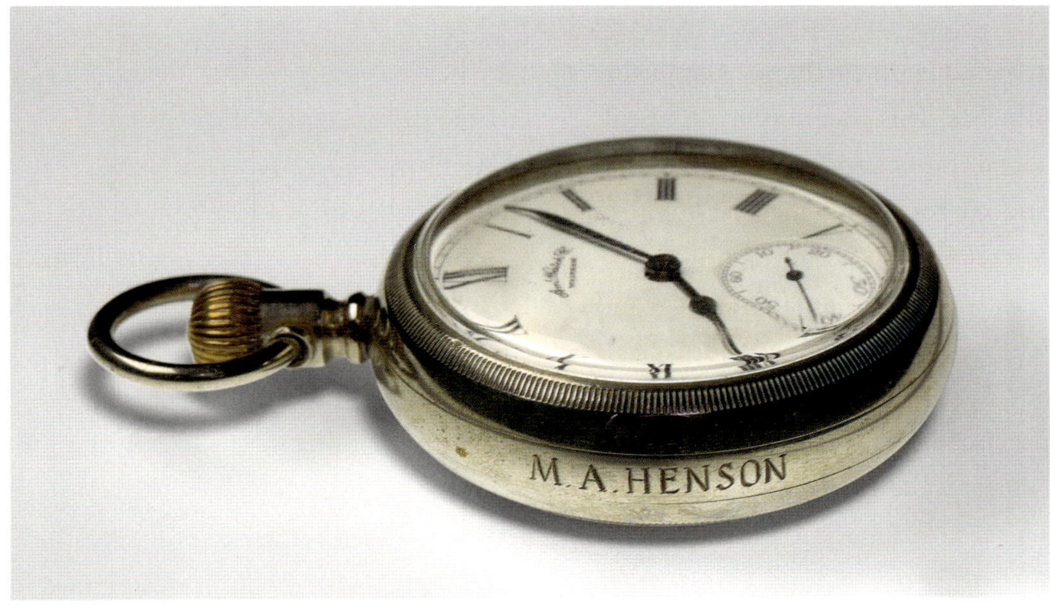

Pocket watch likely carried by Matthew Henson in 1908–09 Arctic expedition, 1888–89; inscribed 1908 or 1909, nickel, metal, and glass, manufactured by American Watch Company, Collection of the Smithsonian National Museum of African American History and Culture, 2017.31

Finally, in 1987, many years after he died and was buried in a modest plot in New York City, Henson was reinterred with full military honors at Arlington National Cemetery, near a monument to Robert Peary. In 2000, the National Geographic Society posthumously awarded Henson the Hubbard Medal, its highest honor, and the same award that Peary received almost one hundred years earlier.

Johnson placed Henson at the center of the composition, standing tall beside Peary at the site of their achievement, thus affirming the African American explorer's rightful place in history. Assorted tools at Henson's feet allude to the explorers' technical and navigational skill, while an American flag signifies the country for which the men claimed victory.

—EHR

HISTORICAL SCENE

ca. 1945
oil on fiberboard
39 ⅛ × 37 ⅛ in.
Smithsonian American Art Museum
Gift of the Harmon Foundation

AT THE CENTER of this painting, in a green suit, is George Baker Jr. (1876–1965), or "Father Divine," founder of the International Peace Mission Movement, an idiosyncratic religion that attracted many thousands of followers during the Great Depression. Born in Rockville, Maryland, to formerly enslaved parents, Baker worked as a gardener in Baltimore while preaching and developing his unique theology. He drew from eclectic sources, including Methodism, Catholicism, Pentecostalism, and the twentieth-century New Thought movement, which promoted positive thinking and maintained that the divine exists in all people. Baker took this notion further, claiming to be God personified and preaching to his followers that heaven itself was achievable on earth, not just in the afterlife. This theology had radical social implications. Father Divine and his followers rejected the notion of racial difference altogether, and they lived communally in "heavens" where men and women enjoyed equal status, shared resources, and practiced strict temperance and celibacy. The Peace Mission operated a series of successful businesses to support its work, including restaurants where patrons could buy meals for as little as five cents. They also hosted so-called heavenly meals, lavish banquets that any member of the public could attend for free. During the lean years of the Great Depression, this material assistance was significant—particularly to African Americans living in urban centers in the Northeast—and it drew thousands into the Peace Mission's ranks.

Johnson situated Father Divine among depictions of the many Peace Mission "heavens" that dotted the country in the 1930s and '40s. An outsized American flag hangs above the prophet-minister, perhaps alluding to the patriotic streak that ran through his teachings; Divine believed that only under the American blend of capitalism and democracy could God's earthly kingdom be realized. Multihued hands wave exuberantly in the painting's foreground, emphasizing the diversity of his following. During an era of strict segregation, the Peace Mission's integrated membership and message of racial unity were revolutionary.

—EHR

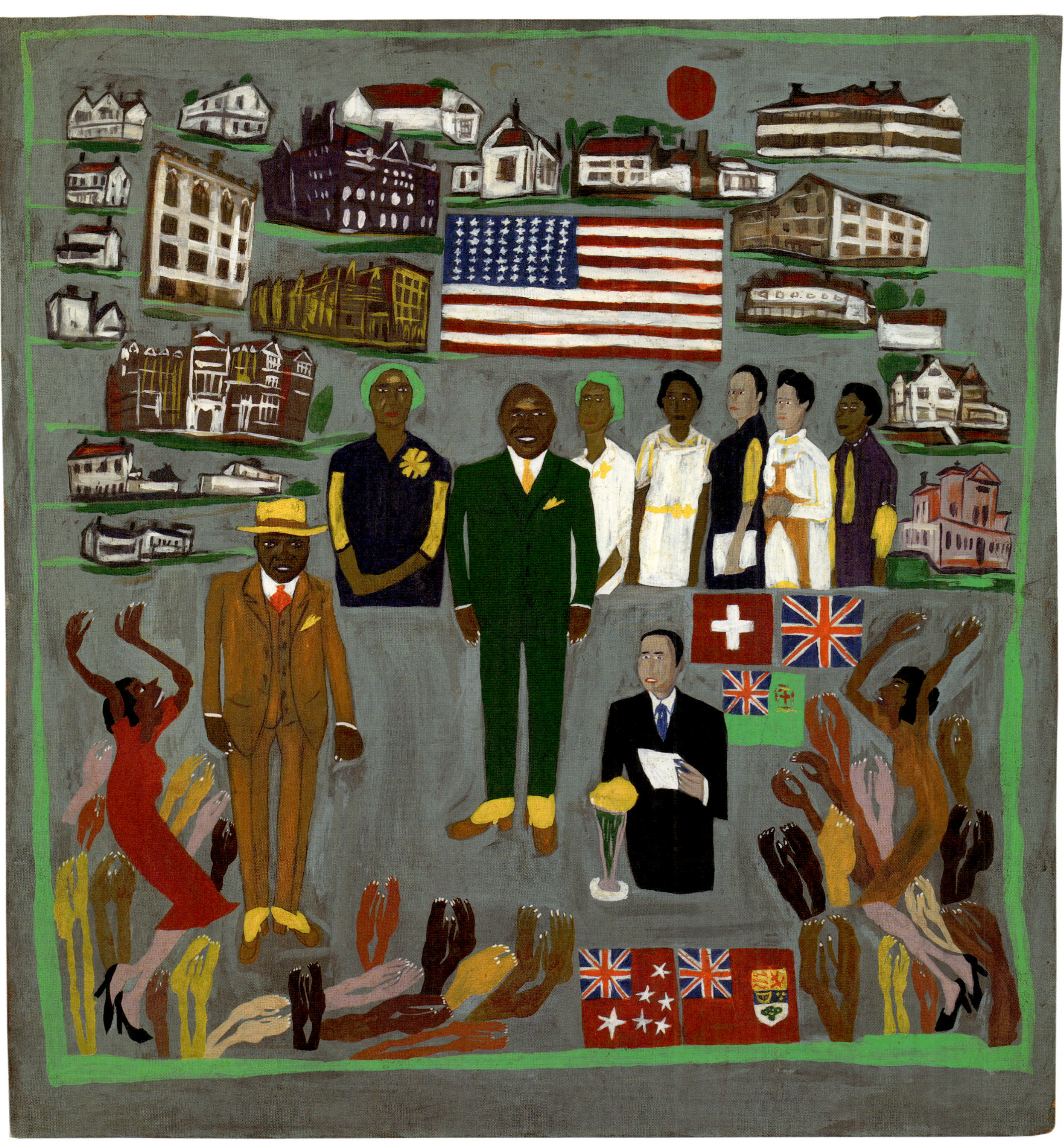

MARCUS GARVEY

ca. 1945
oil on paperboard
35 ¾ × 28 ⅞ in.
Smithsonian American Art Museum
Gift of the Harmon Foundation

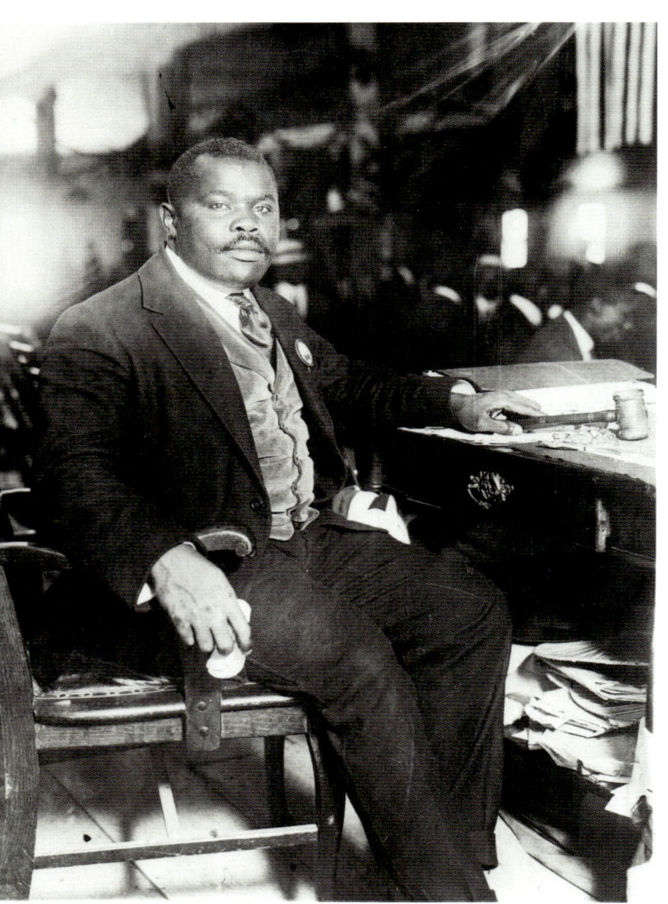

Marcus Garvey, ca. 1924, Library of Congress Prints and Photographs Division, Bain Collection

JAMAICA-BORN Marcus Garvey (1887–1940) had a bold vision for Black empowerment. With his fraternal organization, the United Negro Improvement Association and African Communities League (UNIA-ACL), founded in Kingston in 1914, he sought to "unite into one solid body the four hundred million negroes of the world." This concept of solidarity among all people of African descent came to be known as Pan-Africanism.

Garvey's chief inspiration was Booker T. Washington, whose autobiography *Up from Slavery* he read as a young man. The book's message of self-sufficiency—that Black people should rely on only themselves to build up economic and political power—resonated with the enterprising Garvey. He took it one step further, arguing that his fellow African-descended people should relocate to Africa to find true independence and establish a new political stronghold. After moving to the United States in 1916, Garvey, a spellbinding speaker, crisscrossed the country preaching his message of pride and empowerment. Within just a few years he attracted tens of thousands of members to the UNIA-ACL's ranks and established the organization's weekly newspaper, *Negro World*.

To further his Pan-African dream, Garvey established the Black Star Line steamship company (its name a response to the British-owned White Star Line shipping company). According to Garvey's plan, the company's fleet of luxury vessels would transport Black passengers

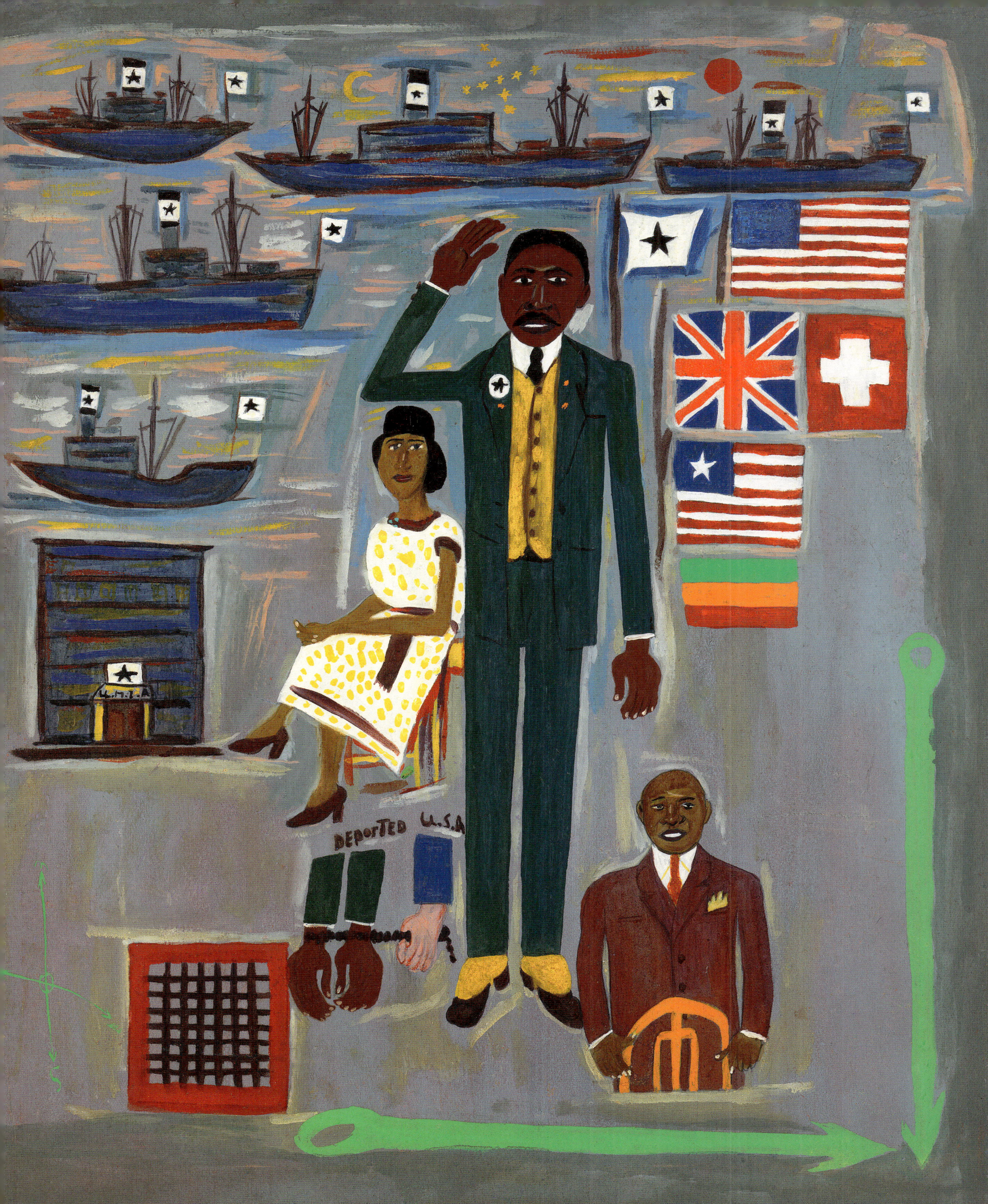
U.N.I.A
DEPORTED U.S.A

Smithsonian Connections

This stock certificate, dated September 18, 1919, issued Miss Amy McKenzie two shares of stock in Black Star Line, Inc., the steamship company founded by Marcus Garvey. Garvey created the shipping line to facilitate the exchange of goods among global Black economies, and he intended to eventually transport African Americans to Africa to establish their own nation-state. The illustration on the certificate depicts a man who points to a globe bearing the words "Africa: The Land of Opportunity," with an ocean liner to its right. While the Black Star Line ultimately failed, Garvey's ideas inspired new generations of activists to further his vision of Black pride and self-empowerment.

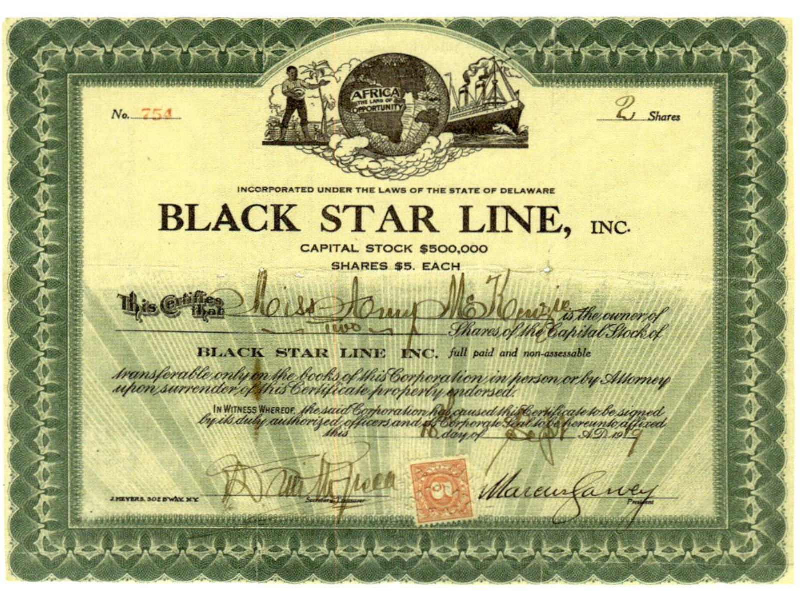

2 Shares

AFRICA THE LAND OF OPPORTUNITY

INCORPORATED UNDER THE LAWS OF THE STATE OF DELAWARE

BLACK STAR LINE, INC.

CAPITAL STOCK $500,000

SHARES $5. EACH

This Certifies that Miss Amy McKenzie is the owner of Shares of the Capital Stock of BLACK STAR LINE INC. full paid and non-assessable transferable only on the books of this Corporation in person or by Attorney upon surrender of this Certificate properly endorsed.

In Witness Whereof, the said Corporation has caused this Certificate to be signed by its duly authorized officers and its Corporate Seal to be hereunto affixed this 18 day of Sept A.D. 1919

Black Star Line stock certificate to Amy McKenzie, 1919, ink on paper, Collection of the Smithsonian National Museum of African American History and Culture, 2012.46.41

from Europe and the United States to West Africa, where they could make a new start. In Johnson's painting, ships bearing the Black Star Line flag surround Garvey and his second wife, Amy Jacques Garvey, an author and advocate for the UNIA and Black women. The figure at lower right could be Joshua Cockburn, captain of the Black Star Line's inaugural ship, the S.S. *Yarmouth*.

Thousands of people, most of them working-class, bought into the Black Star Line's promise of hope and liberation, offering donations and purchasing honorary shares in the company for five dollars each. But it would never come to pass. A pair of shackled hands and a barred window at the bottom of the painting allude to Garvey's downfall. After years of surveillance by federal authorities (including a young J. Edgar Hoover), Garvey was convicted of mail fraud related to Black Star Line stock sales and deported to Jamaica in 1927. Johnson nevertheless celebrates Garvey as a man of great ambition and inspiration.

—EHR

Amy Jacques Garvey, ca. 1945, pencil on paper, 15 × 20 1/8 in., Smithsonian American Art Museum, Gift of the Harmon Foundation, 1967.59.531R–V

Marcus Garvey, ca. 1945, pencil and carbon transfer on paper, 11 1/4 × 17 5/8 in., Smithsonian American Art Museum, Gift of the Harmon Foundation, 1967.59.542R-V

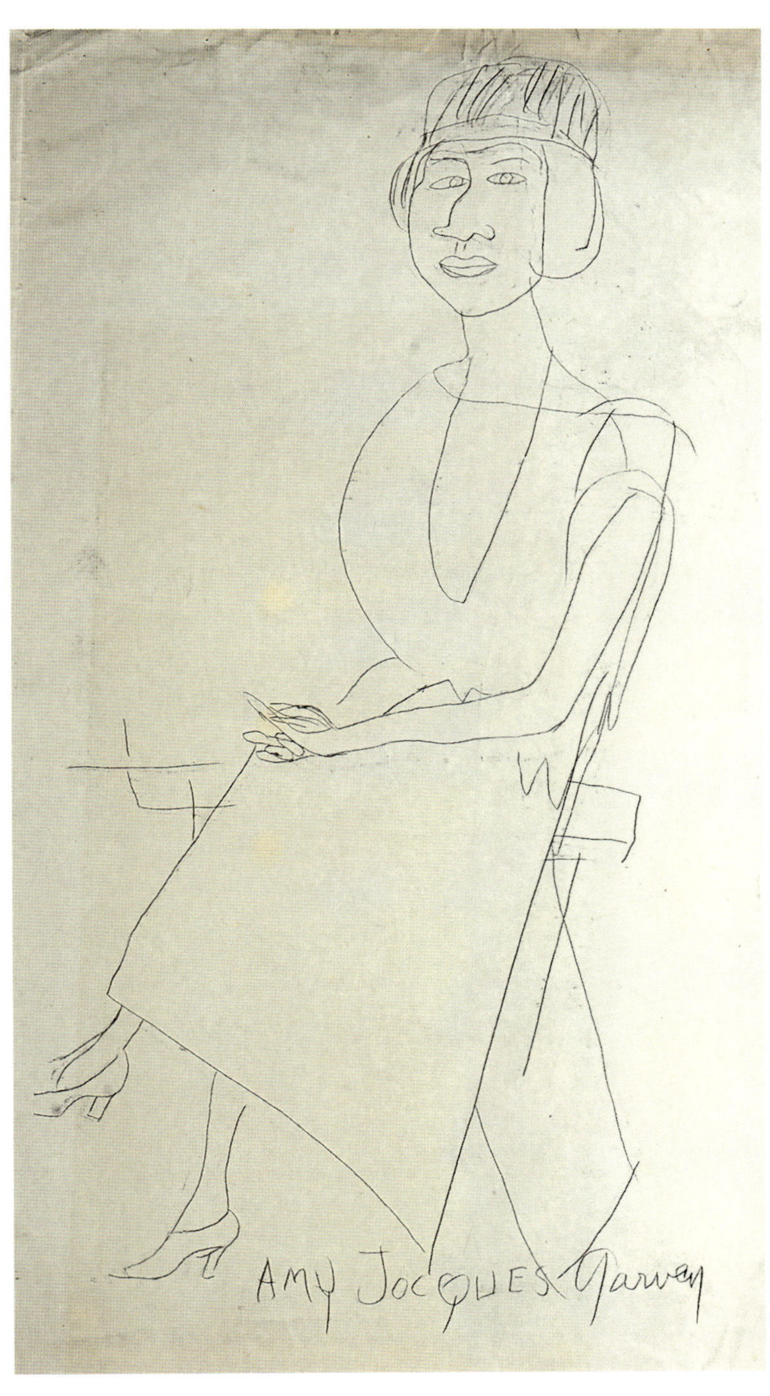

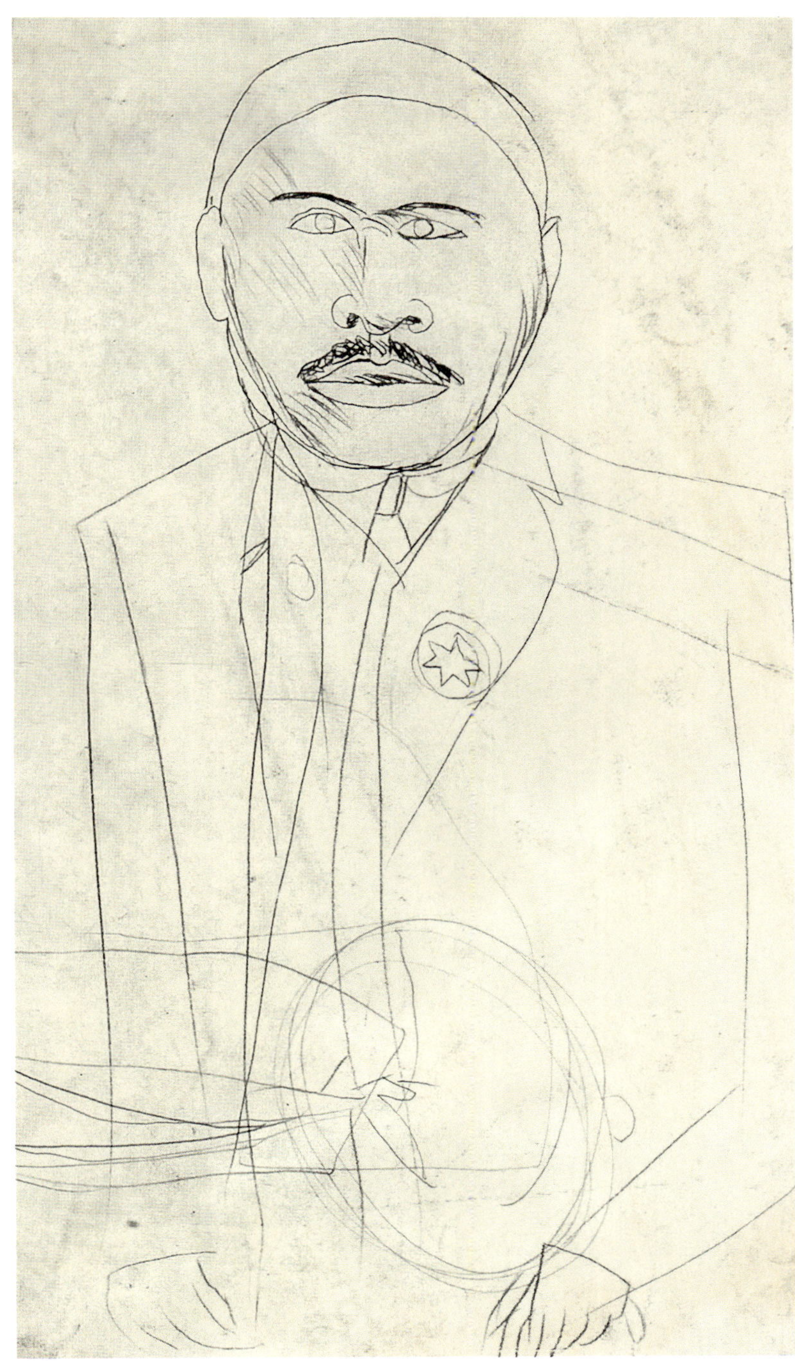

WOMEN BUILDERS

1945
oil on paperboard
37 5/8 × 34 1/8 in.
Smithsonian American Art Museum
Gift of the Harmon Foundation

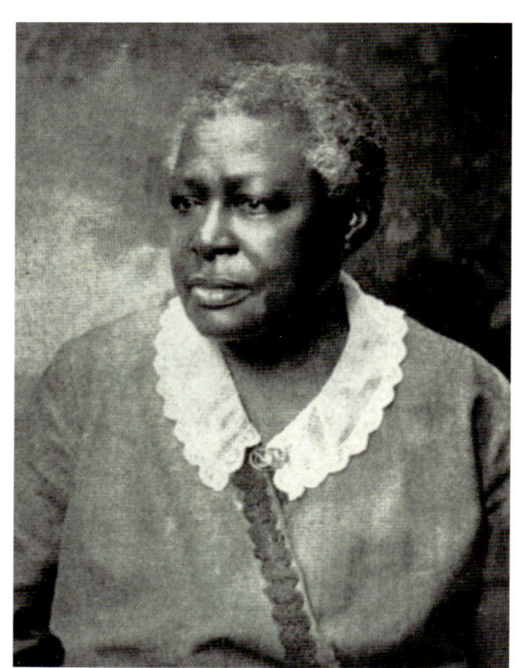

Lucy Craft Laney, photograph from Sadie Iola Daniel's *Women Builders* (1931)

WOMEN BUILDERS depicts a constellation of inspiring and enterprising African American women. Johnson sourced these portraits from Sadie Iola Daniel's 1931 book of the same name. The painting's eight figures include the author Daniel (middle row, right) and others who provided services and opportunities in African American communities. After the abolition of slavery, many areas of the United States legalized segregation of the races (enacting what are called Jim Crow laws), which left many African American communities without schools, banks, housing, and other resources. These important women filled the void. To underscore the book's "builders" theme, Johnson paired the women's portraits with buildings from their organizations.

Lucy Craft Laney (top row, left, and at left) created the first school for African American children in Augusta, Georgia. Another educator, Charlotte Hawkins Brown (top row, middle), founded the Palmer Memorial Institute, a boarding school in Sedalia, North Carolina. In 1903, Maggie Lena Walker (top row, right) became the first African American woman to charter a bank, the St. Luke Penny Savings Bank in Richmond, Virginia. Trained as a nurse, Jane Edna Hunter (middle left) eventually formed a residence for African American women in Cleveland, Ohio, to ensure their safety and help find jobs for those who had moved from the South. Now well-known, Mary McLeod Bethune (bottom left) founded a school and college in Florida today called Bethune-Cookman University (p. 108). Social

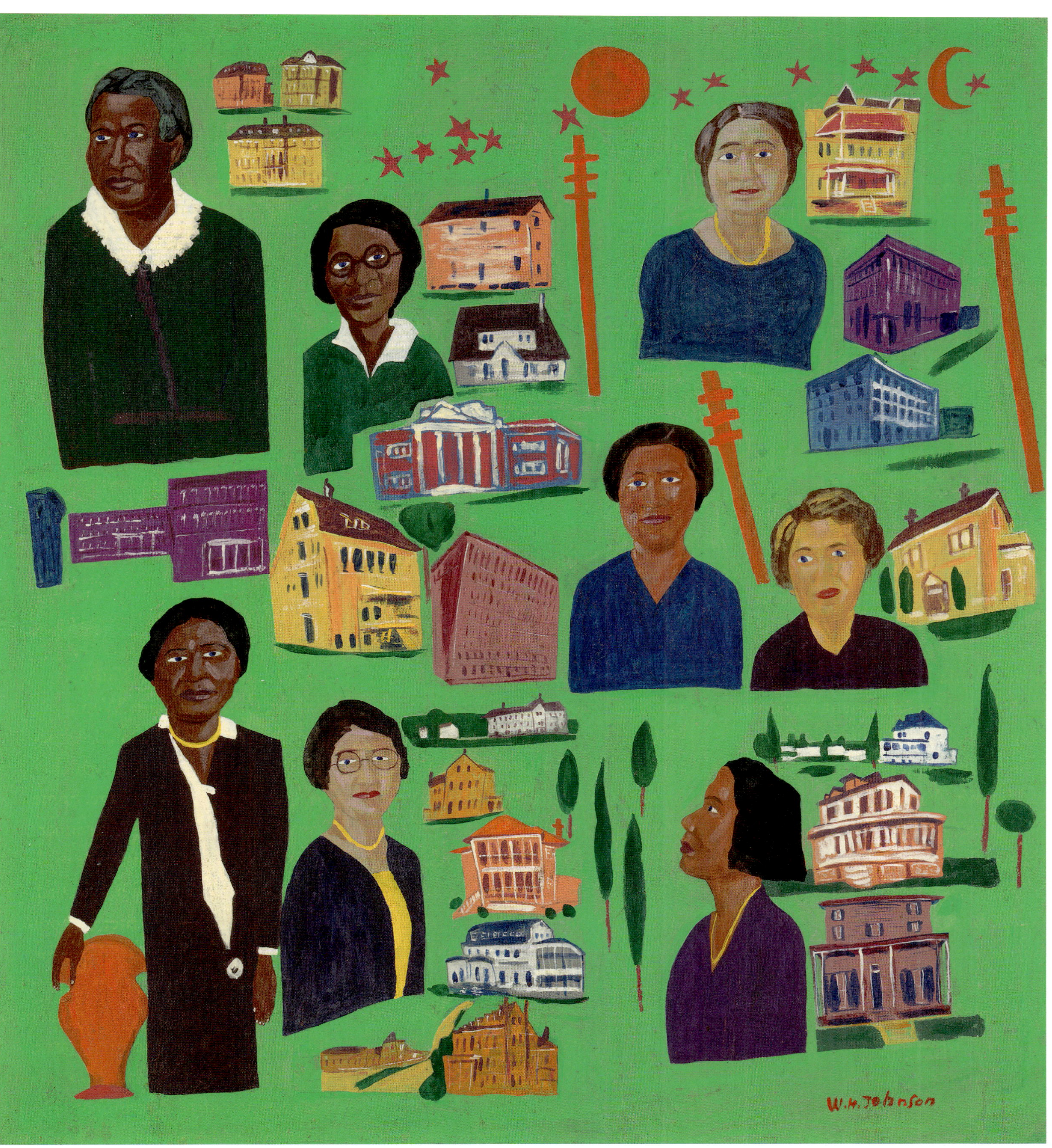
W.H. Johnson

Smithsonian Connections

Nannie Helen Burroughs (1879–1961, bottom right in *Women Builders*) used this cash register at the National Training School for Women and Girls, an institution she founded in 1909. The school was unique in its mission to provide professional training for working-class African American women, preparing them for careers beyond domestic labor and fostering independence through financial literacy. In addition to vocational training, students were required to complete courses in African American history. Burroughs's cash register, embellished with her name, reflects the pride she took in her hard-earned professional success, as well as her dedication to future generations of women.

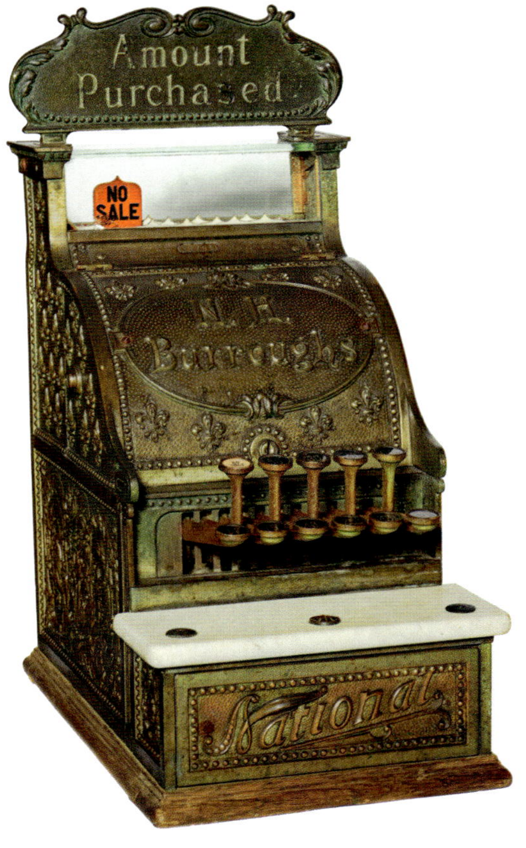

Cash Register, 1904, glass, wood, and marble, manufactured by National Cash Register Company, Nannie Helen Burroughs School, National Museum of American History, Smithsonian Institution, 1978.0342.009

worker Janie Porter Barrett (bottom middle) built a settlement house in Hampton, Virginia, and a reform school for African American girls in Hanover, Virginia.

Pictured in profile, Nannie Helen Burroughs (bottom right) was an educator, civil rights activist, and orator. Born in Orange, Virginia, Burroughs spent most of her life in Washington, DC. After she was denied a job as a public school teacher, purportedly because her skin was too dark, she vowed to create her own school. Her fund-raising campaign sought support from Black citizens, religious groups, and businesses; banker Maggie Lena Walker (pictured above Burroughs) gave five hundred dollars to the cause. After the National Baptist Convention bought land for the school in northeast Washington, DC, Burroughs founded the National Training School for Women and Girls. The curriculum offered vocational and academic courses, and Burroughs was the school's president for the rest of her life.

Burroughs's skyward gaze suggests her religious convictions and moral vision for racial equality. She assumed leadership roles in the National Baptist Convention, its Woman's Auxiliary, and the National Association of Colored Women, which fought for women's suffrage. Some consider her activism a forerunner to the Civil Rights Movement of the 1960s and '70s. A gifted intellectual, Burroughs was also a writer and orator. Her description of the Allied effort in World War II (from a circa 1943 radio address) could also summarize her own life's work: "to make the world large enough for democracy and too small for race prejudice, discrimination, injustice and hate."

—TDF

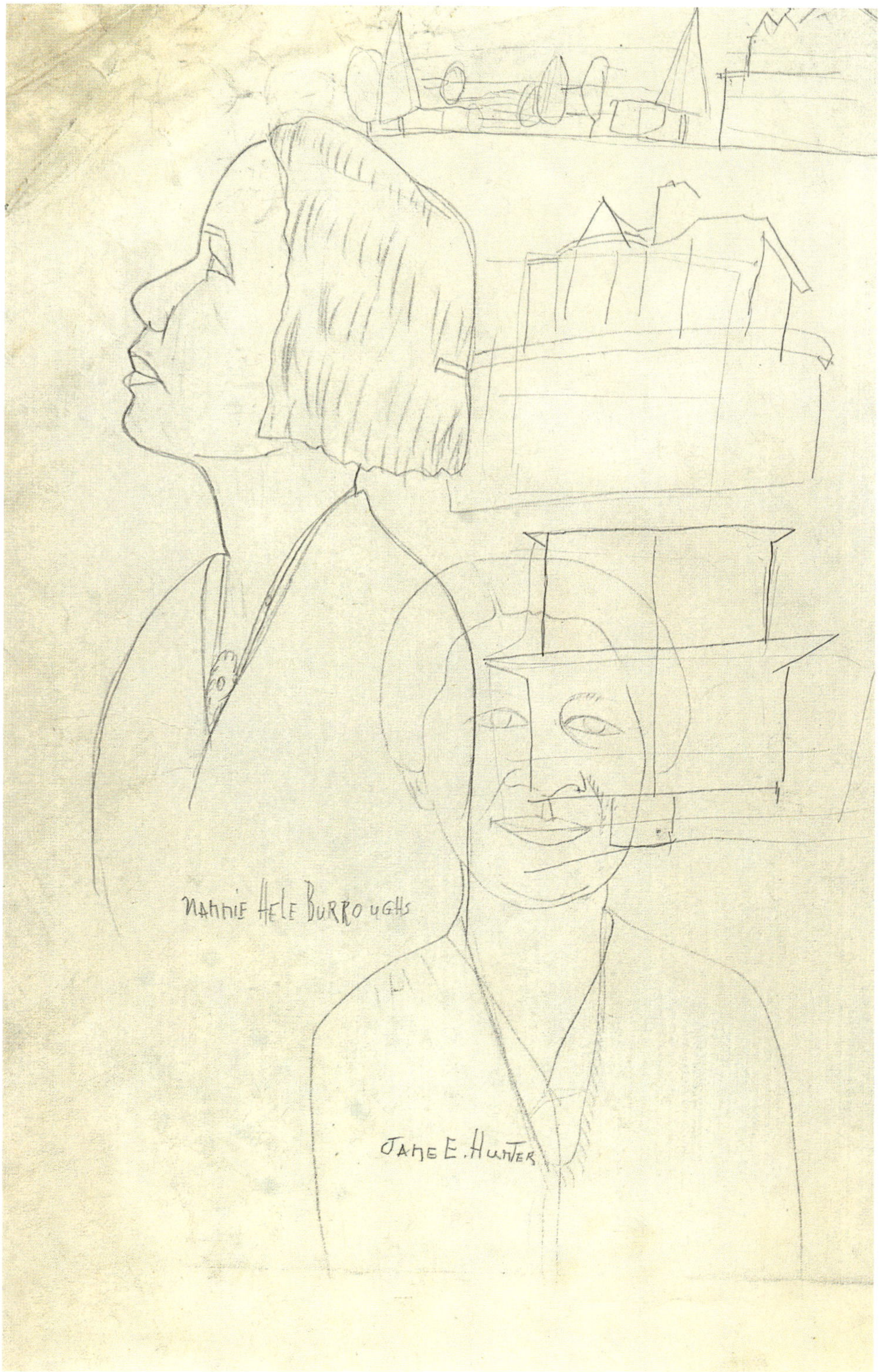

Nannie H. Burroughs, and Jane E. Hunter, ca. 1945, carbon tracing on paper, 16 1/8 × 11 1/4 in., Smithsonian American Art Museum, Gift of the Harmon Foundation, 1967.59.489R–V

Nannie Helen Burroughs, photograph from Sadie Iola Daniel's *Women Builders* (1931)

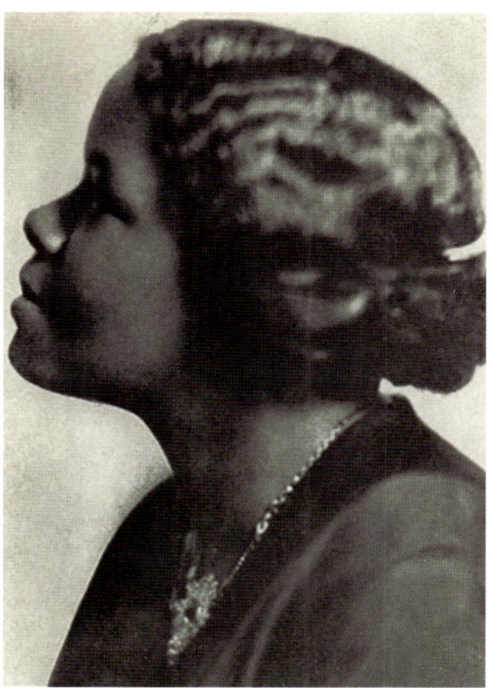

HISTORICAL SCENE WITH MARY McLEOD BETHUNE

ca. 1945
oil on paperboard
37 ½ × 28 ½ in.
Smithsonian American Art Museum
Gift of the Harmon Foundation

MARY McLEOD BETHUNE (1875–1955)—an educator, women's and civil rights champion, and presidential adviser—was one of the most effective and influential freedom fighters of the twentieth century. Like others in this series, her success was hard won. Her parents could afford to send only one of their seventeen children to a segregated mission school nearby; they chose Mary. She then won a scholarship to a segregated seminary in North Carolina. Dedicated to empowering African American women, she became a teacher. By 1904, she founded a boarding school

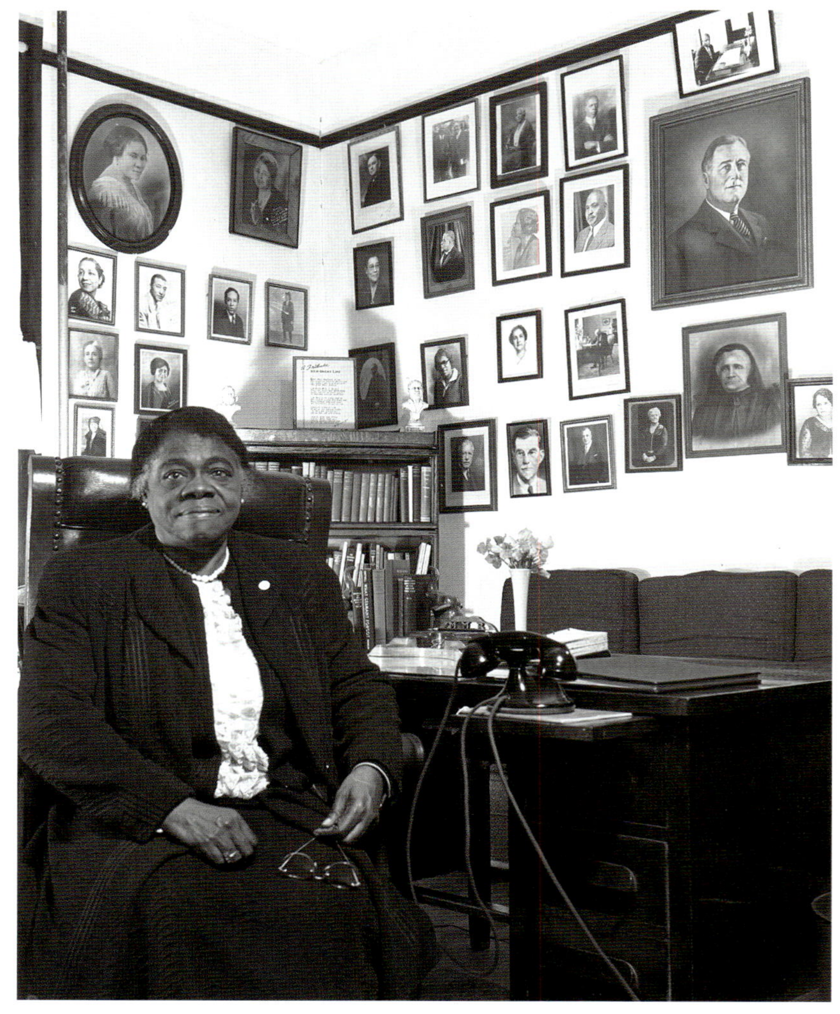

Gordon Parks, *Daytona Beach, Florida. Bethune-Cookman College. Dr. Mary McLeod Bethune, founder and former president and director of the NYA (National Youth Administration) Negro Relations*, 1943, gelatin silver print, 13 7⁄16 × 10 ½ in., National Gallery of Art, Corcoran Collection (The Gordon Parks Collection), 2016.117.120

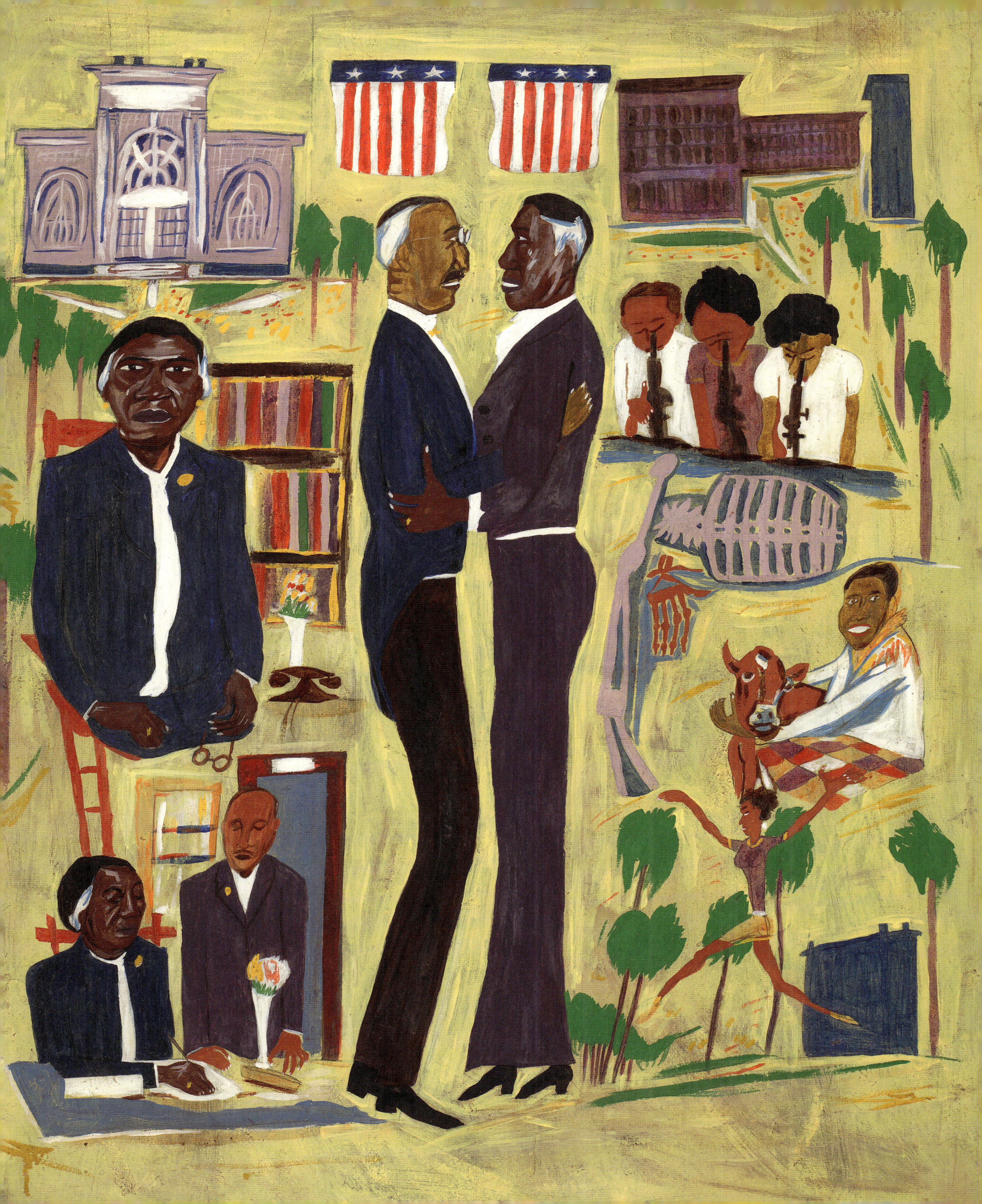

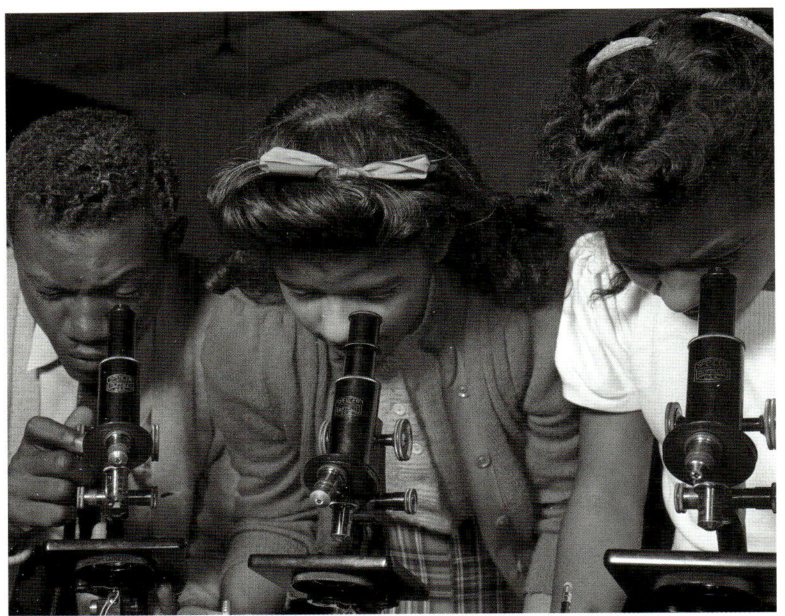

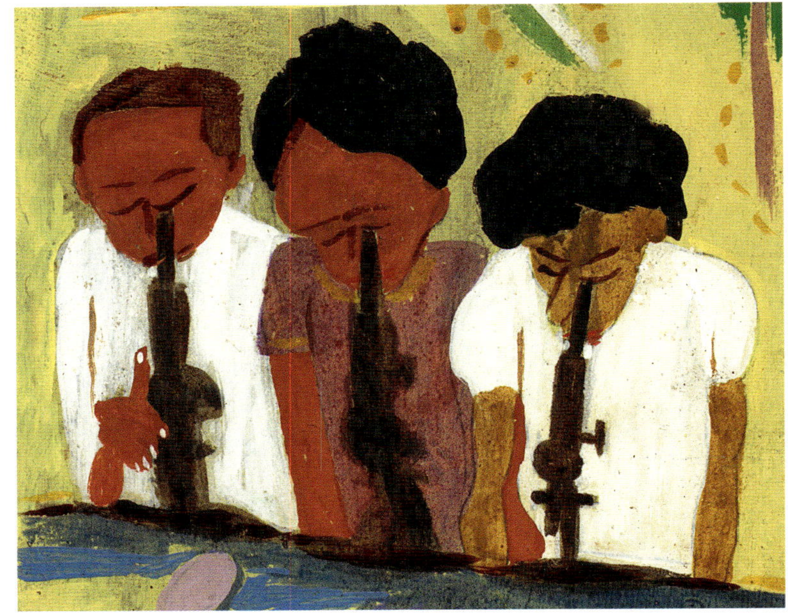

in Florida, the Daytona Literary and Industrial Training School for Negro Girls. In 1923 the Daytona School merged with the all-male Cookman Institute in Jacksonville to form what is now called Bethune-Cookman University. Bethune served as president from its founding until her retirement in 1942.

Bethune's vision targeted political change as well. While she led the school, she joined women's clubs and headed national educational organizations. After the 1920 passage of the Nineteenth Amendment, which granted women the right to vote, she assisted voter registration drives for African American women despite threats of violence. Bethune's political activism led to a friendship with Franklin Delano Roosevelt and his wife, Eleanor, even before they occupied the White House. After Roosevelt was elected president, Bethune served as an adviser, the only woman in the so-called Black Cabinet, which ensured that Depression-era programs helped African Americans. In 1936 she became director of Negro Affairs for the National Youth Administration, a New Deal agency that created employment and educational opportunities for young people. As the first African American woman to head a division of a federal agency, Bethune fought for equal opportunity not only in the federal workforce but also in private companies. Working with others, she laid the groundwork for executive orders in the 1940s banning discrimination and segregation in many government sectors, including defense contracting, civilian jobs, and finally, in 1948, the U.S. military.

William H. Johnson captured Bethune's dedication to inclusion and uplift in a multifaceted view of Bethune-Cookman College, as it was known in the 1940s. The vignettes around the painting's border come

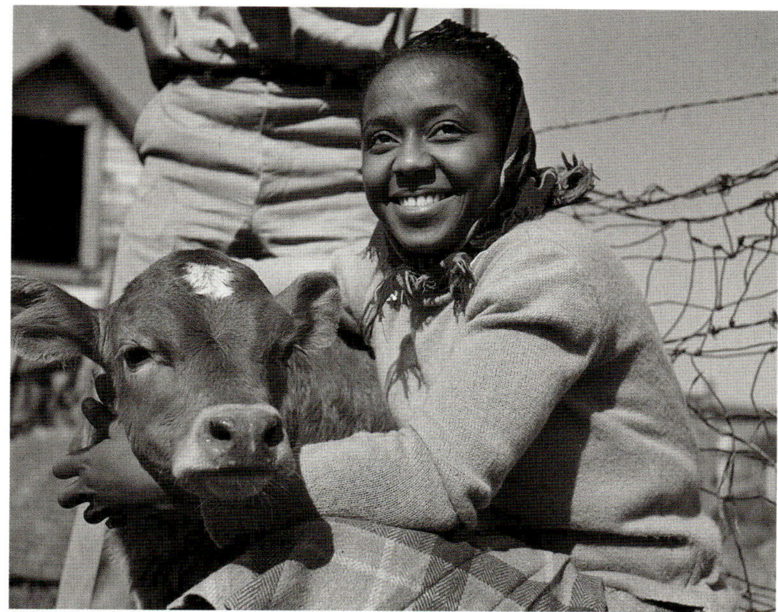

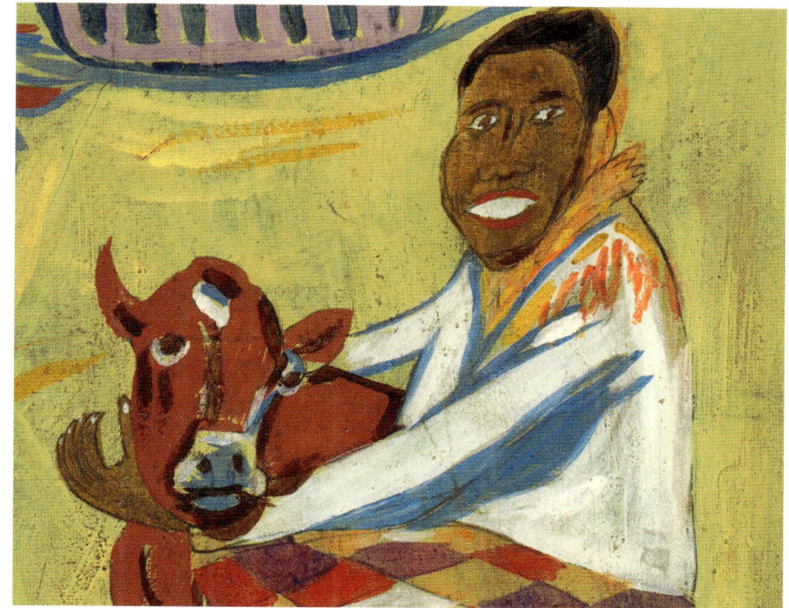

from photographs taken by Gordon Parks, who visited the school in early 1943 on assignment for the Farm Security Administration. On the right are science students with microscopes (opposite), a youth at the agricultural school with a cow (above), and a modern dance instructor. At the bottom left, Bethune transfers the presidency to her successor, James Colston. Above that, Bethune is seated at her home on the grounds of the college, surrounded by books and her telephone, a sign of her continuing activism. Faith Hall, a building on campus, hovers at top left. The embracing figures at center might refer to the merging of the two schools or a civil rights milestone of the 1940s—such as the founding of the United Negro College Fund in 1944, another of Bethune's many causes.

As Bethune faced her mortality in 1955, she wrote an article for *Ebony* magazine in the form of a will. Distilling her life's work, she described a legacy of love and hope, a thirst for education and racial dignity, and a responsibility to young people—but also faith. She wrote, "Faith is the first factor in a life devoted to service. Without it, nothing is possible. With it, nothing is impossible."

—TDF

Gordon Parks, *Daytona Beach, Florida. Bethune-Cookman College. Students using microscopes*, February 1943, nitrate negative, Library of Congress Prints and Photographs Division

Gordon Parks, *Daytona Beach, Florida. Bethune-Cookman College. Student holding a young calf on the agricultural school farm*, February 1943, nitrate negative, Library of Congress Prints and Photographs Division

Historical Scene with Mary McLeod Bethune (details); see page 109

BOXERS

ca. 1945–46
oil on paperboard
32 7/8 × 28 7/8 in.
Smithsonian American Art Museum
Gift of the Harmon Foundation

IN *BOXERS*, heavyweight champions Jack Johnson (1878–1946) and Joe Louis (1914–1981) seem to hop, jab, and weave about the composition, much as they did in the ring. Their stylized stances and athletic builds were likely based on the many photographs and sketches, especially of Joe Louis, that the painter kept among his papers. A preparatory drawing (p. 114) identifies the figure holding the hat at lower center as Joe Louis, and the cabin at the upper center as Louis's boyhood home near Buckalew Mountain, Alabama. Both Johnson and Louis overcame systemic racism to reach the pinnacle of boxing, and, as shown in the painting, they both defeated white challengers in highly publicized matches.

The first African American heavyweight boxing champion, Jack Johnson held the title from 1908 to 1915, when the sport and U.S. society were segregated. Outspoken after his wins and flamboyant with his money, Johnson confronted racism in many forms, including the taboo against interracial dating and marriage; white resentment flared. Exploiting racial tensions for match hype, promoters sought white boxers to challenge him and called for a "Great White Hope." Former heavyweight champ James Jeffries, who had previously refused to fight African Americans, came out of retirement to square off against Johnson on July 4, 1910. Johnson was victorious with a knockout in the fifteenth round before a crowd of twenty thousand in Reno, Nevada. African Americans celebrated, but some whites rioted in cities across the nation.

Similarly, Joe Louis won dozens of professional matches leading up to a 1937 title bout against James J. Braddock to become heavyweight champion, a title he held for a record twelve years. Unlike Johnson, however, Louis became a hero to all. His tremendous skills in the ring along with sophisticated marketing and the threat of war in Europe unified Americans behind him. Back in June 1936, Louis had surprisingly lost a match against German boxer Max Schmeling. Within two years, Adolf Hitler had annexed Austria, and the German threat to Europe was palpable. Even though Schmeling was not a member of the Nazi Party, the 1938 rematch was billed as an international battle of ideologies and races, the American "Brown Bomber" against Hitler's "Aryan master race."

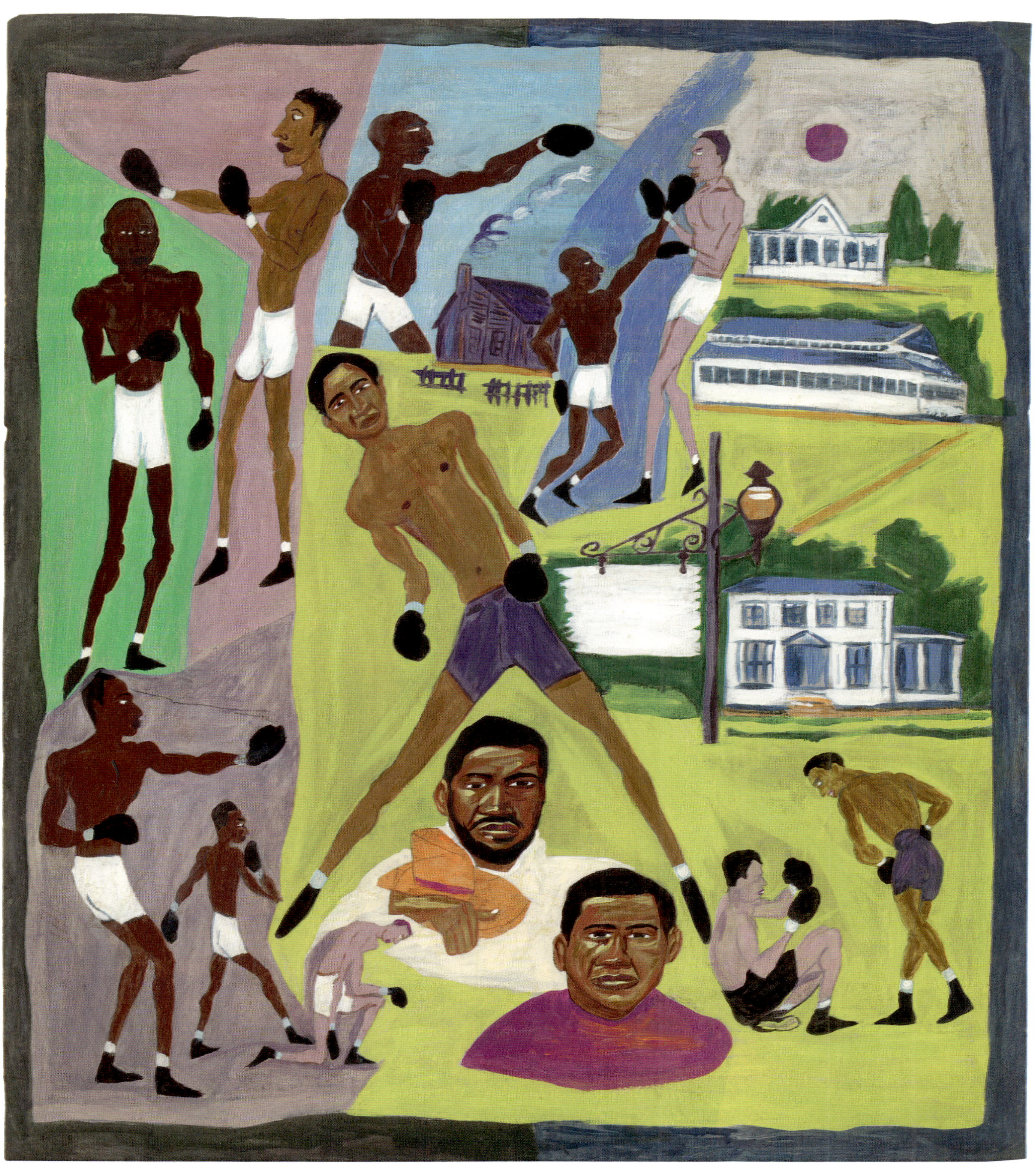

Opposite: *Joe Louis and Unidentified Boxer,* ca. 1939–42, tempera and pen and ink on paper, 18 × 12 in., Smithsonian American Art Museum, Gift of the Harmon Foundation, 1967.59.173R–V

Joe Louis and Buckalew Mountain, ca. 1945, pencil on paper, 9 ¾ × 5 in., Smithsonian American Art Museum, Gift of the Harmon Foundation, 1967.59.389

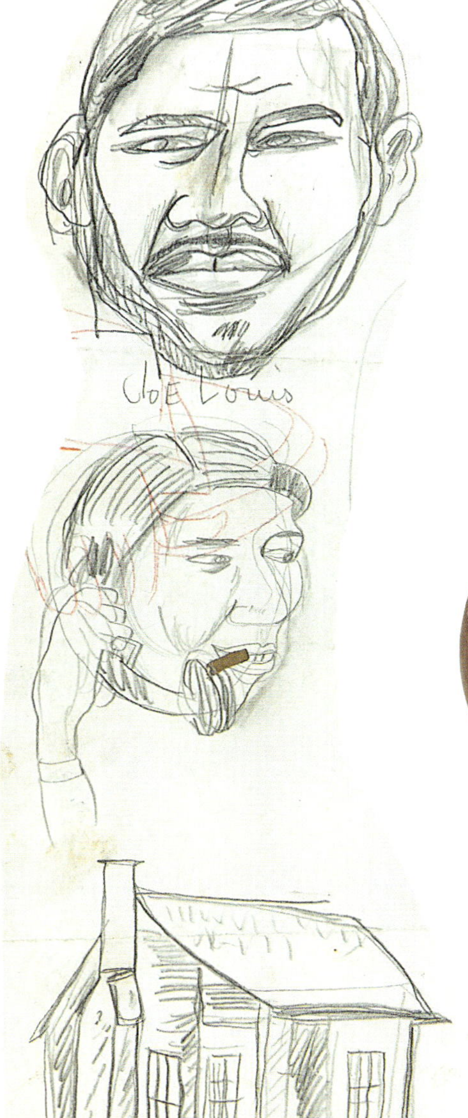

Smithsonian Connections

Jack Johnson never backed down from a fight. The first African American heavyweight boxing champion, Johnson likewise struck a powerful blow to racism and inequality outside the ring. "He stood up and challenged the ideas that African Americans couldn't assert themselves, couldn't live lavishly," says Damion Thomas, curator of sports at the Smithsonian's National Museum of African American History and Culture. This signed glove is from an exhibition match later in Johnson's career. It reads "Jack Johnson / Former Heavyweight / Champion / of the world / U.S.A," reflecting his significance as one of the greatest champions in the sport. His success challenged racial hierarchies and symbolized possibility for future generations of African Americans.

Boxing glove signed by Jack Johnson, 1919–45, leather, cotton, manufactured by Ken-Wel Sporting Goods Company, Collection of the Smithsonian National Museum of African American History and Culture, 2013.115

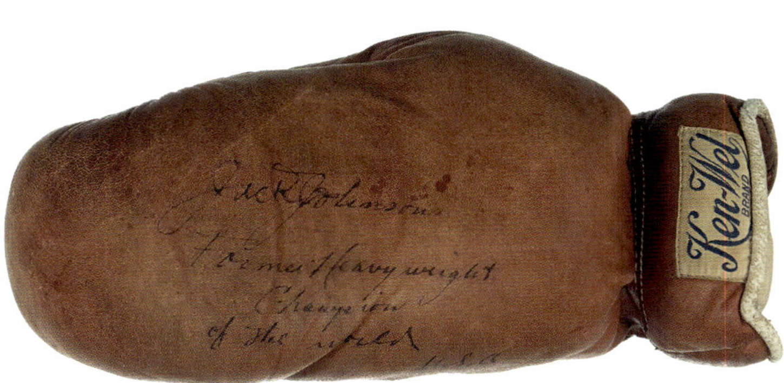
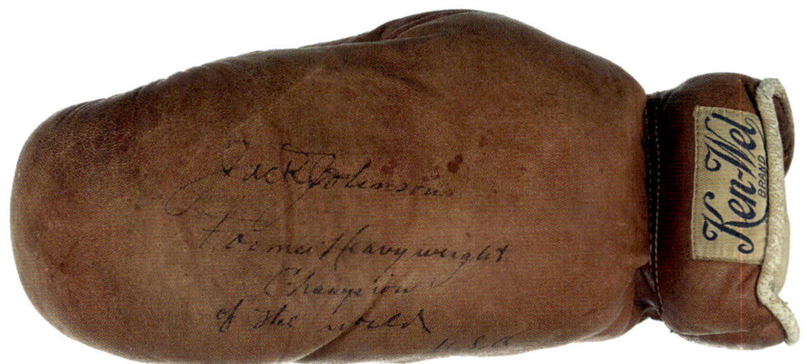

Sixty million Americans listened on the radio; another one hundred million tuned in worldwide. Two minutes into the first round, the referee called a technical knockout. Joe Louis, on the side of democracy, had defeated Schmeling, the stand-in for Nazi fascism. After the United States entered World War II in December 1941, Louis enlisted in the U.S. Army. As a soldier, he fought exhibition matches and visited wounded GIs. By the time he was discharged in 1945, he had entertained more than two million soldiers at home and abroad. Joe Louis's patriotism had become as celebrated as his masterful boxing.

—TDF

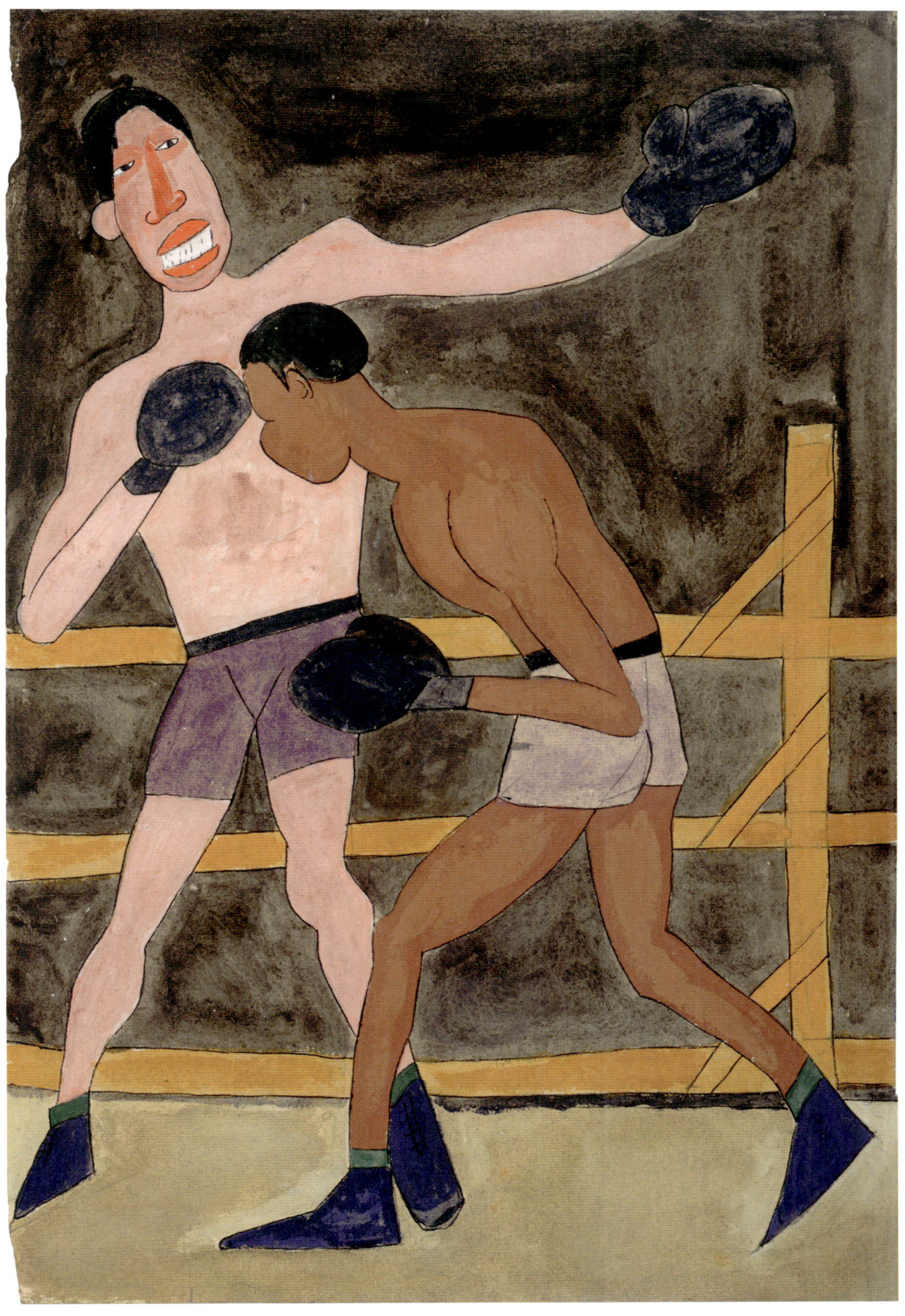

THREE GREAT DANCERS

ca. 1945
oil on paperboard
33 5⁄8 × 28 1⁄2 in.
Smithsonian American Art Museum
Gift of the Harmon Foundation

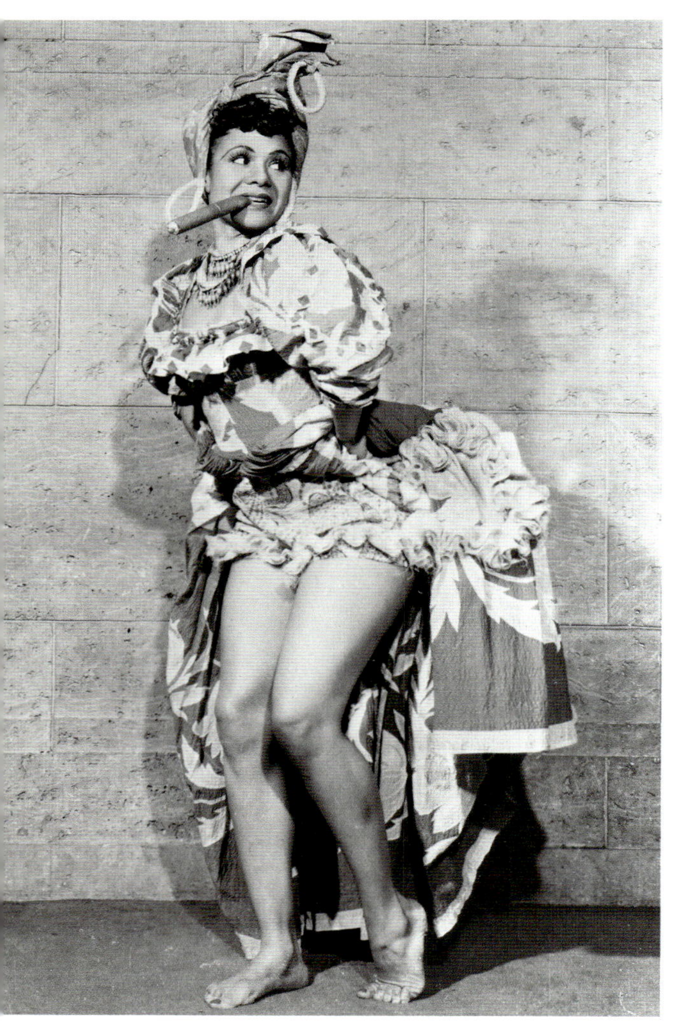

Katherine Dunham as Woman with a Cigar from the ballet *Tropics—Shore Excursion*, ca. 1943, Jerome Robbins Dance Division, The New York Public Library

THIS VIBRANT, DYNAMIC composition celebrates African American dancers Josephine Baker and Katherine Dunham. Like a theater set, Johnson's palm trees, drums, and bananas evoke African and Caribbean settings as well as Afro-Caribbean music and culture. Swaying and leaping figures conjure those rhythms and the exuberance of the women's performances.

In the painting, Josephine Baker (1906–1975) takes center stage as three figures with kiss curls. Born in St. Louis, Missouri, she performed with Black vaudeville shows from a young age. In 1921, Baker went to New York City, where she appeared in the chorus line for *Shuffle Along*, a landmark Broadway show created by African Americans with an all-Black cast. Four years later she performed in Paris with other Black musicians and dancers in *La Revue Negre*. The liberation and frenetic energy of her movements in that show's "Danse Sauvage" catapulted her to fame. She went on to star in *La Folie du Jour* at Paris's famed cabaret the Folies Bergère, where she donned her iconic banana skirt. Finding more freedom and acceptance in Parisian society, she became a French citizen and spent much of her life and career there.

Katherine Dunham (1909–2006) (shown in the lower left in a blue top and with a cigar) formed one of the first African American dance companies in the United States and many dance schools. An anthropology major

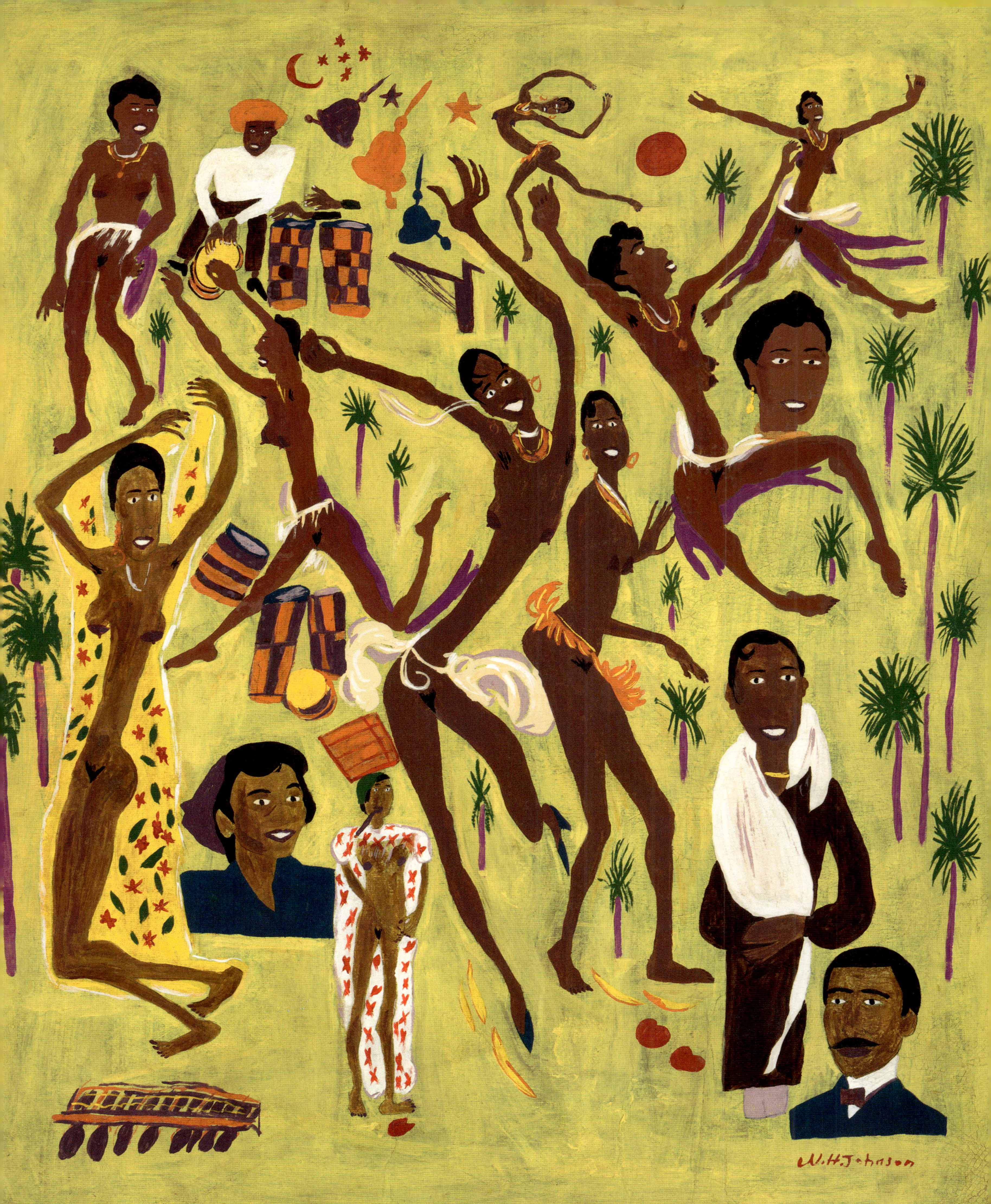
W.H.Johnson

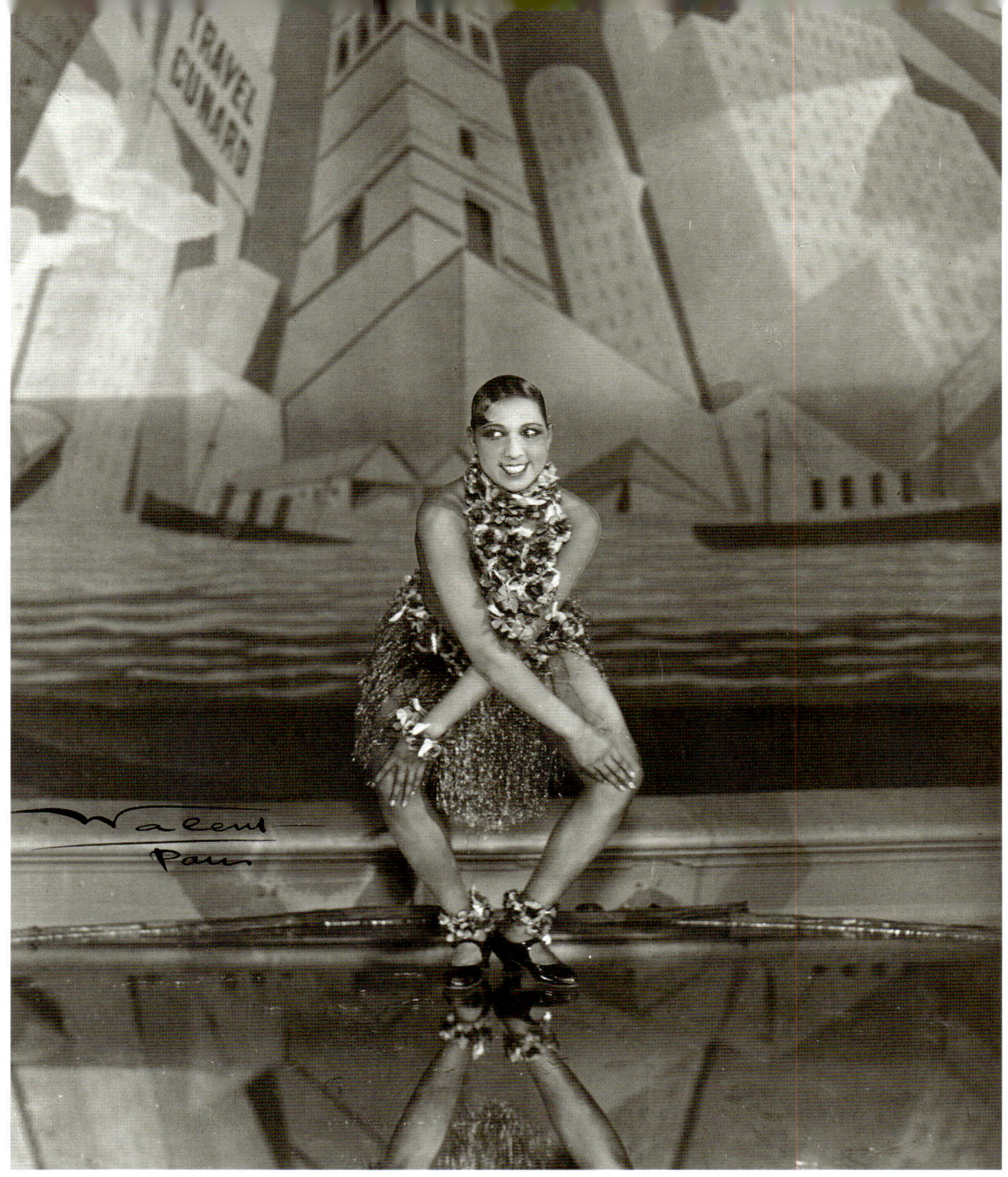

Smithsonian Connections

Josephine Baker was not only a dancer, singer, and actor, but also a civil rights activist. She pushed back against stereotypes about Black women throughout her career in France, embracing her sexuality with confidence and agency in her expressive dance moves. Fighting against racial discrimination, she refused to perform for segregated audiences. During World War II, she utilized her fame and charisma to smuggle secrets on behalf of the French Resistance. Baker received numerous accolades for these efforts, including the French Resistance Medal, Croix de Guerre, and Legion of Honor. In 2021, she posthumously received France's highest honor with her induction into the Panthéon, the nation's mausoleum for heroes. Baker is the first Black woman, American, and performer to be included.

Stanislaus Julian Walery, *Josephine Baker*, 1926, gelatin silver print, 8 $^{3}/_{4}$ × 6 $^{3}/_{8}$ in., National Portrait Gallery, Smithsonian Institution, NPG.95.105

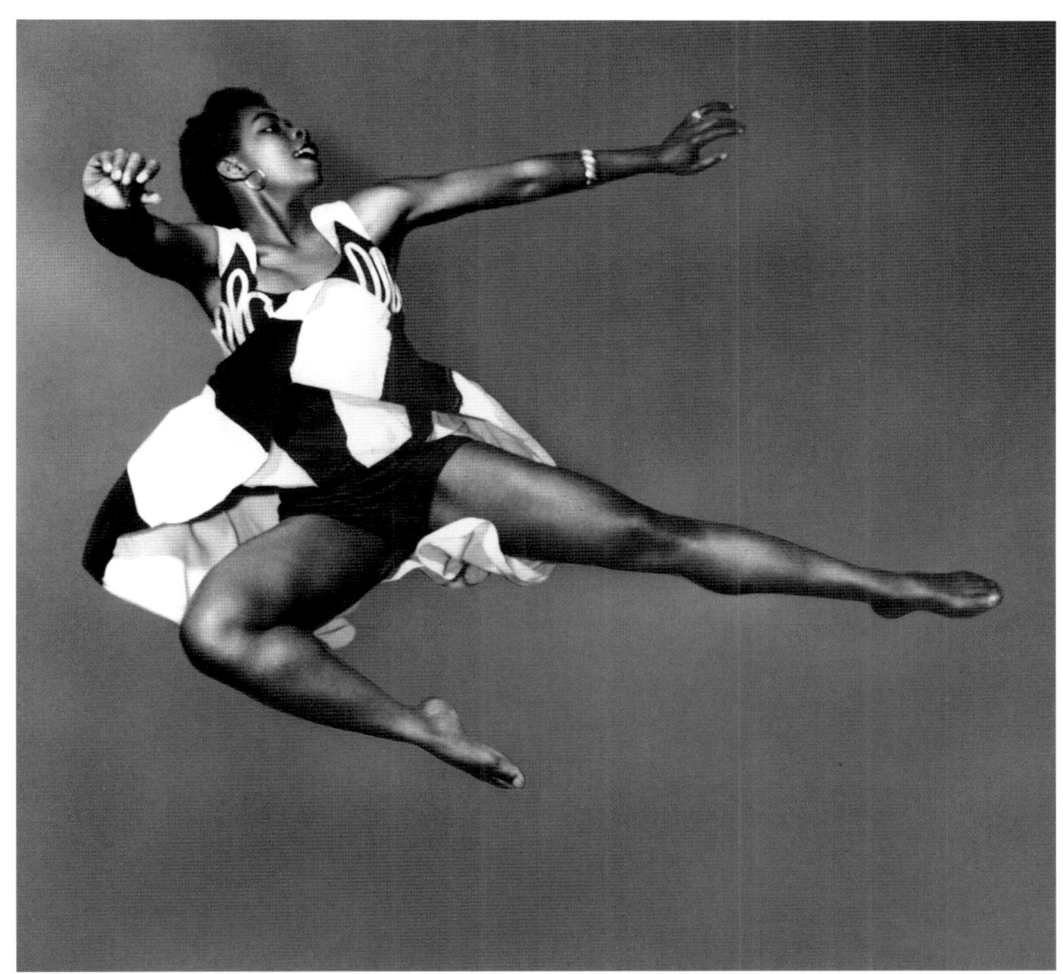

Gerda Peterich, *Pearl Primus*, 1945, Syracuse University Archives

at the University of Chicago, she won scholarships to film folk dances in the Caribbean in 1935. During nine months in Haiti, in particular, she began to understand the African roots of the country's dance traditions, and she used that knowledge to develop a new form of African American dance. In 1940, she and her company debuted her *Tropics and Le Jazz Hot (From Haiti to Harlem)*, based on Caribbean and Mexican sources and early African American social dances. For this work, Dunham created a seductress named Woman with a Cigar. In a revised version of the show, called *Tropical Revue* (1943), she smoked the cigar and carried a bird cage on her head, as she saw women in Cuba do.

The third "great dancer" in Johnson's title is likely Pearl Primus (1919–1994), whose works protested racism and discrimination. She choreographed and performed *Strange Fruit* (1943), for example, accompanied not by music, but the words of the anti-lynching poem. *Hard Time Blues* (1945) protested southern sharecropping and featured Primus's signature athletic jumps. One reviewer wrote that her dance "was exultant with the mastery over the law of gravitation." Primus won a scholarship in 1948 to study dance in West Africa, which influenced her later choreography and the dance schools she founded. Like Dunham, Primus studied anthropology and went on to earn a PhD from New York University. All three of these remarkable dancers overcame systemic racism and discrimination to create new techniques, dance companies, and schools that revolutionized modern dance.

—TDF

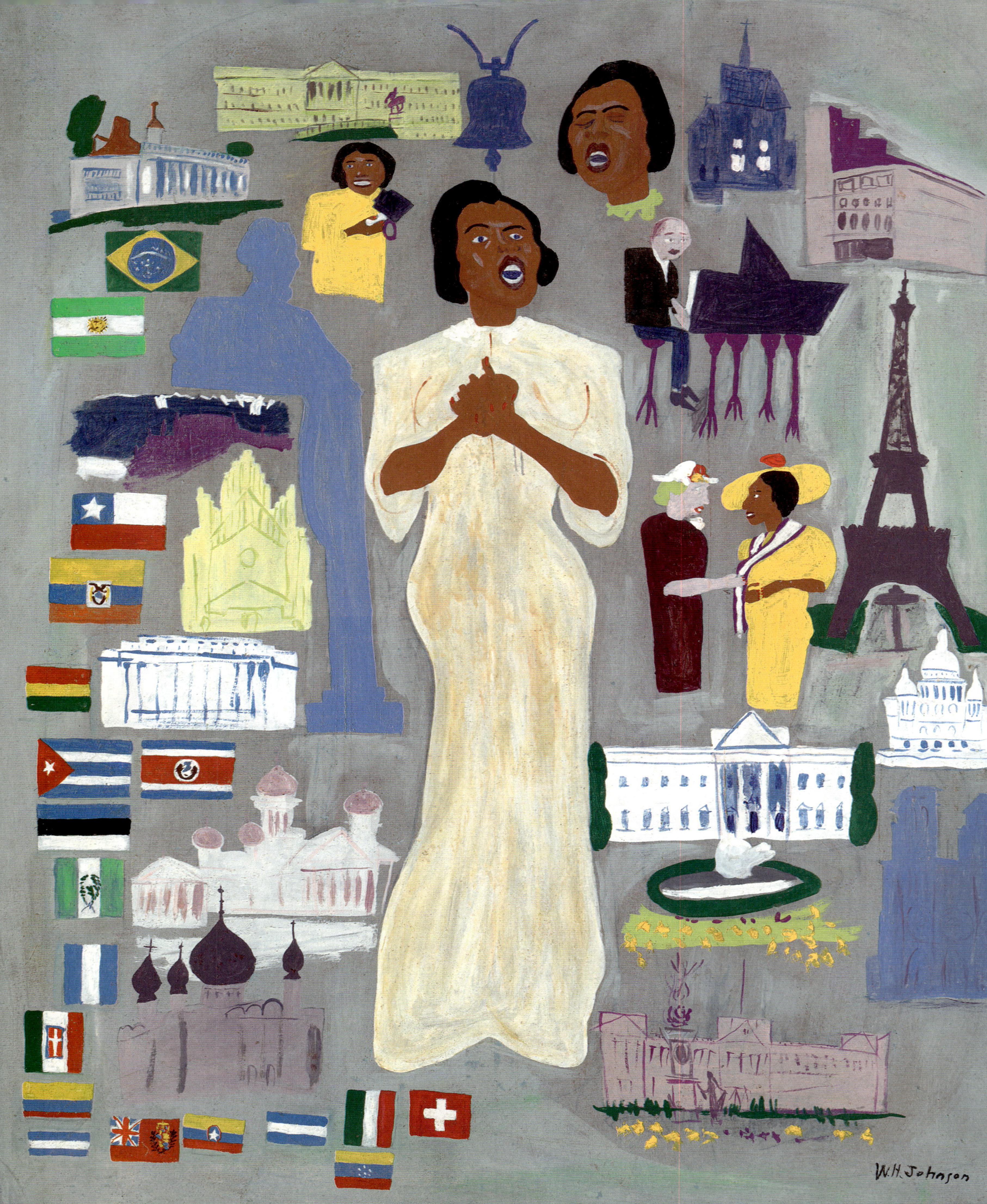
W.H. Johnson

MARIAN ANDERSON

ca. 1945
oil on paperboard
35 5/8 × 28 7/8 in.
Smithsonian American Art Museum
Gift of the Harmon Foundation

IN 1939, MARIAN ANDERSON (1897–1993)—an internationally acclaimed contralto renowned for her operatic arias, spirituals, and gospel music—was barred by the Daughters of the American Revolution (DAR) from performing at Washington, DC's Constitution Hall because of her race. Three years earlier, Anderson had performed at the White House—the first African American to do so—launching a friendship with First Lady Eleanor Roosevelt. On hearing of Anderson's rejection, the First Lady resigned her membership in the DAR in protest. The National Association for the Advancement of Colored People (NAACP), the Brotherhood of Sleeping Car Porters, the American Federation of Labor, and other national organizations also rallied in support of Anderson. Within weeks Secretary of the Interior Harold L. Ickes invited Anderson to sing on the steps of the Lincoln Memorial. Organizers and civil rights leaders leveraged the symbolism of the memorial as a stage—with the marble figure of the "Great Emancipator" gazing out from behind the performer. Anderson was initially reluctant: "I said yes, but the yes did not come easily or quickly.... As I thought further, I could see that my significance as an individual was small in this affair. I had become, whether I liked it or not, a symbol, representing my people." Attendance at the concert justified her decision. More than seventy-five thousand people came to hear her perform; millions more listened on the radio.

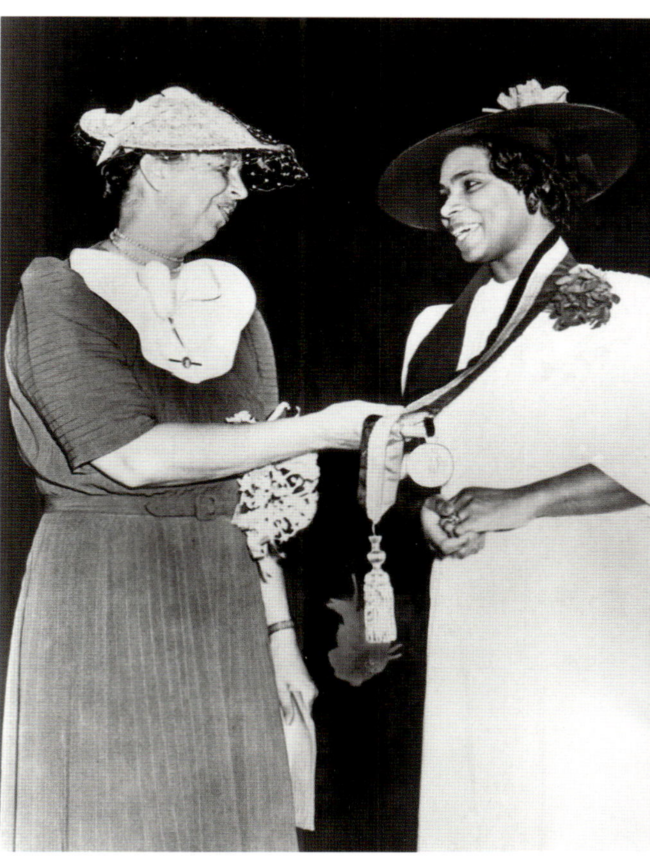

Eleanor Roosevelt awarding Marian Anderson the NAACP's Spingarn Medal for outstanding achievement by an African American, 1939

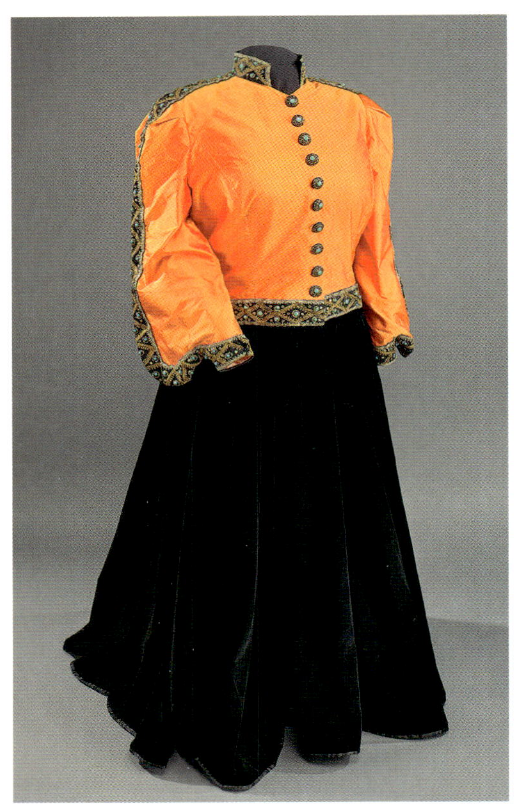

Ensemble associated with Marian Anderson's 1939 Lincoln Memorial concert, 1939; modified 1993, jacket: silk, metal, thread, sequin; skirt: nylon velveteen, tulle, metal, cloth, Collection of the Smithsonian National Museum of African American History and Culture, Gift of Ginette DePreist in memory of James DePreist, 2014.27.2

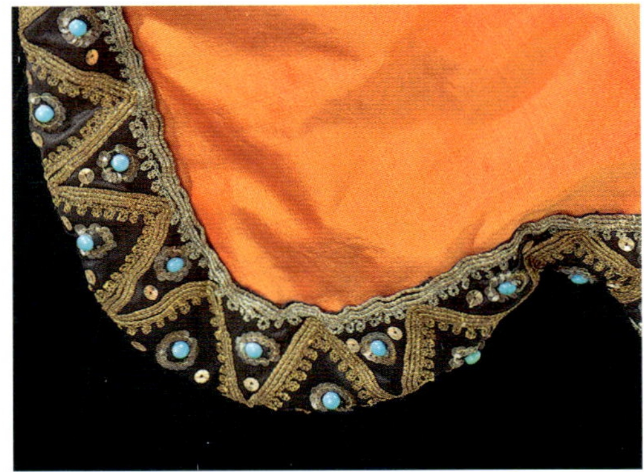

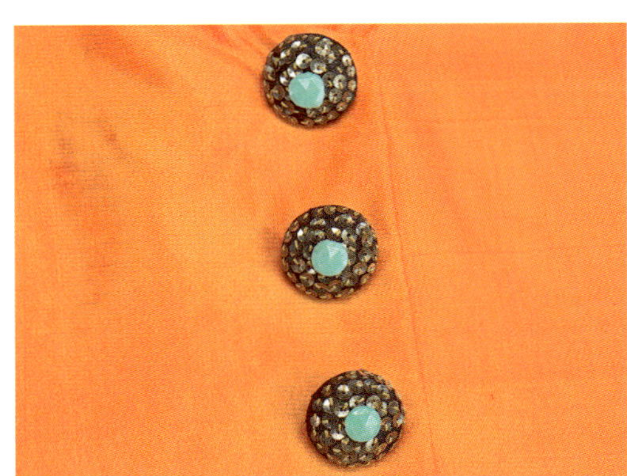

Smithsonian Connections

Wearing a long black velvet skirt with a slight train and an orange tailored jacket with embellished buttons and trim beneath her fur coat, Marian Anderson stood bravely on the steps of the Lincoln Memorial on Easter Sunday, April 9, 1939. In front of a racially integrated crowd of seventy-five thousand people, she sang "My Country, 'Tis of Thee"—a song representing freedom, justice, and equality.

Anderson broke down color barriers throughout her international career as a contralto, refusing to sing to segregated audiences, and paving the way for future African American performers. She prided herself on her sense of style, recognizing it as a symbol of racial progress and possibility. By 1993, the original orange velvet jacket was disintegrating and needed repair. With Anderson's permission, it was remade using an exact color match in silk fabric, along with the original collar, trim, and buttons.

In his introduction Ickes praised Anderson, stating, "Genius draws no color line." However, even after the success of her Lincoln Memorial concert, Anderson continued to face racial bias in the United States. It wasn't until 1955 that she became the first African American soloist to perform at the Metropolitan Opera in New York City. Nevertheless, she continued touring and sang at the 1961 inauguration of President John. F. Kennedy. In 1963 she won the Presidential Medal of Freedom, the nation's highest civilian honor—the same year she again performed at the Lincoln Memorial for the March on Washington for Jobs and Freedom. There she sang the spiritual "He's Got the Whole World in His Hands," during the same program in which Dr. Martin Luther King Jr. gave his "I Have a Dream" speech. Soon thereafter the Civil Rights Act

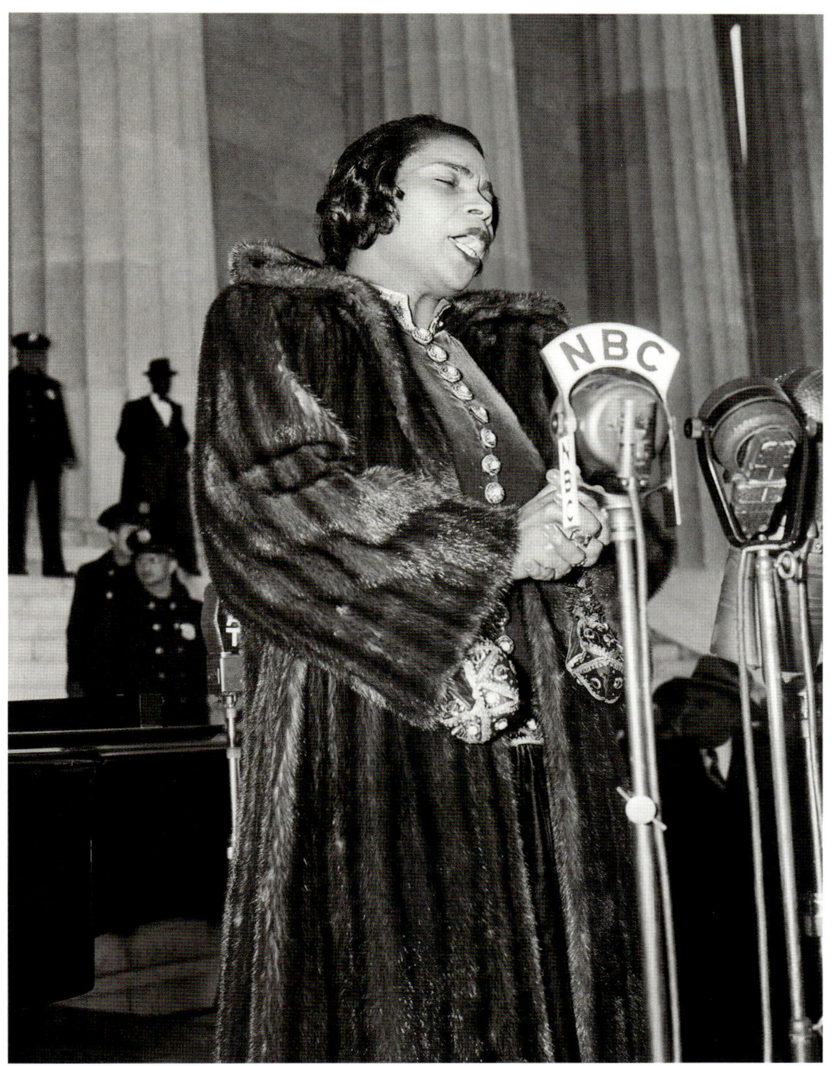

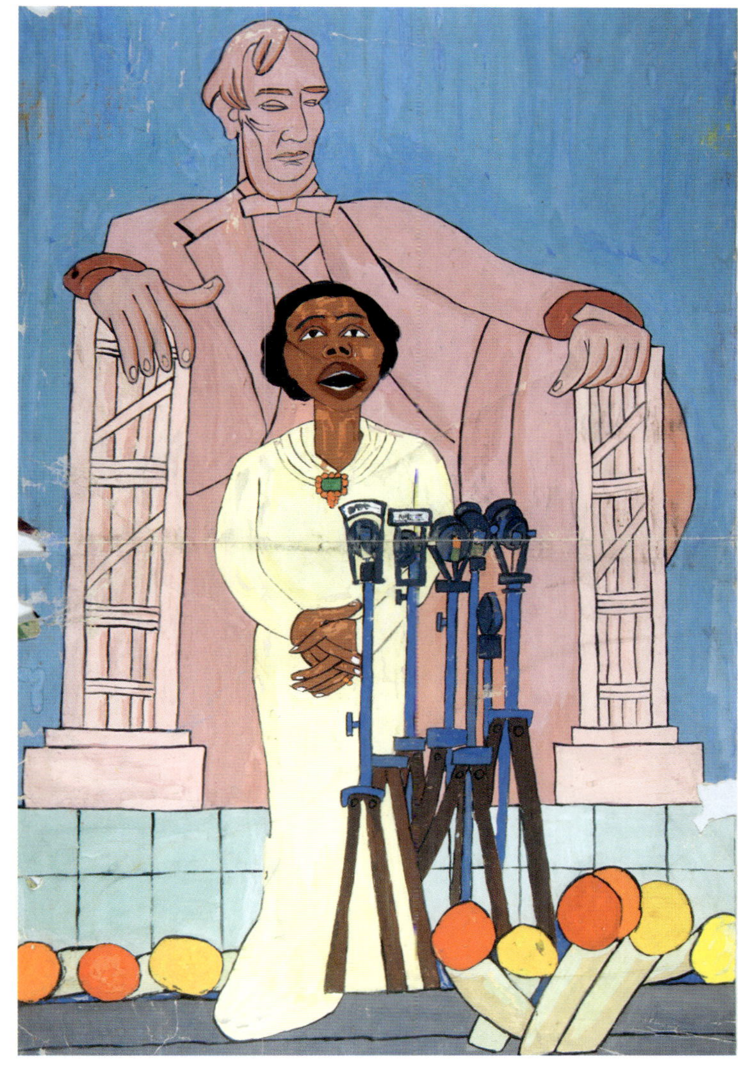

Anderson performing on the steps of the Lincoln Memorial, April 9, 1939

Marian Anderson #1, ca. 1939, tempera on paper, 37 ⅝ × 20 ⅝ in., Smithsonian American Art Museum, Gift of the Harmon Foundation, 1967.59.318R-V

of 1964 made it illegal to discriminate on the basis of race, color, religion, sex, or national origin.

Johnson painted at least three portraits of this trailblazing performer and civil rights activist. Two show Anderson standing in front of the Lincoln Memorial. This one includes symbols of her international fame. Brazilian, Chilean, and other flags represent her tour of South America. The Eiffel Tower in Paris, St. Basil's Cathedral in Moscow, and other monuments track her popularity across Europe. Johnson also flanks Anderson with the White House and Lincoln Memorial, honoring her fight for equality at home. Among her many degrees and awards, Anderson, in yellow, is shown receiving the Spingarn Medal of the NAACP from First Lady Eleanor Roosevelt in July 1939.

—TDF

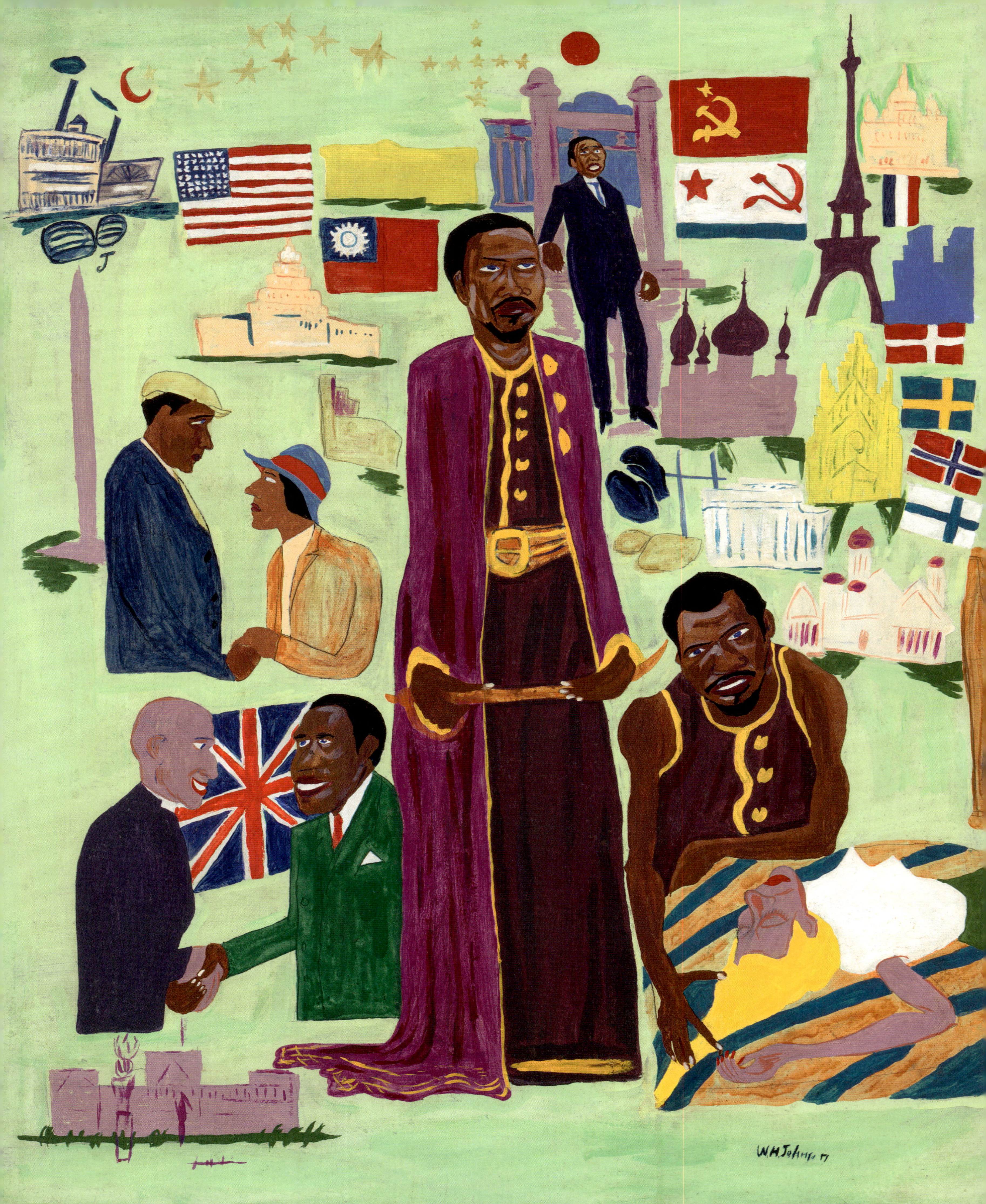

PAUL ROBESON'S RELATIONS

ca. 1945
oil on fiberboard
36 3/8 × 28 5/8 in.
Smithsonian American Art Museum
Gift of the Harmon Foundation

RENOWNED SINGER AND ACTOR Paul Robeson (1898–1976) excelled in academics and athletics at Rutgers University and earned a law degree at Columbia University before he became a theatrical star. Robeson was also a political activist who fought against oppression worldwide. In this painting, Johnson centered Robeson in costume as the protagonist in Shakespeare's play *Othello: The Moor of Venice*. Even though the drama spotlights a main character with dark skin, that role had traditionally been cast with white actors. Robeson made history as the first African American to assume the title character in a major U.S. production, from 1943 to 1944 on Broadway. He had previously starred in a staging of *Othello* at the Savoy Theatre, in London's West End, in 1930. Significantly, Johnson depicts Robeson in Othello's robes from the New York City performances. The contract for that show gave Robeson the final say "solely and exclusively" in not only casting decisions but also costuming; such was his fame and power in the theater world at that time. The lower right corner shows Robeson as Othello with the character's white wife, Desdemona, in the tragic moment after he has killed her and before he takes his own life.

Surrounding the Othello portraits are symbols of the actor's varied accomplishments. The steamboat at top left refers to Robeson's role as Joe in the musical *Show Boat*. He starred in the 1928 London stage production and in the 1936 Hollywood film adaptation. Jerome Kern and Oscar Hammerstein II wrote

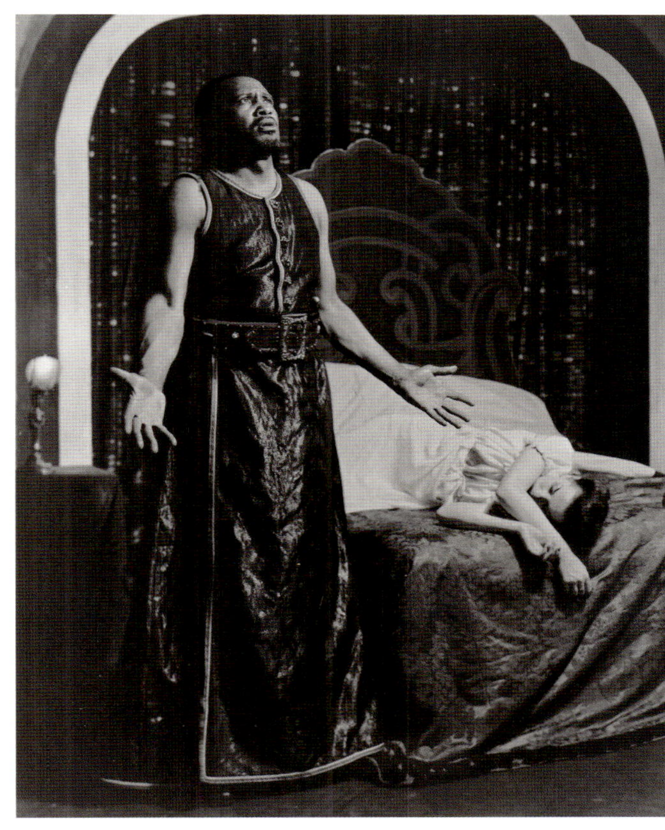

Scene from *Othello* with Paul Robeson in the title role and Uta Hagen as Desdemona, Theatre Guild production, ca. 1943–44, Library of Congress Prints and Photographs Division

the song "Ol' Man River" specifically for Robeson's rich, expressive voice. The baseball bat at the painting's far right refers to Robeson's talks with Major League Baseball leaders in late 1943, in which he successfully pressed for Black players to be admitted to the league. Leveraging his celebrity status to speak out against injustice in the United States before the Civil Rights Movement was formally organized, he also refused to sing to racially segregated audiences in the Jim Crow South (opposite right).

The woman at the left, in the blue hat, is Robeson's wife, Eslanda Goode Robeson (1895–1965), who had a successful career in her own right (opposite left). She studied chemistry at Columbia and worked as head chemist in the surgical pathology department at a New York City hospital before she became Robeson's business manager in 1926. Eslanda went on to study anthropology in London, travel to Africa several times, and publish books and articles, while also working in motion pictures. The scene depicted in Johnson's painting comes from the Robesons' avant-garde silent film from 1930, *Borderline*, in which they played Pete and Adah Marond, a married couple caught in an interracial love triangle.

Living in Great Britain and performing in Europe in the 1930s, Paul Robeson experienced Nazism in Germany and fascism during the Spanish Civil War. Consequently, he became an international political crusader, fighting for workers' rights in Britain and denouncing authoritarian leaders in Europe. His activism extended to Pan-African issues as well. In 1937, Robeson cofounded the Council on African Affairs (originally named the International Committee on African Affairs), a nonprofit based in New York City that publicized problems on the continent, especially the

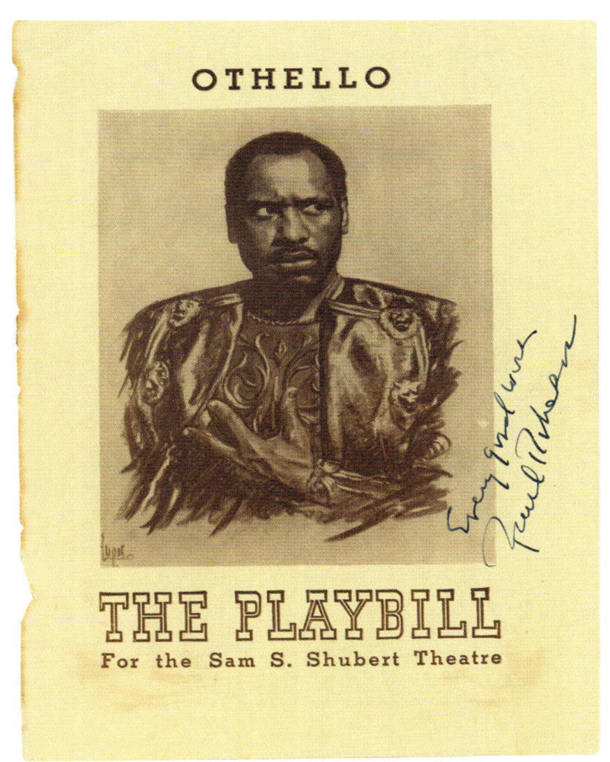

Smithsonian Connections

Actor, singer, and activist Paul Robeson made history in 1943 as the first African American man to play the lead in a major U.S. production of Shakespeare's *Othello*. This playbill from Broadway's Shubert Theatre, signed by Robeson, commemorates his groundbreaking performance. At a time of widespread segregation and hostility toward interracial relationships, it was risky for an African American man to play the lover and eventual murderer of the white Desdemona on stage. Critics praised Robeson's performance, noting that its real life racial dynamics gave increased weight to Othello's motivations. Audiences were likewise captivated by the production, which remains the longest-running Shakespeare play on Broadway.

Program for *Othello* signed by Paul Robeson, 1944, ink on paper, National Portrait Gallery, Smithsonian Institution, Gift of June Barnes, AD/NPG.99.2

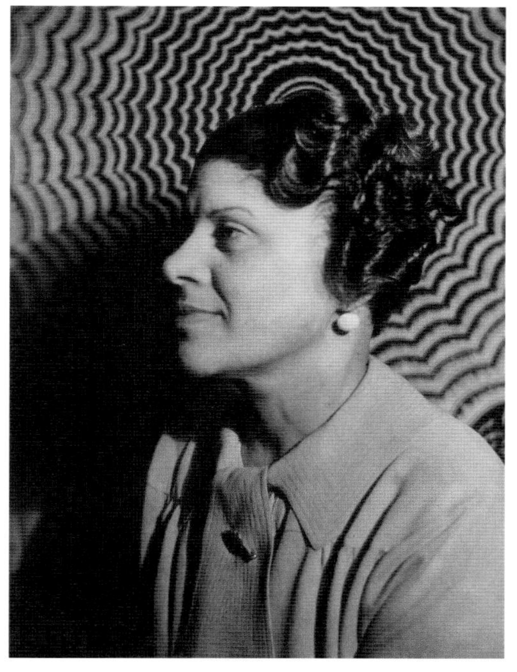

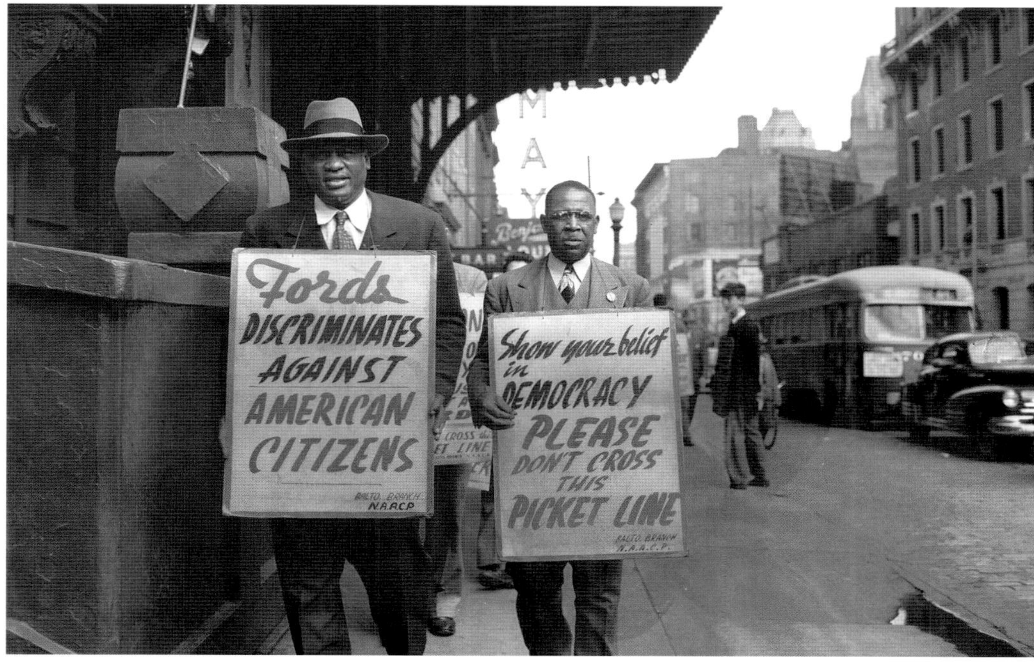

Carl Van Vechten, *Eslanda G. Robeson, from the unrealized portfolio "Noble Black Women: The Harlem Renaissance and After,"* 1936, printed 1983, photogravure, 8 7/8 × 6 in., Smithsonian American Art Museum, Transfer from the National Endowment for the Arts, 1983.63.141

Paul S. Henderson, *Paul Robeson and Dr. John E. T. Camper protesting Ford's Theatre Jim Crow admission policy,* 1948, H. Furlong Baldwin Library, Maryland Center for History and Culture, Paul S. Henderson Photograph Collection

exploitation of people under colonial rule. Eslanda joined him in campaigning for freedom for Africa's people.

This painting likely had personal significance for William H. Johnson because he had met Robeson in Denmark in 1936. Robeson bought two of Johnson's paintings from a New York exhibition as well. The flags on the far right side refer to Robeson's concert tours to Nordic countries, including Denmark (the red and white flag below the Eiffel Tower). After performing in the Soviet Union (referenced by the onion domes of St. Basil's Cathedral in Moscow and the red Soviet flag above it), Robeson said that there, for the first time in his life he was treated "not as a Negro, but as a human being." Robeson's time in the Soviet Union and his political activism made him a target of investigations during the Red Scare, when many U.S. policymakers sought out suspected American communists, whom they feared were disloyal. In 1950 the State Department revoked the Robesons' U.S. passports because of suspicions of Communist Party affiliation, preventing the singer from earning income abroad. When the Supreme Court ruled such actions illegal in 1958, their passports were returned. This political targeting, or "blacklisting," damaged his performing career at the time, though Robeson is now widely respected for his advocacy for peace and social justice.

—TDF

HAILE SELASSIE

ca. 1945
oil on plywood
32 7/8 × 25 1/2 in.
Smithsonian American Art Museum
Gift of the Harmon Foundation

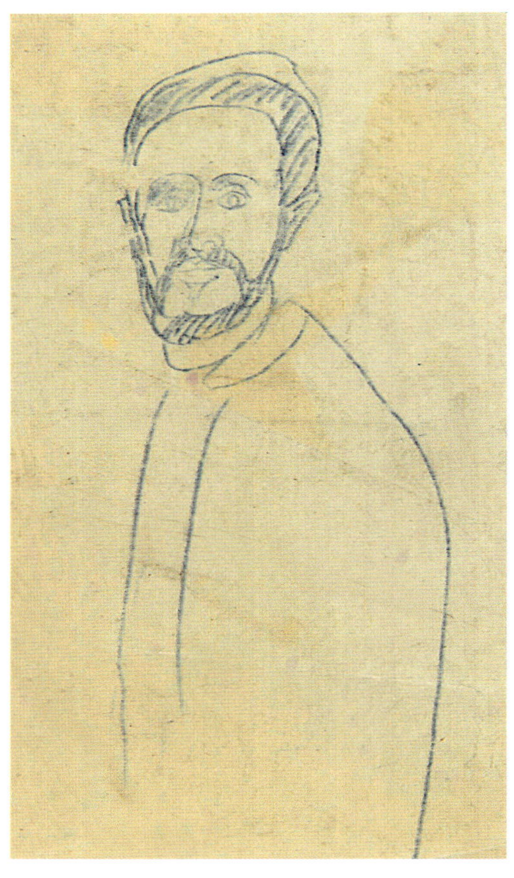

Haile Selassie, ca. 1945, carbon tracing on paper, 7 1/8 × 3 3/4 in., Smithsonian American Art Museum, Gift of the Harmon Foundation, 1967.59.412

HAILE SELASSIE was a well-known figure in the United States by the time Johnson featured him as a Fighter for Freedom. *Time* magazine had named him Man of the Year for 1935 and called him "the best and wisest ruler ancient Ethiopia has ever had." As Ethiopia's regent before becoming emperor, Selassie had gained the country's admission to the League of Nations, the international organization formed after World War I to promote cooperation among member countries. In 1930, Selassie was crowned "King of Kings" of Ethiopia. Within eight months, he introduced the country's first written constitution and took the initial steps to establish a democratic form of government. Selassie also fended off attempts by Great Britain and Italy to economically exploit Ethiopia. He inspired the Rastafari movement, an Afrocentric religious and social movement founded in Jamaica in the 1930s that considered Selassie's emperorship to be the fulfillment of a biblical prophecy—Ras [Prince] Tafari had been his title as regent.

Selassie's early success at avoiding colonialist incursions in Ethiopia was short-lived, however. In December 1935, Benito Mussolini's Italian troops invaded the country; in the spring they overran the capital of Addis Ababa and declared Ethiopia an Italian province. With little recourse, Selassie headed for Switzerland to address the League of Nations. He spoke eloquently about international morality; without collective action, he said, aggression on the part of large countries with unlimited access to "death-dealing weapons"

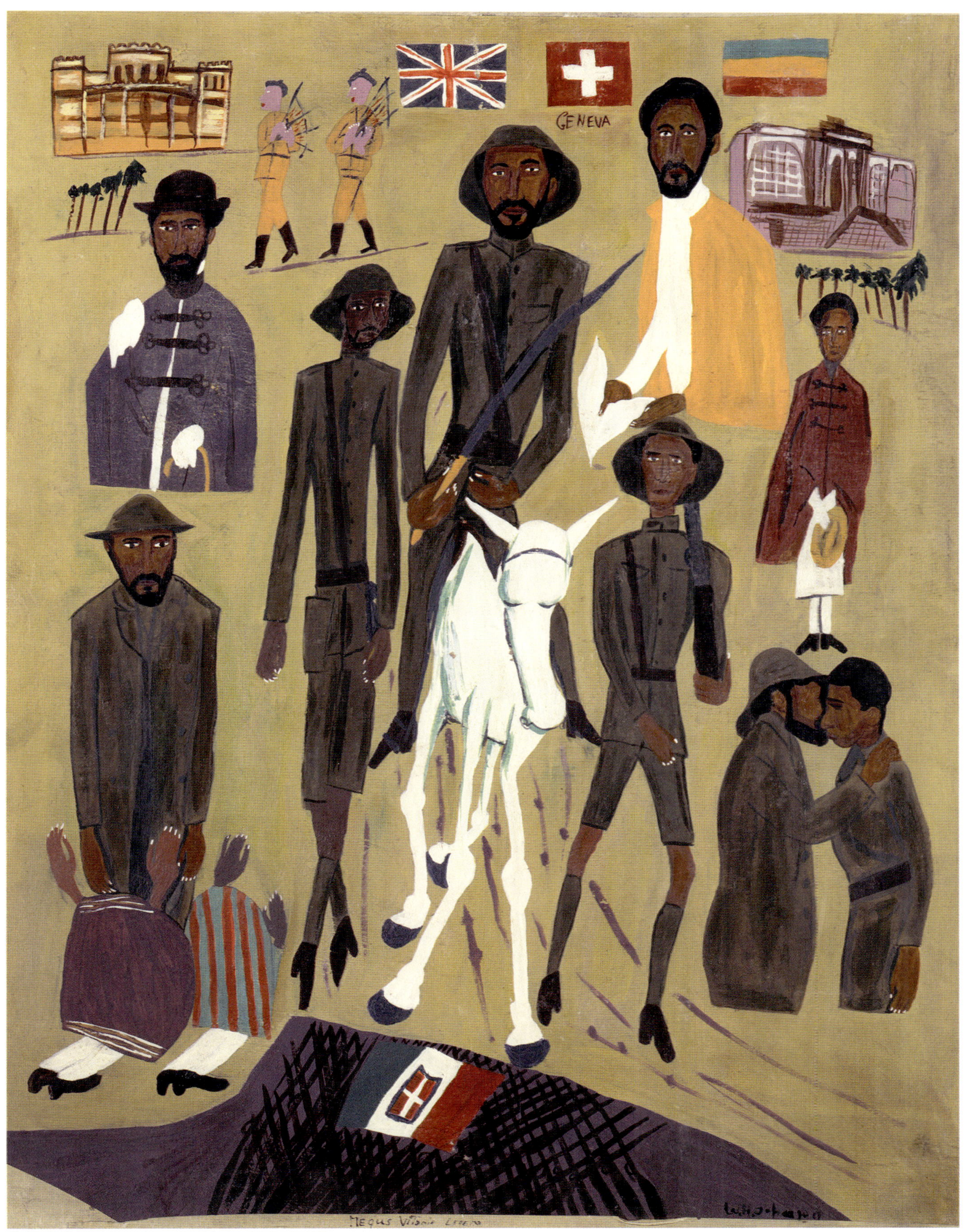
GENEVA

Opposite: Cover of *Time* magazine featuring Haile Selassie as Man of the Year, January 6, 1936

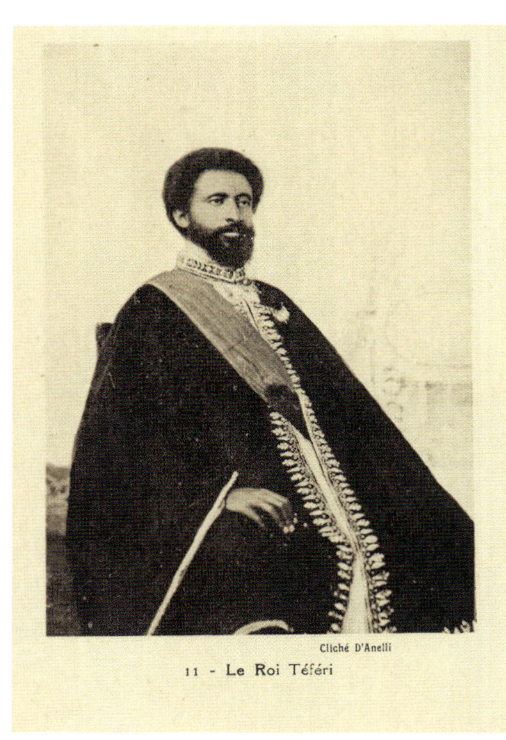

"Le Roi Téféri," postcard featuring Haile Selassie, ca. 1925, collotype, 5 ½ × 3 ½ in., Eliot Elisofon Photographic Archives, National Museum of African Art

threatened all small nations. Italian aircraft sprayed chemical weapons in Ethiopia that killed all living things in their wake, poisoning water and destroying crops.

Although at first the British offered little support against the Italians, after Mussolini joined forces with Adolf Hitler, they welcomed Selassie as a political exile. He spent the next five years in Bath, England, where he combatted Italian propaganda and nurtured relationships with friendly nations. In 1937, for example, Selassie delivered a radio address to the American people to thank them for their support and affirm that all peace-loving people should work to promote international harmony. In January 1941, once the Italian invaders were defeated, Selassie returned to the throne. A year later, on August 26, 1942, he abolished slavery, which had been practiced in Ethiopia for more than a thousand years.

Johnson had great respect for Selassie, whom he presented in multiple roles—as a military leader astride his iconic white horse, as a wise civilian leader holding the constitution in his hand, and, at the lower left, as a man adored by his people. At the top of the painting, Johnson featured flags of countries where Selassie had his greatest impact: his own country of Ethiopia (the green, yellow, and red banner) and Switzerland (identified by the word Geneva), where he had addressed the League of Nations. Beside the flag of Great Britain, where Selassie had lived in exile, he included two soldiers carrying bagpipes.

—VMM

FIFTEEN CENTS

January 6, 1936

TIME

The Weekly Newsmagazine

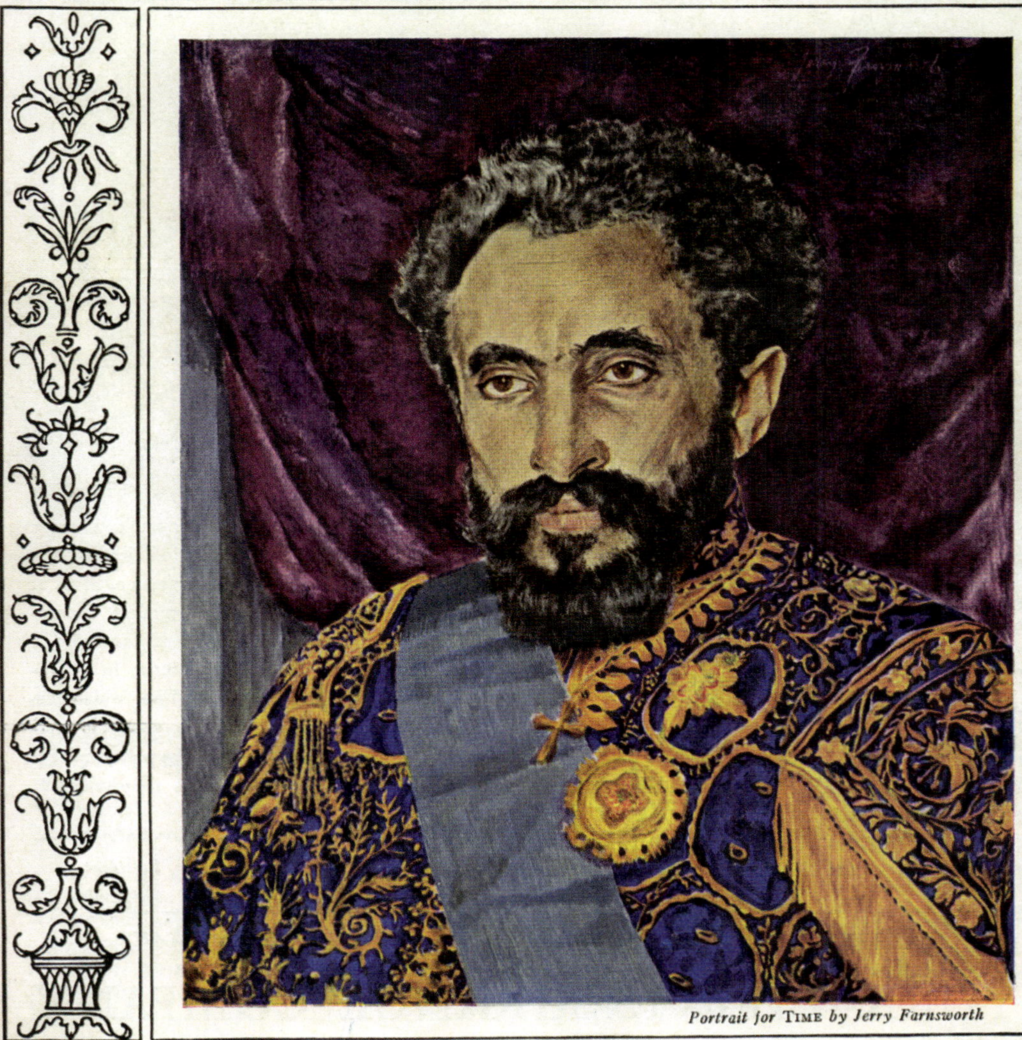

Portrait for TIME *by Jerry Farnsworth*

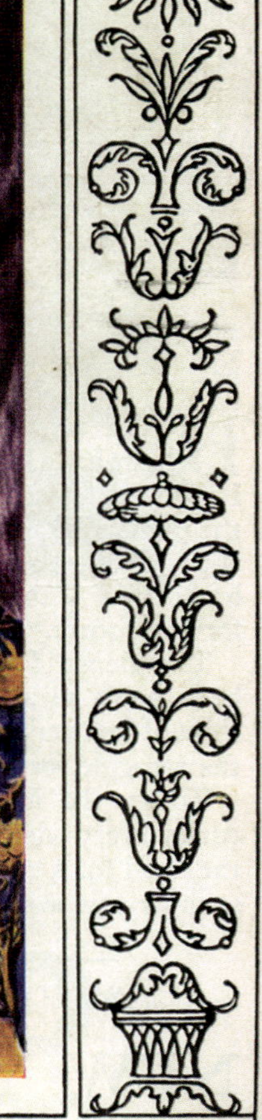

Volume XXVII

MAN OF THE YEAR

"... subject to negotiation."

(See FOREIGN NEWS)

Number 1

Circulation Office, *350 East 22nd Street, Chicago.* (Reg. U. S. Pat. Off.) Editorial and Advertising Offices, *135 East 42nd Street, New York.*

KING IBN SAUD

ca. 1945
oil on paperboard
35 5/8 × 28 5/8 in.
Smithsonian American Art Museum
Gift of the Harmon Foundation

BY THE TIME he met with President Franklin Roosevelt in February 1945, King Abdul Aziz ibn Saud was a legendary figure, a "self-made man on a heroic scale," according to *LIFE* magazine, which featured him on the cover of its May 31, 1945, issue. Born into the Saud royal family but raised impoverished in exile, Ibn Saud determined to expel those who had ousted his family and unite Saudi Arabia. Over the course of two decades he reconquered territory, and in 1932 he formed the peninsula's largest kingdom in over one thousand years.

As king, the renowned warrior was esteemed by his people for his commitment to Islam and deep belief in the Arab principles of generosity and hospitality—sharing one's possessions with those in need. He set up a centralized soup kitchen, irrigated

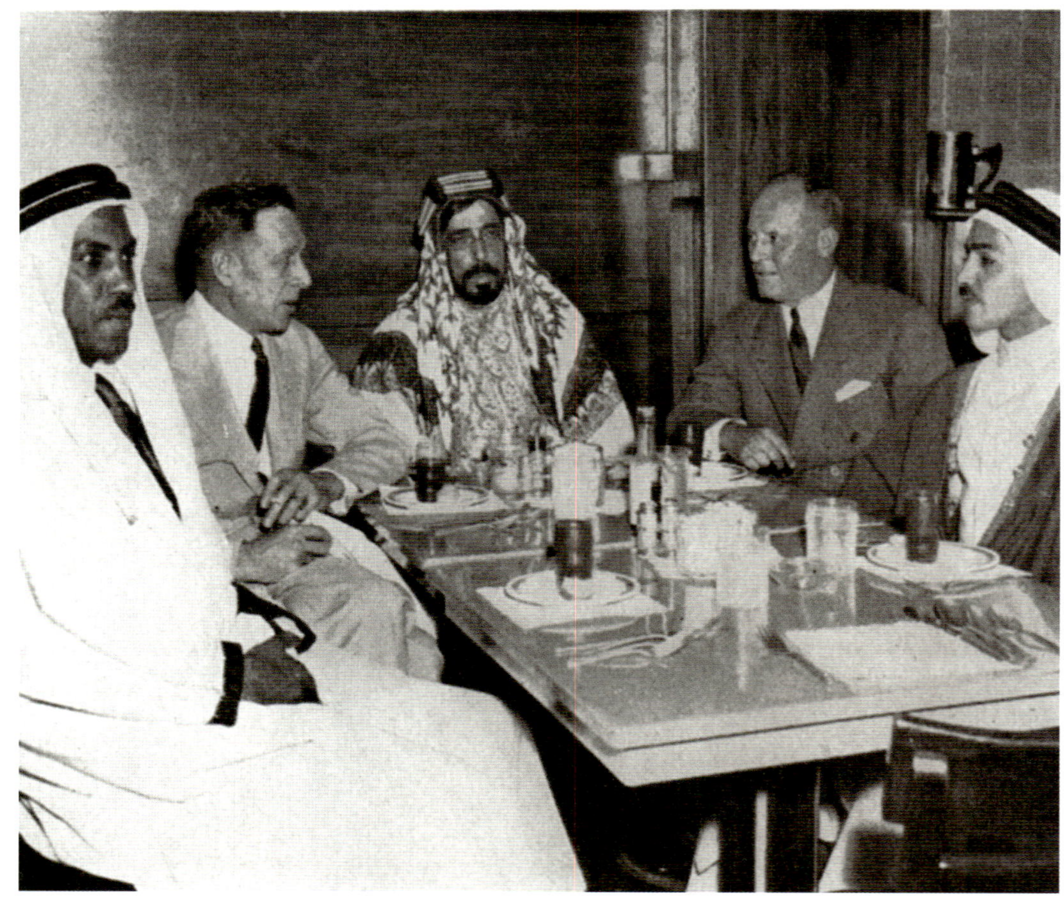

Photograph from "King of Arabia Sells His Oil for Profit, Not Politics, to U.S. Company," *LIFE* magazine, August 21, 1939. Johnson reproduced this grouping in the upper right of *King Ibn Saud.*

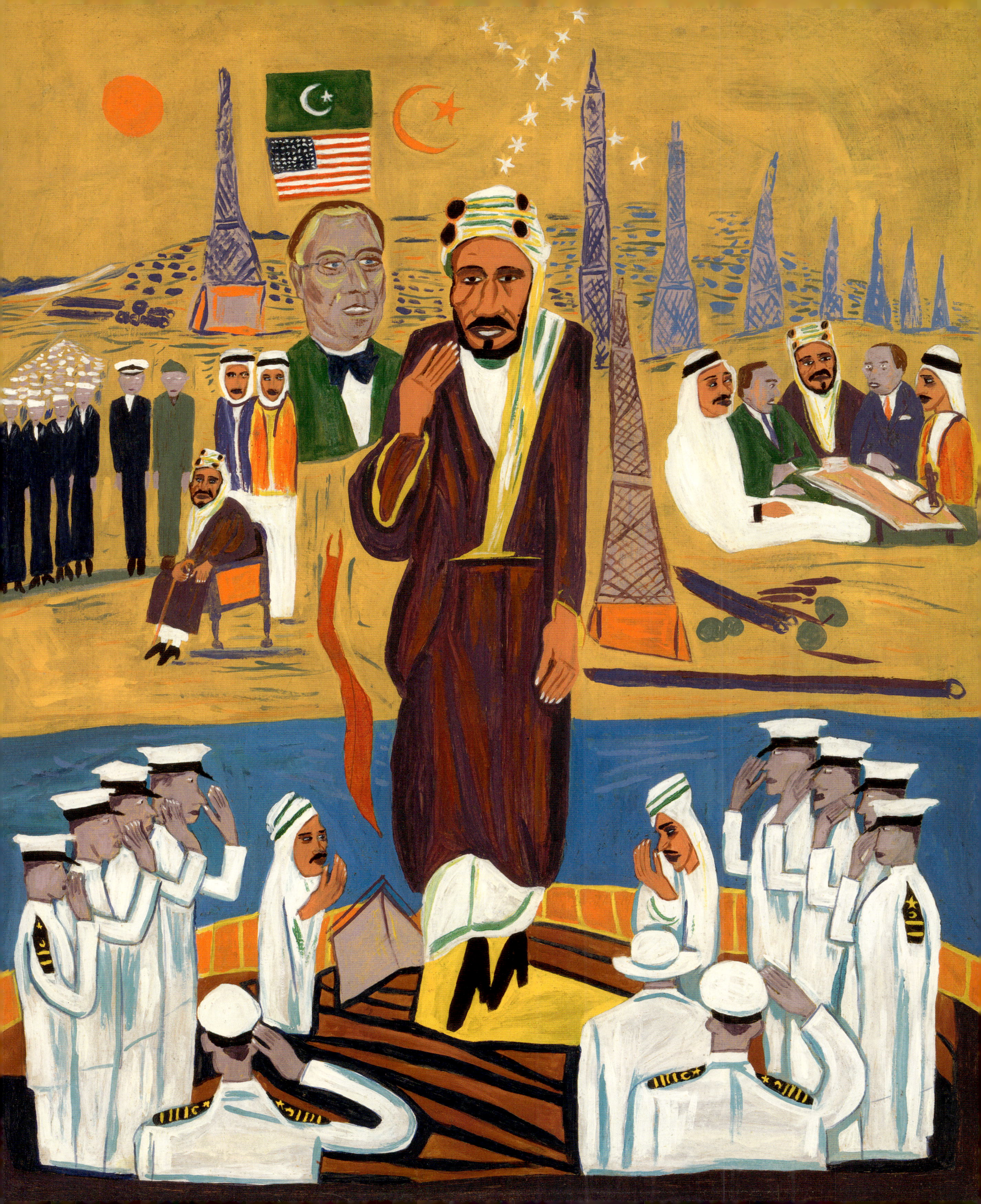

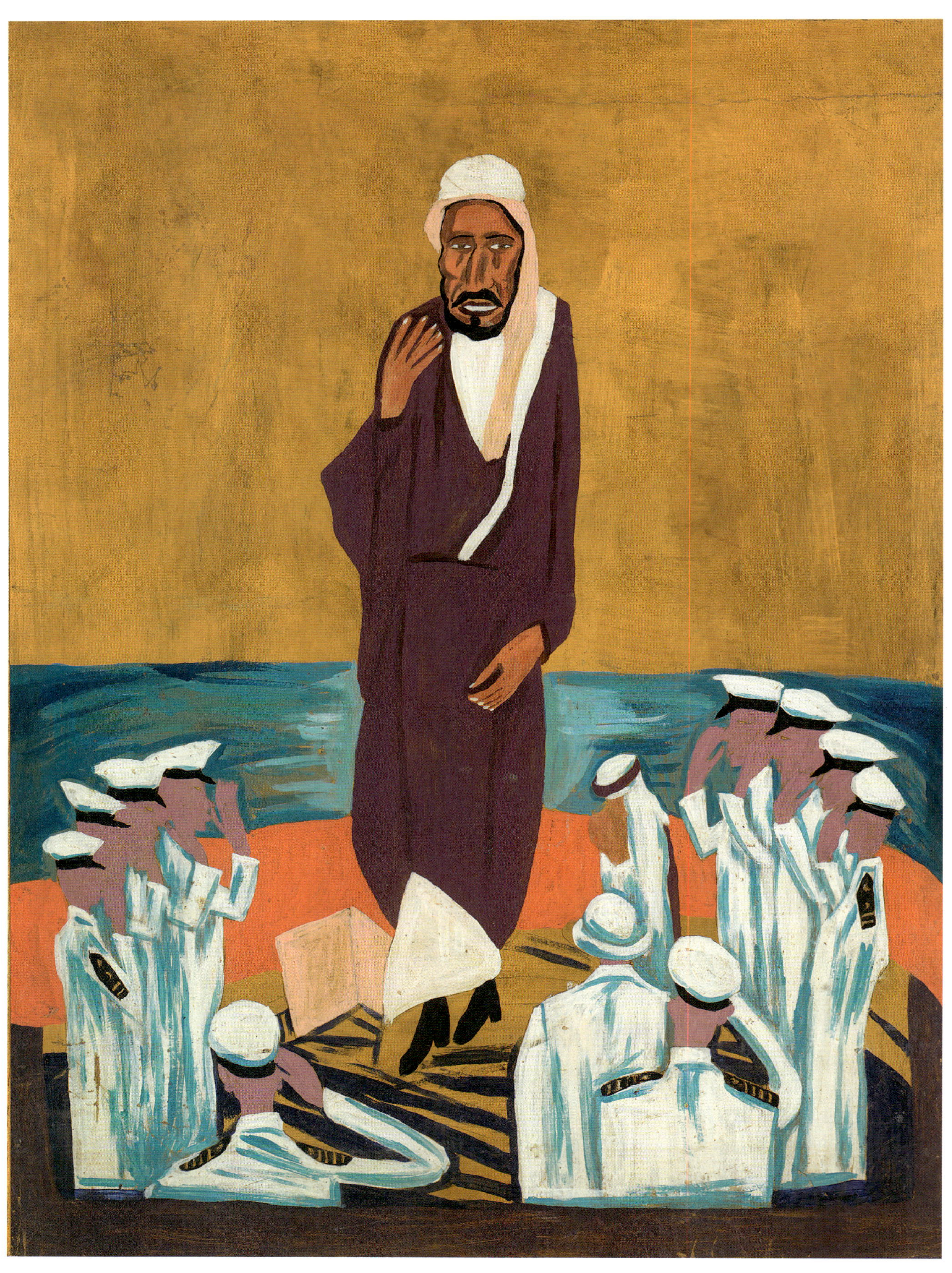

Opposite: *King Ibn Saud*, ca. 1944–45, oil on paperboard, 32 × 23 ⅞ in., Smithsonian American Art Museum, Gift of the Harmon Foundation, 1967.59.661

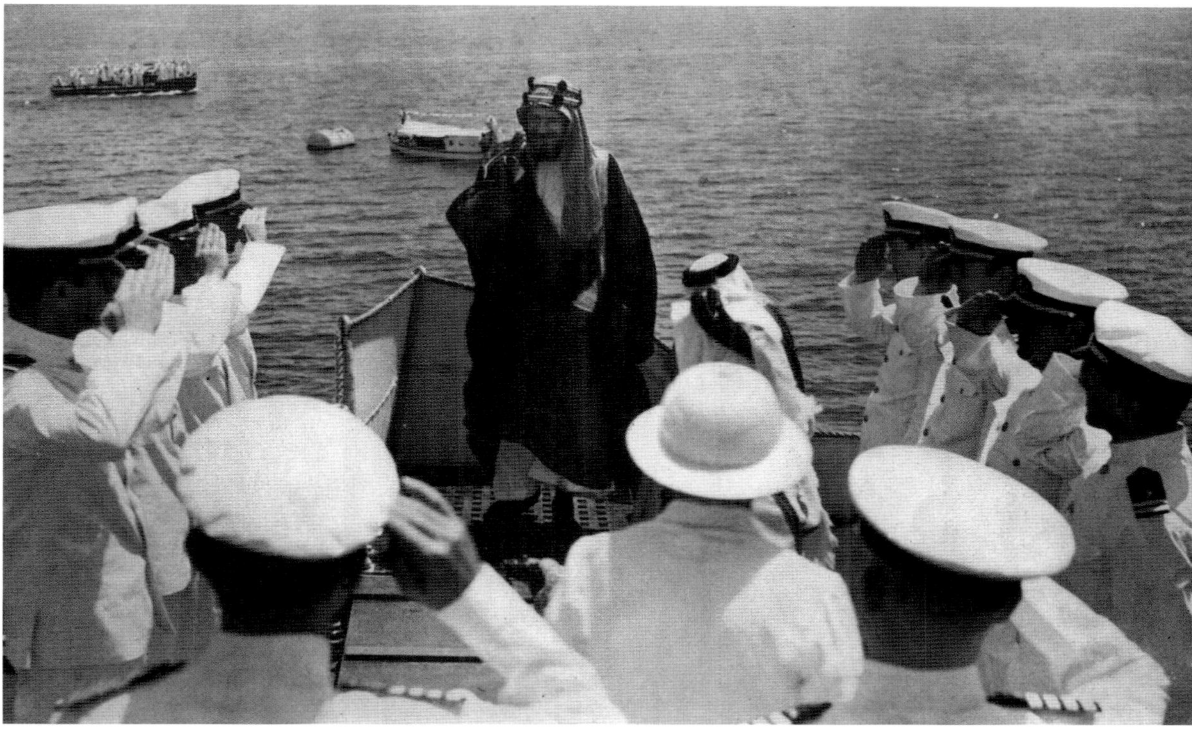

Ibn Saud saluted by American sailors aboard the U.S. tanker *Scofield*. Photograph from *LIFE* magazine, August 21, 1939

land for agriculture, and asserted the integrity of individual property rights—all with an eye to developing national unity. Understanding that modern communications technology was essential to implementing reform, he built the country's first radio towers and broadcast scripture over the airwaves.

Standing over six feet tall, King Ibn Saud was absolute monarch over one of the world's richest but mostly untapped oil fields. Recently discovered oil was bringing wealth to neighboring Bahrain, so, in 1933, Ibn Saud leased 165,000 square miles to an American partnership to explore for oil. Rather than accept more lucrative offers from Britain, France, Germany, Italy, or Japan, he signed with the consortium of U.S. oil companies because the Americans offered a business proposition with no political strings attached. By May 1939, Saudi oil was pumping through a forty-three-mile pipeline the Americans had built from eastern Saudi Arabia to the Persian Gulf.

The king's meeting with President Roosevelt was historic. Held in secret aboard the USS *Quincy* in the Suez Canal, the conference cemented a relationship between the king, who wanted to preempt colonialist political entanglements, and Roosevelt, who was concerned about wartime oil consumption and the depletion of reserves in the Americas.

Johnson borrowed both the images of Ibn Saud saluted by American naval officers and the figures seated around a table on the right side of the painting from a *LIFE* magazine article published in 1939, less than a year after the artist moved back to New York from Scandinavia. The desert landscape behind Ibn Saud is punctuated by a row of towers receding into the distance, a reference to his radio broadcasting initiative. At the king's right is a portrait of Franklin Roosevelt; above their heads are flags of the United States and Egypt, where the meeting took place. (The Suez Canal is controlled by Egypt.) Johnson kept a scrapbook and folders of magazine and newspaper clippings that served as source material for his paintings. Those he used for *King Ibn Saud* indicate that Johnson had been thinking of the Arabian king for several years before including him in his constellation of freedom fighters.

—VMM

NEHRU AND GANDHI

ca. 1945
oil on paperboard
33 ⅞ × 27 ⅞ in.
Smithsonian American Art Museum
Gift of the Harmon Foundation

IN *NEHRU AND GANDHI*, Johnson honored two men who spent their lives working to free India from British colonial rule. Gandhi (right), the spiritual leader, pushed nonviolent protest and civil disobedience as effective tactics of resistance; the far-sighted Nehru drafted laws and, in 1947, the new nation's constitution. For two decades, Nehru and Gandhi defied British authority and were intermittently imprisoned for doing so. The British government's pushback was fierce. In 1942, after becoming prime minister, Winston Churchill declared that he had not become the country's leader "to preside over the liquidation of the British empire."

Mohandas Karamchand Gandhi (1869–1948), known as the Mahatma ("great-souled"), studied law in London before taking a job in the British colony of South Africa in 1893. On arriving he was stunned by the discrimination he faced. He was not allowed to ride with white passengers on public transportation and was once thrown off a train for refusing to leave the first-class compartment. For the next twenty-one years he campaigned for the civil rights of both Indian and Black South Africans. He organized nonviolent actions to protest unfair laws and was beaten and jailed for his efforts. When he returned to India in 1915, Gandhi's profound belief in nonviolent resistance shaped his political and social actions, and as president of the Indian National Congress in the early 1920s he launched campaigns to address the country's desperate poverty, expand women's rights, and improve the lot of the people called "untouchables,"

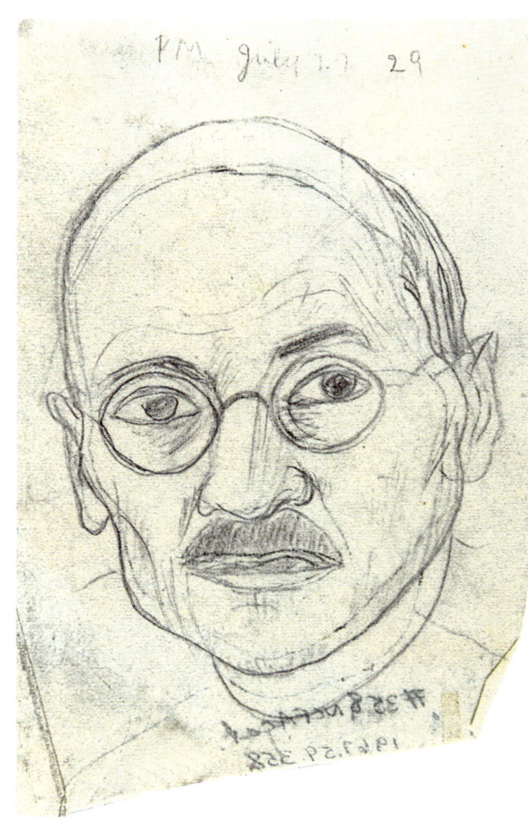

Gandhi, ca. 1945, colored pencil and pencil on paper, 6 ⅝ × 4 ½ in., Smithsonian American Art Museum, Gift of the Harmon Foundation, 1967.59.358R–V

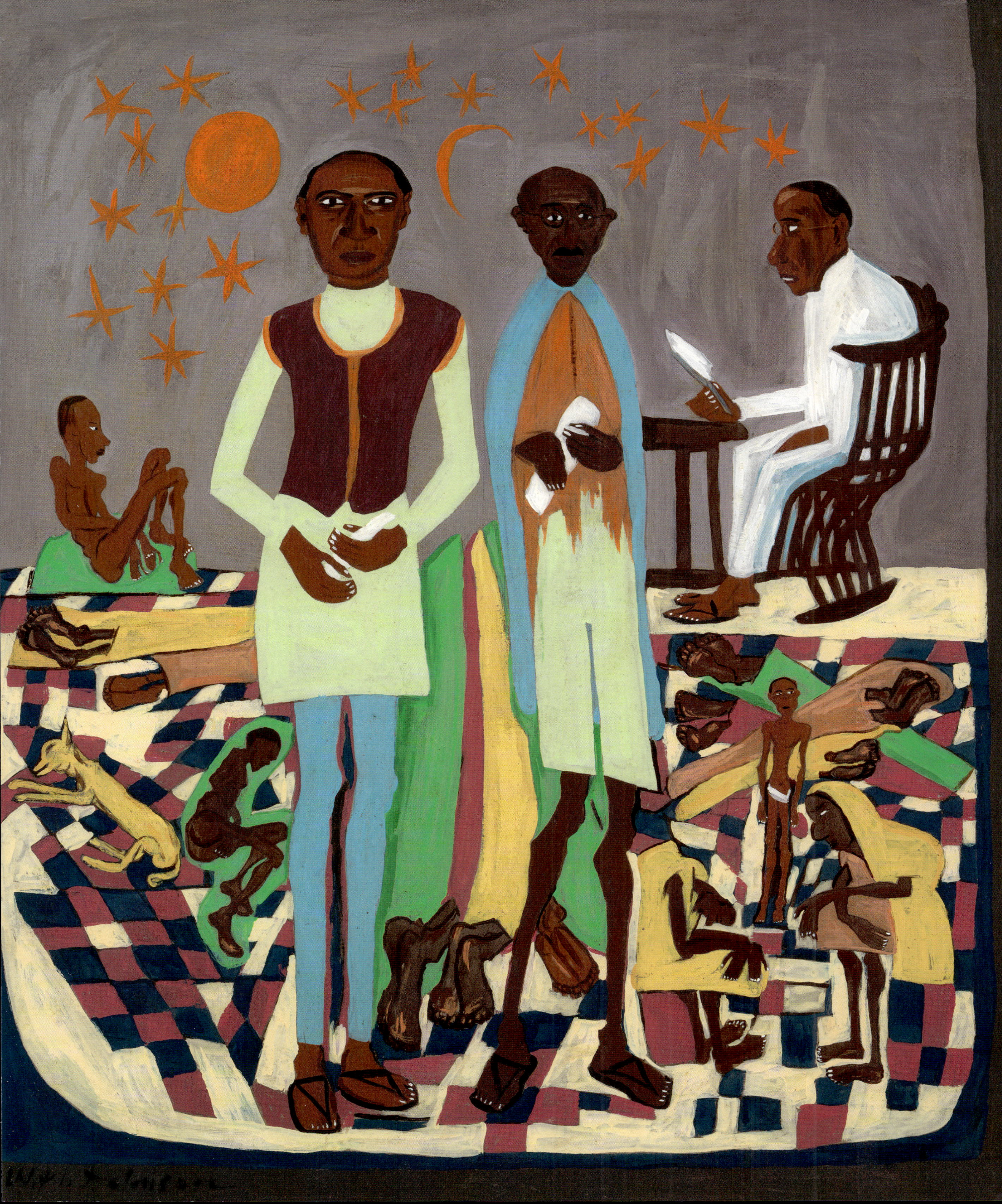

Gandhi, ca. 1945, carbon tracing on paper, 20 ⅛ × 15 in., Smithsonian American Art Museum, Gift of the Harmon Foundation, 1967.59.540R–V

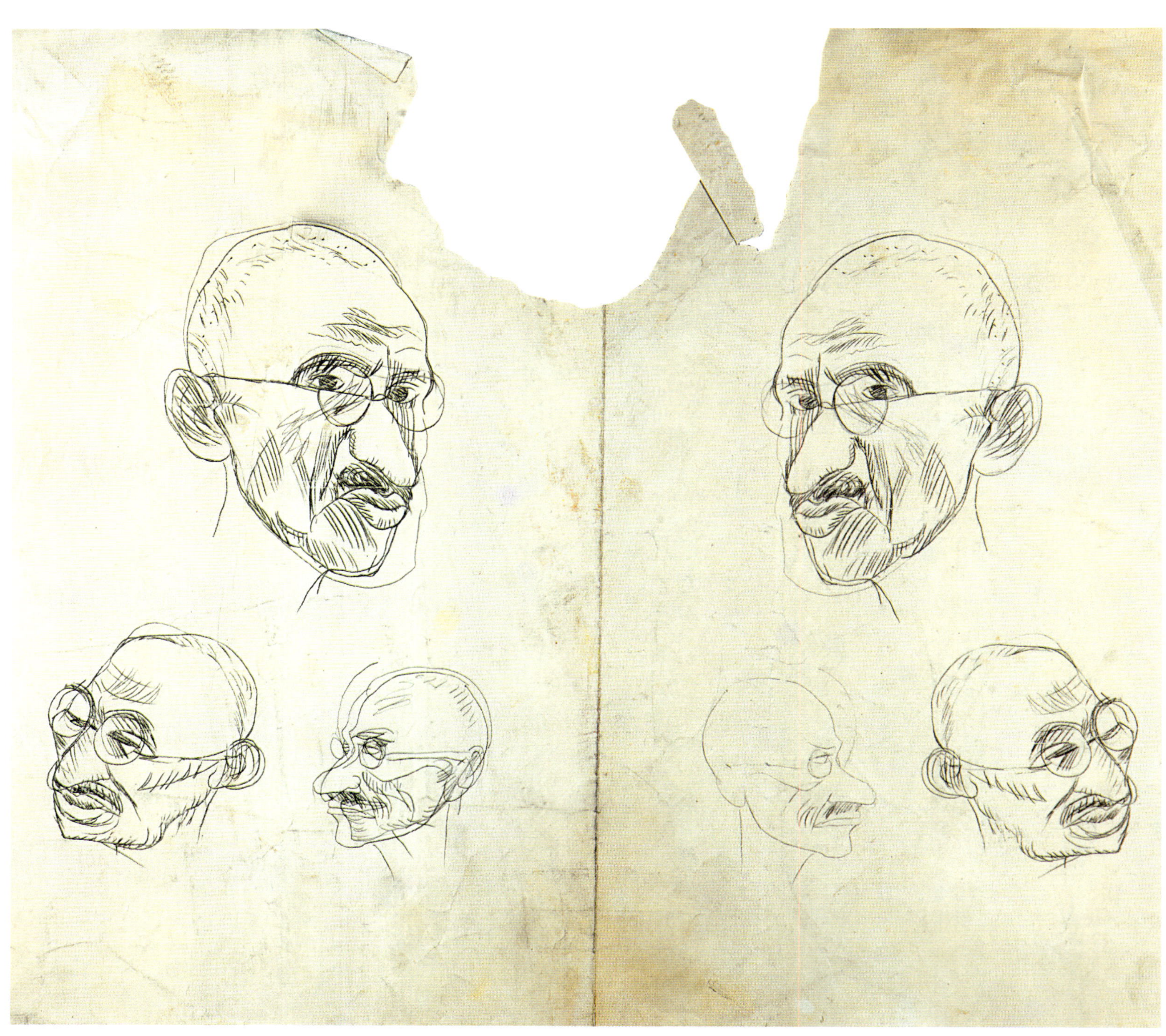

whom Gandhi called "children of God." He also advocated noncooperation, urging Indians to boycott British products, ignore British laws, and refuse to pay taxes. Rejecting Western dress, he spun cloth and adopted the clothes of the poor, becoming a visual reflection and a powerful voice of the country's masses.

Jawaharlal Nehru (1889–1964), who like Gandhi trained as a lawyer in London, envisioned a country free from British control and campaigned against indentured servitude and other forms of discrimination Indians faced as colonial subjects. In the 1920s he took up Gandhi's mission to transform the Indian National Congress from an elite body comfortable with British rule into a political force that demanded equal treatment of all of India's citizens. He began meeting with diplomats from other countries that were also struggling against colonialism. In 1929, when he became president of the Indian National Congress, Nehru wrote a declaration of independence for India that called for freedom of religion, freedom of expression, and equality for everyone, without distinction. He also joined with Gandhi on the Salt March, a nonviolent, direct-action protest that took place in 1930 and resulted in a brutal police attack on the unresisting demonstrators. More than sixty thousand participants, Nehru included, were imprisoned.

Two decades of protest and civil disobedience came to a head in 1942 when the National Congress adopted the Quit India resolution. The document demanded that Britain renounce possession of the subcontinent. Nehru and Gandhi, along with other senior political leaders, were sentenced to prison, and Nehru joined Gandhi as a national hero. In 1944, after Nehru was released from prison for the last time, the British finally made plans to withdraw. Nehru became India's first prime minister when the country achieved independence in 1947. He used his great political skill to guide India from its colonial status to recognition as a modern nation-state.

Johnson portrayed the two activists and friends against a star-filled sky. In the upper right quadrant, Johnson included an image of Nehru seated at a desk reviewing a document that probably represents India's constitution. The emaciated bodies that surround the two men are a haunting reference to the horrific Bengal famine of 1943 to 1944 in which more than one million people died. (Among Johnson's papers is a magazine article describing the famine.) They are also clues to the challenges Nehru and Gandhi faced in creating a modern India.

—VMM

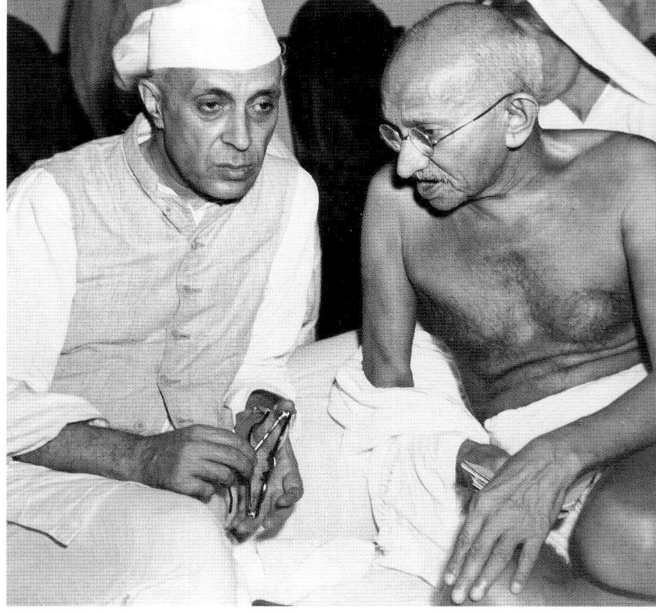

Dave Davis (Acme correspondent), "Gandhi with all India Congress's new president [Jawaharlal Nehru], Bombay, India," 1946, Library of Congress Prints and Photographs Division, New York World Telegram & Sun Collection

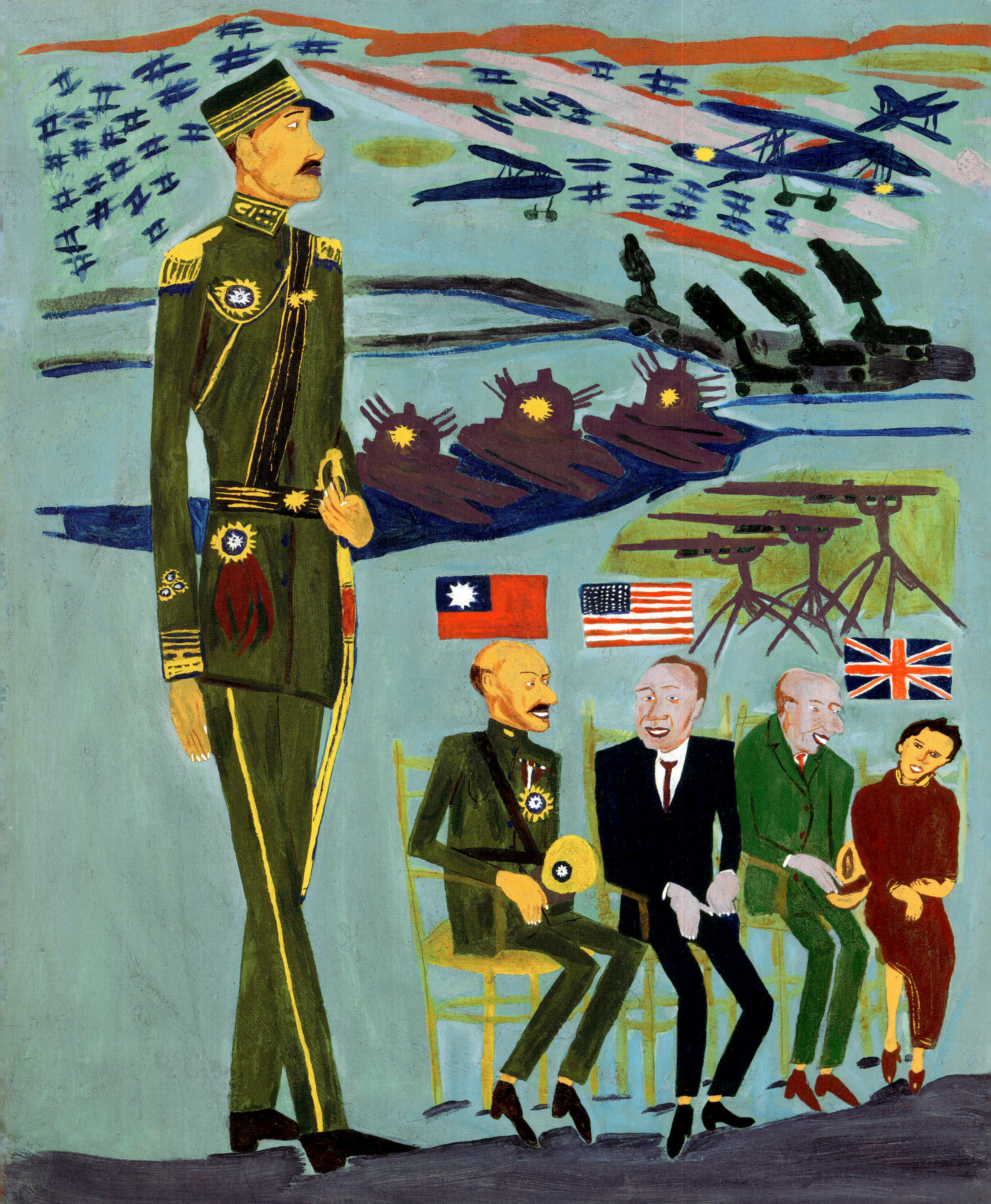

HISTORICAL SCENE—WW II

ca. 1945
oil on paperboard
32 ½ × 24 ¾ in.
Smithsonian American Art Museum
Gift of the Harmon Foundation

IN *HISTORICAL SCENE—WW II*, Johnson showed Generalissimo Chiang Kai-shek, president of Nationalist China, surveying a landscape filled with machines of war. In 1931, Japan invaded China's northern territory of Manchuria, but tensions went as far back as the late nineteenth century, tied, in part, to competition for dominance over China's northern provinces as well as the Korean Peninsula. In July 1937, within weeks of a clash at the Marco Polo Bridge near Beijing, Japan occupied the city. By December, invading forces had taken Shanghai, decimated the capital of Nanjing (Nanking), and slaughtered more than two hundred thousand soldiers and civilians. With inadequate equipment and poorly trained troops, the government retreated to the country's interior. By 1943, after Japan occupied the British colony of Burma (now Myanmar) and blockaded Chinese seaports, the primary supply lines China relied on to bring armaments and ammunition, as well as food and humanitarian supplies, were cut off.

At the left of the painting Chiang Kai-shek stands tall. Warplanes pockmark the sky, while tanks, artillery, and machine guns dominate the landscape. We can only guess whether Johnson meant for *Historical Scene—WW II* to represent the Chinese leader's nightmare of continued Japanese incursions, or his greatest hope—the arrival of tanks, planes, and armaments from the Allies that would allow China to repulse further invasion.

At the lower right Johnson included in miniature a scene from the 1943 Cairo Conference. In addition to the three heads of state he pictured in *Three Allies in Cairo* (p. 147), he included American-educated Madame Chiang Kai-shek, who served as interpreter and adviser to her husband. A savvy strategist and skilled diplomat, Madame Chiang Kai-shek addressed the U.S. Congress in spring 1942. Her impassioned statement of shared values and urgent plea for U.S. support for the Chinese cause convinced many in American political circles to back Roosevelt's decision to provide war supplies to China.

Johnson made multiple sketches of these world leaders, drawing many of them from press photographs to ensure his viewers could identify the characters in the dramatic scene. The composition underscores Roosevelt's conviction that peace could only come through collaboration and compromise.

—VMM

FOR INDIA AND CHINA

ca. 1944–45
oil on paperboard
32 ⅛ × 23 ⅝ in.
Smithsonian American Art Museum
Gift of the Harmon Foundation

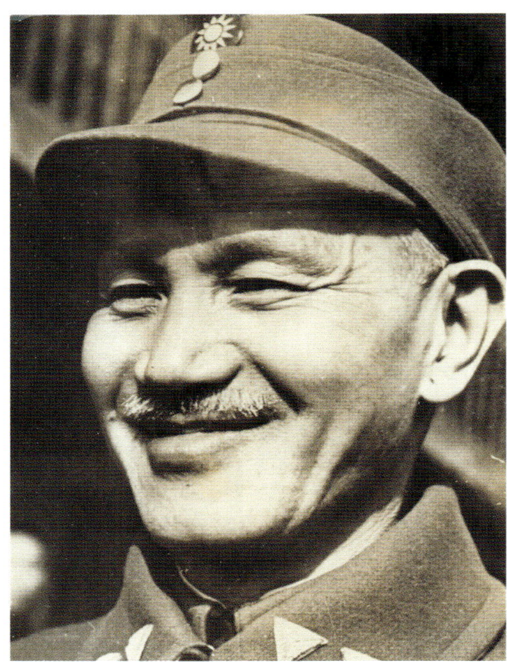

Generalissimo Chiang Kai-Shek, ca. 1945, gelatin silver print, 6 ⅛ × 4 ⅜ in., National Museum of American History, Smithsonian Institution, 2013.0327.1031

IN FEBRUARY 1942 Generalissimo Chiang Kai-shek and his wife, Soong Mei-ling, traveled to Calcutta, India, to meet with Mohandas Gandhi and Jawaharlal Nehru, head of the Indian National Congress. Nehru had visited the Chiangs in China three years earlier and shared a bunker with them during a Japanese bomber attack; the Chiangs, in turn, continued the friendship by writing to Nehru when he was imprisoned following a civil disobedience campaign.

There were multiple reasons for the 1942 meeting, which Nehru arranged. His primary purpose was to introduce Gandhi to the Chinese leaders for the first time, but he also wanted to clarify the two countries' relationship at a critical point during the Second World War.

By the time Johnson painted *For India and China*, both countries had been engaged in internal and external struggles for more than a decade. In China, Nationalist leader Chiang Kai-shek was under attack by Chinese communist forces, who defied his government. Externally he fought the Japanese invasion of his country (see *Historical Scene—WW II* and *Three Allies in Cairo*). In India, the Indian National Congress, led by Gandhi and Nehru, fought against British colonial rule and over whether, when the time came, the country would remain whole or be split into separate Hindu and Muslim nations.

Chiang Kai-shek had long stood up for India's independence from British rule and sought Indian support against the Japanese invasion of his country.

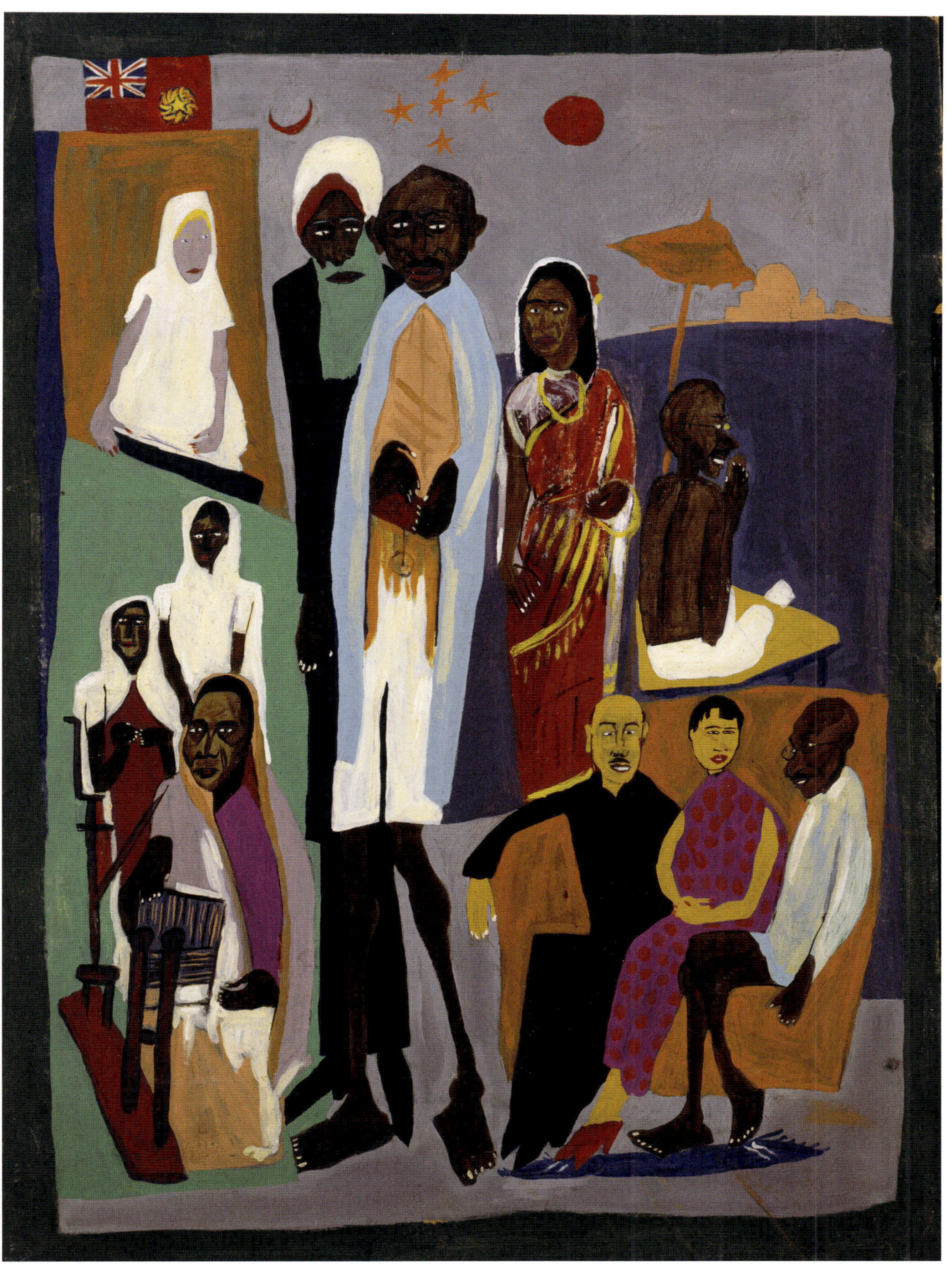

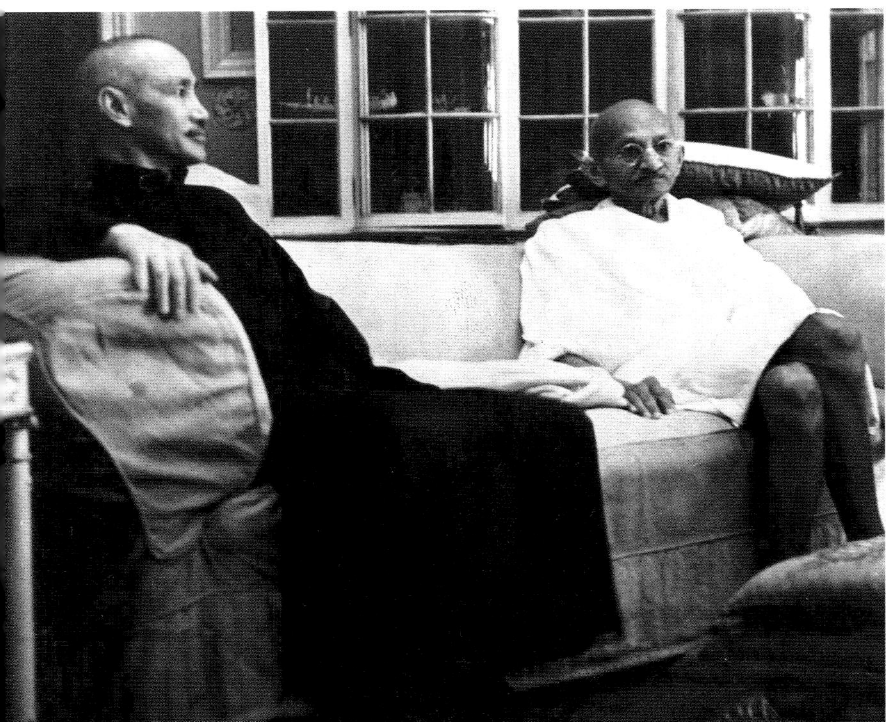

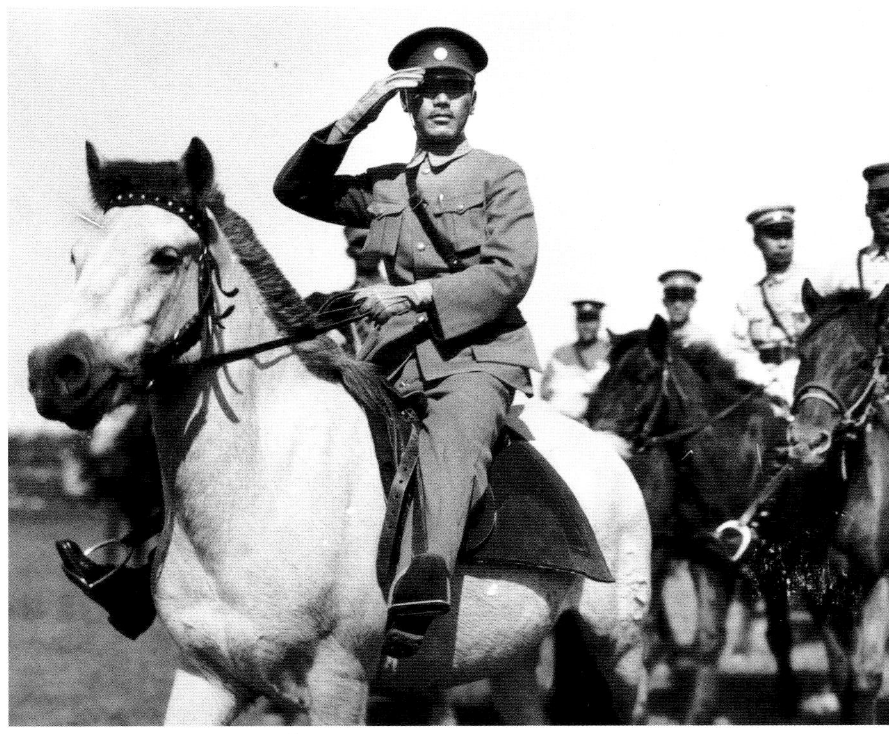

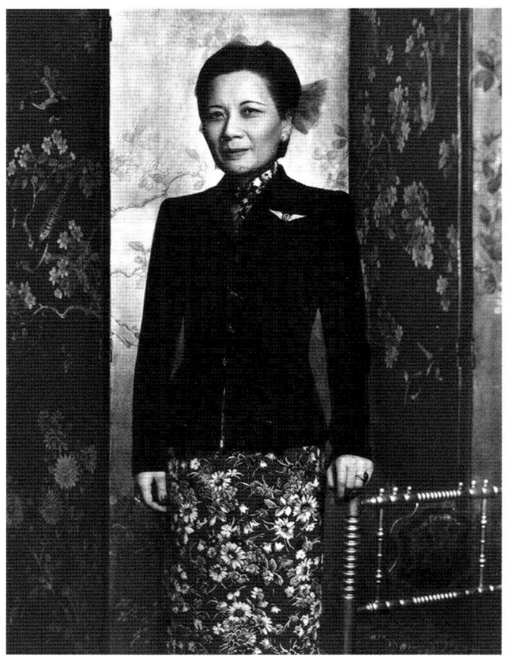

Yousuf Karsh, *Mme. Chiang Kai-shek*, 1943, gelatin silver print, 13 1/16 × 9 13/16 in., National Portrait Gallery, Smithsonian Institution, Gift of Estrellita Karsh in memory of Yousuf Karsh, NPG.2012.77.55

By the 1942 meeting, the need for an alliance was urgent. The Japanese had overrun Burma (today Myanmar), a British colony that shared borders with both India and China, and cut off the primary supply line the Allies used to send munitions and equipment to China. Chiang needed to discuss a new supply line and to determine India's willingness to support China's war against Japan. No commitments were made during the meeting, but in an open letter to the Chinese people Nehru confirmed that China's freedom was inextricably intertwined with that of India. "To the people of China and their great leaders, Generalissimo and Madame Chiang Kai-shek," he wrote, "[I] pay homage to the heroism which has shown like a bright star during their past five years of war and infinite suffering."

In *For India and China*, Johnson created a composite image that links multiple people and events. Gandhi, in the center, wears the homespun clothes he had adopted as a tribute to Indians who lived in poverty. At the right is Kasturba, his wife of sixty-two years, who was sentenced to hard labor for protesting the ill-treatment of Indian immigrants when the couple lived in South Africa. After they returned to India, she was often jailed for civil disobedience. The image at right, of Gandhi seated on a mat, represents the many fasts he undertook in his nonviolent campaign against British rule. Behind him stands poet Rabindranath Tagore, a lifelong advocate for Indian independence and the

Opposite, top left: "Mahatma Gandhi with Chinese leader Chiang Kai-shek, Calcutta, India, Asia," February 18, 1942

Opposite, top right: *Chiang Kai-shek*, 1933, black and white photograph on paper, 6 3/4 × 9 1/4 in., National Portrait Gallery, Smithsonian Institution, Gift of *Time* magazine, NPG.84.TC120

Chiang Kai-shek, ca. 1945, pencil on paper, 12 5/8 × 5 5/8 in., Smithsonian American Art Museum, Gift of the Harmon Foundation, 1967.59.354

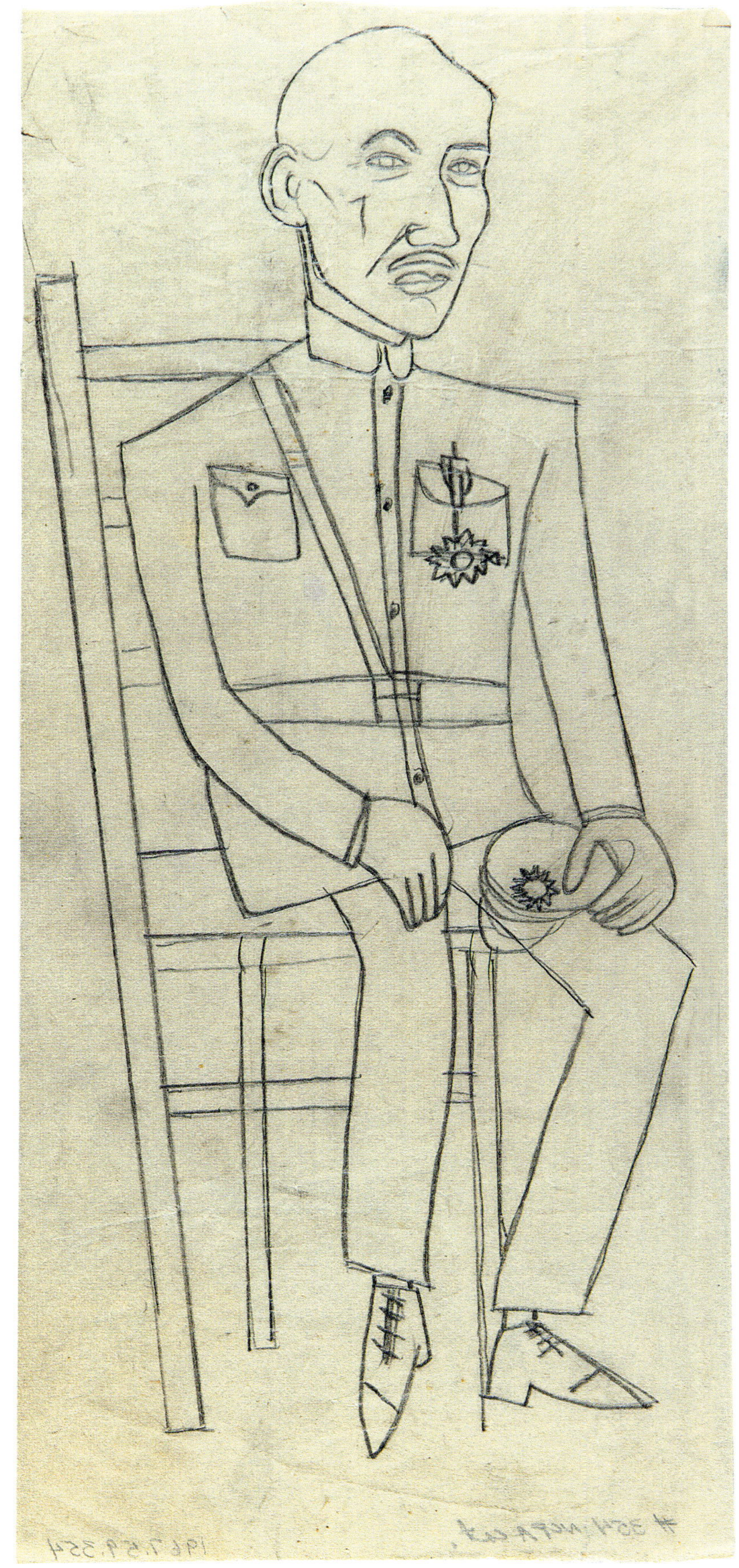

first non-European to win the Nobel Prize in Literature. At the lower right, the small scene of Generalissimo and Mrs. Chiang seated on a sofa beside Gandhi represents the 1942 meeting. At the lower left is Gandhi's spinning wheel, which he gave to Madame Chiang Kai-shek. The woman in white could be Madeleine Slade, known as Mirabehn, a British-born follower of Gandhi and supporter of the Indian Independence Movement, or possibly Margaret Bourke-White, the *LIFE* magazine photographer whose pictures of Gandhi were widely published. The tiny building with the dome at the top right is the British Viceroy's palace. Johnson included it, along with a British Indian flag at upper left, as a reminder of the country's colonial status.

—VMM

CAIRO AND TEHRAN CONFERENCES

IN NOVEMBER 1943, President Franklin Roosevelt scheduled back-to-back meetings with British, Chinese, and Soviet heads of state to develop plans for defeating Japan in the Pacific and Germany in Europe. He also wanted to propose a blueprint for global power dynamics in the postwar world and, through face-to-face meetings, develop personal relationships that would dispel long-standing suspicions among the parties.

Chiang Kai-Shek, Nationalist president of China, and British prime minister Winston Churchill (with Mrs. Chiang Kai-shek present as interpreter) joined President Roosevelt in Cairo from November 22 to 26, 1943, to strategize about retaking British colonial territories Japan had seized in Asia (Burma, today called Myanmar, was one) and to bolster support for under-equipped and undertrained Nationalist Chinese forces.

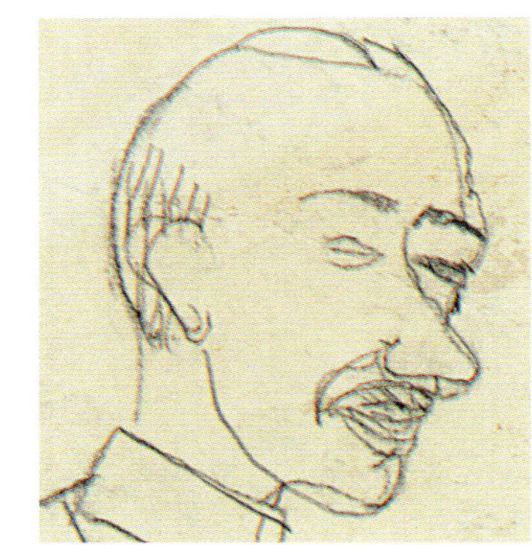

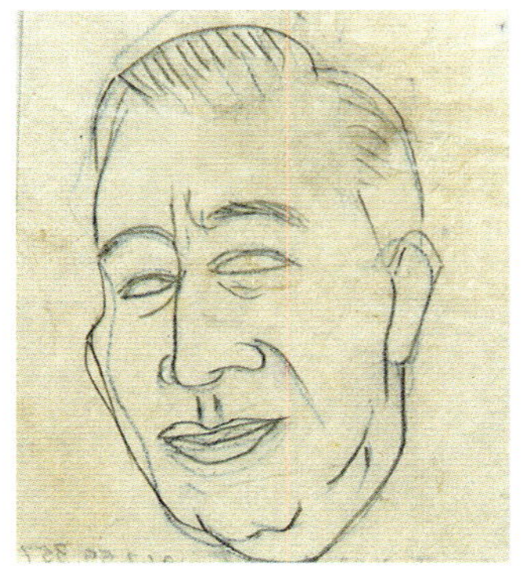

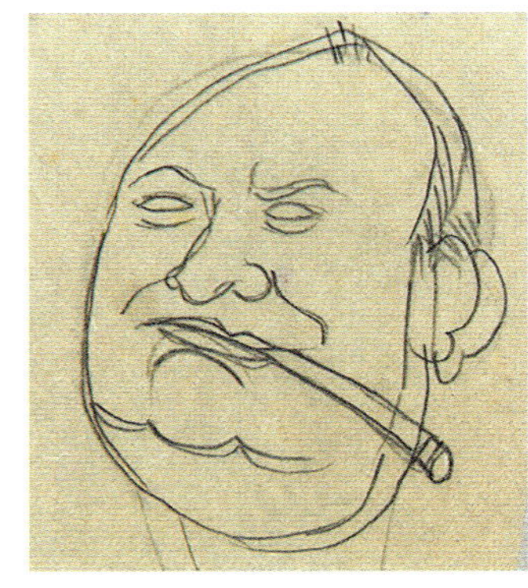

Both U.S. and Chinese interests were at stake. On December 8, 1941, the day after bombing Pearl Harbor, Japanese troops invaded the Philippines and captured Manila. Within three months Japan took some seventy-five thousand U.S. and Filipino troops prisoner. China's war with Japan went back more than a decade, to 1931, when Japan occupied Manchuria, Inner Mongolia, and Korea.

The challenges facing the three leaders were immense. Chiang Kai-shek needed to secure continued Allied support as his country suffered shortages of munitions, food, and humanitarian goods. Churchill

Sketch details, from left:

Chiang Kai-shek from *Chiang Kai-shek, Roosevelt, Churchill and Madame Chiang Kai-Shek, Cairo Conference,* ca. 1945, pencil and carbon tracing on paper, 13 1/8 × 13 1/4 in., Smithsonian American Art Museum, Gift of the Harmon Foundation, 1967.59.502

Franklin Delano Roosevelt, ca. 1945, 3 1/2 × 3 1/8 in., pencil and carbon tracing on paper, Smithsonian American Art Museum, Gift of the Harmon Foundation, 1967.59.357

Winston Churchill, ca. 1945, pencil on paper, 4 3/4 × 3 1/2 in., Smithsonian American Art Museum, Gift of the Harmon Foundation, 1967.59.361

Three Allies in Cairo
ca. 1945
oil on paperboard
28 ⅝ × 36 ½ in.
Smithsonian American Art Museum
Gift of the Harmon Foundation

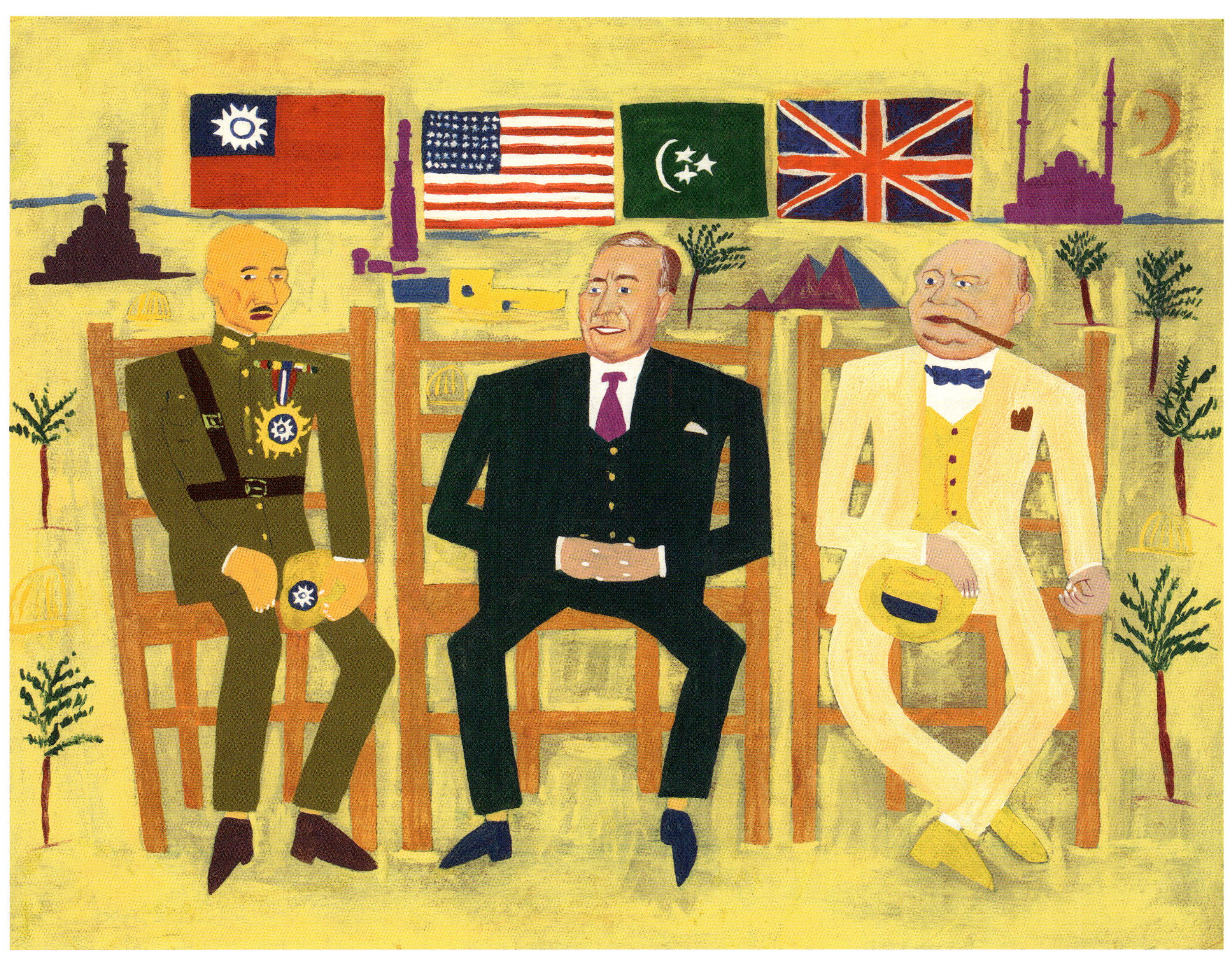

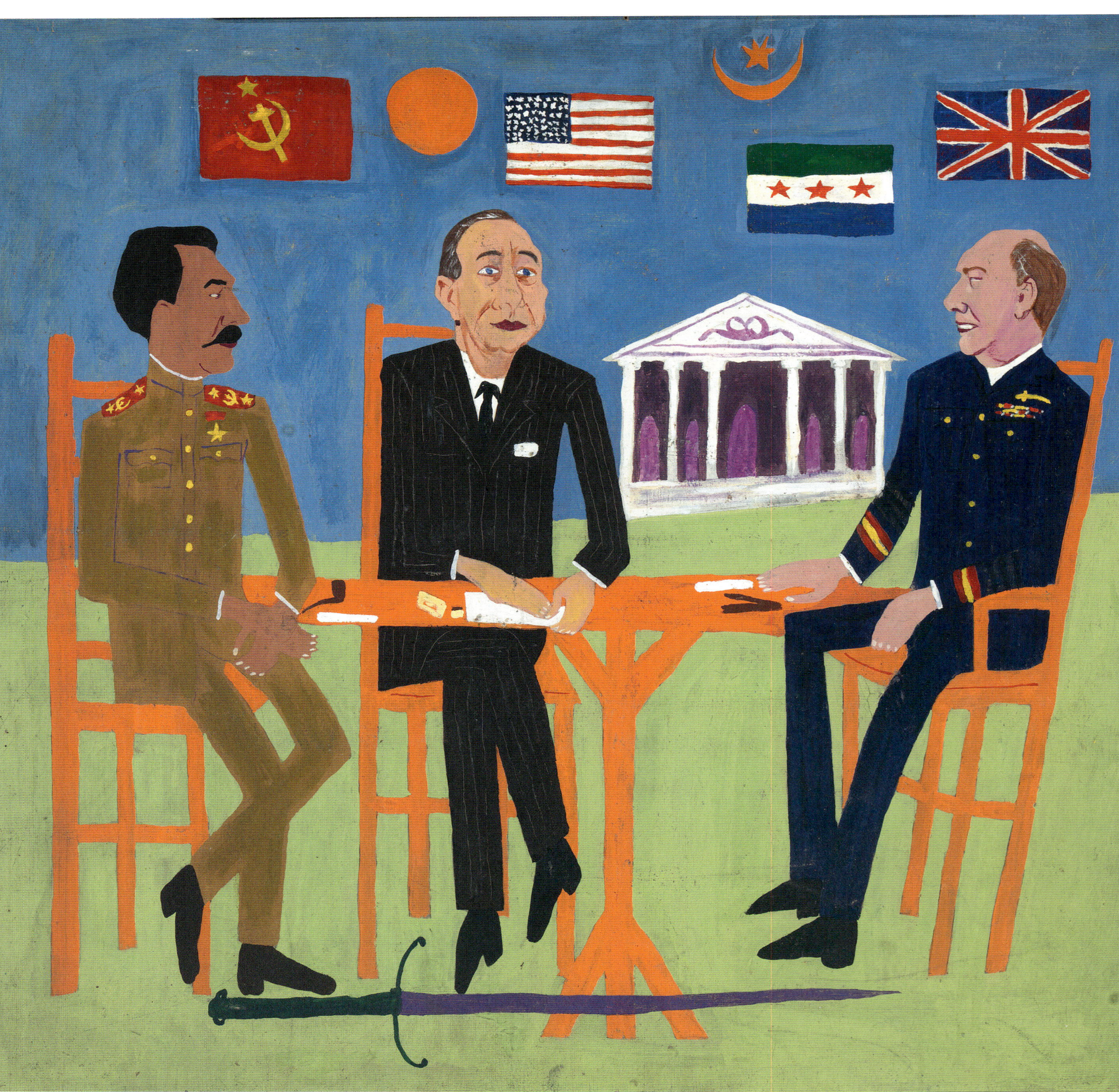

Tehran Conference
ca. 1945
oil on plywood
34 3/8 × 37 in.
Smithsonian American Art Museum
Gift of the Harmon Foundation

wanted to ensure British involvement in decisions about the postwar balance of power, and Roosevelt hoped to persuade Churchill to relinquish long-held British colonial territory. After five days of negotiations, the three committed to a total defeat of Japan and a return to its 1895 territorial borders.

From Cairo, Roosevelt and Churchill headed to Tehran to meet with Joseph Stalin, general secretary of the Soviet Union's Communist Party (p. 43). Stalin had been pushing the United States and Great Britain to launch a major assault on Germany, which would open a second front in the European war. The previous two years had taken a brutal toll on Soviet troops and civilians alike. In August 1942, the Germans had launched airstrikes against the industrial center of Stalingrad, leaving the city in ruins. Losses on both sides numbered in the millions, before the German army, surrounded during a brutally cold winter and facing starvation, surrendered. When the Tehran Conference ended on December 1, 1943, Roosevelt and Churchill had committed to invading German-occupied northern France. Stalin, in turn, agreed to launch an offensive on Germany's eastern flank and to declare war against Japan after the Germans surrendered.

Press reports of the Tehran Conference considered the meetings successful. Stalin called Churchill and Roosevelt his "fighting friends," and Churchill presented the Soviet premier with a hand-forged ceremonial longsword, the Sword of Stalingrad, as a tribute from the British people to those who had, at huge loss, defended the Russian city.

Johnson created his paintings of these historic meetings based in part on an article from a December 20, 1943, issue of *LIFE* magazine he saved in his scrapbook. *Three Allies in Cairo* shows Roosevelt seated between Chiang Kai-shek on the left and Winston Churchill on the right, as in the press photograph. The palm trees, pyramids, and green Egyptian flag that identify the location are devices Johnson used to expand his narrative. A preliminary sketch for the painting shows the British prime minister smoking one of his trademark cigars even though that detail doesn't appear in the picture released to the press.

In his depiction of the Tehran Conference, Johnson added the table at which the three are seated and cigars adjacent to the uniformed Churchill. The Sword of Stalingrad appears at the bottom of the painting.

—VMM

POTSDAM MEETING

ca. 1945
oil on paperboard
37 ½ × 28 ½ in.
Smithsonian American Art Museum
Gift of the Harmon Foundation

POTSDAM MEETING presents three world leaders—President Harry Truman of the United States (center), Premier Joseph Stalin of the Soviet Union (right), and Prime Minister Clement Attlee of Great Britain (left)—standing on a Nazi flag with hands joined in victory.

The three met in Potsdam, about twenty miles from Berlin, from July 17 to August 2, 1945, to negotiate terms of peace after Germany surrendered on May 8. The cast of characters at Potsdam was new: Truman replaced Franklin Roosevelt, who died in April; Attlee replaced Churchill midway through the meeting when Attlee's landslide general election victory was announced.

The basic terms of the agreements made in Potsdam had been worked out by Roosevelt, Churchill, and Stalin in a meeting at Yalta on the Crimean Peninsula the previous February. Anticipating that the war in Europe would soon be over, they had issued a "Declaration on Liberated Europe" that called for the unconditional surrender and demilitarization of Germany and free elections in countries it had occupied.

In Potsdam, senior officials from the three countries met to decide how to implement the earlier agreements. Major questions about territorial boundaries in Eastern and Western Europe had to be negotiated, as did the deportation of Germans living in previously occupied territories and payment of reparations. The three heads of state also confirmed that Germany would be divided into four spheres of influence to be controlled by the Soviet Union, Great Britain, the United States, and France, as had been discussed at several previous meetings.

Truman's highest priority was ending the war in Asia. On August 6, shortly after the conference concluded, the United States dropped an atomic bomb on the city of Hiroshima. Stalin declared war on Japan on August 8. After a second bomb decimated Nagasaki on August 9, Japan surrendered.

Johnson found no need to add small descriptive elements to identify Attlee, Truman, or Stalin or the reason for the meeting. Flags representing the three victorious countries and the German flag beneath the leaders' feet send a clear message. The simplicity of *Potsdam Meeting* makes it one of Johnson's most declarative paintings.

—VMM

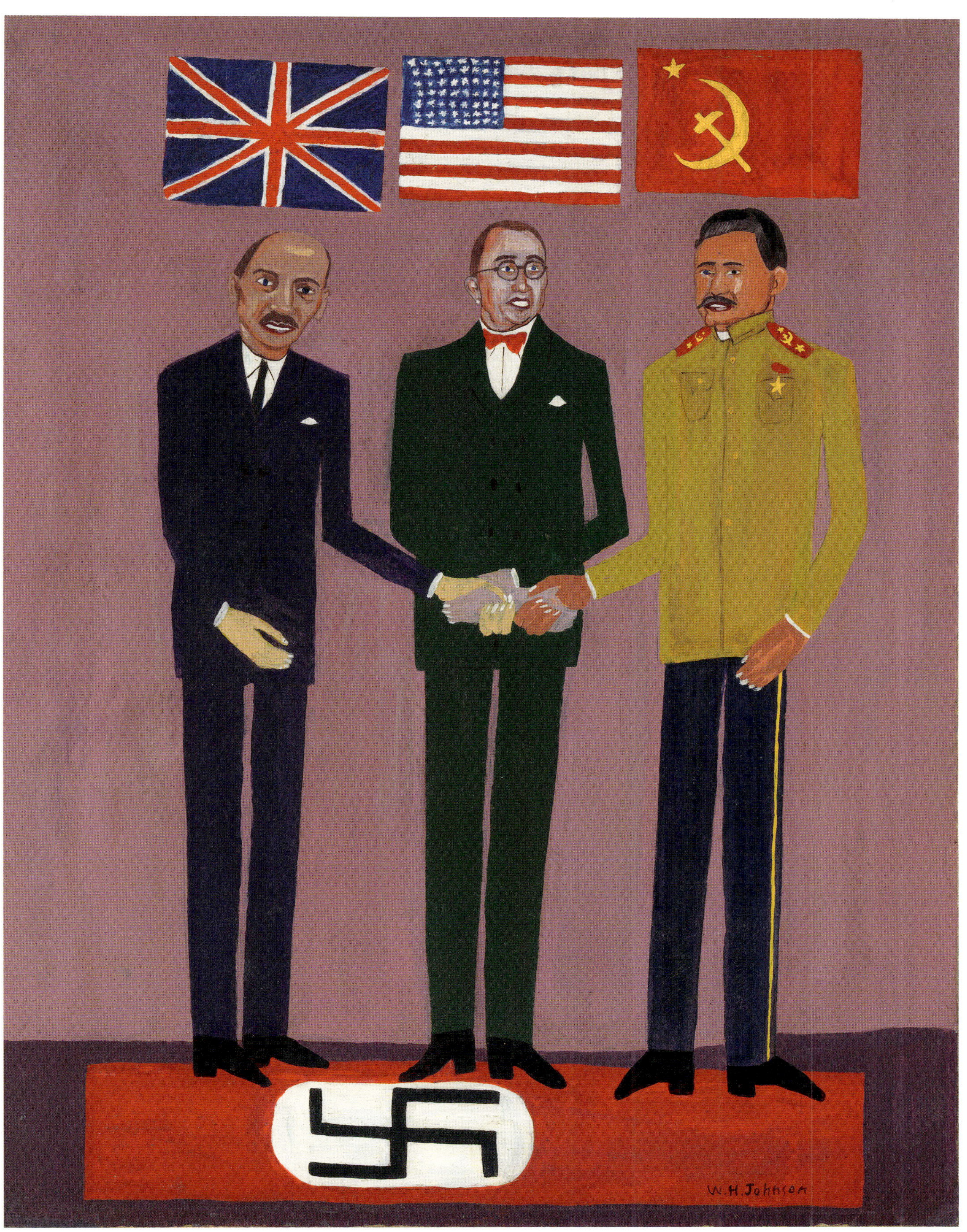
W.H.Johnson

FDR AND U.N.

1945
oil on plywood
37 × 39 in.
Smithsonian American Art Museum
Gift of the Harmon Foundation

ON JUNE 26, 1945, representatives of fifty nations from around the world signed the United Nations Charter. They had been working since April to craft the mission and structure of an organization that would prevent the horror of future wars. In the preamble to the charter they affirmed the equal rights of individuals and nations and pledged to practice tolerance and promote the economic and social advancement of all people. The conference, which was held in San Francisco, was the culmination of meetings going as far back as 1941. President Franklin Roosevelt of the United States and British prime minister Winston Churchill led the initial effort; the Soviet Union, China, and the governments-in-exile of countries under German occupation soon signed on. Over the next four years, meetings in Moscow, Cairo, London, Tehran, Yalta, Potsdam, and other far-flung cities considered the conduct of the war, terms for Germany's and Japan's surrender, postwar spheres of influence in Europe and Asia, and the formation of an international organization that would address world peace. At a fall 1944 conference at the Dumbarton Oaks estate in Washington, DC, the organizational structure was decided, but it took another meeting at Yalta on the Crimean Peninsula in February 1945 for Churchill, Roosevelt, and Stalin to resolve issues related to veto protocols and the Soviet Union's role in the nascent organization.

Johnson placed Franklin Roosevelt standing at the center of *FDR and U.N.*, even though the president died two weeks before the charter conference began. It is a triumphant painting that acknowledges Roosevelt's central role in establishing the UN. Forming an international organization was on the agenda for his meetings in Cairo with Winston Churchill and Chiang Kai-shek in 1943 (the group at the lower left) and again for the Tehran Conference with Churchill and Joseph Stalin (at the lower right). The background is alive with flags representing member and observer countries. With this painting Johnson memorialized Roosevelt as a peacemaker whose legacy would live on.

—VMM

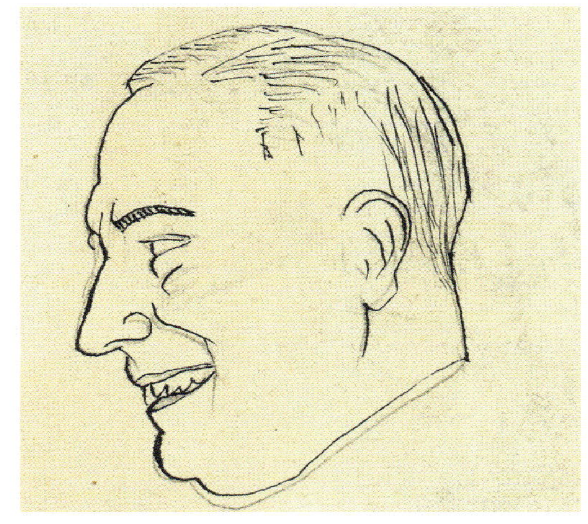

Franklin Delano Roosevelt, ca. 1945, pen and ink, pencil, and carbon tracing on paper, 5 ½ × 6 in., Smithsonian American Art Museum, Gift of the Harmon Foundation, 1967.59.381

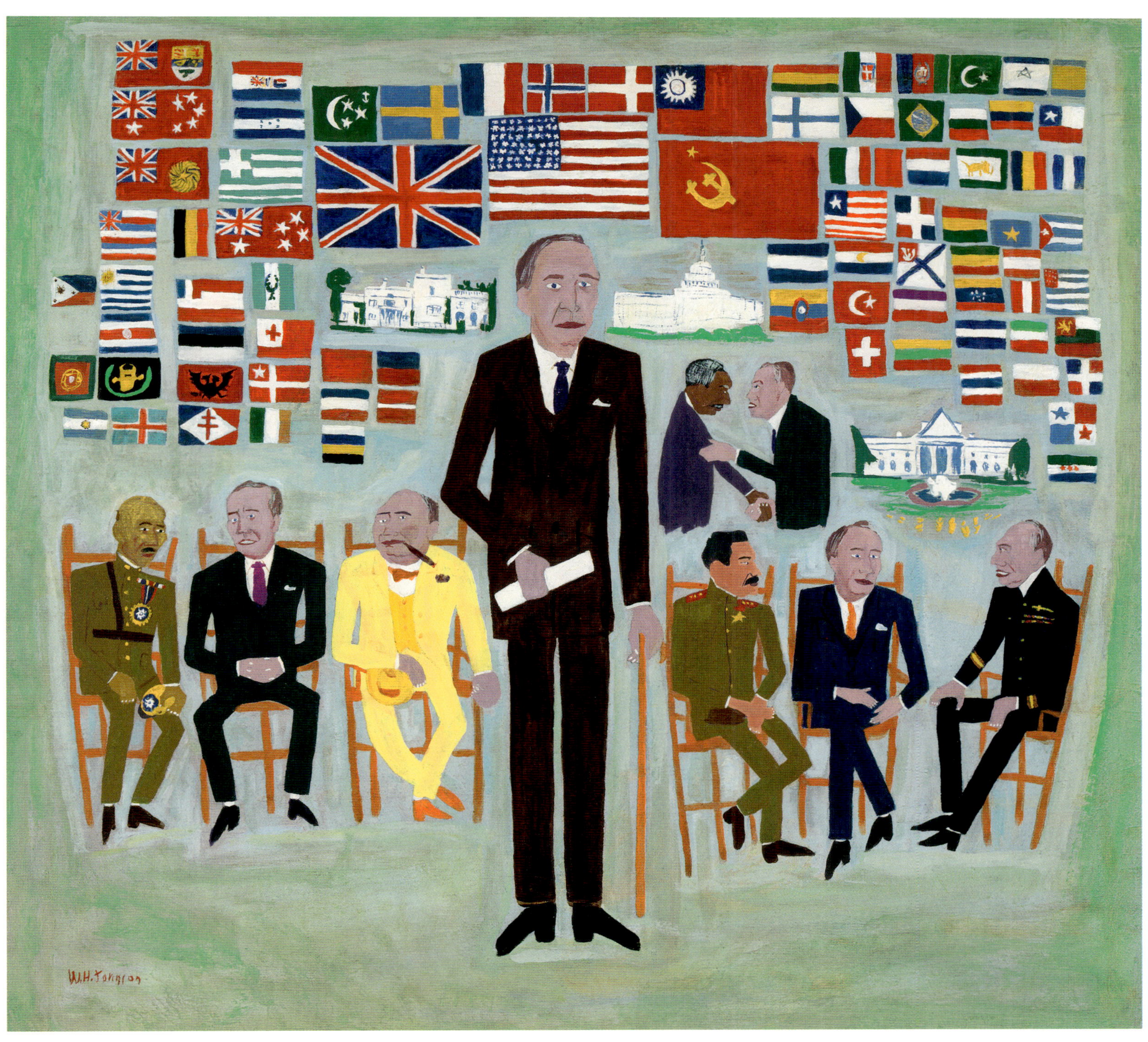
W.H.Johnson

AGAINST THE ODDS

ca. 1945
oil on paperboard
29 ¾ × 27 ⅛ in.
Collection of the
Hampton University Museum

IN 1944, Edwin R. Embree, president of the Julius Rosenwald Fund, a philanthropic organization dedicated to supporting African American and Jewish causes, published *13 Against the Odds*. The book presented biographies of thirteen African Americans who, in the author's words, embodied "success stories in the best American tradition…good tough personalities, with the joys and sorrows common to all men, with the extra pain that comes from the prejudices of their neighbors, and the added zest that comes with climbing from special depths to the pinnacles of distinction." To determine which individuals would be featured, Embree polled two hundred people, some Black, some white, to identify living African Americans who had the most transformative impact on American life.

Johnson illustrated Embree's entire pantheon of Black achievers. The top row features Paul Robeson (p. 124), Mary McLeod Bethune (p. 108), and George Washington Carver (p. 90). Below them (left to right) are Joe Louis (p. 112) and Marian Anderson (p. 120) along with Harlem Renaissance poet and author Langston Hughes; Walter White, president of the National Association for the Advancement of Colored People (NAACP); and W. E. B. Du Bois, founder and editor of *The Crisis*, the first magazine written by and for African Americans. Across the bottom are Richard Wright, author of the novel *Native Son*; A. Philip Randolph, activist and president of the Brotherhood of Sleeping Car Porters; Charles S. Johnson, influential sociologist and president of Fisk University; Howard University president Mordecai Johnson; and composer William Grant Still, whose *Afro-American Symphony* (1930) was then the most widely performed symphony ever written by an American.

Against the Odds is probably the last *Fighters for Freedom* painting Johnson completed. With the addition of these leaders to his community of Fighters, Johnson touched the full range of human endeavor. In the fall of 1946, he wrote: "I [have] now completed it all.…Great men, women—fighter[s] for Freedom.…who accomplished great deeds for the freedom [fight]. Now all this completed—all!"

—VMM

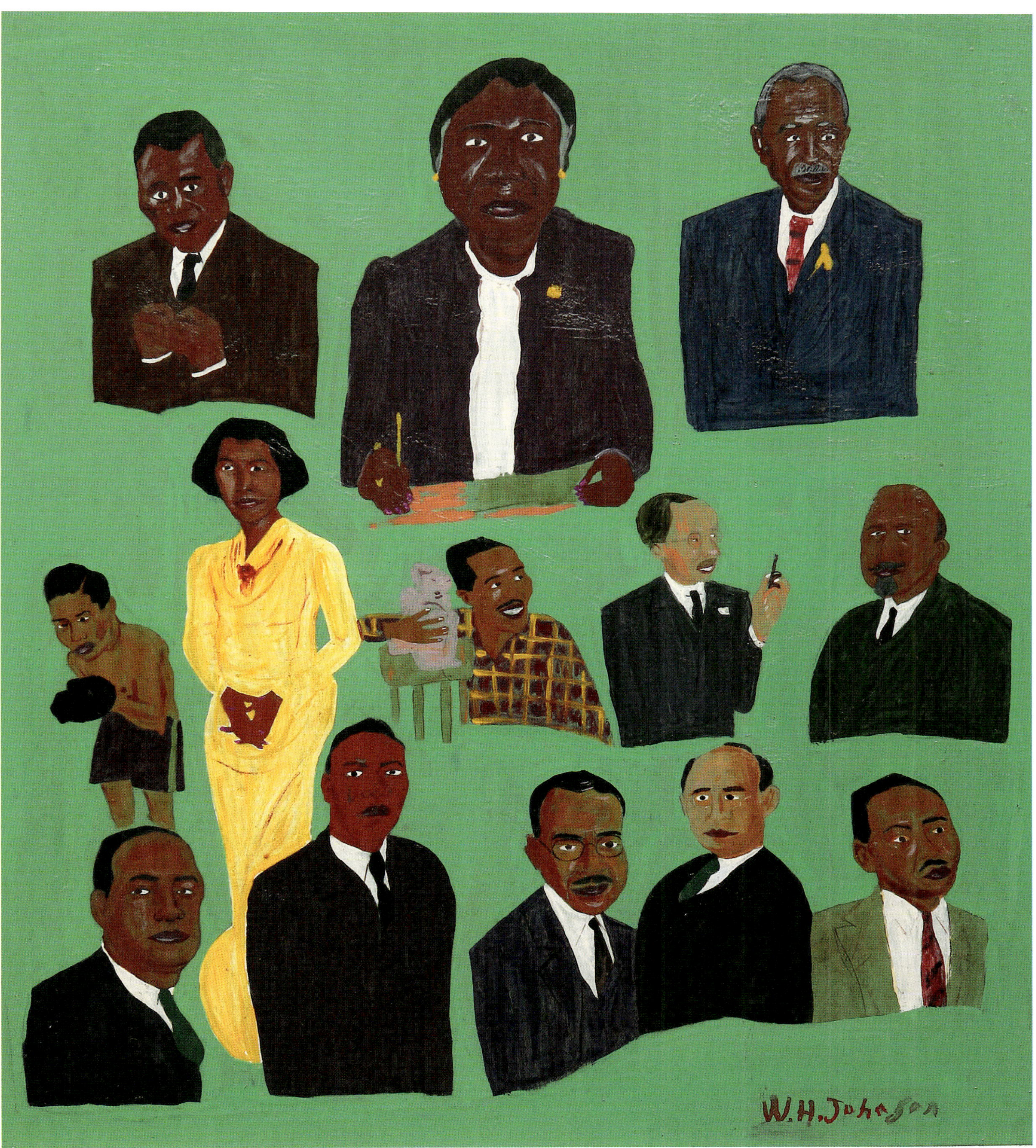
W.H.Johnson

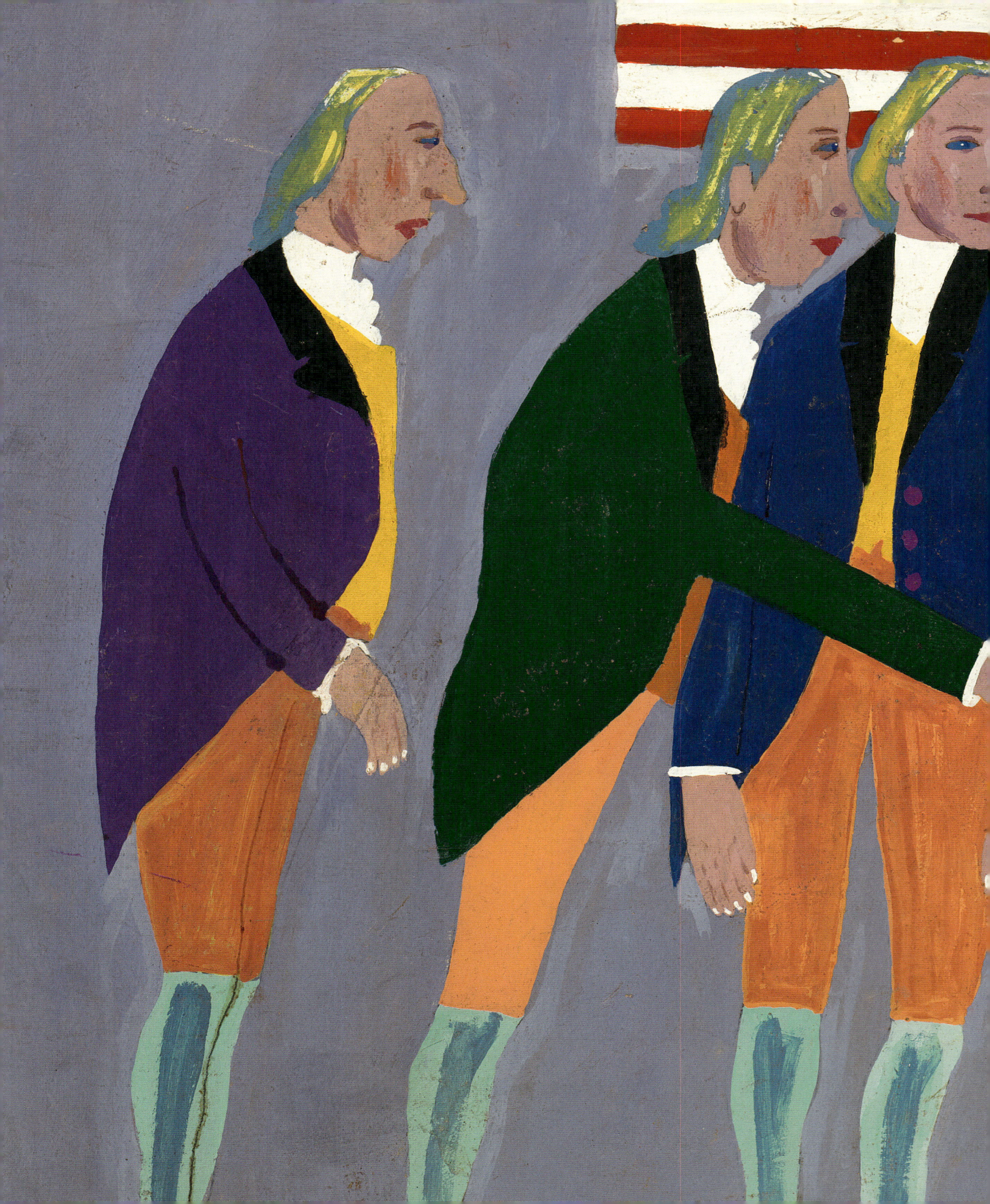

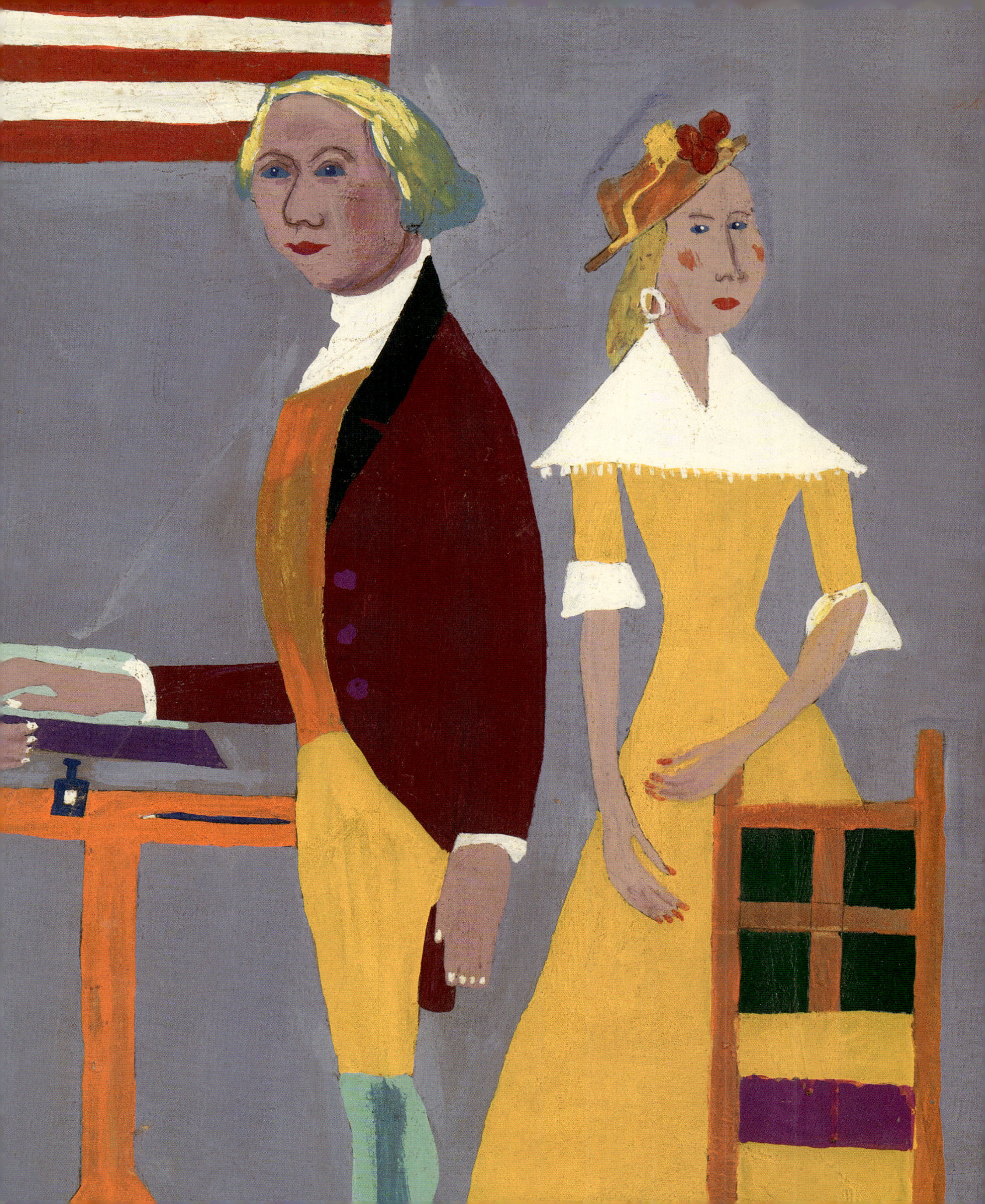

EXHIBITION CHECKLIST

William H. Johnson created all the paintings and sketches illustrated in this book.

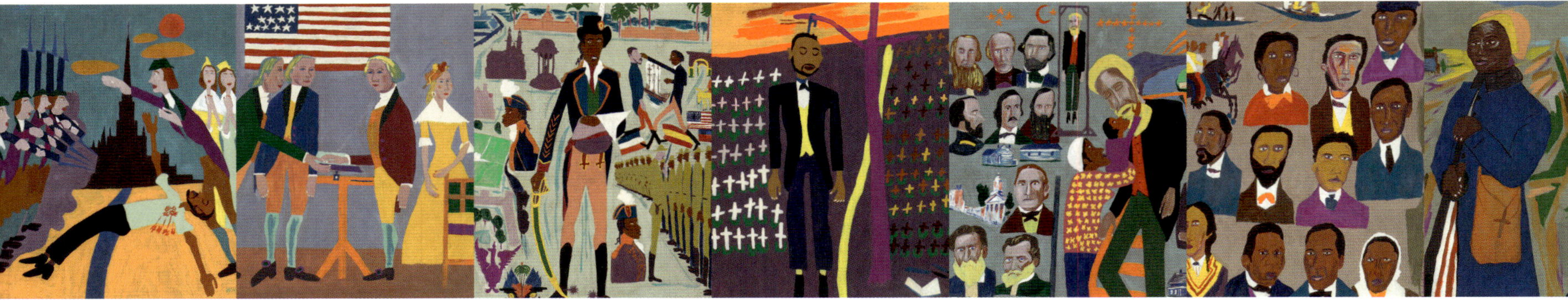

34 *Self-Portrait with Pipe* † §
ca. 1937
oil on canvas
35 × 28 in.
Smithsonian American Art Museum
Gift of the Harmon Foundation
1967.59.913

52 *Crispus Attucks*
ca. 1945
oil on paperboard
29 1/2 × 30 7/8 in.
Smithsonian American Art Museum
Gift of the Harmon Foundation
1983.95.53

57 *Swearing in George Washington*
ca. 1945
oil on paperboard
27 5/8 × 31 7/8 in.
Smithsonian American Art Museum
Gift of the Harmon Foundation
1967.59.653

60 *Toussaint l'Ouverture, Haiti*
ca. 1945
oil on paperboard
38 1/4 × 30 1/8 in.
Smithsonian American Art Museum
Gift of the Harmon Foundation
1967.59.1154

63 *Nat Turner*
ca. 1945
oil on paperboard
31 3/8 × 25 7/8 in.
Smithsonian American Art Museum
Gift of the Harmon Foundation
1967.59.658

67 *John Brown Legend*
ca. 1945
oil on paperboard
38 5/8 × 36 1/4 in.
Smithsonian American Art Museum
Gift of the Harmon Foundation
1967.59.1145

69 *Underground Railroad*
ca. 1945
oil on paperboard
33 3/8 × 36 3/8 in.
Smithsonian American Art Museum
Gift of the Harmon Foundation
1967.59.645

73 *Harriet Tubman*
ca. 1945
oil on paperboard
28 7/8 × 23 3/8 in.
Smithsonian American Art Museum
Gift of the Harmon Foundation
1967.59.1146

77 *Three Great Freedom Fighters* †
ca. 1945
oil on paperboard
41 1/2 × 33 3/8 in.
Collection of the
Hampton University Museum

† On view in the Washington, DC, exhibition only

§ Artwork is not part of the *Fighters for Freedom* series

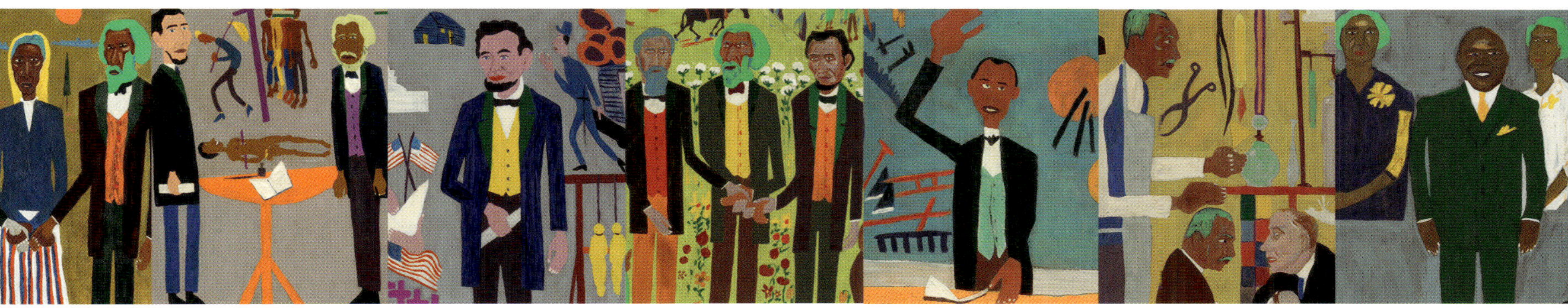

79 *Let My People Free*
ca. 1945
oil on fiberboard
38 1/4 × 30 in.
Smithsonian American Art Museum
Gift of the Harmon Foundation
1967.59.649

83 *Abraham Lincoln*
ca. 1945
oil on paperboard
36 1/4 × 33 3/8 in.
Smithsonian American Art Museum
Gift of the Harmon Foundation
1967.59.643

85 *Three Great Abolitionists: A. Lincoln, F. Douglass, J. Brown*
ca. 1945
oil on paperboard
37 3/8 × 34 1/4 in.
Smithsonian American Art Museum
Gift of the Harmon Foundation
1983.95.51

87 *Booker T. Washington Revelation*
ca. 1945
oil on fiberboard
39 7/8 × 30 7/8 in.
Smithsonian American Art Museum
Gift of the Harmon Foundation
1967.59.1143

88 *Booker T. Washington Legend*
ca. 1944–45
oil on plywood
32 5/8 × 25 1/4 in.
Smithsonian American Art Museum
Gift of the Harmon Foundation
1967.59.664

90 *Dr. George Washington Carver*
ca. 1945
oil on paperboard
35 1/2 × 28 1/2 in.
Smithsonian American Art Museum
Gift of the Harmon Foundation
1967.59.1142

93 *Dr. George Washington Carver*
ca. 1945
oil on plywood
32 1/2 × 26 3/4 in.
Smithsonian American Art Museum
Gift of the Harmon Foundation
1967.59.597

95 *Commodore Peary and Henson at the North Pole*
ca. 1945
oil on paperboard
27 5/8 × 35 1/2 in.
Smithsonian American Art Museum
Gift of the Harmon Foundation
1983.95.54

99 *Historical Scene*
ca. 1945
oil on fiberboard
39 1/8 × 37 1/8 in.
Smithsonian American Art Museum
Gift of the Harmon Foundation
1967.59.646

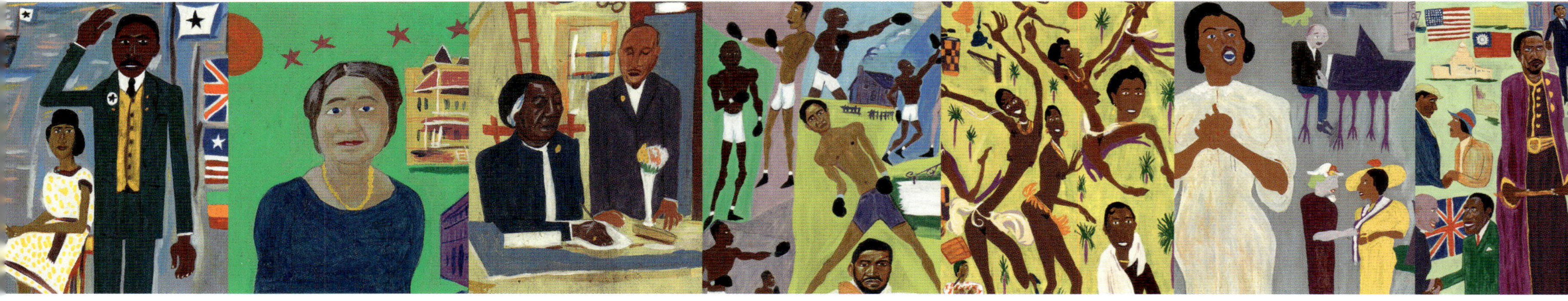

101 *Marcus Garvey*
ca. 1945
oil on paperboard
35 3/4 × 28 7/8 in.
Smithsonian American Art Museum
Gift of the Harmon Foundation
1967.59.648

105 *Women Builders*
1945
oil on paperboard
37 5/8 × 34 1/8 in.
Smithsonian American Art Museum
Gift of the Harmon Foundation
1967.59.1150

109 *Historical Scene with Mary McLeod Bethune*
ca. 1945
oil on paperboard
37 1/2 × 28 1/2 in.
Smithsonian American Art Museum
Gift of the Harmon Foundation
1967.59.651

113 *Boxers*
ca. 1945–46
oil on paperboard
32 7/8 × 28 7/8 in.
Smithsonian American Art Museum
Gift of the Harmon Foundation
1967.59.652

117 *Three Great Dancers*
ca. 1945
oil on paperboard
33 5/8 × 28 1/2 in.
Smithsonian American Art Museum
Gift of the Harmon Foundation
1967.59.667

120 *Marian Anderson*
ca. 1945
oil on paperboard
35 5/8 × 28 7/8 in.
Smithsonian American Art Museum
Gift of the Harmon Foundation
1967.59.657

124 *Paul Robeson's Relations*
ca. 1945
oil on fiberboard
36 3/8 × 28 5/8 in.
Smithsonian American Art Museum
Gift of the Harmon Foundation
1967.59.666

129 *Haile Selassie*
ca. 1945
oil on plywood
32 7/8 × 25 1/2 in.
Smithsonian American Art Museum
Gift of the Harmon Foundation
1967.59.607R-V

133 *King Ibn Saud*
ca. 1945
oil on paperboard
35 5/8 × 28 5/8 in.
Smithsonian American Art Museum
Gift of the Harmon Foundation
1967.59.650

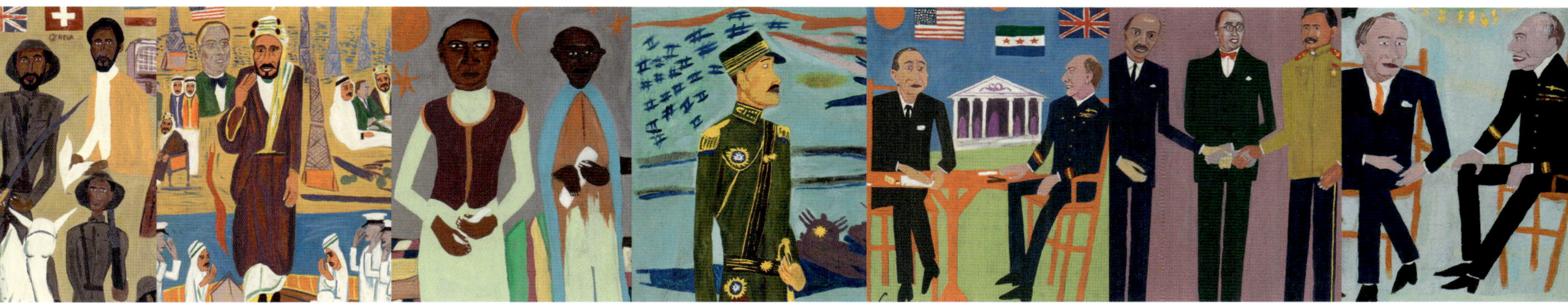

137 *Nehru and Gandhi*
ca. 1945
oil on paperboard
33 7/8 × 27 7/8 in.
Smithsonian American Art Museum
Gift of the Harmon Foundation
1967.59.665

140 *Historical Scene—WW II*
ca. 1945
oil on paperboard
32 1/2 × 24 3/4 in.
Smithsonian American Art Museum
Gift of the Harmon Foundation
1967.59.659

143 *For India and China*
ca. 1944–45
oil on paperboard
32 1/8 × 23 5/8 in.
Smithsonian American Art Museum
Gift of the Harmon Foundation
1967.59.662

147 *Three Allies in Cairo*
ca. 1945
oil on paperboard
28 5/8 × 36 1/2 in.
Smithsonian American Art Museum
Gift of the Harmon Foundation
1967.59.663

148 *Tehran Conference*
ca. 1945
oil on plywood
34 3/8 × 37 in.
Smithsonian American Art Museum
Gift of the Harmon Foundation
1967.59.647

151 *Potsdam Meeting*
ca. 1945
oil on paperboard
37 1/2 × 28 1/2 in.
Smithsonian American Art Museum
Gift of the Harmon Foundation
1967.59.655

153 *FDR and U.N.*
1945
oil on plywood
37 × 39 in.
Smithsonian American Art Museum
Gift of the Harmon Foundation
1967.59.644

155 *Against the Odds* †
ca. 1945
oil on paperboard
29 3/4 × 27 1/8 in.
Collection of the
Hampton University Museum

FURTHER READING

William H. Johnson

Best, Makeda. "Cut Aesthetics: William H. Johnson's Scrapbook History Paintings." *Archives of American Art Journal* 58, no. 1 (Spring 2019): 1–96.

Breeskin, Adelyn D. *William H. Johnson (1901–1970).* Washington, DC: Smithsonian Institution Press for the National Collection of Fine Arts, 1971.

Gionis, Teresa G., ed. *William H. Johnson: An American Modern.* Jacob Lawrence Series on American Artists. Washington, DC: Smithsonian Institution Traveling Exhibition Service (SITES); Baltimore, MD: James E. Lewis Museum of Art, Morgan State University, 2011.

LeFalle-Collins, Lizzetta. *Novae: William H. Johnson and Bob Thompson.* Los Angeles: California Afro-American Museum Foundation, 1990.

Powell, Richard J. *Homecoming: The Art and Life of William H. Johnson.* Washington, DC: National Museum of American Art, Smithsonian Institution, 1991.

Rodgers, Kenneth G. *William H. Johnson: Revisiting an African American Modernist.* Durham: North Carolina Central University Art Museum, 2006.

The Fighters

Crispus Attucks

Kachun, Mitch. *First Martyr of Liberty: Crispus Attucks in American Memory.* New York: Oxford University Press, 2017.

Kaplan, Sidney. *The Black Presence in the Era of the American Revolution, 1770–1800.* Rev. ed. Amherst: University of Massachusetts Press, 1989.

Nell, William Cooper. *The Colored Patriots of the American Revolution.* New York: Arno, 1968. First published 1855 by Robert F. Wallcut (Boston).

George Washington

Burns, James MacGregor, and Susan Dunn. *George Washington.* The American Presidents. New York: Times Books, 2004.

Chernow, Ron. *Washington: A Life.* New York: Penguin, 2010.

Johnson, Paul. *George Washington: The Founding Father.* Eminent Lives. New York: HarperCollins, 2005.

Toussaint L'Ouverture

Bell, Madison Smartt. *Toussaint Louverture: A Biography.* New York: Pantheon, 2007.

Girard, Philippe. *Toussaint Louverture: A Revolutionary Life.* New York: Basic Books, 2016.

Hazareesingh, Sudhir. *Black Spartacus: The Epic Life of Toussaint Louverture.* New York: Farrar, Straus and Giroux, 2020.

James, C. L. R., *The Black Jacobins: Toussaint L'Ouverture and the San Domingo Revolution.* Rev. ed. New York: Vintage Books, 1989.

Nat Turner

Aptheker, Herbert. *Nat Turner's Slave Rebellion, including the 1831 "Confessions."* New York: Dover, 2006. First published 1965 by Humanities Press (New York).

Breen, Patrick. *The Land Shall Be Deluged with Blood: A New History of the Nat Turner Revolt.* New York: Oxford University Press, 2015.

Encyclopedia Virginia. "Nat Turner's Revolt." Accessed April 24, 2023. https://encyclopediavirginia.org/entries/turners-revolt-nat-1831/.

Roth, Sarah N. "The Nat Turner Project." Widener University Department of History. Accessed April 24, 2023. https://www.natturnerproject.org.

John Brown

Carton, Evan. *Patriotic Treason: John Brown and the Soul of America.* New York: Free Press, 2006.

Cox, Clinton. *Fiery Vision: The Life and Death of John Brown.* New York: Scholastic, 1997.

Du Bois, W. E. B. *John Brown.* New York: Oxford University Press, 2017. First printed 1909 by G. W. Jacobs (Philadelphia).

Reynolds, David S. *John Brown, Abolitionist: The Man Who Killed Slavery, Sparked the Civil War, and Seeded Civil Rights*. New York: Vintage Books, 2006.

Villard, Oswald Garrison. *John Brown, 1800–1859: A Biography Fifty Years Later*. Boston: Houghton Mifflin, 1910.

Underground Railroad

Blight, David W., ed. *Passages to Freedom: The Underground Railroad in History and Memory*. Washington, DC: Smithsonian Books in association with the National Underground Railroad Freedom Center, 2004.

Diemer, Andrew K. "The Forgotten Father of the Underground Railroad." *Smithsonian Magazine*, November 9, 2022. https://www.smithsonianmag.com/history/the-forgotten-father-of-the-underground-railroad-180981088/.

———. *Vigilance: The Life of William Still, Father of the Underground Railroad*. New York: Alfred A. Knopf, 2022.

Still, William. *The Underground Railroad Records: Narrating the Hardships, Hairbreadth Escapes, and Death Struggles of Slaves in Their Efforts for Freedom*. Philadelphia: Porter & Coates, 1872. Reprinted with a foreword by Quincy T. Mills and an introduction by Ta-Nehisi Coates. New York: Modern Library, 2019.

Walters, Kerry S. *The Underground Railroad: A Reference Guide*. Santa Barbara, CA: ABC-CLIO, 2012.

Harriet Tubman

Bradford, Sarah H. *Harriet Tubman: The Moses of Her People*. Reprint with an introduction by Butler A. Jones. Gloucester, MA: Peter Smith, 1981. First published 1886 by Geo. R. Lockwood & Son (New York).

Clinton, Catherine. *Harriet Tubman: The Road to Freedom*. New York: Little, Brown, 2005.

George, Alice. "Why Harriet Tubman's Heroic Military Career is Now Easier to Envision." *Smithsonian Magazine*, June 8, 2020. https://www.smithsonianmag.com/smithsonian-institution/why-harriet-tubmans-heroic-military-career-now-easier-envision-180975038/.

Larson, Kate Clifford. *Bound for the Promised Land: Harriet Tubman, Portrait of an American Hero*. New York: Ballantine, 2004.

Sernett, Milton C. *Harriet Tubman: Myth, Memory, and History*. Durham, NC: Duke University Press, 2007.

Abraham Lincoln

Delbanco, Andrew, ed. *The Portable Abraham Lincoln*. Viking Portable Library, New York: Viking, 1992.

Foner, Eric. *The Fiery Trial: Abraham Lincoln and American Slavery*. New York: W. W. Norton, 2010.

McPherson, James M. *Abraham Lincoln*. New York: Oxford University Press, 2009.

National Park Service. "Lincoln Speeches." Last updated April 10, 2015. https://www.nps.gov/liho/learn/historyculture/speeches.htm.

Frederick Douglass

Blight, David W. *Frederick Douglass: Prophet of Freedom*. New York: Simon & Schuster, 2018.

Oakes, James. *The Radical and the Republican: Frederick Douglass, Abraham Lincoln, and the Triumph of Antislavery Politics*. New York: W. W. Norton, 2007.

Voss, Frederick S. *Majestic in His Wrath: A Pictorial Life of Frederick Douglass*. Washington, DC: Smithsonian Institution Press for the National Portrait Gallery and the National Park Service, 1995.

Booker T. Washington

Harlan, Louis R. *Booker T. Washington: The Making of a Black Leader, 1856–1901*. New York: Oxford University Press, 1972.

Harlan, Louis R., and Raymond W. Smock, eds. *The Booker T Washington Papers Digital Edition*. Charlottesville: University of Virginia Press, Rotunda, 2021. https://rotunda.upress.virginia.edu/founders/BTWN-01-04-02-0122.

Norrell, Robert J. *Up from History: The Life of Booker T. Washington*. Cambridge, MA: Belknap Press of Harvard University Press, 2009.

Washington, Booker T. *Up from Slavery: An Autobiography*. New York: Penguin, 1986. First published 1901 by Doubleday (New York).

———. *My Larger Education: Being Chapters from My Experience*. New York: Doubleday, 1911.

George Washington Carver

Holt, Rackham. *George Washington Carver: An American Biography*. New York: Doubleday, 1943.

Kaufman, Rachel. "In Search of George Washington Carver's True Legacy." *Smithsonian Magazine*, February 21, 2019. https://www.smithsonianmag.com/history/search-george-washington-carvers-true-legacy-180971538/.

Vella, Christina. *George Washington Carver: A Life*. Baton Rouge: Louisiana State University Press, 2015.

Matthew Henson

Dolan, Edward F., Jr., *Matthew Henson: Black Explorer*. New York: Dodd, Mead, 1979.

Henson, Matthew A. *A Negro Explorer at the North Pole*. With a foreword by Robert E. Peary and an introduction by Booker T. Washington. Portland, OR: Mint Editions, 2021. First published 1912 by Frederick A. Stokes (New York).

Mills, James. "The Legacy of Arctic Explorer Matthew Henson." *National Geographic*, February 28, 2014. https://www.nationalgeographic.com/adventure/article/the-legacy-of-arctic-explorer-matthew-henson.

Father Divine

Watts, Jill. *God, Harlem, U.S.A.: The Father Divine Story*. Berkeley: University of California Press, 1992.

Weisbrot, Robert. *Father Divine and the Struggle for Racial Equality*. Urbana: University of Illinois Press, 1983.

Marcus Garvey

Clarke, John Henrik, ed. *Marcus Garvey and the Vision of Africa*. Baltimore: Black Classic Press, 2011. First printed 1974 by Vintage Books (New York).

Grant, Colin. *Negro with a Hat: The Rise and Fall of Marcus Garvey*. New York: Oxford University Press, 2008.

Martin, Tony. *Race First: The Ideological and Organizational Struggles of Marcus Garvey and the Universal Negro Improvement Association*. Westport, CT: Greenwood Press, 1976.

Women Builders

Daniel, Sadie Iola. *Women Builders*. 1931. Rev. ed. Washington, DC: Associated Publishers, 1970.

McCluskey, Audrey Thomas. *A Forgotten Sisterhood: Pioneering Black Women Educators and Activists in the Jim Crow South*. Lanham, MD: Rowman & Littlefield, 2014.

Mary McLeod Bethune

Bethune, Mary McLeod. "My Last Will and Testament." *Ebony*, August 1955.

———. "What Does American Democracy Mean to Me?" Radio address delivered on *America's Town Meeting of the Air*, November 23, 1939. http://americanradioworks.publicradio.org/features/sayitplain/mmbethune.html.

Hanson, Joyce Ann. *Mary McLeod Bethune and Black Women's Political Activism*. Columbia: University of Missouri Press, 2018.

National Museum of African American History and Culture. "Mary McLeod Bethune: 'First Lady of Negro America.'" Published July 15, 2022. https://nmaahc.si.edu/explore/stories/mary-mcleod-bethune.

Joe Louis
Jack Johnson

Hietala, Thomas R. *The Fight of the Century: Jack Johnson, Joe Louis, and the Struggle for Racial Equality*. New York: M. E. Sharpe, 2002.

Roberts, Randy. *Joe Louis: Hard Time Man*. New Haven, CT: Yale University Press, 2010.

Rundstetler, Theresa. *Jack Johnson, Rebel Sojourner: Boxing in the Shadow of the Global Color Line*. Berkeley: University of California Press, 2012.

Josephine Baker
Katherine Dunham
Pearl Primus

Baker, Jean-Claude, and Chris Chase. *Josephine Baker: The Hungry Heart*. New York: Random House, 1993.

Cohen-Stratyner, Barbara. "Pearl Primus in 'Strange Fruit.'" New York Public Library. Published August 29, 2016. https://www.nypl.org/blog/2016/08/29/pearl-primus-strange-fruit.

Durkin, Hannah. *Josephine Baker and Katherine Dunham: Dances in Literature and Cinema*. Urbana: University of Illinois Press, 2019.

Library of Congress. "Katherine Dunham Timeline." Accessed April 24, 2023. https://www.loc.gov/collections/katherine-dunham/articles-and-essays/katherine-dunham-timeline/.

Risner, Vicky J. "Katherine Dunham: A Life in Dance." Library of Congress Performing Arts Encyclopedia. Accessed April 24, 2023. https://www.loc.gov/item/ihas.200152685/.

Schwartz, Peggy, and Murray Schwartz. *The Dance Claimed Me: A Biography of Pearl Primus*. New Haven, CT: Yale University Press, 2011.

Marian Anderson

Anderson, Marian. *My Lord, What a Morning: An Autobiography*. Urbana: University of Illinois Press, 2002. First published 1956 by Viking Press (New York).

Arsenault, Raymond. *The Sound of Freedom: Marian Anderson, the Lincoln Memorial, and the Concert that Awakened America*. New York: Bloomsbury Press, 2009.

Keiler, Allan. *Marian Anderson: A Singer's Journey*. Urbana: University of Illinois Press, 2002.

Paul Robeson

Duberman, Martin Bauml. *Paul Robeson*. New York: Knopf, 1989.

Hovde, Sarah. "A Contract for Othello." Folger Shakespeare Library, February 26, 2016. https://www.folger.edu/blogs/shakespeare-and-beyond/a-contract-for-othello-paul-robeson/.

Robeson, Paul. *Here I Stand*. Boston: Beacon Press, 1988. First published 1958 by Othello Associates (New York).

Stewart, Jeffrey C., ed. *Paul Robeson: Artist and Citizen*. New Brunswick, NJ: Rutgers University Press, 1998.

Against the Odds

Embree, Edwin R. *13 Against the Odds*. New York: Viking, 1945.

Haile Selassie

Asserate, Asfa-Wossen. *King of Kings: The Triumph and Tragedy of Emperor Haile Selassie I of Ethiopia*. Translated by Peter Lewis. London: Haus Publishing, 2015.

Selassie, Bereket Habte. *Emperor Haile Selassie*. Athens: Ohio University Press, 2014.

Selassie, Haile. *My Life and Ethiopia's Progress, 1892–1937: The Autobiography of Emperor Haile Selassie*. 6th ed. London: Oxford University Press, 2013.

Ibn Saud

Darlow, Michael, and Barbara Bray. *Ibn Saud: The Desert Warrior Who Created the Kingdom of Saudi Arabia*. New York: Skyhorse, 2015.

Mohandas Gandhi

Guha, Ramachandra. *Gandhi: The Years That Changed the World, 1914–1948*. New York: Knopf, 2018.

Tidrick, Kathryn. *Gandhi: A Political and Spiritual Life*. 2nd ed. London: Verso, 2013.

Jawaharlal Nehru

Kohlsa, Madhav, ed. *Letters for a Nation: Jawaharlal Nehru to His Chief Ministers, 1947–1963*. New York: Penguin, 2014.

Nehru, Jawaharlal. *Jawaharlal Nehru: An Autobiography*. New Delhi: Penguin, 2004. First published 1936 by John Lane (London).

Tharoor, Shashi. *Nehru: The Invention of India*. New York: Arcade, 2003.

Chiang Kai-shek
Madame Chiang Kai-shek

Mitter, Rana. *Forgotten Ally: China's World War II, 1937–1945*. Boston: Houghton Mifflin Harcourt, 2013.

Pakula, Hannah. *The Last Empress: Madame Chiang Kai-shek and the Birth of Modern China*. New York: Simon & Schuster, 2009.

Taylor, Jay. *The Generalissimo: Chiang Kai-shek and the Struggle for Modern China*. Cambridge, MA: Belknap Press of Harvard University Press, 2009.

Franklin Delano Roosevelt

Dallek, Robert. *Franklin D. Roosevelt: A Political Life*. New York: Viking, 2017.

———. *Franklin D. Roosevelt and American Foreign Policy, 1932–1945*. New York: Oxford University Press, 1979.

Daniels, Roger. *Franklin Delano Roosevelt: The War Years, 1939–1945*. Urbana: University of Illinois Press, 2016.

Goodwin, Doris Kearns. *No Ordinary Time: Franklin and Eleanor Roosevelt: The Home Front in World War II*. New York: Simon & Schuster, 1994.

Miscamble, Wilson D. *From Roosevelt to Truman: Potsdam, Hiroshima, and the Cold War*. Cambridge: Cambridge University Press, 2007.

For Young Readers

Brandenberg, Aliki. *A Weed Is a Flower: The Life of George Washington Carver.* New York: Aladdin, 1988.

Caraventes, Peggy. *The Many Faces of Josephine Baker: Dancer, Singer, Activist, Spy.* Chicago: Chicago Review Press, 2018.

Cline-Ransome, Lesa. *Words Set Me Free: The Story of Young Frederick Douglass.* New York: Simon & Schuster, 2011.

Cortez, Rio. *The ABCs of Black History.* New York: Workman, 2020.

de la Peña, Matt. *A Nation's Hope: The Story of Boxing Legend Joe Louis.* New York: Dial, 2011.

Davis Pinkney, Andrea. *Let It Shine: Stories of Black Women Freedom Fighters.* San Diego: Gulliver, 2000.

Draper, Sharon M. *Stella by Starlight.* New York: Atheneum, 2015.

Elster, Jean Alicia. *I Have a Dream, Too!* Valley Forge, PA: Judson, 2002.

Everett, Gwen. *Li'l Sis and Uncle Willie.* Washington, DC: National Museum of American Art; New York: Rizzoli, 1994.

———. *John Brown: One Man Against Slavery.* With paintings by Jacob Lawrence. New York: Rizzoli, 1993.

Gandhi, Arun, and Bethany Hegedus. *Be the Change: A Grandfather Gandhi Story.* New York: Atheneum, 2016.

Greenfield, Eloise. *Mary McLeod Bethune.* New York: HarperCollins, 1977.

Greenfield, Eloise. *Paul Robeson.* Rev. ed. New York: Lee & Low, 2009.

Harrison, Vashti. *Little Leaders: Bold Women in Black History.* New York: Hachette, 2017.

Hudson, Cheryl Willis. *Brave, Black, First: 50+ African American Women Who Changed the World.* New York: Crown, 2020.

Lawrence, Jacob. *Harriet and the Promised Land.* New York: Aladdin Paperbacks, 1993.

Levine, Ellen. *Henry's Freedom Box: A True Story from the Underground Railroad.* New York: Scholastic, 2002.

McCalman, George. *Illustrated Black History: Honoring the Iconic and the Unseen.* New York: HarperOne, 2022.

Muñoz Ryan, Pam. *When Marian Sang: The True Recital of Marian Anderson.* New York: Scholastic, 2002.

Powell, Patricia Hruby. *Josephine: The Dazzling Life of Josephine Baker.* San Francisco: Chronicle, 2014.

Reynolds, Peter H. *Say Something!* New York: Scholastic, 2019.

Ringgold, Faith. *Aunt Harriet's Underground Railroad in the Sky.* New York: Crown, 1992.

Robbins, Dean. *Two Friends: Susan B. Anthony and Frederick Douglass.* New York: Scholastic, 2016.

Robeson, Susan. *Grandpa Stops a War.* New York: Triangle Square, 2019.

Sanchez Vergara, Maria Isabel. *Harriet Tubman.* Little People, BIG DREAMS. London: Frances Lincoln, 2019.

———. *Josephine Baker.* Little People, BIG DREAMS. London: Frances Lincoln, 2018.

———. *Mahatma Gandhi.* Little People, BIG DREAMS. London: Frances Lincoln, 2020.

Shange, Ntozake. *Freedom's a-Callin' Me.* New York: Amistad, 2012.

Smith, Charles R., Jr. *Black Jack: The Ballad of Jack Johnson.* New York: Roaring Brook, 2010.

Weatherford, Carol Boston. *Moses: When Harriet Tubman Led Her People to Freedom.* New York: Hyperion Books for Children, 2006.

INDEX

Page numbers in *italics* indicate illustrations. Titles of paintings without parenthetical attribution are by Johnson.

O

P

Q

R

S

T

Image Credits

Unless otherwise specified, all photographs were provided by the owners/collections of the artworks noted in the captions and are used with permission. Every effort has been made to obtain permissions for all copyright-protected work used in this book.

Front cover flap and p. 6 National Archives and Records Administration, Harmon Foundation Collection, H-HN-JOHW-15_003 Fig. 1 William H. Johnson papers, Archives of American Art, Smithsonian Institution, box 2, folder 11 (hereafter Johnson papers) Fig. 4 Johnson papers, box 2, folder 11 Fig. 5 Johnson papers, box 2, folder 6 Fig. 9 Johnson papers, box 1, folder 12 Fig. 12 Johnson papers, box 2, folder 5 Fig. 23 Johnson papers, box 2, folder 11 Fig. 24 General Research Division, The New York Public Library: b17637669 Fig 25 Johnson papers, box 1, folder 16 © 1943 *Time* Inc., all rights reserved, reprinted/translated from *LIFE* magazine and published with permission of Time Inc., reproduction in any manner in any language in whole or in part without written permission is prohibited Fig. 27 Everett Collection Historical/Alamy Stock Photo: CWAF5W Fig. 28 Getty Images/Hulton Archive/Stringer, 2696327 Fig. 30 Johnson papers, box 1, folder 14 Fig. 31 Smithsonian Institution Archives: SIA2023-020265 Fig. 32 Smithsonian Institution Archives: SIA2023-020268r01; photo by Ellsworth Davis Fig. 33 Smithsonian Institution Archives: SIA2023-020269 p. 54 Schomburg Center for Research in Black Culture, Manuscripts, Archives and Rare Books Division, The New York Public Library: b10228377 p. 64 (left): Schomburg Center for Research in Black Culture, Manuscripts, Archives and Rare Books Division, The New York Public Library: b15262566 p. 64 (right): Courtesy of Documenting the American South, University Library, The University of North Carolina, VCC326.92 T95 1831 p. 65 photograph by Michael R. Barnes p. 70 Schomburg Center for Research in Black Culture, Manuscripts, Archives and Rare Books Division, The New York Public Library, b11664210: (left) 1167940, (right) 1222689, (bottom) 1222685 p. 71 Schomburg Center for Research in Black Culture, Manuscripts, Archives and Rare Books Division, The New York Public Library, b11664210: 1222659 p. 72 General Research Division, The New York Public Library: b11616598 p. 75 Alpha Historica/Alamy Stock Photo; Library of Congress, JK1881.N357 sec. XVI, no. 3-9 NAWSA Coll p. 79 Library of Congress: LOT 14043-2, no. 647 [P&P] p. 81 Library of Congress: LC-DIG-ppmsca-23718 p. 89 Library of Congress: LOT 13164-B, no. 72 [P&P] p. 91 © Tuskegee University Archives, Tuskegee, AL p. 96 Library of Congress: LC-USZ62-68223 p. 100 Library of Congress: LC-USZ61-1854 pp. 104, 107 General Research Division, The New York Public Library: b17637669 p. 110 Library of Congress: LC-USW3-016829-E [P&P] LOT 684 p. 121 Everett Collection Inc./Alamy Stock Photo: BTJEX1 p. 123 Getty Images/Bettmann Archive, 515166886 p. 111 Library of Congress: LC-USW3-017132-C [P&P] LOT 682 p. 117 Jerome Robbins Dance Division, The New York Public Library: ps_dan_cd58_864 p. 119 Gerda Peterich Papers, University Archives, Special Collections Research Center, Syracuse University Libraries p. 121 Everett Collection Inc./Alamy Stock Photo: BTJEX1 p. 123 Getty Images/Bettmann Archive, 515166886 p. 125 Library of Congress: LC-USW33-054945-C [P&P] p. 127 Photograph © Van Vechten Trust; Compilation/Publication © Eakins Press Foundation. From *'O, Write My Name': American Portraits, Harlem Heroes* (Eakins, 2015) p. 130 African Postcard Collection, Eliot Elisofon Photographic Archives, National Museum of African Art: ET-15-01, EEPA ET 2011-14 p. 131 © 1936 Time Inc., all rights reserved, reprinted from *LIFE* magazine and published with permission of Time Inc., reproduction in any manner in any language in whole or in part without written permission is prohibited pp. 132, 135 © 1939 Time Inc., all rights reserved, reprinted/translated from *LIFE* magazine and published with permission of Time Inc., reproduction in any manner in any language in whole or in part without written permission is prohibited p. 139 Library of Congress: LC-USZ62-111090 p. 144 (clockwise from top left) Dinodia Photos/Alamy Stock Photo, © International Photo Agency, © Yousuf Karsh

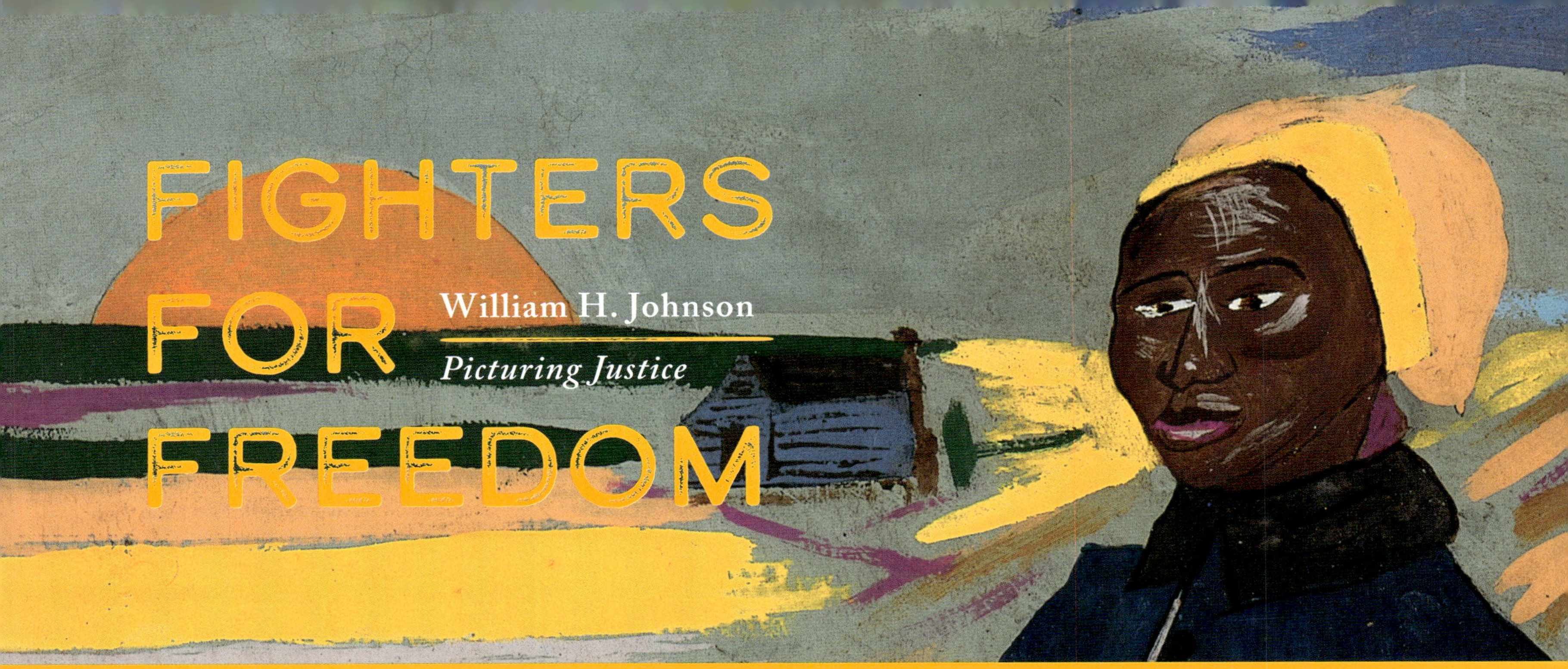

Published in conjunction with the exhibition of the same name, on view at the Smithsonian American Art Museum, Washington, DC, March 8 to September 8, 2024; Patricia and Philip Frost Art Museum, Miami, FL, September 28, 2024 to January 5, 2025; Weatherspoon Art Museum, Greensboro, NC, September 6 to November 9, 2025; and Dayton Art Institute, Dayton, OH, June 27 to September 13, 2026.

Previously traveled to the Gibbes Museum of Art, Charleston, SC, January 21 to August 7, 2022; Albany Museum of Art, Albany, GA, September 1 to December 10, 2022; Oklahoma City Museum of Art, February 18 to May 14, 2023; Rockwell Museum, Corning, NY, June 2 to September 5, 2023; Wichita Art Museum, Wichita, KS, October 7, 2023 to January 14, 2024.

The Smithsonian American Art Museum is home to one of the largest collections of American art in the world. Its holdings—more than 46,000 works—represent the most inclusive collection of American art of any museum today.

It is the nation's first federal art collection, predating the 1846 founding of the Smithsonian Institution. The museum shares the stories of our nation through American art and craft to inspire reflection, spark dialogue, and build connection.

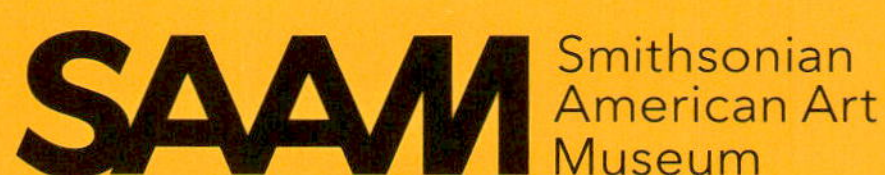

Produced by the Publications Office, Smithsonian American Art Museum

Tiffany D. Farrell, *Head of Publications*
Emily H. Rohan, *Editorial Assistant*
Denise Arnot, *Designer*
Janell Blackmon Pryor, *Researcher and Reviewer*
Emily K. Berg, *Kress Interpretive Fellow*
Phoebe Hillemann, *Teacher Institutes Educator*
Mary Cleary, *Proofreader*
Riche Sorensen and Aubrey Vinson, *Image and Permissions Coordinators*
Kate Mertes, *Indexer*

Published by the Smithsonian American Art Museum in association with Scala Arts Publishers, Inc.

First published in 2024 by

Scala Arts Publishers, Inc.
1301 Avenue of the Americas, 10th floor
New York, NY 10019
scalapublishers.com
Scala—New York—London

Smithsonian American Art Museum
8th and G Streets, NW
Washington, DC 20001
americanart.si.edu

Distributed in the book trade by

ACC Art Books
8 West 18th Street, 4th floor
New York, NY 10011

This book was typeset in Adobe Caslon, Roc Grotesk, and Calder. The paper is Symbol Matte Plus, 170 gsm. Printed and bound in Verona, Italy by Opero.

IMAGE DETAILS

cover and above *Harriet Tubman*; see p. 73
pp. 2–3 *Booker T. Washington Legend*; see p. 88
p. 4 *Booker T. Washington Revelation*; see p. 87
pp. 20–21 *Three Great Abolitionists: A. Lincoln, F. Douglass, J. Brown*; see p. 85
pp. 50–51 *Three Great Freedom Fighters*; see p. 77
pp. 156–57 *Swearing in George Washington*; see p. 57

LIBRARY OF CONGRESS
Cataloging-in-Publication Data

NAMES Smithsonian American Art Museum, author, host institution. | Mecklenburg, Virginia M. (Virginia McCord), author. | Farrell, Tiffany D., contributor. | Rohan, Emily H., contributor. | Bunch, Lonnie G., III, writer of preface. | Patricia & Phillip Frost Art Museum, host institution.

TITLE Fighters for freedom: William H. Johnson picturing justice | Virginia M. Mecklenburg; with a preface by Lonnie G. Bunch III; contributions by Tiffany D. Farrell, Emily H. Rohan.

IDENTIFIERS LCCN 2023032904 | ISBN 9781785515354 (paperback)

SUBJECTS LCSH: Johnson, William H., 1901–1970. Fighters for freedom—Exhibitions. | Johnson, William H., 1901–1970—Exhibitions. | African Americans—Portraits—Exhibitions. | Leadership in art—Exhibitions. | Social justice in art—Exhibitions. | Painting—Washington (D.C.)—Exhibitions. | Smithsonian American Art Museum—Exhibitions.

CLASSIFICATION LCC ND1329.J65 A64 2024 | DDC 759.13—dc23/eng/20231018

LC record available at https://lccn.loc.gov/2023032904

10 9 8 7 6 5 4 3 2 1